# Working with Children

## 2004–05

edited by
**Clare Horton**

**SocietyGuardian**

the children's charity

Published by Guardian Books
Guardian Books is an imprint of Guardian Newspapers Ltd

The Guardian and SocietyGuardian are trademarks of the
Guardian Media Group plc and Guardian Newspapers Ltd

Copyright © NCH
Copyright in Directory © Guardian Newspapers Ltd 2003
Copyright in introduction and chapter overviews ©
Guardian Newspapers Ltd 2003

A CIP record for this book is available from the
British Library

ISBN 184354 327 3

Distributed by Atlantic Books,
an imprint of Grove Atlantic Ltd, Ormond House,
26-27 Boswell Street, London WC1N 3JZ

Directory researched on behalf of the Guardian
by Toni Hanks
Cover Design: Guardian Development
Text and graphics by carrstudio  www.carrstudio.co.uk

# Contents

*Working with Children* is published by SocietyGuardian in association with NCH and replaces *Factfile*, NCH's annual statistical compendium. Essential facts and figures about children and families in the UK are combined with informative articles on a range of children's issues. A fully comprehensive list of contact details makes this guide an indispensible reference tool for anyone who works with children.

**Clare Horton** is Deputy Editor of SocietyGuardian.co.uk

## Acknowlegements

Thanks to all at NCH, especially Caroline Abrahams, Tina Webb, Amanda Allard, Jacqui McCluskey and George McNamara; Al Aynsley-Green and Ruth Johnstone; Adam Sampson and Matt Cornish at Shelter; Sharon Moore and Andrew Cooper at the Children's Society; David Walker, Polly Toynbee, David Batty, Polly Curtis at the Guardian.

# Introduction

## By David Walker

When, last year, children's minister Margaret Hodge was pilloried over her handling of a child abuse scandal while leader of Islington council, it was evidence of a certain kind of "joining up". How could she speak on nursery provision, the commentariat asked, when she had allegedly condoned failures in child protection? The answer was that, at last, a single minister had wide responsibilities for childcare and for children whether poor, well-off or in local authority care. Mrs Hodge's accumulated experience, not all of it positive, made her a strong candidate for this new job.

Of course her remit was still limited. You can go round the departments of Whitehall and see how responsibilities for children remain broken in fragments: their income dealt with by Inland Revenue, Treasury and Department for Work and Pensions; "bad" children the object of Home Office policy; sick children in the Department of Health; and, even within the Department of Education and Skills, older and younger children and their schooling and welfare split between divisions and ministers.

And Whitehall departments are just the outward manifestation of deeper ambiguities in public policy towards children. In schools the replacement of exams by course work relies on a notion of children selecting from a menu, then being left relatively free to structure their work.

Labour's national childcare strategy and its Sure Start programme have a core idea. Detached from family, it suggests, children will thrive; in social programmes they will realise themselves, unimpeded by the disadvantages of their homes.

But last year's children's green paper emphasised children's vulnerability and dependence and the need to build institutional walls against their victimhood. The flaring of debate, for example over children being driven to school rather than getting there under their own steam, shows this old conflict between autonomy and dependence is no nearer resolution.

Administratively speaking, would it even be wise to brigade together all the interests of all children in a single administrative entity? Might this end up pitting the interests of children against, say, those of older citizens or ethnic minorities or other groups that might claim similar bureaucratic recognition? A single "Department for Children" could not be justified on the back of persisting incoherence in public attitudes towards children.

Over the last two decades, opinion certainly moved in favour of children, with a 15% increase in the number of those saying their top priority for any extra public spending would be children - more than the 12% who put more for pensioners at the top of their list. But what's this? In the same period there was a 7% drop in the numbers of those who would reserve any incremental spending for single mothers and a huge 20% drop in those favouring the unemployed. Where do poor children live? They tend to live in workless households and with partnerless parents. Some evidence of lack of joining up in the public mind, perhaps.

That's just one of the problems with public opinion. For all the attention we in the media give poll findings, we rarely stop to point out the public's inconsistencies and, often, downright ignorance. Solid research-based evidence about the effectiveness of early years interventions — active roles for health visitors, nurseries, wraparound care and the like — routinely gets rejected by people who prefer the wisdom of personal experience.

Nursery provision faces an uphill struggle in the polling stakes. As the 2003 British Social Attitudes survey found, at an inopportune time for the government, a higher proportion of the population seems to favour spending on higher education than pre-school provision. What on earth explains the halving of public support for incremental spending on nurseries in the years since the mid-1990s?

The answer is likely to be complex. Recent years have been troubling for parents, grandparents and all those professionally involved with children - and all the more troubling because of the disparity between their day-to-day experience with children and what "public opinion" says seems to have grown. How rational has been the panic over paedophiles; how well founded the response to a tiny number of murders of children? At no other point in their lives are girls aged between five and 15 less likely to die from any cause. The homicide rate for school-age girls is lower than for any other group in society, including, of course, boys of the same age. Only one in 35 of all accidental deaths happens to children.

Facts and figures will not, in and of themselves, stop the contradictory pulls between policies based on ideas of children's autonomy and those emphasising their dependence. Dependence is expensive in terms of parental time and energy. Autonomy fits the modern, consumerist lifestyle better, as well as the claims of the children's rights movement and modern pedagogy.

Children's violent deaths suddenly shift the fulcrum, however exceptional they are as events, and we are all left confused. Can the child who must not be allowed out to play because of lurking dangers really be the same child exercising mature selection of subject and method in the classroom, the same child thriving in out-of-hours classes so mum can work?

Still, with a collection of data such as this to hand, there is no excuse either for exaggeration – or for minimising the plight of many children. Numbers will not trump prejudice but they offer a way into rational discussion. And we do need more and better national conversation about children - less preoccupied by protection - joining up what people say and how parents actually behave, giving expression to the necessary compromises between autonomy and authority, development and direction. It is a conversation not just for adults either, for no conversation about children can be complete without children's voices joining in and being attended to.

**David Walker** is the Guardian's specialist on the government's delivery agenda

# About NCH
## who we are and what we do

NCH, the children's charity, helps children and young people facing difficulties or challenges in their lives. Through more than 500 projects we work with over 100,000 vulnerable children, young people and their families. We work in partnership with them, ensuring their voices are heard and that services are designed with their needs in mind. Above all, we aim to ensure that all children and young people get the support and opportunities they need to reach their full potential.

NCH improves the lives of the UK's children and young people by offering them innovative, responsive and increasingly integrated services. Our services vary because they are developed in response to local needs, through partnerships with many statutory and voluntary agencies across the health, education and social care sectors.

Our services fall into the following categories:

For children at risk we provide:
- Family centres that specialise in helping families where there is a child protection concern
- Assessment services
- Sexual abuse treatment centres
- Residential, foster care and adoption services
- Independent visitors and advocacy services for children in care
- schools for children with special educational needs

For vulnerable young people we provide:
- Leaving care services
- Youth justice services
- Youth homelessness projects
- Projects that prevent truancy and school exclusion

For families in need of support we provide:
- Neighbourhood family and community centres
- Short break projects that support disabled children and their families
- Young carers projects
- Child-focused mediation for divorcing and separating parents
- Early years services including Sure Start

Many NCH projects are in disadvantaged neighbourhoods in the inner cities and outer estates, but we are also the largest UK provider of children's services in rural areas. The government has pledged to end child poverty by 2020 and we estimate that we work with more children who stand to gain from this than any other organisation.

NCH also works to improve children's lives by lobbying and campaigning for change, drawing on the views of our service users and our experience on the ground. In 2004 we will be focusing, among many other issues, on children and young people with mental health problems, families in need of support, young people in care and leaving care, and on the voluntary sector's contribution to improving children's services since the green paper, Every Child Matters, was published last year. Much of this work will happen in partnership with both statutory and voluntary organisations that share our campaigning objectives.

To find out more about our work, please visit our website at www.nch.org.uk

# Chapter 1

# Population

# Population

The number of people living in the United Kingdom has risen by 8.6 million over the last 50 years. This trend is set to continue with the UK population reaching a peak of around 64 million in 2040. By 2014 it is expected that, for the first time, the number of people aged 65 and over will exceed those aged under 16. By 2025 there will be 1.6 million more people of retirement age than those aged under 16. The 2001 census found that there were already more people aged over 60 than children aged under 16 in the UK, for the first time.

Source: Social Trends 33, ONS, the Stationery Office, 2003

## Actual and projected population of the UK (millions)

|  | 1951 | 1991 | 2001 | 2011 | 2021 | 2025 |
|---|---|---|---|---|---|---|
| England | 41.2 | 48.2 | 49.2 | 50.9 | 52.7 | 53.4 |
| Wales | 2.6 | 2.9 | 2.9 | 2.9 | 3 | 3 |
| Scotland | 5.1 | 5.1 | 5.1 | 5 | 4.9 | 4.8 |
| Northern Ireland | 1.4 | 1.6 | 1.7 | 1.7 | 1.8 | 1.8 |
| United Kingdom | 50.2 | 57.8 | 58.8 | 60.5 | 62.4 | 63 |

Source: ONS; Government Actuary's Department; General Register Office for Scotland; Northern Ireland Statistics and Research Agency, reported in Social Trends 33, ONS, the Stationery Office, 2003

In 2001-02, 8% of people in the United Kingdom described themselves as belonging to a minority ethnic group. In general, the minority ethnic population is of a younger age profile than the white population, with 38% of the Bangladeshi group being under the age of 16, double the proportion of the white group. However, 55% of the mixed ethnic group are aged under 16, considerably more than any of the other ethnic groups.

Source: Social Trends 33, ONS, the Stationery Office, 2003

## Population[1] by age and ethnic group, Great Britain, 2001-02

Age group (as a percentage of ethnic group)

|  | Under 16 | 16-34 | 35-64 | 65 and over |
|---|---|---|---|---|
| White | 19 | 25 | 40 | 16 |
| Mixed | 55 | 27 | 16 | 2 |
| **Asian or Asian British** | | | | |
| Indian | 22 | 33 | 38 | 6 |
| Pakistani | 35 | 36 | 25 | 4 |
| Bangladeshi | 38 | 38 | 20 | 3 |
| Other Asian | 22 | 36 | 38 | 4 |
| **Black or black British** | | | | |
| Black-Caribbean | 25 | 25 | 42 | 9 |
| Black-African | 33 | 35 | 30 | 2 |
| Other black groups[2] | 35 | 34 | 26 | - |
| Chinese | 18 | 40 | 38 | 5 |
| Other | 20 | 37 | 39 | 4 |
| All ethnic groups[3] | 20 | 26 | 39 | 15 |

[1] Population living in private households

[2] Sample size too small for reliable estimate of the 65 and over age group

[3] Includes those who did not state their age group

*Source: Annual Local Area Labour Force Survey, ONS, reported in Social Trends 33, ONS, the Stationery Office, 2003*

In 2001 there were 11.9 million children aged under 16 in the UK: 6.1 million boys and 5.8 million girls.

*Source: Social Trends 33, ONS, the Stationery Office, 2003*

## Number of children aged under sixteen (thousands)

| England | 9,900.40 |
|---|---|
| Wales | 586.7 |
| Scotland | 970.3 |
| Northern Ireland | 397.1 |

Source: Social Trends 33, ONS, the Stationery Office, 2003

## Trends in the number of live births

There were 596,122 live births in England and Wales in 2002 - an increase of 0.25% on 2001, when there were 594,634. This is the first increase since 1996. Apart from 2001, this annual total is still the lowest since 1977 when there were 569,259.

If the 2002 patterns of fertility by age were to remain unchanged, as represented by the total fertility rate (TFR), then an average of 1.65 children would be born per woman. This rate is marginally higher than that of 2001 (1.64).

*Source: Birth Statistics: Births and Patterns of Family Building England and Wales, Series FM1, ONS 2003 (Note: 2001 is the most recent year to which the contents refer)*

## Fertility rates

Changes in fertility patterns influence the size of households and families and also affect the age structure of the population. At the beginning of the 20th century there were about 115 live births per 1,000 women aged 15 to 44 in the UK, but in 2001 there were fewer than 55 births per 1,000 women of childbearing age.

There is an overall trend toward childbearing later in life. In England and Wales the average age of childbirth has increased by three years since 1971 from 26.2 years to 29.1 years in 2000. The average age of fathers at childbirth has also risen, from 27.2 years in 1971 to 31.7 years in 2001 for births registered to both parents.

*Source: Social Trends 33, ONS, the Stationery Office, 2003*

## Births outside marriage

More than four in 10 children in the United Kingdom were born outside marriage in 2001, compared with one in 10 in 1979. This increase is mainly due to the increasing number of cohabiting couples since the late 1980s. In 2001, three in four births outside marriage were jointly registered by both parents; three-quarters of these births were to parents living at the same address.

*Source: Social Trends 33, ONS, the Stationery Office, 2003*

# Children in families

| Percentage of children living in different family types, Great Britain | | | |
|---|---|---|---|
| | **1981** | **1992** | **2002** |
| **Couple families** | | | |
| 1 child | 18 | 18 | 17 |
| 2 children | 41 | 39 | 37 |
| 3 or more children | 29 | 27 | 24 |
| **Lone mother families** | | | |
| 1 child | 3 | 4 | 6 |
| 2 children | 4 | 5 | 7 |
| 3 or more children | 3 | 4 | 6 |
| **Lone father families** | | | |
| 1 child | 1 | 1 | 1 |
| 2 or more children | 1 | 1 | 1 |
| All children | 100 | 100 | 100 |

Source: General Household Survey and Labour Force Survey, ONS

Over the last 20 years there has been a decrease in the number of couple families and an increase in lone mother families. In 2002, one fifth of dependent children in Great Britain were living in lone parent households, almost twice the proportion in 1981.

*Source: Social Trends 33, ONS, the Stationery Office, 2003*

# Ethnicity and family structure

Different demographic structures, cultural traditions and economic characteristics of various ethnic groups in the United Kingdom underlie distinctive patterns of family structures across ethnic groups. In spring 2002, of families with dependent children 61% of those headed by a person of mixed origin and 54% headed by a person of black Caribbean origin were lone parent families. This compared with 23% headed by a white person and 9% headed by an Indian person.

Family size also varies by ethnicity, with Pakistani and Bangladeshi households being the largest. In spring 2002, the average size of Bangladeshi households was 4.7 people per household and for Pakistani households was 4.2 people. Such households may contain three generations, with grandparents living with a married couple and their children.

*Source: Social Trends 33, ONS, the Stationery Office, 2003*

# Partnerships

Although most people in Great Britain still marry, the proportion who do so has fallen over the last 30 years. In 1971, 71% of men and 65% of women in Great Britain were married; by 2000 this had fallen to 54% of men and 52% of women. Over the same period, the proportion who were divorced increased and was eight times greater for men and nine times greater for women, to reach almost a tenth of each group. The proportion remaining single has also increased, from a quarter of men and a fifth of women in 1971 to a third of men and a quarter of women in 2000. The proportions who cohabit have also increased. Between 1979 and 2000-01, the proportion who were cohabiting almost tripled, from 11% to 30%. In Great Britain a quarter of non married adults aged 16 to 59 were cohabiting in 2000-01.

*Source: ONS; General Register Office for Scotland, reported in Social Trends 33, ONS, the Stationery Office, 2003*

# Marriage

In 2000 there were 306,000 marriages in the UK, a 2% increase on the numbers in 1999. This was the first year that marriages had increased since 1992. There has been a long-term decline in the numbers of marriages since 1972, when 480,000 took place.

The number of first marriages in the UK peaked in 1970 at almost 390,000 and has since then reduced by about half - 180,000 in 2000. Since the 1960s first marriages have been taking place later in life. In 1961 the average age at first marriage in England and Wales was 26 for men and 23 for women. By 2000, this had increased to 31 and 28 respectively. The growth in pre-marital cohabitation helps to explain the recent trend towards later marriage, but other factors such as increased and longer participation in further and higher education, particularly among women, have also contributed. The number of remarriages has remained relatively constant over the last 25 years. In 2000 there were 126,000 remarriages, two-fifths of all marriages.

The marriage rate in the UK in 2000 was around the EU average of 5.1 per 1,000 people. Within the EU Denmark has the highest rate of 6.6 marriages per 1,000 people and Sweden the lowest at 4 marriages per 1,000 people.

*Source: ONS and Eurostat, reported in Social Trends 33, ONS, the Stationery Office, 2003*

# Divorce

There were 157,000 divorces in the UK in 2001, the first time there had been a rise since 1996. Average divorce rates across the EU have more than trebled since 1961, from 0.5 divorces per 1,000 population to 1.9 per 1000 population in 2001.

Source: Social Trends 33, ONS, the Stationery Office, 2003

# Children and divorce

In 2002, 149,000 children under 16 were affected by divorce, nearly twice as many as in 1971 but fewer than the highest figure recorded of 176,000 in 1993. Around one in four was under five years old and seven in 10 were under 10 years old. Almost one in four children born in 1979 had experienced divorce by the age of 16.

A survey of children in divorce has found that:

- Only one in 20 believes their parents' separation was properly explained to them.
- Instead, it was their grandparents and school friends who turned out to be their greatest sources of comfort.
- A quarter felt that no one had talked to them at all about the reasons for their parents' separation.
- Only one in 20 said they had been encouraged to ask questions.
- Children now living with lone mothers enjoyed just as warm a relationship with them as those in two-parent families, and had more shared activities.
- More than half of the children who spent time in two different households took a positive view of the arrangement. However, they expressed a desire to see the non-resident parent more often.

Source: Population Trends, 113 Report: Divorces in England and Wales during 2002, ONS 2003; One Parent Families Today: The Facts, National Council for One Parent Families, 2001; Children's Views Of Their Changing Families by Dunn J and Deater-Deckard K, Joseph Rowntree Foundation, 2001.

# Grandparents who raise their grandchildren

A recent survey of the experiences of grandparents who raise their grandchildren has found that:

- They all said the love they give to and receive from their grandchildren was the most rewarding aspect. Those who had stepped in after a crisis emphasised the importance of providing a safe and stable home within the family.

- 85% had to make financial sacrifices, with 71% saying this had led to financial hardship.
- A third had given up work to care for their grandchildren so had seen deficits in their pension provision: 14% had been forced to continue with work, some well past retirement age.
- 48% were coping with long-term health problems.
- For grandparents from minority ethnic communities there was little evidence of extended family stepping in, with most grandparents reliant on the immediate family.
- Most grandparents from minority ethnic communities were unaware of the services available locally and those who had tried to access help had been unsuccessful.

Source: Second Time Around: A Survey of Grandparents Raising Their Grandchildren, Family Rights Group, 2001.

# Stepfamilies

Stepfamilies can be either married or cohabiting couples. In 2000-01 stepfamilies where the head of the family was aged under 60 in Great Britain accounted for 8% of families with dependent children. Almost nine in 10 stepfamilies consisted of a couple with at least one child from a previous relationship of the female partner.

Source: General Household Survey, ONS, quoted in Social Trends 33, ONS, the Stationery Office, 2003

# Lone parenthood

Lone parents headed about 21% of all families with dependant children in Great Britain in spring 2002. There was an increase in the number of lone parent families until the mid-1980s, after which there was a more

| Lone parents with dependent children in GB | | |
|---|---|---|
| | Percentage of population | |
| 1971 | 3% | (600,000) of households |
| 1981 | 5% | (1,000,000) of households |
| 1991 | 6% | (1,300,000) of households |
| 2002 | 6% | (1,500,000) of households |

Source: Social Trends 2003

rapid rise. A large part of the increase up to the mid-1980s was due to divorce, while after 1986 the number of lone mothers grew at a faster rate with growth in the proportion of live births outside marriage. A lone mother heads a majority of lone parent families, with only 10% of lone parent families being headed by a lone father.

*Source: Social Trends 33, ONS, the Stationery Office, 2003*

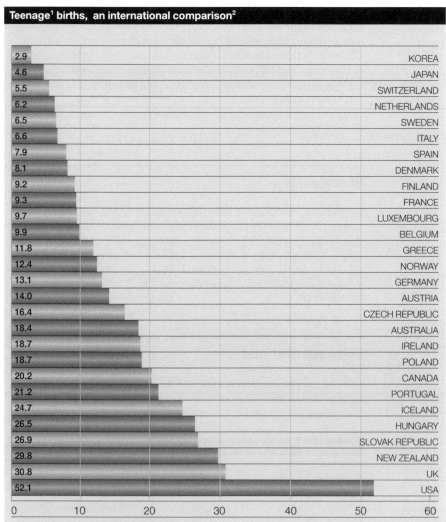

**Teenage[1] births, an international comparison[2]**

| Value | Country |
|---|---|
| 2.9 | KOREA |
| 4.6 | JAPAN |
| 5.5 | SWITZERLAND |
| 6.2 | NETHERLANDS |
| 6.5 | SWEDEN |
| 6.6 | ITALY |
| 7.9 | SPAIN |
| 8.1 | DENMARK |
| 9.2 | FINLAND |
| 9.3 | FRANCE |
| 9.7 | LUXEMBOURG |
| 9.9 | BELGIUM |
| 11.8 | GREECE |
| 12.4 | NORWAY |
| 13.1 | GERMANY |
| 14.0 | AUSTRIA |
| 16.4 | CZECH REPUBLIC |
| 18.4 | AUSTRALIA |
| 18.7 | IRELAND |
| 18.7 | POLAND |
| 20.2 | CANADA |
| 21.2 | PORTUGAL |
| 24.7 | ICELAND |
| 26.5 | HUNGARY |
| 26.9 | SLOVAK REPUBLIC |
| 29.8 | NEW ZEALAND |
| 30.8 | UK |
| 52.1 | USA |

[1] Births to women aged below 20 per 1,000 15 to 19 year-olds

[2] Data are for 1998, the most recent year for which comparable information is available from all countries.

*Source: Innocenti report card, Unicef, 2001*

## Teenage parenthood

Despite the overall trend towards later childbearing, the proportion of teenage girls becoming pregnant rose in the 1980s after fluctuating during the 1970s. In England and Wales in 2000 there were 98,000 conceptions to teenage girls aged under 20. 61% of these led to a maternity and 39% to abortions. There were 8,000 conceptions to girls under the age of 16. Of these conceptions almost 400 were to girls under the age of 14, 160 of which led to maternities.

Teenage births in the UK have remained at or above the level of the early 1980s. The UK, with an average live birth rate of 29 live births per 1,000 girls aged 15 to 19 in 2000, had the highest rate in the EU. This was more than two-fifths higher than Portugal, the country with the next highest rate. Italy and Sweden had the lowest rates at seven live births per 1,000 girls aged 15 to 19, and Denmark and the Netherlands had rates of almost eight live births per 1,000 young women.

*Source: Social Trends 33, ONS, the Stationery Office, 2003*

# Chapter 2

# Children's services

# Children's services: the key facts

## Expenditure

A Eurostat analysis across the EU has found that the expenditure on social protection benefits in the UK was £3,870 per head in 1999, close to the EU average of £3,810. Countries such as Luxembourg, Denmark, Sweden and the Netherlands spent more per head, while countries such as Greece, Portugal, the Irish Republic and Spain spent the least. (Social protection includes the NHS and social security system, as well as the personal social services).

*Source: Social Trends 33, ONS, the Stationery Office, 2003*

More than £40bn is estimated to be spent annually on delivering (all) services for children in England.

*Source: Report of the cross-cutting review on children at risk for Spending Review 2002, HMT 2002*

In 2000-01, £3.1bn was spent on personal social services for children by local authorities in England, up from £2.3bn in 1997-98 and £2.56bn in 1998-99.

*Source: PSS Current Expenditure Statistical Bulletins, Department of Health, 1997-2003*

The latest Children in Need census found that services provided to children in need by social services departments in England cost on average £61m per week: £37m per week on children looked after and £24m per week on other children in need. The average child looked after who received a service cost social services £600 a week and other children in need who received a service around £145 a week. These costs increased by about 23% between October 2001 and February 2003.

*Source: Children in Need in England: Preliminary results of a survey of activity and expenditure, ONS, Department for Education and Skills 2003*

In 1999-2000, voluntary organisations spent £367m on delivering "social protection services" to children in the UK. Charities helping children experienced the biggest increase in spending of all types of charity between 1996-97 and 1999-2000.

*Source: Charities Aid Foundation 2003, reported in Social Trends 33*

In 2002-03, total expenditure on education and training in England was an estimated £44.6bn in cash prices, up from £30.8bn in 1997-98. Between 1997-98 and 2002-03, revenue funding in maintained schools rose in real terms by £730 per pupil - 25%.

Source: Education and Training Expenditure Since 1993-94 Statistical Bulletin, DfES 2003

Between 2003-04 and 2005-06, the government will spend £1.5bn on Sure Start, early years and childcare.

Source: DfES annual report 2003

## Workforce issues

Research conducted by the Employers' Organisation for local government suggests that more than 4 million people in England currently work with children, or support those working with children (aged up to and including 18). This figure includes around 2.4 million paid staff and 1.8 million unpaid staff and volunteers.

**Estimated number of people working with children** (England)

|  | Paid education, care and support staff | Unpaid staff/volunteers |
|---|---|---|
| Education | 1,500,000 | 190,000 |
| Social care | 80,000 | 70,000 |
| Early years | 380,000 | 50,000 |
| Justice & probation | 20,000 |  |
| Sports, recreation and allied occupations | 480,000 | 1,480,000 |
| Total | 2,460,000 | 1,790,000 |

Note: health workers were omitted from this survey.

Source: Working With Children (interim report), the Employers' Organisation for local government, 2003

## The social care workforce

The social care workforce in England is estimated to include:

- 43,100 care staff employed in local authority social services departments.
- 16,500 professional staff, 18,500 administrative staff and 71,500 unpaid staff and volunteers employed in the voluntary sector.
- 37,000 foster families (UK estimate).

Source: Working With Children (interim report), the Employers' Organisation for local government, 2003

The most recent social services workforce survey (at September 30 2002) shows that in England:

- Children's social worker vacancies fell to 9.2% in 2002, down from 11.3% in 2001.
- Turnover rates within social work were particularly high for care staff working in children's homes (17.3% in 2002, up from 15.3% in 2001).
- Half the local authorities responding to the survey said they were currently experiencing difficulties in recruiting children's social workers and almost one in three said they were currently having difficulties in retaining them.
- There were significant regional variations with regard to the scale of these recruitment and retention difficulties. Although London and the south-east fared least well overall in their recruitment of social work and care staff, the south-west and Yorkshire and Humberside reported the greatest current difficulties in recruiting field social workers for children.
- Social services departments were using a wide range of strategies to try to overcome these problems. A fifth had recruited children's social workers from abroad - particularly Australia, South Africa, Zimbabwe and Canada. Others had raised rates of pay.
- The employment of long-term agency staff to cover vacancies cost social services £228m between 2001 and 2002, and 13% of all social work staff in London were from agencies.

*Source: Social Services Workforce Survey 2002, report no. 31, social and health care workforce group, the Employers' Organisation for local government, 2003*

## The education workforce

The education workforce in England is estimated to include:

- 437,200 (full-time equivalent) teachers employed by local education authorities.
- 731,700 non-teaching staff employed by local education authorities and schools.
- 187,400 volunteers working in local authority schools.
- 68,900 teachers and 21,000 support staff employed in the independent sector.

*Source: Working With Children (interim report), the Employers' Organisation for local government, 2003*

**Turnover and recruitment rates of LEA full-time permanent teachers (1999-2002)**
(England and Wales)

Turnover and recruitment rates (percentages of employment)

| | Female | | | | Male | | | | Total | | | |
|---|---|---|---|---|---|---|---|---|---|---|---|---|
| | 1999 | 2000 | 2001 | 2002 | 1999 | 2000 | 2001 | 2002 | 1999 | 2000 | 2001 | 2002 |
| **Turnover** | | | | | | | | | | | | |
| Primary | 10.2 | 12.6 | 12.5 | 11.6 | 10.7 | 13.6 | 15.6 | 12.5 | 10.3 | 12.8 | 13 | 11.7 |
| Secondary | 10 | 13.5 | 14.1 | 12.8 | 8.6 | 11.9 | 12.7 | 12 | 9.4 | 12.7 | 13.5 | 12.5 |
| Total | 10.1 | 13 | 13.2 | 12.1 | 9.1 | 12.3 | 13.4 | 12.2 | 9.8 | 12.8 | 13.2 | 12.1 |
| | | | | | | | | | | | | |
| **Recruitment** | | | | | | | | | | | | |
| Primary | 6.8 | 7.2 | 9 | 7.9 | 7.5 | 6.7 | 9.8 | 7.7 | 6.9 | 7.1 | 9.1 | 7.9 |
| Secondary | 9.9 | 12.8 | 15.3 | 14 | 7.2 | 9.4 | 12.1 | 11 | 8.6 | 11.2 | 13.8 | 12.6 |
| Total | 8.1 | 9.5 | 11.5 | 10.4 | 7.3 | 8.7 | 11.5 | 10.2 | 7.8 | 9.2 | 11.5 | 10.3 |

Source: Provisional results from the survey of teacher resignations and recruitment, calendar year 2002, the Employers' Organisation for local government, 2003

# Early years workforce

The early years workforce is estimated to include 274,500 paid childcare staff; between 75,000 and 100,000 nannies; 14,300 support (non childcare) staff; and 46,000 volunteers and unpaid trainees.

Source: Working With Children (interim report), the Employers' Organisation for local government, 2003

# Youth work workforce

The youth work workforce is estimated to include 11,100 workers employed by local education authorities and 39,900 youth workers employed outside local government.

Source: Working With Children (interim report), the Employers' Organisation for local government, 2003

# Service provision for children, young people and families

## Children in need and the services provided to assist them

In a typical calendar week in England in 2003:

- There were approximately 384,200 children in need. Of these 69,100 (18%) were looked after and 315,100 (82%) were in families or living independently – termed "other children in need" to differentiate them.
- Social services provided services for around 224,000 (58%) children in need
- 90% (62,100) of children looked after and 52% (162,300) of other children in need received a service or had money spent on their behalf
- The single main need for social service intervention for children is cases of "abuse and neglect" which account for just over half (55%) of all children looked after and 26% of other children in need.

*Source: Children in Need In England: Preliminary results of a survey of activity and expenditure, ONS, Department for Education and Skills, 2003*

## Childcare and early years services

Between 1997 and December 2002, 367,000 new childcare places were added to the stock available in England, taking turnover and other factors into account.

By April 2003, 450 Sure Start programmes had been established - with a further 74 in development and due to be up and running by summer 2003. When they are fully operational, it is estimated that they will cover approximately 400,000 children under four and about a third of children aged under four living in poverty in England.

*Source: DfES annual report 2003*

## Services for young people

From April 2002 to January 2003, more than 2.7 million interventions were carried out by the Connexions service with young people aged 13-19 in England.

*Source: DfES, 2003*

## Family support services

The first attempt at mapping family support services in England and Wales found:

- 47% of services have been established for 10 years or more but 40% have been established only in the last five years.
- The voluntary sector provides 49% of family support services, most of them funded by local authorities.
- There are twice as many services for families of children under five as for families of children aged five to 10.
- Only 2% of services are aimed specifically at minority ethnic groups.

*Source: National Mapping of Family Services in England and Wales, by Henricson C, Katz I, Sandison M and Tunstill J, National Family and Parenting Institute, 2001*

# Chapter 3

# Children's health

# Children's health: an overview

**By Professor Al Aynsley-Green**

Every Child Matters, the government's recently published green paper on children, outlines a long overdue and most welcome series of proposals to transform the standing of children, young people and families in government policy. Children really do matter.

Not only do they represent between 20 and 25% of local communities, but they are citizens now. They are not people of the future, and they deserve to have an appropriate focus in policy and resource allocation. Furthermore, nothing matters more to families than the health, welfare and future success of their children, and our national survival depends upon healthy children becoming healthy adults.

There is incontrovertible fact that so much adult ill health and disease have their roots in childhood. While it is true that the vast majority of children and young people lead rich and fulfilled lives, nonetheless, there are widening inequalities of health, wealth and education, with many children, young people and families not benefiting from society.

That all has not been well with the standing and quality of health and social care services provided for them has been exposed by the public inquiries chaired by Sir Ian Kennedy and Lord Laming into the outcome of children having cardiac surgery and into the murder of eight-year-old Victoria Climbié respectively.

In order to speak effectively for children, young people and families, the starting point has to be a firm foundation of fact on contemporary child life and health. This book, with its collation of the most recent research and data about children's services together with details of the action that government is taking in these areas is very welcome and will provide essential reading for those engaged in policy formulation and in developing effective services at the local level.

This data source will be a relevant toolkit for all who are concerned with implementing not only Every Child Matters, but also Getting the Right Start – the national service framework for children, young people and maternity services.

There are outstanding opportunities now to improve the lives and health of children in contemporary society. Effective advocacy is dependant on access to key information.

**Professor Al Aynsley-Green** is the national clinical director for children; chair of the children's taskforce, Department of Health, London; Nuffield Professor of Child Health, Institute of Child Health and Great Ormond Street Hospital, University College London.

# Children's health: the key facts

## Infant mortality

One of the major factors contributing to increased life expectancy over the past century has been the huge fall in infant mortality. In 1921, 84.0 children per 1,000 live births in the UK died before the age of one; by 2002 the rate had fallen to 5.3. This decline in infant mortality can be largely attributed to improvements in children's diet, improvements in sanitation and hygiene, better antenatal and postnatal care and the development of vaccines and immunisation programmes.

*Source: Social Trends 33, ONS, the Stationery Office 2003*

There were 3,168 infant deaths (under one year of age) in England and Wales in 2002, compared with 3,240 in 2001.

There were 3,372 still births in England and Wales in 2002 and 1,633 perinatal deaths (of children aged under seven days).

There were wide regional variations within England and the West Midlands had the highest infant mortality rate at 8.1 deaths per 1,000. The lowest rate, 4.4 deaths per thousand, was in the south-east. The West Midlands also had the highest rates of neonatal (deaths under four weeks) and perinatal mortality (still births and deaths under one week).

Boys are more likely to die than girls. There were six deaths per 1,000 boys under one and 4.6 per 1,000 girls.

*Source: Health Statistics Quarterly 19, Department of Health, Autumn 2003*

For those children dying within the first 28 days of life, the main causes were conditions related to prematurity, such as very low birthweight or respiratory distress of the newborn and congenital anomalies.

*Source: Mortality Statistics: Childhood, infant and perinatal 2001, Series DH3, No.34, ONS*

The 2002 infant death rate in the UK is still higher than the 2001 rate in France, Germany, Italy and Spain and although falling is the second worse in EU, beaten only by Greece.

*Source: The State of the World's Children 2002, Unicef 2003.*

## Sudden infant deaths

There were 187 sudden infant deaths in England and Wales in 2002, compared with 240 in 2001, a decrease of 22%. The sudden infant death rate fell from 0.40 per 1,000 live births in 2001 to 0.31 in 2002. The sudden infant death rate was highest for babies of mothers aged under 20 at the time of the child's birth (0.97 per 1,000 live births).

In the period 1998-2002, 61% of all sudden infant deaths occurred amongst boys, who comprised 51% of all live births. In the same period, 89% of sudden infant deaths occurred in babies aged less than six months and 61% occurred in babies aged less than three months.

Source: Sudden Infant Deaths 2002, Health Statistic Quarterly 19, autumn 2003, ONS

## Childhood mortality

There were 1,420 deaths of children aged between one and 14 years in England and Wales in 2001, giving a death rate of 15 deaths per 100,000 children in this age group, the same as in 2000. For one to four-year-olds, the rate was 24 deaths per 100,000 children, while for five to nine-year-olds it was less than half this at 11 per 100,000.

The main causes of deaths in 2001 among children aged one to 15 years were cancer and injury and poisoning. Cancer accounted for 21% of deaths among girls and 18% among boys in the age group, but boys were far more likely to die from injury and poisoning than girls, 27% and 18% respectively.

Source: Mortality Statistics: Childhood, Infant and Perinatal, 2001, series DH3, No.34, ONS

## Causes of death in childhood

In 1998-2000, cancers were the most common cause of death among girls aged five to 15 in England and Wales, accounting for 23% of the total in this age group. They were the second most common cause among boys in this age group, accounting for 24% of deaths. Between 1985 and 2000 cancer mortality rates in the age group five to 15 fell by a third, even though the incidence of cancers changed little.

In 1998-2000 accidents were the most common cause of death among boys aged 5 to 15, representing 27% of the total. At 17%, accidents were the second most common cause of death among girls in this age group. Most of these deaths were caused by transport accidents, accounting for 61% of accidental deaths among boys and 73% among girls.

Infections were a more common cause of death in children aged one to four years than in older children, causing around a tenth of deaths in both boys and girls. Deaths caused by cancers and accidents each accounted for around a sixth of deaths among both boys and girls in this age group.

**Main causes of child mortality 1998-2000** (England and Wales)

| | Percentages | | | |
|---|---|---|---|---|
| | **Males** | | **Females** | |
| | **1-4** | **5-15** | **1-4** | **5-15** |
| Infections | 10 | 4 | 9 | 6 |
| Cancers | 15 | 24 | 13 | 23 |
| Nervous system & sense organs | 13 | 15 | 13 | 16 |
| Circulatory system | 6 | 5 | 8 | 5 |
| Respiratory system | 11 | 6 | 9 | 8 |
| Congenital anomalies | 13 | 6 | 16 | 8 |
| Accident | 16 | 27 | 15 | 17 |
| Other | 17 | 13 | 16 | 16 |
| All deaths | 1,153 | 1,773 | 855 | 1,239 |

Source: Social Trends 33, ONS, the Stationery Office 2003

# Childhood morbidity

A survey involving more than 10,000 young people between the ages of 11 and 16 revealed that headaches and emotional distress are the most common symptoms of ill-health in this age group. In terms of gender, girls suffer more headaches and stomach aches than boys.

Source: Young People and Health: Health Behaviour in School-Aged Children, Health Education Authority, 1999

The median number of GP consultations of 10 to 15-year-olds was two per year for young men and three per year for young women.

Source: Socio-economic Differences in Childhood Consultation Rates in General Practice in England and Wales, by Saxena S, Majeed A and Jones M, British Medical Journal, 318, 642-647 1999

The latest survey of 10 to 15-year-olds in the UK by the Schools Health Education Unit found that:

- 26% of 14 to 15-year-old girls report health problems and 42% would turn to their mother for support.

- About 27% of the children reported visiting their GP within the previous month, and about 50% of all the young people had done so within the previous three months.
- 25% of 12 to 15-year-old females reported feeling "quite uneasy" or "very uneasy" on their last visit to the doctor.
- Up to 18% of the 10 to 15-year-olds report having asthma.
- Around 60% of females report "wheezing" and have trouble breathing when they run.
- 53% of the 14 to 15-year-old females had taken painkillers on at least one day during the previous week. 31% of 14 to 15-year-old males also report taking painkillers. 40% of 12 to 13-year-old females and 25% of 12 to 13-year-old males said they took painkillers "at least one day in the last week".
- During the previous year, around 40% of the males had an accident that needed treatment from a doctor or at a hospital. Most accidents for males occur while playing sport. Females are more likely to report accidents that occur at home.
- The majority of children surveyed feel they are in control of their health. At least a quarter do not think they can influence their health by their own efforts.

Source: Young People in 2002, Schools Health Education Unit, 2003

## Accidents

10% of boys and 7% of girls reported having at least one major accident in the previous six months. The proportion reporting more than one accident was 1%. Annual major accident rates per 100 persons were 23 in boys and 17 in girls.

5% of boys and 3% of girls reported having at least one minor accident in the previous fortnight. The proportion reporting more than one accident was minimal. Children's minor accident rates were 149 per 100 boys and 131 per 100 girls. A peak in minor accidents was seen at age 14 to 15 for both sexes (243 per 100 boys and 222 per 100 girls).

Source: Health Survey for England 2001, Non-fatal Accidents, the Stationery Office, 2003

## Asthma

Asthma is the most common chronic condition in children. However, in the last five years there has been a decline in the number of new cases of asthma diagnosed in both sexes. Among both sexes, new attacks are far more common during childhood particularly between the ages of one and four years. Incidences of asthma in childhood tend to be higher for boys than for girls.

## New episodes[1] of asthma (England and Wales)

Rates per 100,000 population

|  | 1996 | 1998 | 2000 | 2001 |
|---|---|---|---|---|
| **Males** | | | | |
| Under 1 | 106.9 | 74.6 | 48.5 | 42.3 |
| 1-4 | 151.9 | 113.6 | 90.2 | 74.8 |
| 5-14 | 78.8 | 71.2 | 56.1 | 49.9 |
| 15-24 | 40.0 | 33.1 | 26.0 | 23.1 |
| **Females** | | | | |
| Under 1 | 56.9 | 37.0 | 29.6 | 31.0 |
| 1-4 | 111.9 | 93.5 | 56.6 | 56.4 |
| 5-14 | 65.0 | 58.5 | 42.1 | 32.9 |
| 15-24 | 56.8 | 53.2 | 43.4 | 37.6 |

[1] Mean weekly incidence. A diagnosis for the first time or a previously diagnosed asthmatic person having a new attack.

*Source: Social Trends 33, ONS, the Stationery Office, 2003*

# Diabetes

Diabetes is the third most common chronic condition in children after asthma and cerebral palsy with at least 20,000 children and young people in the UK suffering with it. The large majority of children and young people with diabetes have type 1, which nearly always occurs in childhood, adolescence or young adulthood. Incidence of type 1 is increasing but epidemiological studies have not been able to explain exactly why. A small but growing number of adolescents have developed type 2 diabetes which is usually associated with people over 40 and with obesity and a sedentary lifestyle.

*Source: Injection of Hope, Zero2Nineteen magazine, July 2003*

# Immunisation

Over the past 50 years, a key factor in the reduction of infectious diseases and the associated morbidity and mortality has been the development of childhood vaccination programmes. Current government immunisations targets are for 95% of children to be immunised against tetanus, diptheria, poliomyelitis, whooping cough (pertussis) and measles, mumps and rubella. In 1988 the measles, mumps, rubella (MMR) vaccine was introduced. Notifications of measles fell to their lowest recorded annual total of under 3,000 in 2001. The number of children who have received the MMR vaccine by their second birthday has fallen from 91% in 1997-98 to 88% in 2000-01. It is likely that media reports speculating on a link between MMR, Crohn's disease and autism have contributed to this decline.

**Immunisation of children** (UK)

| | | | | | Percentages | |
|---|---|---|---|---|---|---|
| | 1981[1] | 1991-92 | 1994-95 | 1998-99 | 1999-00 | 2000-01 |
| Tetanus | 83 | 94 | 93 | 96 | 95 | 95 |
| Diptheria | 83 | 94 | 95 | 95 | 95 | 95 |
| Poliomyelitis | 82 | 94 | 95 | 95 | 95 | 95 |
| Whooping cough | 45 | 88 | 95 | 94 | 94 | 94 |
| Measles, mumps, rubella[2] | 54 | 90 | 91 | 89 | 88 | 88 |

[1] Data excludes Scotland

[2] Includes measles-only vaccine for 1981. Combined vaccine was not available prior to 1988.

Source: Social Trends 33, ONS, the Stationery Office, 2003

## Children and young people's mental health

The 1999 National Statistics survey is the most recent comprehensive study of the mental health of children and adolescents aged five to 15-years-old in Great Britain. The survey found:

- 11% of boys and 8% of girls had a mental disorder (mental disorders are a clinically recognisable set of symptoms or behaviour associated with considerable distress and substantial interference with personal functions).
- Among children aged five to 10 years, 10% of boys and 6% of girls had a mental disorder.
- At 11 to 15 years 13% of boys and 10% of girls had a mental disorder.
- Among children aged five to 15 years, 5% had clinically significant conduct disorders, 4% were assessed as having emotional disorders such as anxiety and depression, and 1% were rated as hyperactive.
- While the rates of emotional disorders were similar for boys and girls, the prevalence of conduct disorder was approximately twice as common among boys than girls, and for hyperkinetic disorders the ratio was even greater; 2% among boys of all ages compared with about 0.5% of girls.
- Nearly 10% of white children and 12% of black children were assessed as having a mental health problem whereas the prevalence rates among Asian children were 8% of the Pakistani and Bangladeshi and 4% of the Indian samples.

- Although the overall prevalence of mental disorders among children and adolescents was 10%, the rate among children in well functioning families was 7% compared with 18% among poorly functioning families.
- Although children with a mental disorder were more likely than other children to have had one stressful life event: 82% compared with 70%, they were far more likely to have experienced three or more events: 31% compared with 13%.

*Source: The Mental Health of Children and Adolescents in Great Britain, by Meltzer H et al, ONS, the Stationery Office, 2000*

## Characteristics of children with mental disorders

- One in five children has officially recognised special educational needs – those with a disorder are about three times more likely than other children to have special needs (49% compared with 15%).
- Those with a mental disorder are about four times more likely than other children to have played truant (33% compared with 9%). Children with conduct disorders had the highest rate of truancy at 44%.
- 25% of 11 to15-year-olds reported that they had been in trouble with the police at least once: this includes 43% of children with a mental disorder and 21% of children with no disorder.
- Children with a mental disorder are far more likely to be frequently punished than children with no disorder: 18% compared with 8% were frequently sent to their rooms; 17% compared with 5% were frequently grounded; and 42% compared with 26% were frequently shouted at.
- 50% of children with a mental disorder had at one time experienced the separation of their parents, compared with 29% of children who did not suffer from a mental disorder.

*Source: Mental Health of Children and Adolescents in Great Britain by Meltzer H et al, ONS, the Stationery Office, 2000*

## Family and household characteristics of children with mental disorders

The prevalence rates of mental disorders were greater among children in:

- Lone parent compared with two parent families (16% compared with 8%).
- Reconstituted families rather than those with no stepchildren (15% compared with 9%).

- Families with five or more children compared with two children (18% compared with 8%).
- Families in which parents had no educational qualifications compared with a degree level or equivalent qualification (15% compared with 6%).

*Source: Mental Health of Children and Adolescents in Great Britain by Meltzer H et al, ONS, the Stationery Office, 2000*

**Note:** links between childhood mental disorders and socio-economic disadvantage are reported in the chapter on poverty and social exclusion.

## Children and adolescents who try to harm, hurt or kill themselves

### Five to 10-year-olds

- According to parents, approximately 1.3% of five to 10-year-olds had ever tried to harm, hurt or kill themselves. The lowest rate, 0.4% was found among five to seven-year-old girls rising to 2.1% of 8 to 10-year-old boys.
- The rate of self-harm among the sample of young children with no mental disorder was 0.8%. The rate increased dramatically to 6.2% of children diagnosed as having an anxiety disorder and 7.5% of those who had a conduct disorder, hyperkinetic disorder or a less common mental disorder.

The prevalence of self-harm among five to 10-year-olds was greater for children in:

- Lone parent compared with two-parent families (1.9% and 1.1%).
- Single child families compared to those with 3 or more children (1.8% and 1.1%).
- Social class V families (unskilled manual) (2.6%) compared with social class I families (professional) (0.9%).
- Families who were social housing tenants or private renters (1.8-2.1%) compared with owner occupiers (1.0%).
- England (1.4%) rather than Scotland (0.8%) or Wales (0.7%).

The prevalence of self-harm among five to 10-year-olds increased with:

- An increase in the number of stressful life events: 0.8% among those with none compared with 2.3% of children who had experienced 3 events and 13.3% among five to 10-year-olds who had had five or more stressful life events.
- An increase in the degree of family discord: 1.1% among children with no family discord (healthy functioning) rising to 3.7% of children in the most dysfunctional families.
- An increase in the frequency of punishment: 1.0% of children seldom or occasionally punished compared with 1.8% of those frequently punished.

## 11 to 15-year-olds

- According to parents, approximately 2.1% of 11 to 15-year-olds had ever tried to harm, hurt or kill themselves. The highest rate, 3.1%, was found among 13 to 15-year-old girls.
- The rate of self-harm among the sample of 11 to 15-year-olds with no mental disorder was 1.2%. The rate increased markedly to 9.4% of those with anxiety disorders, 18.8% of children diagnosed as having depression, 12.6% of those who had a conduct disorder and 8.5% among children with a hyperkinetic disorder.

The prevalence of self-harm among 11 to 15-year-olds was greater for children in:

- Lone parent compared with two-parent families (3.1% and 1.8%).
- Families with stepchildren as distinct from those without (3.7% and 1.8%).
- Families with five or more children compared with those with fewer children (6.2% and 2.0%).
- Families who were social sector tenants (3.7%) or private renters (3.2%) compared with owner occupiers (1.5%).
- Wales (2.8%) and England (2.2%) rather than Scotland (1.0%).

The prevalence of self-harm among 11 to 15-year-olds increased with:

- An increase in the number of stressful life events: 1.2% among those with none compared with 3.6% of children who had experienced three events and 9.5% among 11 to 15-year-olds who had had five or more stressful life events.
- An increase in the degree of family discord; 1.5% among children with no family discord (healthy functioning) to 8.4% of children in the most dysfunctional families.
- An increase in the frequency of punishment: 1.9% of children seldom or occasionally punished compared with 2.9% of those frequently punished.

*Source: Children and Adolescents who try to Harm, Hurt or Kill Themselves, ONS, 2001*

---

# Suicide

In 2000 a total of 555 young men in the UK between the ages of 15 and 24 took their lives. Suicide rates for young men in England and Wales have fallen from 16 per 100,000 in 1997 to 12 per 100,000 in 2000. However, in Scotland rates for young men have risen from 23 per 100,000 in 1990 to 36 per 100,000 in 2000.

*Source: Key Data on Adolescence 2003 by Coleman J & Schofield S, the Trust for the Study of Adolescence, 2003*

# Diet and lifestyle

## National diet and nutrition survey

This survey of children and young people aged four to 18 found:

- The foods most commonly consumed by children and young people in the survey (over 80%) were white bread; savoury snacks; potato chips; boiled, mashed and jacket potatoes and chocolate confectionery.
- Boys eat, by weight, more than four times as many biscuits as leafy green vegetables and girls eat, by weight, more than four times as many sweets and chocolate as leafy green vegetables.
- The most commonly consumed fruits were apples and pears, eaten by more than half the group, followed by bananas, eaten by just under 4%. A quarter of young people ate citrus fruit and a third ate "other" fruit (mainly soft fruit). Whereas 33% of 15 to 18-year-old girls smoke, only 20% eat citrus fruit.
- Three-quarters drank standard carbonated soft drinks and 45% drank low calorie versions. Girls drink two-thirds more fizzy drinks than milk.
- The average proportion of food energy derived from total fat was 35% for boys and 36% for girls, close to the Committee on Medical Aspects of food and nutrition policy (COMA) recommendation of 35%. The average proportion of food energy derived from saturated fatty acids was 14.2% for boys and 14.3% for girls, above the COMA recommendation of 11%.
- Non-milk extrinsic sugars (NMES) provided on average 16.7% of food energy for boys and 16.4% for girls, which exceeded the COMA recommended average of no more than 11%. The main source of NMES intake was carbonated soft drinks, followed by chocolate confectionery.
- Indicators of socio-economic status such as receipt of benefits, household income and social class showed that children, particularly boys, in households of lower socio-economic status had lower intakes of energy, fat, some other macronutrients and most vitamins and minerals.

Source: National Diet and Nutrition Survey of Children and Young People aged four to 18, Food Standards Agency, 2000

# Food choices and weight

A survey of 10 to 15-year-old children in the UK found that:

- 20% of the 14 to 15-year-old females had nothing at all for breakfast on the morning of the survey and 16% of the 14 to 15-year-old females ate no lunch on their previous day at school.
- 28% of the 14 to 15-year-old females who had nothing to eat at breakfast that morning had nothing to eat at lunch the previous day at school.
- 61% of 14 to 15-year-old females and 54% of the 12 to 13-year-old females "would like to lose weight". The proportion of the 14 to 15-year-old females who missed breakfast and lunch and "would like to lose weight" was 22%.
- Over 66% of older pupils have dairy products regularly. Females, from 10 to 15 years, show a greater preference for fresh fruit, salads and vegetables.
- Females are more likely than males to take health into account when choosing what to eat. 24% of the 14 to 15-year-old males say they never do.

Source: Young People in 2002, Schools Health Education Unit, 2003

# Exercise and activities

A survey by the Schools Health Education Unit found that:

- At least 53% of 10 to 15-year-old in the UK walk to school, 22-29% go by car and 19% go by school bus.
- Up to 69% of 10 to 11-year-old pupils think they are "fit" or "very fit". 26% of the 14 to 15-year-old females describe themselves as "unfit" or "very unfit". Perceived fitness declines with age in both males and females.
- Over 80% of 10 to 15-year-olds had exercised to the level of "breathing hard" at least once in the previous week. The gap is seen to widen between males and females among the frequent exercisers as they get older. More than 10% of 10 to 15-year-olds never exercise.
- The most common evening activity is television watching (between 71 and 85%). Other popular activities for 10 to 15-year-old males include computer games, meeting with friends and playing sport. Popular activities with 10 to 15-year-old females include reading a book and caring for pets.
- Up to 71% of the males, compared with up to 35% of the females, spent some time playing computer games on the previous evening.

- Up to 87% of 14 to 15-year-olds and more than 78% of all 10 to 15-year-olds have internet access. At least 57% of children have access to the internet at home. 71% of 14 to 15-year-old males browse without adult supervision.

*Source: Young People in 2002, Schools Health Education Unit, 2003*

- Most children and young people were inactive. Girls were less active than boys and activity levels fell with increasing age. About a third of boys and over half of girls aged seven to 14 failed to meet the HEA recommendation for children to participate in at least moderate intensity activity for one hour a day.
- About 50% walked to school, about one third travelled by car and about 20% by bus. Between 1% and 6% cycled to school. Boys were significantly more likely to cycle to school than girls. Older children were significantly less likely to travel by car. Boys from families in receipt of benefits had significantly lower activity scores than other boys.

*Source: National Diet and Nutrition Survey of Children and Young People aged four to 18, Food Standards Agency, 2000*

## Obesity

The growth in the number of people in the population who are overweight and obese is of increasing concern in most developed countries of the world. While obesity is more common in older age groups the growth in the proportion of overweight and obese children is a major concern.

- In 2001 8.5% of six-year-olds and 15% of 15-year-olds were obese.
- Between 1996 and 2001 the proportion of overweight children increased by 7% and obese children by 3.5%.
- Particularly worrying is that maturity onset (or type 2) diabetes, which previously was seen only in middle and older age, is now being seen among teenagers for the first time, thought to be as a result of childhood obesity.
- Obesity is responsible for 9,000 premature deaths each year in England, and reduces life expectancy by, on average, nine years.

*Source: Health Check: On the State of the Public Health, annual report of the Chief Medical Officer 2002, Department of Health 2003*

# Substance misuse

## Smoking

A recent survey commissioned by the Department of Health found:

- In 2002 10% of pupils aged 11 to 15 in England were regular smokers (defined as usually smoking at least one cigarette a week). The proportion of regular smokers has been quite stable since 1998.
- Prevalence of smoking was strongly related to age. Only 1% of 11-year-olds were regular smokers compared with 23% of 15-year-olds.
- In the early 1980s, boys and girls were equally likely to smoke. Since then, girls have been consistently more likely to smoke than boys. In 2002, 11% of girls were regular smokers, compared with 9% of boys.
- Although girls were more likely to smoke than boys, boys smoked more cigarettes than girls. Among regular smokers, boys smoked an average of 52 cigarettes in the last seven days, compared with 48 for girls.
- 69% of regular smokers usually bought cigarettes from a newsagent. The most common source of cigarettes for occasional smokers was friends (72%).
- Between 1990 and 2002, the proportion of pupils who had attempted to purchase cigarettes from a shop in the last year decreased from 32% to 18%.

*Source: Smoking, Drinking & Drug Use Among Young People in England in 2002, summary of key findings, Boreham R & McManus S (eds), ONS, 2002*

According to the Schools Health Education survey of children in the UK aged 10 to 15 years old:

- 27% of the 14 to 15-year-old females and 20% of the 14 to 15-year-old males smoked at least one cigarette during the previous week.
- Between 12 to 13 years and 14 to 15 years, the number of regular smokers more than triples. Up to 65% will have smoked by year 10. The majority of current smokers say they would like to stop. 57% of the year 10 females have a close friend who smokes. Around 50% of all 10 to 15-year-olds live in a "smoky" home.

*Source: Young People in 2002, Schools Health Education Unit, 2003*

## Alcohol

A survey commissioned by the Department of Health found:

- 24% of pupils aged 11 to 15 in England said they had had an alcoholic drink in the previous week (25% of boys and 23% of girls).
- Drinking was strongly related to age: 5% of 11-year-olds had drunk alcohol in the last week compared with 47% of 15-year-olds.
- The average amount of alcohol consumed over a week has risen steadily from 5.3 units of alcohol in 1990 to 9.9 units in 1998, and has fluctuated at this level since then. In 2002, pupils who drank in the last week consumed an average of 10.5 units.
- Among those who drank in the last week, boys consumed an average of 11.5 units in 2002 compared with 9.6 units for girls.
- 15-year-olds who drank consumed 12.9 units in the last week, compared with 6.8 units for 11 to 13-year-olds.
- The type of alcohol drunk has changed over time: in 2002, beer, lager and cider were still the most common type of drink (drunk by 71% of drinkers in the last week) but the prevalence of alcopops has increased in recent years from 55% in 1996 to 68% of drinkers in 2002. The proportion of drinkers who had drunk spirits in the last week increased from 35% in 1990 to 61% in 2002, whereas the prevalence of drinking shandy, wine or fortified wine in the last week has decreased in recent years.
- Among pupils who drink, 48% reported they never buy alcohol. The most common sources of alcohol in 2002 were friends or relatives and off-licences, reported by 17% and 16% respectively of all pupils who drink. There has been a shift in recent years towards purchasing from friends or relatives (from 9% in 1998 to 17% in 2002) and away from purchasing from off-licences (from 27% in 1996 to 16% in 2002).

*Source: Smoking, Drinking & Drug Use Among Young People in England in 2002, summary of key findings, Boreham R & McManus S (eds), ONS, 2002*

According to the Schools Health Education survey of children in the UK aged 10 to 15 years old:

- Between 13% and 21% of 10 to 11-year-olds, 28% of 12 to 13-year-olds, and 47% of 14 to 15-year-olds had consumed at least one alcoholic drink in the previous week.
- 27% of the males and 10% of the females aged 14 to 15 drank at least one pint of beer or lager during the previous week.
- 24% of the 14 to 15-year-old females drank at least one small bottle of alcopops during the previous week. 20% of the 14 to 15-year-old females had drunk at least one glass of wine during the previous week. Since 1996, older females have overtaken males as spirit drinkers with

20% of 14 to 15-year-old females drinking one or more spirit measures in the past week.

- Almost twice as many males as females aged 14 to 15 drank 15 or more units of alcohol in the previous week. 19% of the older males drank over 11 units.
- Most "drinkers" drank at home and substantial numbers of 14 to 15-year-olds used other venues including friends' homes, discos, clubs, pubs and outside in public places. Of those who drank at home, about half did so with their parents always knowing about it.

*Source: Young People in 2002, Schools Health Education Unit, 2003*

## Drugs

According to the most recent Department of Health survey:

- Among pupils in England aged 11 to 15, the prevalence of having ever taken drugs decreased between 2001 and 2002 from 29% to 26%, with a corresponding decrease in drug taking in the last year (from 20% to 18%). The proportion of pupils who reported taking drugs in the last month was 11% in 2002, a similar level to 2001 (12%).
- Between 2001 and 2002, the proportion of girls who had taken drugs in the last month fell from 11% to 9% and the proportion who had taken drugs in the last year decreased from 19% to 17%. Among boys in 2002, 12% had taken drugs in the last month (13% in 2001) and 20% in the last year (21% in 2001). As in previous surveys, boys were more likely than girls to have taken drugs.
- Older pupils were much more likely to take drugs: 3% of 11-year-olds had taken drugs in the last month, but 22% of 15-year-olds had. 45% of 15-year-olds had ever tried drugs at some point and 36% had taken drugs in the last year.
- Cannabis was by far the most widely taken drug, with 13% of pupils having taken it in the last year. 6% had sniffed volatile substances. No other individual drug had been taken by more than 4% of pupils, with a total of 4% taking any class A drugs in the last year.
- Prevalence of taking cannabis in the last year increased with age from 1% of 11-year-olds to 31% of 15-year-olds. Prevalence of taking class A drugs in the last year also increased with age, but not to the same extent as cannabis, from 1% of 11-year-olds to 8% of 15 year olds.
- Among younger pupils (11 and 12-year-olds), sniffing glue or other solvents was more common than taking cannabis. Among 11-year-olds, 1% had taken cannabis in the last year, compared with 5% who had sniffed glue or other solvents.

*Source: Smoking, Drinking & Drug Use Among Young People in England in 2002, summary of key findings, Boreham R & McManus S (eds), ONS, 2002*

## Drug use by 11 to 15-year-olds[1] (England)

| | Percentages | | | | |
|---|---|---|---|---|---|
| | **1998** | **1999** | **2000** | **2001** | **2002** |
| Any drug | 11 | 12 | 14 | 20 | 18 |
| Cannabis | 10 | 11 | 12 | 13 | 13 |
| **Stimulants** | | | | | |
| Cocaine | 1 | 1 | 1 | 1 | 1 |
| Crack | 0 | 1 | 1 | 1 | 1 |
| Ecstasy | 1 | 1 | 1 | 2 | 1 |
| Amphetamines | 2 | 1 | 1 | 1 | 1 |
| Poppers | 1 | 2 | 2 | 3 | 4 |
| **Psychedelics** | | | | | |
| LSD | 1 | 1 | 1 | 1 | 1 |
| Magic mushrooms | 1 | 1 | 1 | 2 | 1 |
| **Opiates** | | | | | |
| Heroin | 0 | 0 | 1 | 1 | 1 |
| Methadone | 0 | 0 | 1 | 1 | 1 |
| Glue, gas and other solvents | 1 | 3 | 3 | 7 | 6 |
| Other drugs | 1 | 0 | 1 | 1 | 0 |
| Any class A drug | 3 | 2 | 4 | 4 | 4 |

[1] Use of drugs in the last year.

Source: Statistics on Young People and Drug Misuse: England, 2002, Statistical Bulletin 2003/14, Department of Health, July 2003

According to the latest Schools Health Education Unit survey of children aged between 10 and 15 in the UK:

- About one in four pupils in year 10 (14 to 15-year-olds) – four times as many as in year 8 – has tried at least one drug.
- Cannabis is by far the most likely drug to have been tried, with 29% of 14 to 15-year-old males, 27% of 14 to 15-year-old females, and up to 8% of 12 to13-year-olds reporting having taken it.
- Up to 19% of 14 to 15-year-olds have mixed drugs and alcohol "on the same occasion".
- Up to 62% of 14 to 15-year-olds are "fairly sure" or "certain" they know a drug user.

Source: Young People in 2002, Schools Health Education Unit, 2003

# Drug use among 16 to 24-year-olds

Among 16 to 24-year-olds in England and Wales in 2002:

- 30% had used drugs in the last year and 19% in the last month.
- 27% had used cannabis in the last year, 7% ecstasy, 5% amphetamines, 5% cocaine, 4% poppers and 1% crack. In total 9% had used class A drugs in the last year.
- The proportion that had used drugs in the last year was about the same level in 1994, 1996, 1998, 2000 and 2002 (around 30%). The only drugs to have shown a significant increase between 1994 and 2002 were cocaine used in the last year (from 1% to 5%) and ecstasy used in the last year (from 4% to 7%). During this time the use of amphetamines in the last year has fallen from 10% to 5% and LSD from 6% to 1%.

*Source: Statistics on Young People and Drug Misuse: England, 2002, Statistical Bulletin 2003/14, Department of Health, July 2003*

# Relationships between smoking, drinking and drug use

The strongest relationship was between recent use of cannabis and cigarettes. There were strong relationships between recent use of cigarettes and alcohol, alcohol and cannabis, cigarettes and class A drugs, and cannabis and class A drugs, but a less strong relationship between recent use of alcohol and class A drugs. Recent sniffing of volatile substances showed a relatively weak relationship with recent use of other substances.

Pupils who started smoking, drinking or taking cannabis at an earlier age were more likely than those who started at a later age to have taken class A drugs. Pupils who had not smoked, drunk or taken cannabis were least likely to have taken class A drugs. For example, 17% of 15-year-olds who first smoked aged 10 or younger had taken class A drugs before they were 15, compared with 4% who had first smoked aged 14 and 1% who had not smoked by the time they turned 15. Although 17% of 15-year-olds who had first smoked aged 10 or younger had taken class A drugs before 15, 83% had not done so. There are other factors involved which influence whether pupils smoke, drink, take cannabis and class A drugs such as socio-economic, cultural and peer group factors.

*Source: Smoking, Drinking & Drug Use Among Young People in England in 2002, summary of key findings, Boreham R & McManus S (eds), ONS, 2002*

## Ethnicity and substance misuse

White pupils and pupils from mixed ethnic groups were more likely than black or Asian pupils to have drunk in the last week or to be regular smokers, and these differences were greater for drinking than for smoking. Differences in prevalence of taking drugs in the last month were less pronounced than for smoking or drinking, with Asian pupils being the least likely to have taken drugs in the last month.

While white pupils and pupils from mixed ethnic groups were substantially more likely to have drunk alcohol in the last week than to have taken drugs in the last month, this pattern was not found among pupils in black and Asian groups. Among Asian girls the reverse was true, as they were slightly more likely to have taken drugs in the last month than to have drunk alcohol in the last week.

Source: Smoking, Drinking & Drug Use Among Young People in England in 2002, summary of key findings, Boreham R & McManus S (eds), ONS, 2002

## Substance misuse and truancy and exclusion

Pupils aged 11 to 15 who had ever truanted were considerably more likely than those who had not to be regular smokers (35% compared with 5%), to have drunk alcohol in the last week (53% compared with 18%) and to have taken drugs in the last month (35% compared with 6%). Similar patterns were found for pupils who had ever been excluded. It is not possible to draw conclusions about causality from these results. It is not clear whether playing truant or being excluded makes children and young people more likely to smoke, drink or take drugs, or whether those who already partake in these behaviours are more likely to start playing truant or be excluded from school.

Source: Smoking, Drinking & Drug Use Among Young People in England in 2002, summary of key findings, Boreham R & McManus S (eds), ONS, 2002

## Parental drug use

An inquiry by the Advisory Council on the Misuse of Drugs estimated that:

- Between 250,000 and 350,000 children in England and Wales have at least one parent with a serious drug problem.
- This represents about 2-3% of children under 16.
- Only 37% of the fathers and 64% of the mothers were still living with their children.

- Most children not living with their birth parents were living with other relatives. About 5% of all children were in care.
- The inquiry also estimated that in Scotland there are between 41,000 and 59,000 children with a parent with a drug problem. This represents about 4 to 6% of all children in Scotland aged under 16.

*Source: Hidden Harm – Responding to the Needs of Children of Problem Drug Users, Advisory Council on the Misuse of Drugs, Home Office, 2003.*

# Sexual health

## Sexual behaviour

The National Survey of Sexual Attitudes and Lifestyles (Natsal), a 10-yearly survey of sexual behaviour patterns and the most recent report published in December 2001, reported that:

- Average age of first intercourse has fallen for women and men from 17 to 16.
- Among 16 to 24-year-olds the prevalence of first intercourse before age 16 was higher in single parent families, among those whose parents were manual workers and those whose main source of information about sex was not school.
- 8% of those aged 16 to 24 reported peer pressure as the main reason for having sex and 8.5% put drunkenness as the main reason.

Source: The National Survey of Sexual Attitudes and Lifestyles 1999-2001, December 2001

The Schools Health Education Unit survey of 10 to 15-year-olds in the UK found that:

- Between 12 and 15 years of age, there is a trend away from parents and school lessons and towards friends as a source of information about sex. Parents and/or school lessons should be the main source of information according to these young people.
- Up to 37% of 14 to 15-year-olds and nearly 45% of 12 to 13-year-olds felt unable to respond positively to a question about their knowledge of methods of contraception. Similarly, up to 47% of 14 to 15-year-olds and up to 57% of 12 to 13-year-olds could not decide which contraceptive methods were reliable to stop infections like HIV/Aids.
- 37% of the 14 to 15-year-old females knew about birth control services and knowledge grew with age. 49% of the older males did not know of a source of free condoms whereas two-thirds of the females said they did know.

Source: Young People in 2002, Schools Health Education Unit, 2003

# Teenage pregnancy

**Note:** teenage parenthood statistics are in the population section

In 2001, there were 38,439 conceptions to under-18s in England and 7,396 of these conceptions were to under 16-year-olds. The under-18 conception rate for 2001 is 42.3 per thousand, 3.5% lower than in 2000, and is 10% below the 1998 rate. The under-16 conception rate for 2001 is 7.9 per thousand, 4.5% lower than the 2000 rate, and is 11% below the 1998 rate. The percentage of conceptions leading to abortion rose to 46.0% for under-18s, and 55.9% for under-16s, continuing the upward trend observed since 1995.

*Source: Teenage Pregnancy Unit, Department of Health, 2003*


# Teenage pregnancy and alcohol

There is a strong association between drinking alcohol, having risky sex and teenage pregnancy. Studies suggest that when young people have been drinking, they are less likely to use contraception

Three quarters of 16 to 20-year-olds use contraception while sober, compared to 59% who are moderately intoxicated and just 13% of those who are strongly intoxicated.

Among 15 to 16-year-olds, one in 14 said they had unprotected sex after drinking, and one in seven 16 to 24-year-olds said they had done so.

*Source: Alcohol and Teenage Pregnancy, Alcohol Concern, 2002*


# Sexually transmitted infections

The last decade has witnessed a dramatic rise in diagnoses of sexually transmitted infections (STIs), especially among young people. One in 10 of the UK population has at some time had an STI. In 2001, genital chlamydia was the most common sexually transmitted infection diagnosed in genito-urinary clinics in England and Wales, with a total of just under 70,200 cases, a 10% increase compared with 2000 and more than double the 30,400 cases diagnosed in 1995. Between 1995 and 2001 the increase was greatest among those aged under 25. Among young women the number of cases diagnosed rose from 11,800 to 28,900; for young men it increased from 5,700 to 15,200.

*Source: Social Trends 33, ONS, the Stationery Office, 2003*

## New episodes of genital chlamydia (England and Wales)

Numbers

| | 1995 | 1997 | 1999 | 2001 |
|---|---|---|---|---|
| **Males** | | | | |
| 0-15 | 45 | 50 | 74 | 85 |
| 16-19 | 1,181 | 1,866 | 2,969 | 4,148 |
| 20-24 | 4,462 | 5,480 | 7,534 | 10,978 |
| **Females** | | | | |
| 0-15 | 394 | 519 | 711 | 950 |
| 16-19 | 4,896 | 7,478 | 10,262 | 13,256 |
| 20-24 | 6,516 | 8,306 | 10,788 | 14,695 |

Source: Social Trends 33, ONS, the Stationery Office 2003

42% of females with gonorrhoea and 36% with genital chlamydial infection were under 20 years of age. Among 12 to 15-year-old females diagnosed with gonorrhoea, almost a quarter will return with another episode of the disease within a year.

Source: Health select committee report, Sexual Health Volume 1, third report of session 2002-03, the Stationery Office, 2003

# Chapter 4

# Education

# Education: an overview

**By Polly Curtis**

"Education, education, education" was New Labour's mantra when it came to power in 1997. And standards - particularly in literacy and numeracy - have definitely improved. But critics say the improvements have been undermined by the government's real focus: testing, targets and tables.

The headline figures are startling. In 2003, 52.6% of pupils achieved five or more GCSEs; in 1997 that figure was 45.1%. Also in 2003, 68% of 14-year-olds achieved Level 5 (the target level) or above in English and science, and 70% of pupils achieved Level 5 or above in mathematics - the highest since standard assessment test (Sats) were launched in the early 1990s.

However, targets for seven and 11-year-olds have not been so easy to crack with results stalling and targets missed, leading some to declare that the target regime had reached its limits. And girls continue to outstrip boys, who at seven years of age lag eight points behind girls in reading and 11 points behind in writing. By 14, boys are 13 points behind in both reading and writing.

Teachers have also been critical of the three Ts. Many believe that, along with the national primary literacy and numeracy strategies, the regime is "squeezing" the creativity out of the curriculum. Parent campaigning groups and teacher unions are calling for Westminster to follow the example of Wales and Scotland, which are already heading towards phasing out the tests.

The worry is that a tighter curriculum - constrained, its critics say, by the first ever national literacy and numeracy strategy and Sats-focused teaching - is failing to excite children enough. A major review is planned of the 14-19 curriculum to try to keep young people engaged. However, following the A-level crisis of 2002, where problems with marking the new modular Curriculum 2000 A-level threatened to undermine confidence in the qualification, everyone is eager to avoid more upheaval.

While the curriculum has been shifting, the shape of the schools in which it is taught has also been rapidly transformed. Central to this has been the specialist schools programme - whereby schools develop a specialism, such as the arts, sciences or information communication technology, and are given extra government money once they raise a minimum from private sources.

The government has hailed specialist schools a success, raising standards across the curriculum. In specialist schools, 56.1% of pupils achieved A*-C at GCSE, compared with 48.7% in non-specialist schools. Fears that this would lead to a two-tier system of schooling have been soothed with the lifting of the cap on the number of schools that can apply for specialist status.

New schools are now routinely privately financed and City Academies - secondary schools built with a mixture of taxpayer and industry cash - have been introduced to develop new schools in inner city areas.

Meanwhile, the workforce in schools has also been radically changed. The 2003 signing of the school workforce agreement saw the first steps towards guaranteeing teachers time out of the classroom for preparation. It also led to the greatest ever rift between the biggest teachers' union, the National Union of Teachers, and the government after the NUT refused to sign the agreement, citing fears that the extension of the role of the teaching assistant would undermine the teaching profession.

But teacher numbers have risen. In January 2003, there were 25,000 more teachers than in 1997 and an 80,000 increase in support staff. Experienced classroom teachers will earn £28,005 a year from September 2005, compared with £21,318 in September 1997, a real terms increase of 8%.

The last year has also seen one of the biggest shifts in schools policy with the widening of the role of schools. Margaret Hodge (controversially) became the first ever children's minister within the Department for Education and Skills, with a remit extending from child protection to early years provision, and the government pushed forward with plans for extended schools. The new schools will see health and welfare workers brought on site with training for parents, GPs and social workers providing all-round family services from one place.

Full-time police officers are now being deployed in schools facing the worst problems of crime, bad behaviour and truancy. The government is cracking down on truancy with truancy sweeps and fast-track prosecution for the parents of persistent truants. The first ever target to reduce exclusions was met in 2002, but subsequently dropped. A slight rise in exclusions followed, despite schools being given further options for providing for all children through outside pupil behaviour centres and more centralised local authority support.

Meanwhile, significant overall improvements have masked a worrying trend: reports by schools inspectorate the Office for Standards in Education (Ofsted), comparing achievement in inner city secondary schools in 1993 with 2003, reveal that pupils in the most deprived areas are still being left behind. Pupils from deprived urban backgrounds are twice as likely as others to leave without any GCSEs. Despite millions of pounds worth of initiatives designed to target inner city schools, the stubborn gap in achievement has yet to be bridged.

**Polly Curtis** is a specialist correspondent on EducationGuardian.co.uk

# Education: the key facts

## Schools and pupils

There are just over 10 million full and part-time pupils in schools in the UK. The declining birth rate during the late 1970s led to a fall in pupil numbers in the 1980s and early 1990s. Numbers then increased until 2000-01, but there was a decline in the last year: numbers are still below the peak level of the 1970s.

All publicly-funded secondary schools in Scotland and Wales are comprehensive. In Northern Ireland, secondary education is largely organised along selective lines and in 2001-02, 40% of Northern Irish pupils attended grammar schools.

*Sources: Social Trends 33, ONS, the Stationery Office, 2003*

**School pupils[1] by type of school[2]** (UK)

| | Thousands | | | | |
|---|---|---|---|---|---|
| | 1970-71 | 1980-81 | 1990-91 | 2000-01 | 2001-02 |
| **Public sector schools** | | | | | |
| Nursery & primary | 5,952 | 5,260 | 5,060 | 5,450 | 5,395 |
| Secondary Modern | 1,164 | 233 | 94 | 112 | 103 |
| Grammar | 673 | 149 | 156 | 205 | 209 |
| Comprehensive | 1,313 | 3,730 | 2,843 | 3,340 | 3,390 |
| Other secondary | 403 | 434 | 300 | 260 | 247 |
| All public sector schools | 9,507 | 9,806 | 843 | 9,367 | 9,344 |
| Non-maintained schools | 621 | 619 | 613 | 626 | 635 |
| Special schools | 103 | 148 | 114 | 113 | 112 |
| Pupil referral units | | | | 10 | 10 |
| All schools | 10,230 | 10,572 | 9,180 | 10,116 | 10,102 |

[1] Head counts

[2] Main categories of educational establishments and stages of education

Source: DfES, National assembly for Wales, Scottish executive, Dept of Education Northern Ireland. Reported in Social Trends 33, ONS, the Stationery Office 2003

# Daycare

Daycare is provided for young children by childminders, voluntary agencies, private nurseries and local authorities, as well as nannies and relatives. In 2001 there were more than a million places with childminders, in day nurseries and playgroups.

## Daycare places for children[1] in England, Wales and Northern Ireland (thousands)

| Provision | 1987 | 1992 | 1999 | 2000 | 2001 |
|---|---|---|---|---|---|
| Day nurseries | | | | | |
| Local authority provided[2] | 29 | 24 | 16 | 18 | 19 |
| Registered | 32 | 98 | 235 | 261 | 282 |
| Non-registered[3] | 1 | 1 | 12 | 2 | 2 |
| All day nursery places[4] | 62 | 123 | 262 | 281 | 304 |
| After school clubs[5] | - | - | 119 | 153 | 165 |
| Childminders | | | | | |
| Local authority provided[2] | 2 | 2 | 9 | 3 | 3 |
| Other registered person | 159 | 275 | 360 | 349 | 331 |
| All childminder places[4] | 161 | 277 | 369 | 353 | 338 |
| Playgroups | | | | | |
| Local authority provided | 4 | 2 | 3 | 2 | 7 |
| Registered | 434 | 450 | 383 | 391 | 347 |
| Non-registered[2] | 7 | 3 | 3 | 1 | 1 |
| All playgroup places[4] | 444 | 455 | 489 | 394 | 369 |

1 Under the age of eight in England and Wales. Under the age of 12 in Northern Ireland.

2 England and Wales only.

3 England only before 2000; England and Wales only from 2000.

4 Figures do not add to totals. Total figures for England include an imputed figure for missing values.

5 For children aged five to seven in England and Wales. In Northern Ireland for children aged four to eight.

*Source: DfES; National assembly for Wales; Department of Health, Social Services and Public Safety, Northern Ireland*

The number of day nursery places has risen steadily over the last 15 years with nearly five times as many places in 2001 as in 1987. During the same period, the number of playgroup places fell by 20%, although there was a sharp rise in the number of local authority provided playgroups between 2000 and 2001 - from 2,000 to 7,000. There was a large increase in the number of childminder places during the 1990s but this has tailed off slightly with numbers falling by 9% since 1999. Since their introduction, after school club places have increased rapidly by 39% to 165,000.

Historically, the provision of daycare in the UK has lagged behind that in other EU countries: research published during 2001 acknowledged the recent advances that have been made in the UK but pointed out that early education provision in the UK is moving towards two years' part-time provision, while most European countries seek three years' full-time.

A survey published in 2001 also found that childcare costs in Britain are the highest in the EU. Some families on low incomes are entitled to help towards their childcare bills through the childcare tax credit, but they still have to find 30% of the cost themselves. Only 20,000 children can access services funded by local authorities, leaving many children in workless households without access to childcare. This, in turn, makes it impossible for their parents to enter the labour market and so helps to keep them trapped in poverty.

The typical cost of a full-time nursery place for a two-year-old is £128 per week (more than £6,650 per year), up 6.7% in the last year. In some areas the costs are much higher: in inner London the average is £168 per week. The average cost of a full-time place with a childminder is £118 per week.

*Sources: Social Trends 33, ONS, the Stationery Office, 2003; The UK at the Crossroads: Towards an Early Years European Partnership (Facing the Future policy paper No2), Moss P, Daycare Trust, 2001*

## Early years education

In recent years there has been a major expansion of pre-school education with an increased emphasis on children beginning school with a basic foundation of literacy and numeracy. In 1970-71, 21% of three and four-year-olds in the UK attended school; by 1999-2000 this had tripled to 63% and has remained at this level.

*Source: Social Trends 33, ONS, the Stationery Office, 2003*

## Class sizes

In January 2003, the average size of classes in primary schools taught by one teacher was 26.3, unchanged from the previous year. 16.3% of pupils in primary classes taught by one teacher were in classes of 31 or more pupils, compared with 17.8% a year earlier. The average size of classes taught by one teacher in secondary schools between January 2002 and January 2003 remained unchanged at 21.9.

*Sources: Statistics of Education: Class Sizes and Pupil Teacher Ratios in England, DfES February, 2003; Pupil Characteristics and Class Sizes in Maintained Schools in England, January 2003 (provisional) DfES, April 2003*

| Class sizes[1] in maintained primary[2] and secondary schools[3,4] 1982-2002 (England) | | | |
|---|---|---|---|
| | **1983** | **1993** | **2003** |
| **Primary** | | | |
| Average class size | 24.8 | 26.6 | 26.3 |
| % of classes with 31+ pupils | 19.9 | 21.6 | 16.3 |
| **Secondary** | | | |
| Average class size | 20.6 | 20.9 | 21.9 |
| % of classes with 31+ pupils | 7.9 | 4.7 | 8 |

[1] Classes as taught during the one selected period in each school on the day of the census in January

[2] Includes middle schools as deemed

[3] Includes middle schools as deemed

[4] Excludes sixth form colleges

*Source: Statistics of Education: Class Sizes and Pupil Teahcer Ratios in England, Department for Education and Skills, February 2003*

## Educational attainment: public examinations

In England and Wales three-quarters of pupils whose parents were in the higher professional group achieved five or more GCSEs at A*-C. Of those pupils whose parents were in the routine group, less than a third achieved the same level. The level of parental qualification also has a marked impact on young people's attainment. 72% of young people whose parents were qualified to degree level achieved five or more GCSEs at A*-C in 2000, compared with 39% of young people whose parents were not qualified to at least GCE A level.

In summer 2003, 5.4% of students left school without a single GCSE pass, about 33,000 young people in total. The government's target was for 95% of students to pass at least one GCSE by 2001-02. The failure rate has been reducing very slowly, falling by just 1.2% since the targets were announced five years ago. Critics say this is partly because league tables force schools to focus on pupils at the C/D margin, to the detriment of the most and least able, and because achieving year-on-year improvements with the least able pupils becomes increasingly difficult.

In summer 2003, 86.3% of pupils achieved five or more grades A*-G, including English and mathematics, at GCSE/GNVQ; this is down from 87.1% in 2002. The government's target is for 92% of pupils to achieve this target by 2004. The government also wants the percentage of 16-year-old pupils achieving five or more GCSE/GNVQs at grades A*-C to increase by an average of 2% per year. In summer 2003, 52.6% of pupils achieved this – an increase of just one percentage point on the figures for the previous year.

## GCSE attainment[1] by parents' socio-economic classification[2], 2000 (England and Wales)

|  | Percentages | | | | |
| --- | --- | --- | --- | --- | --- |
|  | 5 or more GCSE grades A*-C | 1-4 GCSE grades A*-C[3] | 5 or more GCSE grades D-G | 1-4 GCSE grades D-G | None reported |
| Higher professional | 74 | 17 | 6 | 1 | 2 |
| Lower professional | 61 | 22 | 13 | 2 | 2 |
| Intermediate | 51 | 26 | 18 | 3 | 3 |
| Lower supervisory | 36 | 31 | 24 | 4 | 4 |
| Routine | 29 | 34 | 26 | 5 | 7 |
| Other/not classified[4] | 24 | 29 | 26 | 8 | 13 |

[1] For pupils in year 11. Includes equivalent GNVQ qualifications achieved in year 11.

[2] National statistics socio-economic classification.

[3] Consists of those with 1-4 GCSE grades A*-C and any number of other grades.

[4] Includes a high percentage of respondents who had neither parents in a full-time job.

Source: Youth Cohort Study, DfES, reported in Social Trends 33 ONS, the Stationery office, 2003

In 2002-03 girls continued to outperform boys, particularly at the higher grades A*-C; 57.8% of girls achieved five or more grades A*-C, compared with 47.5% of boys.

There has been an increase in the proportion of young people in the UK achieving two or more A levels (or equivalent). The proportion of young women who have achieved this has increased by almost half since 1995-96, to 45.8% in 2001-02. The increase in the proportion of young men achieving this has been slightly more modest, with a rise of 33% over this period to 36.2%.

Sources: GCSE/GNVQ results for young people in England, 2002-03 (provisional), DfES, October 2003; GCE/VCE A/AS examination results for young people in England 2001-02 (provisional), DfES, April 2003

## Educational attainment: performance in national tests

School pupils in England and Wales are now formally assessed at three key stages before GCSE level, at the ages of seven, 11 and 14. The assessments cover the core subjects of English (and Welsh in Wales), mathematics and science. Typically a seven-year-old is expected to achieve level two at key stage 1, an 11-year-old level four at key stage 2, and a 14-year-old between levels five and six (level five in Wales) at key stage 3.

The government target was for 80% of 11-year-olds to achieve level four at key stage 2 for literacy, and 75% for numeracy. Although girls were very close to achieving the required standard, in English boys lagged behind.

As can be seen from the table, boys also lag behind in English at key stage 3. The proportion of pupils achieving the expected level in tests and teacher assessments declined with age for both sexes (the same was also true in Wales). At key stage 1, for example, 81% of boys and 89% of girls in England achieved the expected level in English teacher assessments. By key stage 3, this had fallen to 75% of girls and 59% of boys.

Source: Social Trends 33 ONS, the Stationery Office, 2003

National learning targets for England required 85% of 19-year-olds to be qualified to NVQ level 2 or its equivalent by 2002 (the Learning and Skills Council has adopted the same target for 2004). In 2002, 74.8% of 19-year-olds had a qualification at or equivalent to level 2 or above, representing no change from 2001. This measure is 2.5 percentage points higher than in 1997. The new target is to increase this measure by 3 percentage points by 2003.

The target for 21-year-olds required 60% to be qualified to NVQ level 3 or its equivalent by 2002. In 2002, 53.8% of 21-year-olds had a qualification at or equivalent to level 3 or above. This had not changed from 2001 but is 5.6 percentage points higher than in 1997.

Source: The Level of Highest Qualification Held by Young People and Adults: England 2002, DfES, January 2003

## Pupils reaching or exceeding expected standards: by key stage and sex, 2002 (England)

Percentages

| | Teacher assessment | | Tests | |
|---|---|---|---|---|
| | **Males** | **Females** | **Males** | **Females** |
| **Key stage 1** | | | | |
| English | 81 | 89 | - | - |
| Reading | 81 | 88 | 81 | 88 |
| Writing | 79 | 88 | 82 | 90 |
| Mathematics | 87 | 90 | 89 | 92 |
| Science | 88 | 91 | - | - |
| **Key stage 2** | | | | |
| English | 67 | 78 | 70 | 79 |
| Mathematics | 74 | 75 | 73 | 73 |
| Science | 82 | 83 | 86 | 87 |
| **Key stage 3** | | | | |
| English | 59 | 75 | 58 | 75 |
| Mathematics | 69 | 72 | 67 | 68 |
| Science | 66 | 69 | 66 | 67 |

Source: Social Trends 33 ONS, the Stationery Office, 2003

## Staying on after 16

Over the last decade, more young people have been staying on in education. In 2001, just over three out of four 16 to 18-year-olds in England were in education or training, an increase from just over seven out of 10 in 1991.

*Source: Social Trends 32 ONS, the Stationery Office, 2002*

## Higher education

In 2000-01 there were 2.1 million students in higher education in the UK, 55% of whom were women. The number of enrolments by men on all undergraduate courses more than doubled between 1970-71 and 2000-01. For women the increase was even more dramatic, with nearly five times as many enrolments in 2000-01 as in the early 1970s.

However, an analysis carried out by the National Audit Office has found that the proportion of young people from families on low incomes who are entering higher education is not increasing: the level has remained static at about 28% for the last six years. The number of students from low income groups entering higher education has doubled over this period, but so too have those from higher income groups.

The researchers point out that Britain is the only one of 10 industrialised countries committed to widening participation in higher education to fail to give any mandatory element of grant towards student living costs. The countries that give this aid include Australia, Finland, France, the Netherlands, Spain, Sweden and the United States.

*Sources: DfES, National assembly for Wales, Scottish executive, Northern Ireland department for employment and learning, reported in Social Trends 32, ONS, the Stationery Office, 2002; National Audit Office, 2002*

## Children with special educational needs

Around 251,000 pupils had statements of special educational needs (SEN) in January 2003. The proportion of pupils with statements was 3% in January 2003, the same as in the previous year. The proportion of pupils with statements placed in maintained mainstream schools increased slightly from 60.2% in January 2002 to 60.3% in January 2003. The proportion placed in special schools or pupil referral units (PRUs) decreased from 35.2% in January 2002 to 35.0% in January 2003.

Not all children with SEN have statements. In January 2003, there were 1,170,000 pupils with SEN without statements. The proportion of pupils with SEN without statements decreased from 16.8% in January 2002 to 14.0% in January 2003.

SEN pupils achieve substantially lower results on average than non-SEN pupils with similar prior attainment, at all key stages and in each subject. This applies even for SEN pupils working at or above the expected level at the start of each key stage.

SEN pupils are under-represented in the most successful schools. Researchers examined figures for 3,151 schools and found that overall the average percentage of children with SEN was 2.7%. However, in the schools attaining the best GCSE results the percentage was 0.9%.

*Sources: Pupil Characteristics and Class Sizes in Maintained Schools in England January 2003 (provisional) DfES, 2003; Statistics of Education: Pupil Progress by Pupil Characteristics 2002, DfES, 2003; the Literacy Trust website: www.literacytrust.org.uk*

## Bullying

In a recent large scale survey in Britain, more than half the young people questioned had been bullied and one in 10 had been severely bullied.

- A third of girls and a quarter of boys had at one time been afraid of going to school because of bullying.
- More than 20,000 calls were made to ChildLine about bullying last year and it was the single most cited issue by callers.
- In a survey of project users by NCH, bullying was cited as the biggest problem issue for them at school.
- It has been suggested that girls are more involved in sustained bullying than boys and that it is girls who report more fear of attending school because of bullying.

*Source: Issues: Dealing with Bullies, Independence Educational Publishers Cambridge, 2003; School Let Me Down, NCH, 2003*

## School exclusions

In 2001-02, 9,540 pupils were permanently excluded from schools in England, an increase of 4% from the 9,135 permanent exclusions in the previous year but a decrease of 25% since 1996-97. There were 7,740 permanent exclusions from secondary schools and 1,450 permanent exclusions from primary schools.

An estimated 82% of permanent exclusions in 2001-02 were boys. Exclusions were most common amongst those aged 13 and 14; pupils of these ages accounted for half of all permanent exclusions.

In 2001-02, 41 in every 10,000 black Caribbean pupils were permanently excluded, the highest rate of any ethnic group, compared

## School exclusions by ethnic group (England)

| Ethnic group: | Number of permanent exclusions[1] | Percentage of permanent exclusions | Percentage of school population[2] |
|---|---|---|---|
| White | 7,820 | 82 | 0.13 |
| Black Caribbean | 410 | 4 | 0.41 |
| Black African | 160 | 2 | 0.15 |
| Black other | 220 | 2 | 0.35 |
| Indian | 60 | 1 | 0.03 |
| Pakistani | 170 | 2 | 0.09 |
| Bangladeshi | 80 | 1 | 0.11 |
| Chinese | 10 | 0 | 0.02 |
| Any other ethnic group | 310 | 3 | 0.19 |
| Ethnicity not known [3] | 310 | 3 | - |
| Total number | 9,519 | | |

[1] The number of permanent exclusions of compulsory school age and above in each ethnic group

[2] The number of permanent exclusions of compulsory school age expressed as a percentage of the number (headcount) of pupils of compulsory school age and above in each ethnic group in primary, secondary and special schools (excluding dually registered pupils in special schools) in January 2002.

[3] Includes permanent exclusions of pupils unclassified according to ethnic group including where information was not sought or refused.

Source: Permanent exclusions from schools and exclusion appeals, 2001-02 (provisional) DfES 2003

with only two in 10,000 Chinese pupils, the lowest rate. The rate for black Caribbean pupils does, however, constitute a significant improvement on earlier years: in 1998-99, 60 in every 10,000 pupils were permanently excluded. Over the same period, the number of permanently excluded white pupils decreased from 15 to 13 in every 10,000.

An Ofsted report examining 10 secondary schools across England with higher than average levels of bad behaviour and poor attendance has concluded that some schools treated black pupils less favourably than white ones. The result was that both parents and pupils could be left with the impression that the schools had treated the young people differently because of their ethnicity, whether this was the case or not. The report found that black pupils were typically suspended for five days for "challenging behaviour", while their white classmates were removed for only three days.

Sources: Permanent Exclusions from Schools and Exclusion Appeals, England 2001-02, DfES, 2003; Social Trends 33, ONS, the Stationery Office, 2003; Improving Attendance and Behaviour, Ofsted, 2001

# Truancy

In 2002-03, 0.71% of half ways were missed due ot unauthorised absence from school - the figure for junior schools was 0.43% and in secondary schools 1.08%. The figures for unauthorised absence have decreased by 0.01 percentage points over the last year. An analysis of the Youth Cohort Study has recently found that the proportion of 16-year-olds reporting that they played truant sometime during year 11 fell from 50% in 1989 to 35% in 2000.

Five million schooldays are lost every year in England to a combination of truancy and absences sanctioned by parents.

*Sources: Pupil Absence in Schools in England 2002-03 (provisional), DfES 2003 ; Ofsted annual Rreport 2001-02*

# Children who 'go missing' from the education system

An estimated 10,000 children and young people in England are "missing" from their schools and have left no trace of their whereabouts. They include pupils who have been excluded from school who are either not offered or who fail to attend alternative provision, and those who have opted to start work early. Most of the missing pupils are aged 14 to 16 and in their last two years of schooling.

This research by Ofsted was followed up by a study which tracked 193 excluded young people. Researchers lost contact with more than a quarter (52) of their subjects. The teenagers who could not be traced were disproportionately female and black.

*Source: Ofsted annual report 2001-02; TES April 18 2003*

# Outcomes from truancy and exclusion

Non-attendance at school has implications for educational attainment and for outcomes in adulthood. A Youth Cohort Study report showed that in 1998 just under a third of persistent truants reported they had no qualifications at year 11, compared with about 4% of non-truants.

Persistent truants are four times more likely not to be in education, employment or training at age 16 than other children.

There is a strong association between non-attendance at school and crime. The Home Office has found that truants were more than three times as likely to offend than non-truants. Almost half of all school age offenders have been excluded from school.

Research was published in 2001 concerning the outcomes in secondary education for children excluded from primary schools. This was a follow-up study of earlier research. This had involved 726 children from 10 local education authorities who received permanent, fixed period and indefinite exclusions in 1993-94. The follow-up study focused on 30 case studies and found:

- Nearly half the pupils received further primary school exclusions and more than a third received exclusions in their secondary education.
- Three-quarters were involved with at least one agency associated with difficulties at home, at school or in their community.
- Three in 10 had evidence of offending over the five-year period.
- About one in six had been in public care. Outcomes for these children were poor with 55% of the boys presenting "serious problems" at the end of the period of research.
- Six in 10 of the children had special educational needs.
- A quarter of the children had records of attendance problems.

Sources: Misspent Youth – Young People and Crime, Audit Commission, 1996; Young People and Crime – Home Office research study no. 45, by Graham J. and Bowling B., Home Office, 1995; Truancy and School Exclusion, Social Exclusion Unit, the Stationery Office 1999; Statistical bulletin: pupil absence and truancy from schools in England 1998-99, issue no 15/99, DfEE, the Stationery Office; Youth Cohort Study: the Activities and Experiences of 16 and 17-year-olds: England and Wales, issue no 4, DfEE, 1998, the Stationery Office; Permanent Exclusions from Schools in England 1997-98 and Exclusion Appeals Lodged by Parents in England 1997-98, DfEE, 1999; Truancy and Youth Transitions: Youth Cohort Study report no 34, by Casey B and Smith D, DfEE, 1995; Outcomes in Secondary Education for Children Excluded from Primary School, by Parsons C, Godfrey R, Howlett K and Martin T, DfES, 2001

# Chapter 5

# Children at risk

# Children at risk: an overview

By David Batty

The past year has seen child protection pushed to the forefront of the political agenda. The damning report of the public inquiry into the murder of eight-year-old Victoria Climbié, published in January 2003, exposed serious flaws in the services meant to safeguard children from abuse and neglect. Ministers have responded with proposals for the biggest reform of child welfare services in England for 30 years.

The Climbié inquiry exposed a complete breakdown in the multi-agency child protection system established in the wake of the death of seven-year-old Maria Colwell in 1973. The NHS, councils, the police and a children's charity failed to work together effectively on Victoria's case, missing at least 12 opportunities to save her. Disturbingly, it emerged that there have been at least 70 previous public inquiries into child abuse in Britain since 1945, many of which identified the same flaws.

Lord Laming, the Climbié inquiry chairman, pledged that Victoria's death would mark an "enduring turning point in ensuring proper protection of children in this country". But the first full audit of child protection services in England last summer painted a bleak picture. The investigation, by the government's social services, healthcare and police inspectorates, revealed the same institutional flaws that led to her death still existed across England more than three years later.

Inspectors found that 45% of 150 social services departments were still failing to adequately safeguard vulnerable children. Thirty-four departments had 408 unallocated child protection cases. Similarly worrying variations in NHS child safety procedures were also identified, which potentially put children at risk of harm.

The national inspection underlined the challenges the government will face in implementing its response to the Climbié inquiry – the green paper Every Child Matters - published last September.

The green paper set out a radical overhaul of children's services. The proposed reforms aim to shift child protection away from crisis intervention towards a more preventative agenda.

The children bill, published in March, proposes creating an electronic file on all 11 million children in the country, in a bid to identify and help those at risk of abuse, neglect, deprivation, offending and poor school performance at the earliest possible stage.

However, many councils lack the IT facilities to support such a database, while a pilot scheme to improve information sharing has been dogged by legal and technical difficulties. There are also concerns that trying to keep track of all children will hinder efforts to closely monitor those at most risk.

The bill also proposes integrating children's services in a bid to prevent the buck passing among different agencies and professionals, which marred the Climbié case. The government wants children's trusts, which bring together education, social care and health services, set up across the country by 2006. It believes this will push child protection higher up the agenda of schools and the health service.

But social services leaders fear that education will dominate the new trusts, with the far greater political priority of raising exam performance overshadowing efforts to better safeguard children.

A growing number of child protection experts, including academics, senior social workers and inspectors, also question whether the green paper misses the point. While its vision of ensuring that children at risk have the same opportunities as other children is worthy, the plans skirt addressing the flaws identified by the Climbié inquiry.

Lord Laming's investigation showed that the child protection system had deteriorated significantly since earlier inquiries. The scale of incompetence was breathtaking, with professionals failing to follow basic principles of practice.

The green paper relies on the standard remedy of the past 45 years of inquiry reports: structural reform. But it does not tackle why staff were working to such a low standard.

Abuse scandals since the Climbié inquiry have raised further concern about how well professionals assess the risks posed to children who are under their protection. The majority of high-risk child protection cases now involve families affected by problems such as criminality, drug and alcohol abuse and domestic violence. This requires staff to put considerable intellectual effort into risk assessment. But research shows there is little evidence of this in child protection case conferences.

The government has announced a childcare workforce strategy with the aim of improving training for all professionals who work with children, as well as recruitment and retention. This will be vital to ensuring the safety of children at risk. Nationally, the vacancy rate for children's social workers is 8% - but as high as 40-50% in some inner city areas.

But with the green paper's reforms not backed by any new money, it is unclear how the plans will be paid for. If ministers fail to offer any rewards to persuade more people to undertake increasingly complex and challenging work, child protection will deteriorate further.

**David Batty** is the social care correspondent for SocietyGuardian.co.uk

# Children at risk: the key facts

## Children on child protection registers

Children who are considered to be either suffering or likely to suffer significant harm and for whom there is a child protection plan have their names placed on a central child protection register held by each local social services/social work department in the UK. Registration takes place following a case conference at which a decision has been taken by professionals about whether the level of risk to the child is sufficient for the child's name to be placed on the register.

At March 31 2002 there were 25,700 children on child protection registers in England, a 4% decrease on the previous year. In 2001–02, 27,800 registrations were made to child protection registers in England, representing a slight increase on the figure for the year 2000–01. 10% of the 2001–02 registrations were for sexual abuse, compared with 20% in 1997–98. Part of this fall was due to the introduction of a "mixed" category for children registered as a result of concerns about multiple risks. At March 31 2002 the most commonly recorded risk category was neglect (39%), followed by physical abuse (19%), and then emotional abuse (17%).

Source: 12th annual report of the Chief Inspector of Social Services 2002–03, Department of Health, 2003

There were 28,800 de-registrations in 2001–02. De-registration is not always permanent and, since 1999, each year around 14% of children who are registered have been registered previously. The concern about re-registration is that it suggests that action taken when children were first registered was ineffective. However, some managers argue that it may reflect good practice, since re-registrations may be lower in councils that "play safe" and keep children on the register for a long time.

Sources: Referrals, Assessments and Children and Young People on Child Protection Registers year ending March 31 2002, Department of Health, 2003; Children Act Report 2000, Department of Health, 2001

# Prevalence of abuse, neglect and maltreatment

In order to put the above figures into context, the table below gives the number and ages of children on the child protection register and expresses the number as a percentage of the total number of children of this age in the population.

| Children on the child protection register (England) | | | | | | |
|---|---|---|---|---|---|---|
| | All ages | Age on registration | | | | |
| | | Under 1 | 1-4 | 5-9 | 10-15 | 16 & over |
| Numbers | 27,800 | 4,200 | 7,600 | 7,600 | 7000 | 400 |
| Percentage of population | 0.0025 | 0.0073 | 0.003 | 0.0024 | 0.0018 | 0.0003 |

*Source: Children on Child Protection Registers in England, year ending March 31 2002, Department of Health statistics 2003*

The numbers above seem to indicate that the proportion of children at real risk of significant harm is very small. However, there are some concerns that the percentage of children on child protection registers is not a full reflection of the number who experience abuse. In 2000, the NSPCC published the results of a nationwide survey of nearly 3,000 young people aged 18-24 concerning their experience of a wide range of treatments at home, both positive and negative.

The survey found:

- 7% had been physically abused by a carer.
- 6% had been emotionally and psychologically maltreated as children.
- 6% had been seriously physically neglected.
- 4% had been sexually abused.

Using the same data, a further report found:

- 90% of children have a loving family background, but large numbers suffer parental abuse at some point in childhood, most commonly physical abuse, neglect and emotional maltreatment.
- 80% of physically abused children have also known domestic violence.
- A significant minority of children face repeated pathological and multiple forms of abuse at the hands of parents or carers.

*Sources: Child Maltreatment in the UK: A Study of the Prevalence of Child Abuse and Neglect, NSPCC, 2000; Child Maltreatment in the Family, Cawson P, NSPCC, 2002*

# Court activity

Under the Children Act 1989, a range of private and public law court orders are available.

## Private law:

- Contact order – an order requiring the person with whom a child lives to allow the child to visit or stay with the person named in the order.
- Prohibited steps order – an order which specifies certain actions/decisions affecting children which should not be made without the consent of the court.
- Residence order – an order stating with whom a child should live.
- Specific issue order – an order settling a specific question which has arisen regarding the parenting of a child.
- Family assistance order – arranging assistance for a family, to which they must agree.

**Number of orders made in private law** (England and Wales)

| Type of order | 1993 | 1997 | 1999 | 2001 |
|---|---|---|---|---|
| Residence | 22,314 | 25,841 | 25,574 | 29,546 |
| Contact | 27,780 | 40,660 | 41,862 | 55,030 |
| Prohibited steps | 6,631 | 5,190 | 4,770 | 7,343 |
| Specific issues | 21,563 | 2,108 | 2,036 | 960 |
| Family assistance orders | 913 | 1,009 | 887 | 1,096 |

Source: Children Act Report 2001, Department of Health, July 2002

Although there is a large degree of fluctuation, the number of residence and contact orders made seems to be following an upward trend.

## Public law:

- Contact, prohibited steps, residence and specific issues orders (see above).
- Emergency protection orders and extensions (EPO & ext) – an order giving the applicant parental responsibility for the child and enabling them to take steps to ensure the child's safety.
- Secure accommodation – an order enabling a local authority to place a child in accommodation provided for the purpose of restricting liberty.
- Care – an order placing a child in the care of a designated local authority.
- Supervision – an order placing a child under the supervision of a designated local authority or probation officer.

| Number of orders made in public law (England and Wales) | | | | |
|---|---|---|---|---|
| Type of order | 1993 | 1997 | 1999 | 2001 |
| EPO & ext | 2,546 | 2,393 | 1,516 | 2,127 |
| Prohibited steps | 542 | 55 | 213 | 178 |
| Secure accommodation | 1,106 | 1,086 | 676 | 583 |
| Residence | 1,470 | 921 | 929 | 1,581 |
| Specific issues | 93 | 55 | 56 | 76 |
| Care | 3,221 | 4,537 | 4,124 | 5,984 |
| Supervision | 1,203 | 1,072 | 787 | 1,466 |
| Contact | n/a | n/a | 796 | 1,538 |

Source: Children Act Report 2001, Department of Health, July 2002

# Child prostitution

It has been estimated that 5,000 minors are involved in prostitution in Britain at any one time. The key findings of the most recent authoritative research study on this issue include the following:

## Age of involvement in prostitution
- 64% of the sample became involved in prostitution before they could legally consent to sex.
- the youngest children became involved in prostitution aged 11.
- 48% were involved in prostitution before they were 14.
- 72% thought there were now more children on the streets than when they started out.

## Abuse and family conflict
- 42% said their first sexual experience was of abuse, and of these, 26% said it occurred before they were 10 years old.
- 8% said their first sexual experience took place in the context of prostitution.
- 72% said they experienced conflict or abuse in their family.
- 48% experienced violence at the hands of partners, pimps or punters.

## Looked after children
- Almost two-thirds of those questioned aged 18 or under had been in care compared with a third of over 25s.
- Three-quarters of those who ran away from care became involved in prostitution before they were 14.

### Runaways

- Almost two-thirds (60%) of all those surveyed had run away and a third had become involved in prostitution while on the run from home or care.
- More than a third had become caught up in prostitution to survive while on the run.

### Drug use

- 56% were using drugs such as heroin, crack cocaine, and/or amphetamines.
- 65% of the sample using drugs started after becoming involved in prostitution.

*Source: One Way Street? Retrospectives on Childhood Prostitution, by Melrose M, Barrett D and Brodie I, the Children's Society, 1999*

## Trafficked children

The trafficking of children for cheap labour or for sexual exploitation is a growing global problem. As it is a clandestine activity there is little hard information and it is especially difficult to gather statistics on children. The UN estimates that the number of children trafficked annually, internally and externally, is around 1.2 million. It is known that at least 250 children have been trafficked to the UK in the last five years but the real figure is likely to be far higher.

*Source: Stop the Traffic! Unicef UK, 2003*

## Children and domestic violence

Domestic violence has an impact on children's life chances from the moment of conception.

Research suggests that:

- 40% of violence starts with the first pregnancy and that it escalates during pregnancy.
- 40-60% of pregnant women who are assaulted are hit in the abdomen.
- Pregnant women who are assaulted are twice as likely to miscarry.

*Source: www.avenueswomen.co.uk*

NCH published the first study carried out in Britain on the impact of domestic violence on children. The research found:

- Nearly three-quarters (73%) of mothers said their children had witnessed violent incidents, and 67% had seen their mothers being beaten. 10% of the women had been sexually abused in front of their children.

- Most (91%) of the mothers believed their children were affected in the short-term. A quarter said their children had become aggressive towards them and other children and almost a third had developed problems at school.
- Over 70% said their children had been frightened, 48% that they had become withdrawn and 34% said they had developed bed-wetting problems.
- Around 86% of mothers believed their children were affected in the long term. 33% thought they had become violent, aggressive and harder to control, 29% said they were resentful and embittered and 21% said that their children lacked respect for them.

*Source: The Hidden Victims - Children and Domestic Violence, NCH, 1994*

A more recent British Medical Association report on domestic violence confirmed many of NCH's findings about the impact of domestic violence on children. It concluded that witnessing domestic violence can cause considerable harm to children in both the short and long term. In the short term, children may show a range of disturbed behaviour including withdrawal, depression, increased aggression, fear and anxiety. Boys are more likely to show increased aggression in the longer-term and many children may suffer post-traumatic stress disorder.

*Source: Domestic Violence: a Healthcare Issue? British Medical Association, 1998*

The most recent research on domestic violence found:
- 60% of victims left their partner because they were afraid they would be killed.
- 54% left because they realised the abuse was affecting their children.
- 25% left because they feared for their children's lives.

*Source: Routes to Safety, Women's Aid Federation of England, 2002*

Of huge concern is the fact that children's safety may not be assured by their parents separating. A 1999 survey of 130 victims of domestic violence found that in 76% of cases where the courts had ordered contact with their estranged parent, the children reported they had been abused during contact visits.
- 10% had been sexually abused during contact.
- 15% had been physically assaulted.
- 26% had been abducted or involved in an abduction attempt.
- 36% had been neglected during contact.
- 62% had suffered emotional harm.
- Most of the children were under the age of five.

*Source: Unreasonable Fears? Women's Aid Federation of England, 1999*

# Chapter 6

# Poverty and social exclusion

# Poverty and social exclusion: an overview

**By Polly Toynbee**

This Labour government's pledge to abolish all child poverty by the year 2020 is probably the most ambitious and radical promise ever made by a party in power. When Tony Blair announced it to a room full of economists and poverty specialists, there was jaw-dropping astonishment on every face.

How was it to be done? The task seemed impossible. In most other respects this pledge simply did not fit in with any of the rest of this Labour government's relatively modest, gradualist approach of social change and taxation. As a result, this radical policy does not seem to have entered the national consciousness as a key part of the story the Blair government tells about itself. Out campaigning, it is police, hospitals and schools painted on the battle buses – those services used by all classes. Child poverty is not painted across the stage when Blair or Brown make their big set-piece speeches.

Here is the task: one in three of Britain's children is born poor, below the EU poverty line - which is households living on less than 60% of median income. Britain is near the bottom of the European league, so that one in three of all poor children born in Europe is born in Britain – a shaming record.

How well has Labour done so far? After seven years in power, it will have lifted more than a million children out of poverty, hitting the quarter-way mark by 2005, a remarkable achievement. It has been done through generous tax credits, giving low-earning families around £50 a week each extra, and some much more. It has also increased children's benefit levels by some 80% for non-working families, as well as increasing universal child benefit for all by 25%. Tax credits, tapering away at the top, go quite high up the income scale – up to families on £58,000 - to help compensate for the extra cost of children, just as there was once a tax break for children.

What perplexes economists is how the government is to hit the half-way mark by 2010, let alone abolish all child poverty by 2020 by following existing policies. The only countries that have virtually no child poverty are mainly Nordic nations – Sweden, Denmark, Norway, Finland and Holland – and they have done it over many decades by pursuing very different political policies. They have high taxes, high prices and a far flatter distribution of wages and incomes. Over many years, they have chosen equality as a positive strategy for the good of society – and, incidently, done very well economically out of that decision. With highly educated workforces and no huge tail of poverty's social problems acting as a drag-anchor on the economy, they have thrived far better than Britain, which is one of the most unequal of western democracies, only out-done by the US. Can Britain change its political climate sufficiently to agree to the more equal distribution necessary to abolish all child poverty? It will require powerful political champions to advocate it. So far, very little is ever said by ministers on future tax policies.

The government has added new indicators to the straightforward standard measure of poverty. But generally whichever way you measure it – on incomes, or a basket of goods a family lacks – you still come up with more or less the same numbers living below a standard of living most people regard as acceptable, when the general population is asked in polls. Recent government research shows that contrary to right-wing myths, the extra money families have received has been spent directly on children, greatly improving life for those in the deepest poverty, even if it hasn't always taken them over the poverty threshold.

Money makes a crucial difference, but it takes more than that to kick-start social mobility and ensure poor children get a fair chance in life. Sure Start has been the programme designed to catch babies and toddlers at risk of failure and help struggling families see that their children are ready to learn by the time they enter primary school. It has been a great success, hugely popular and much praised even by opposition MPs seeing it at work in their constituencies.

But it is expensive and as a result it's a very small programme, more of a pilot scheme. Sure Start children's centres are now in the 20% poorest wards but do not cover all the poor children there, and half of all poor children don't live in those wards anyway. The government fully realises its inadequacies. For the first time, the chancellor in his 2003 pre-budget statement said it was Labour's "goal" to make this universal, but with no date attached to the promise and very little extra money, that goal still looks far distant.

But imagine a time when close to every primary school there was a childrens centre where all parents came, with health visitors and baby clinics, with mother and toddler groups, and every support, from parenting help to child speech therapy. It would have affordable childcare for all, with fees according to means. It would have high quality education starting from toddlerdom. Latest research shows that by three, class differences in children's vocabularies all but fix their future trajectory. By the age of five and the start of school, it is far too late. Very early intervention works and poorer parents seize the chance of getting help and learning how to stimulate their young children.

The US Head Start programme was the inspiration for our Sure Start, because it proved that at the age of 30, the children from the programme who had two years' early family help far outstripped those who had no help. Every $1 spent on early years saved the state $7 later in crime, welfare, mental health and job prospects. Similar universal childcare programmes are what helped the Nordic nations abolish child poverty, catching potential problems early: they also ensured those countries alone buck the downward trend in birth-rates, as mothers can manage to juggle work and babies with guaranteed high quality childcare. Family incomes grow when mothers have the childcare they need. Labour knows how to abolish child poverty: but does it have the nerve to persuade the voters to will the expensive means to make it happen?

**Polly Toynbee** is a Guardian columnist

# Poverty and social exclusion: the key facts

## Problems of definition and measurement

Poverty is usually taken to refer to a lack of material resources, in particular, income. Social exclusion, on the other hand, is generally agreed to mean an inability to participate effectively in economic, social, political and cultural life, so that the people affected are unable to enjoy the activities or take advantage of the opportunities that others take for granted.

There are two main approaches to measuring poverty. One sees poverty in absolute terms and tends to emphasise basic physical needs and discount social and cultural norms. The other sees poverty relatively, in terms of generally accepted standards of living in a particular society. At present there is no official measure of poverty. However, the one that is most frequently used, if not universally accepted, in the UK and across the EU, is 50% of average income. People whose incomes are below this line are then defined as (relatively) poor. Some people criticise this, with some justification, on the basis that it is a measure of inequality rather than poverty.

The government's intention - announced in 1999 - to eradicate child poverty by 2020, with immediate targets to halve it by 2010 and to reduce it by a quarter by 2004, prompted the need to establish a single definition of child poverty. Since April 2002, the government has been consulting on how best to measure child poverty and in December 2003 published its final conclusions setting out the criteria that will be used to assess child poverty in the future. The new measure for child poverty consists of (1) absolute low income, (2) relative low income and (3) material deprivation and low income combined. Using this measure, poverty is falling when all three of these indicators are moving in the right direction. This new measure of child poverty will begin from 2004-05.

*Source: Measuring Child Poverty, DWP, 2003*

## Numbers of children living in poverty and exclusion

In 2001-02 the number of children living in households in Great Britian with below 60% of median household income was 2.7 million before housing costs, and 3.8 million after housing costs.

This 2001-02 figure represents a reduction of 300,000 before housing costs compared with 1994-95; of 600,000 since 1996-97; and of half a million children living in poverty (or of 400,000 after housing costs) compared with 1998-99, the base year for the government's public service agreement (PSA) target on child poverty.

This 2001-02 figure represents a reduction of 300,000 compared with 1994-95; of 600,000 since 1996-97; and of half a million children living in poverty before housing costs (or of 400,000 after housing costs) compared with 1998-99, the base year for the government's public service agreement (PSA) target on child poverty. This is equivalent to a fall of 16% before housing costs and 10% after housing costs from the 1998-99 base year.

Translated into percentages, this means that in 2001-02, 21% of children in Great Britain lived in households with below 60% of median income before housing costs; 30% of children lived in households with below 60% of median income after housing costs. Of those children living in lone parent families, 32% were living in households with below 60% of median income before housing costs, rising to 54% after housing costs are taken into account.

Source: Households Below Average Income Statistics 2001-02, DWP, the Stationery Office, 2003

Although there is no agreed way of measuring overall social exclusion, it is possible to give an idea of the scale of different forms of exclusion:

• A fraction of 1% of the population is affected by the most extreme forms of multiple deprivation (for example, becoming pregnant under sixteen, being excluded from school or sleeping rough).
• Almost 10% suffer significant problems (for example, those aged 16-18 who are not in education, employment or training, or who have been in prison).
• As many as one-third or more are in some way at risk (for example, one in three men has a criminal record by age 30).

Source: Preventing Social Exclusion, Social Exclusion Unit, the Stationery Office, 2001

## Longer-term trends in child poverty and inequality

The number of children in households on below half the average income grew from one in 10 to just under one in three between 1968 and 1995-96.

## Child poverty,[1] an international comparison

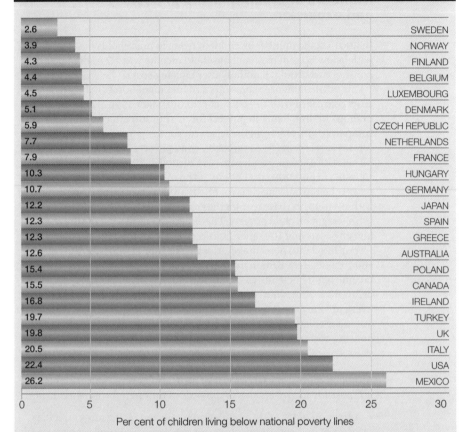

| Per cent | Country |
|---|---|
| 2.6 | SWEDEN |
| 3.9 | NORWAY |
| 4.3 | FINLAND |
| 4.4 | BELGIUM |
| 4.5 | LUXEMBOURG |
| 5.1 | DENMARK |
| 5.9 | CZECH REPUBLIC |
| 7.7 | NETHERLANDS |
| 7.9 | FRANCE |
| 10.3 | HUNGARY |
| 10.7 | GERMANY |
| 12.2 | JAPAN |
| 12.3 | SPAIN |
| 12.3 | GREECE |
| 12.6 | AUSTRALIA |
| 15.4 | POLAND |
| 15.5 | CANADA |
| 16.8 | IRELAND |
| 19.7 | TURKEY |
| 19.8 | UK |
| 20.5 | ITALY |
| 22.4 | USA |
| 26.2 | MEXICO |

Per cent of children living below national poverty lines

[1]The table shows the percentage of children living in 'relative' poverty, defined as households with income below 50 per cent of the national median

*Source: A League Table of Child Poverty in Rich Nations, Unicef, 2000*

In 1968, 9% of children living in two-parent families and 31% of children in lone parent families were poor (below half median income after housing costs).

By 1995-96, 24% of children living in two-parent families and 65% of children in lone parent households were poor.

Over this period, poverty rose twice as fast for families with children (21%) as for those without children (10%).

Over the 20-year period from 1979 to 1999 the incomes of the poorest 10% saw a real rise after housing costs of only 6% compared with a rise of 80% in the mean. The richest 10% experienced a rise in real income after housing costs of 86%.

*Source: Poverty: The Facts, CPAG, 2001*

## Progress in reducing inequality and child poverty since 1997

Since Labour came to power in 1997, measures have been introduced with the aim of reducing the level of income inequality and child poverty. Research by the Institute for Fiscal Studies points to the bottom two quintile income groups having the greatest proportional income gains, followed by the richest group during the period 1997-98 to 2001-02. This compares to the previous 18 years which saw the incomes of the top 20% grow 30 times faster than those of the least well-off.

However, reducing child poverty is proving more difficult than had been hoped. The Treasury claimed the tax and benefit reforms announced in the last parliament (1997-2001) would lift more than 1.2 million children out of relative poverty. However, statistics released in April 2003 showed this figure had only fallen by 600,000 between 1996-97 and 2001-02, a period beyond the lifetime of the last parliament.

*Sources: Inequality Under the Labour Government, the Institute for Fiscal Studies briefing note 33, 2003*

Another recent study has helped to demonstrate why it is so hard to eradicate child poverty. It found that the effect of the policy changes introduced between 1997 and 2003-04 would have been to reduce child poverty by about 1.3 million, other things being equal. But because incomes generally continue to rise, raising the relative poverty threshold, the actual reduction in child poverty is lower: there are likely to be about one million fewer children in poverty in 2003-04 than in 1997.

The researchers conclude that the government could just succeed in reaching its first milestone of reducing child poverty by a quarter by 2004. However, achieving its longer term targets is likely to be much more difficult and will require substantially more redistribution to the poorest and continuing priority to be given to the goal of ending child poverty. The study shows that greater employment, or "work for those who can", has made a real contribution to reducing poverty to date, but that there is a limit to how much further employment measures can contribute.

*Source: Poverty in Britain: The Impact of Government Policy Since 1997 by Sutherland H, Sefton T and Piachaud D, Joseph Rowntree Foundation, 2003*

## The children at greatest risk of poverty

The following children are at greatest risk of living in a low-income household:

- Children in lone parent households (compared with those with two adults).

- Children in workless households.
- Children in large families.
- Children in families with one or more disabled persons.
- Children in families where the mother was aged under 25.
- Children in households headed by someone from an ethnic minority, (particularly someone of Pakistani or Bangladeshi origin).
- Children in inner London had a higher risk of low income than for any other region. Those in the south-east and eastern regions were least at risk.

*Source: DWP, Households Below Average Income 2001-02, DWP, the Stationery Office, 2003*

---

## The cost of a child

It has been estimated that parents spend at least £20,000, excluding childcare, in the first five years of their child's life. The costs of having a child increase with age. Research suggests that between the ages of six and 16, parents spend around £53,000.

The indirect costs of having a child tend to be borne mainly by women. A report to the Women's Unit showed that the gap in lifetime earnings between women with children and those without could be as much as £500,000, with those least skilled losing out the most.

*Source: Study by Pregnancy and Birth magazine 2001; Women's Incomes over a Lifetime: a report to the Women's Unit, by Rake K (ed), the Stationery Office, 2000*

---

## Wealth, savings and debt

It is estimated that the wealthiest 1% of the population owned between a fifth and a quarter of the total wealth of the household sector in the late 1990s. In contrast, half the population shared between them only 6% of total wealth.

Half of all households have less than £1,500 and half of these have no savings at all. Lone parent families are more likely to have no savings than other household types.

Slightly fewer than a quarter of those in low-income households do not have access to a bank account. Lacking access to short-term credit makes it hard to budget, leading to arrears and / or recourse to high-cost moneylenders.

Benefit deductions can be made for social fund loans, overpayment of benefits, debt or fines. In May 2001, 1.22 million income support claimants had one or more deductions from benefit, the largest groups being lone parents (755,000) and disabled people (582,000).

One in seven referrals to the National Association of Citizen Advice Bureaux during 1998-99 concerned debt, up 12% on the previous year.

One in five young people has a bank loan by the age of 18. Research has found that 76% of 16 to 34-year-olds questioned said they think it is "inevitable that you will get into debt nowadays".

*Sources: Households Below Average Income Statistics 1999-2000, DWP; Family Resources Survey statistical report 1999-2000, DWP, 2001; Poverty: The Facts. CPAG, 2001; Income Support quarterly statistical enquiry, DWP, 2001; Undue Distress: CAB Clients' Experience of Bailiffs, NACAB, 2000; Hard Times? How Poor Families Make Ends Meet, by Kempson E, Bryson A and Rowlingson K, PSI, 1994; the Henley Centre, 2002, reported in the Guardian, February 20 2002*

## Child poverty and education

There is a strong correlation between child poverty and poor educational attainment. Children from poor backgrounds lag significantly behind better off children in educational development at 22 months.

Low income, as indicated by eligibility for free school meals, could account for 66% of the difference in GCSE attainment at local authority level.

Despite increased emphasis by the government to improve educational standards for all, socio-economic disadvantage remains a barrier to educational attainment. In 2000 in England and Wales three quarters of pupils whose parents were in the higher professional (highest) group achieved five or more GCSEs at grades A*-C, compared with only a third in the routine (lowest) group.

*Sources: Schools, education and social exclusion, by Sparkes J (ed), Case paper 29, 1999; Youth cohort study, DfES, reported in Social Trends 33, ONS, the Stationery Office 2003*

## Child poverty and health inequalities

Child poverty is also strongly associated with health inequalities.

Life expectancy varies significantly by social class. Given current mortality rates, males born in 1997-99 in England and Wales to parents in the professional group could expect to live, if they remained in that social class, to the age of 78.5. This was seven years longer than males born to parents in the unskilled manual group. Between 1972-76 and 1992-96 the gap between these social classes widened from 5.5 years to 9.5 years. The gap between these two groups then narrowed again to 7.4 years in 1997-99.

There was a similar difference across the social classes for females, with those born to parents in the professional group in 1997-99 having a life expectancy 5.7 years longer than those born to parents in the unskilled manual group. Only females in the unskilled manual group had a lower life expectancy than males in the professional group, and then only since 1987-91.

There has been a huge fall in infant mortality over the last century but socio-economic inequalities still exist. In England and Wales in 2001 the

## Infant mortality[1] by social class[2] (England and Wales)

| | Rates per 1,000 live births | | | |
| | Inside marriage | | Outside marriage[3] | |
| | **1991** | **2001** | **1991** | **2001** |
|---|---|---|---|---|
| Professional | 5.1 | 3.6 | 4.2 | 4.5 |
| Managerial and technical | 5.3 | 3.6 | 6.6 | 4.0 |
| Skilled non-manual | 6.1 | 4.5 | 8.5 | 5.3 |
| Skilled manual | 6.2 | 5.0 | 7.7 | 5.8 |
| Semi-skilled manual | 7.1 | 6.2 | 9.6 | 6.7 |
| Unskilled manual | 8.2 | 7.2 | 11.0 | 7.5 |
| Other | 11.6 | 6.7 | 21.2 | 10.8 |
| | | | | |
| All | 6.3 | 4.6 | 8.8 | 6.1 |

[1] Deaths within one year of birth
[2] Based on father's occupation at death registration
[3] Jointly registered by both parents
*Source: Social Trends 33, ONS, the Stationery Office, 2003*

infant mortality rate among babies born inside marriage whose fathers were in the unskilled manual class was 7.2 per 1,000 live births, twice the rate of those whose fathers were in the professional class. For babies born outside marriage where the birth was jointly registered by both parents there was a similar trend, with an infant mortality rate of 7.5 per 1,000 live births for babies whose fathers were in the unskilled manual class compared with a rate of 4.5 for those whose fathers were in the professional class.

Children under 15 from families in manual classes are more likely to report a long-standing illness than those from professional classes.
*Source: Independent Inquiry into Inequalities in Health, by Acheson D, the Stationery Office, 1998*

In 2000, 30% of lone parent families in Great Britain where the adult worked less than 16 hours a week or not at all and 21% of lone parent families that were eligible for but not receiving working families' tax credit contained one or more children with a long-standing illness or disability. For couple families, the proportions ranged from 27% to 37%.
*2003 Families and Children Study 2000, DWP, reported in Social Trends 33, ONS, the Stationery Office, 2003*

Pupils who received free school meals were more likely than those who did not to be regular smokers (14% compared with 10%) and to have taken drugs in the last month (13% compared with 11%). However, those who received free school meals were less likely than those who did not to have drunk alcohol in the last week (22% compared with 25%).
*Source: Smoking, Drinking & Drug Use Among Young People in England in 2002, summary of key findings, Boreham R & McManus S (eds), ONS, 2002*

A survey of five to 15-year-olds found that 10% had mental health problems. High-risk factors include living in households with weekly incomes under £200, being in social class V, and living in social rented housing, in a lone parent family, and in a family where neither parent is working.

Source: Mental Health of Children and Adolescents in Great Britain, ONS, the Stationery Office, 2000

# Childhood poverty in rural areas

There are significant levels of poverty and social exclusion in rural England and the evidence indicates that this affects a significant number of children. 700,000 children (23% of rural children) live in poverty in the countryside. This represents 18% of all poor children in the UK. 45% of lone parent households in rural areas live on low incomes.

Source: Rural Child Poverty briefing paper, End Child Poverty, 2003

# Worklessness and child poverty

Child poverty is strongly associated with worklessness. About 95% of children in workless households in Great Britain are in the bottom two quintiles, whereas those living in households with one or more working adults are more evenly spread across the income distribution.

The proportion of children under 16 living in workless households stayed constant between 1992 and 1996. Since 1997, this figure has decreased from 16% to 14% in 2003. This means that in 2003 there were 350,000 fewer children living in workless households than in 1997.

Children in lone parent families account for nearly seven out of 10 of children living in workless households. The employment rate of lone parents living in Great Britain has increased by 7% between 1997 and 2003, when it exceeded 50% for the first time in 20 years; however, this still compares badly with other developed countries (eg 82% in France). In comparison, the proportion of children in couple families who are in workless households is just 5%.

In a survey, 90% of lone mothers were either working now or said they wanted to work in the future. The main barriers to work that they identified were the cost of childcare (23%), its availability (16%), not wanting to spend time away from the children (27%), longstanding illness or disability (35%) and health problems among children (35%).

Sources: Households Below Average Income Statistics 2001-02, DWP, the Stationery Office, ONS, 2003; Opportunity For All: Making Progress, Tackling Poverty and Social Exclusion, the third annual report, DWP, the Stationery Office, 2001; Lone Parents and Employment, National Council for One Parent Families, 2001

## Expanding the provision of childcare to help end child poverty

A recent study, using a randomised controlled trial method, has found that mothers who were offered a place at a daycare centre for their children were more likely to find jobs than those who were not, but their reported household incomes were no higher than those whose children had not been given places. In the trial, places at the childcare centre were allocated randomly among a sample of 120 mothers in Hackney. Eighteen months later 67% of mothers whose child had been given a place were in paid work, compared with 60% of the control group of those whose children had not been given a place. But they were no more likely to have a weekly household income of more than £200 than the families who had not been given a place for their child at the centre.

The researchers say the study supports the government's view that daycare provision can increase maternal employment, but argue that this may not be a route out of poverty unless other changes are made. Tackling low pay, changing the benefit structure and reducing the costs of daycare to poor families may be equally important to reducing poverty, they argue.

*Source: Effectiveness of Out-of-Home Care for Disadvantaged Families: randomised controlled trial, by Toroyan T et al, British Medical Journal 2003; 327:906*

## Unemployment

Broadly speaking, unemployment levels follow the economic cycle, albeit with time lags. The most recent peak in unemployment in the UK was in 1993 when it reached nearly 3 million. Since then the number of unemployed people has fallen to 1.5 million people in spring 2002.

A higher proportion of younger people than older people are unemployed. In spring 2002, 22% of economically active men aged 16-17 were unemployed, as were 18.3% economically active women of the same age, compared with only 3.9% of men and 2.7% of women over 50.This is because the rates for young people have remained fairly stable while those for older groups have declined.

People from minority ethnic groups have significantly higher unemployment rates than the white population. 37% of young Bangladeshi people aged between 16 and 24 were unemployed, compared to 11% of young white people.

*Source: Social Trends 33, ONS, the Stationery Office, 2003*

# The New Deal

Participation in the government's New Deal scheme is mandatory for 18 to 24-year-olds who have claimed job seekers' allowance continuously for six months. The scheme also extends to lone parents and the long-term unemployed.

Of those young people in Great Britain leaving the New Deal during the period January 1998 to September 2002, 40% went into sustained employment (13 weeks or more).

Among those leaving the New Deal for people aged 25 and over, a much lower proportion (21%) moved into sustained employment.

*Source: Social Trends 33, ONS, the Stationery Office, 2003*

# In-work poverty

The structure of the labour market and levels of pay can affect the risk of poverty for children whose parents are in work, especially families with young children, large families, certain minority ethnic groups and lone parent families.

By 1995-96 there were twice as many poor children in working families than in 1979 because of greater wage inequality and increasing part-time work.

People living in families with only part-time workers are more than five times more likely to have incomes of less than 60% of the median after housing costs, compared with those with one or more adults working full-time.

The government has taken a number of steps to increase the extent to which work pays, including introducing the working tax credit, child tax credit and the national minimum wage. These measures have helped to lessen the "poverty trap" for people moving from benefits to work. In 1997 almost 750,000 families faced marginal deduction rates of more than 70%. As a result of the government's reforms, this number has now fallen by nearly 500,000.

*Source: Opportunity For All, fifth annual report 2003, DWP; Child Development and Family Income, by Gregg P, Harkness S and Machin S, Joseph Rowntree Foundation, 1999*

# The longer-term impact of poverty on children's life chances

Key findings include:
* Poverty in childhood increases the likelihood of low income in adulthood.
* There is a strong association between children's earnings and those of

their parents. Only a third of boys whose fathers were in the bottom quarter of the income distribution made it to the top half when they grew up, and the pattern is similar for girls. Men whose fathers were unemployed were twice as likely to be unemployed for a year or more between the ages of 23 and 33.

- People's chances of being in a manual occupation, having no access to a car and living in rented accommodation are also higher if their parents were in the same position.

*Sources: Intergenerational and Life Course Transmission of Social Exclusion, by Hobcraft J, Centre for the Analysis of Social Exclusion paper 15, LSE 1998; Childhood disadvantage and Intergenerational Transmission of Economic Status, in Persistent Poverty and Lifetime Inequality: the evidence, Case and HM Treasury; Intergenerational Mobility Among the Rich and Poor: Results from the National Child Development Study, by Johnson P and Reed H, Oxford Review of Economic Policy 1996. All reported in Opportunity For All: Tackling Poverty and Social Exclusion, first annual report, DSS, Stationery Office, 1999*

- A teenage mother with a childhood spent in poverty has six times the risk of remaining unqualified at age 33 as older mothers.

*Source: Childhood Poverty, Early Motherhood and Adult Social Exclusion, by Hobcroft J and Kiernan K, Case, 1999*

# Chapter 7

# Children who are looked after

# Children who are looked after: an overview

By Amanda Allard

A core principle of the Children Act 1989 is that children should be kept with their families whenever consistent with their wellbeing. Local authorities' overarching aim, therefore, is to improve the support available to children and families to ensure that more children can be kept safe and have their needs met at home.

In a minority of cases, the local authority is unable to support children at home. Children come into care when they are "suffering or likely to suffer significant harm", and their welfare cannot be sufficiently safeguarded if they continue to live at home.

This may make it sound as though standards are uniform and decisions are clear cut. In fact recent Department of Health research exploring trends in the numbers of children looked after found a complex picture. In some areas, numbers were increasing either because of better assessment or a better understanding of the impact on children of situations such as domestic violence or parental drug misuse. On a more negative front, staffing difficulties could also lead to an increase because staff did not have the time to devote to getting children out of the looked after system. But lower numbers going into care were not necessarily an indication of poor identification or assessment: there was evidence that those areas which had lower numbers going into care had a higher level of preventative support services.

A key objective for the Department for Education and Skills is to ensure that children are securely attached to carers capable of providing safe and effective care for the duration of childhood. For this reason, once it has been decided that a child needs to be taken into care there is an imperative to minimise the number of placements she or he experiences. Excessive moves undermine the opportunity to establish secure attachments. For this reason there is a target designed to minimise the number of moves in care, discussed in the stability of placements section below. Just as higher levels of support seem to contribute to a decrease in family breakdown with children going into care, so it has been recognised that greater levels of support are required to minimise in care placement breakdowns. Children's services inspections have found that some councils are focusing on working together with carers to achieve continuity and stability and are securing specialist therapeutic inputs to children and their carers in order to support placements.

This objective of secure attachment also underlies the government drive to maximise the contribution that adoption can make to providing permanent families for children. There are two public service agreement targets supporting this drive:

- To increase by 40% the number of looked after children who are adopted, and aim to exceed this by achieving if possible a 50% increase.
- To increase to 95% the proportion of looked after children placed for adoption within 12 months of the decision that adoption is in the child's best interests (up from 81% in 2000-01).

Department of Health analysis of recent trends in the number of children being adopted suggest that councils are making earlier decisions to move children to permanent alternative care where assessments have shown that rehabilitation with their birth family is unlikely to be successful.

One of the driving factors behind the desire to improve placement stability is the link which has been made between high numbers of placement moves and poor outcomes, particularly in education because of the associated risk of disruption in schooling. The poor outcomes for those who have spent time in the care system are now universally acknowledged and there are a number of government targets designed to tackle specific issues. Those relating to education are detailed below. There is also a target relating to youth offending – to reduce to 7.2% by 2004 the proportion of looked after children who have had final warnings or been convicted (the present percentage is 11%). Looked after children are presently three times more likely to have received a final warning or conviction, during the course of a year, than their peers. There is also a national teenage pregnancy strategy with the goals of (i) halving the conception rate among under-18s and (ii) reducing the long term exclusion of teenage parents ensuring 60% are able to re-access education, training or employment by 2010. Young women with a history of being looked after have been shown to be particularly vulnerable to teenage pregnancy.

The recent changes to leaving care legislation, the Children (Leaving Care) Act 2000, has led to a plethora of shortly to be published research looking at the impact of the Act and the outcomes for care leavers. Once all of this research is in the public domain, we may have a better idea about whether or not government initiatives designed to improve the in and leaving care experience and outcomes for young people are yet bearing fruit. Some of the initiatives outlined in the children's green paper, Every Child Matters, such as encouraging more people into foster caring and working with young people may well help. Although, as pointed out by young people at NCH projects who were consulted by the DfES on the green paper, they will need to be the right kind of people.

**Amanda Allard** is a senior public policy officer for NCH

# Children who are looked after: the key facts

Under the Children Act 1989 in England and Wales, a child or young person is "looked after" by a local authority if she or he is placed in their care by a court (under a care order) or provided with accommodation by the authority's social services department for more than 24 hours.

## Number of children looked after in England

Looked after at March 31 2002:

- At March 31 2002, local authorities in England looked after 59,700 children. This is 1% higher than a year earlier (58,900), and 22% higher than in 1993-94 (49,100).

Looked after at any time during the year ending March 31 2002:

- It is estimated that the total number of children looked after during the year 2001-02 was 82,200. This is virtually the same as the revised estimate for the previous year (82,000), and only 2% higher than in 1993-94.

The difference in growth between the snapshot numbers and the numbers for all those looked after during the year can be explained by the fact that there has been a marked increase in the length of time each child is looked after. If children are being looked after for longer then more will be seen on any given day.

In addition to the above figures 11,000 children were looked after during the year 2001-02 under a series of short-term placements. Short-term placements are generally used to provide relief to parents and families; they are often, although not exclusively, used to support the parents of children with disabilities. 72% of children looked after in short-term placements are disabled; 62% are boys. The number of children looked after under a series of short-term placements has risen by 28% since 1993-94.

More boys are looked after than girls - at March 31 2002, 56% of the looked after population were boys, compared with 51% of the population under 18 as a whole.

Up until March 31 2000, the average age of children looked after had been steadily falling for a number of years; since when there has been a slight increase. The average age of children looked after at March 31 2002 was 10-and-a-half, compared with the lowest average age of 10 years and four months in 2000. This compares with 11 years and two months in 1994. At March 31 2002 there were 24,800 children aged under 10 (41% of all children), compared with 18,100 (or 37%) in 1993-94.

*Source: Children Looked After in England at March 31 2002, Department of Health, 2003*

### Children looked after by placement 1997-2002 (England)

| | Numbers | | |
| --- | --- | --- | --- |
| | **1997** | **2000** | **2002** |
| All children [1] | 51,200 | 58,100 | 59,700 |
| Foster placements: | 33,500 | 37,900 | 39,200 |
| Secure units[2, 3] | | | 220 |
| Children's homes [3] | 6,400 | 6,700 | 6,000 |
| Homes and hostels not subject to children's home regulations[3] | 160 | 330 | 540 |
| Placed for adoption[4] | 2,400 | 3,100 | 3,600 |
| Placement with parents | 5,200 | 6,500 | 6,700 |
| Living independently or in residential employment | 1,200 | 1,200 | 1,100 |
| Residential schools | 770 | 1,200 | 1,100 |
| Other accommodation | 1,600 | 1,200 | 1,100 |

[1] Figures for children looked after exclude agreed series of short-term placements

[2] Before 2001 secure units were classified under children's homes

[3] Estimates of numbers of children re-calculated for 1997 to 2000 in line with the new coding structure that came into force on April 1 2000

[4] Increase since 1997 is, in part, a result of improved recording of this type of placement.

*Source: Children Looked After in England at March 31 2002, Department of Health, 2003*

The proportion of looked after children in foster placements rose steadily from 58% in 1992 to 65% in 1996, since when it has remained fairly constant.

In contrast, during the same period there has been a steady decline in the proportion of looked after children in children's homes and residential schools (including secure units). The number fell from 9,700 at March 31 1992 (17% if those in care) to 7,900 at March 31 2002 (13% of children looked after).

At March 31 2002, 6,700 (11%) of all looked after children were placed with parents. The use of this kind of placement has been increasing since 1994-95 when the proportion was 8%. Before this, the numbers had been falling; in 1992 the proportion was 12%.

Source: Children Looked After in England at March 31 2002, Department of Health, 2003

## Stability of placements

In 1999 the government set a target for every local authority of having no more than 16% of children who are looked after with three or more placements in a year, in recognition of the importance of placement stability. Nationally, this was achieved by March 31 2001. At March 31 2002 it was down to 15%. There is however wide variation between individual local authorities from 3% (Kensington & Chelsea) to 43% (Swindon). The percentage of local authorities achieving 16% or less has increased steadily, from 38% in 1998 to 65% in 2002.

Research has shown that children who experienced three or more moves since a care order was made because of placement breakdown had the poorest outcomes. But research also shows that some children will always need to move placement in order to achieve secure attachment to carers; this is why the target is 16% and not 0%. Placement stability should be the consequence of children enjoying secure attachments and it should not be assumed that a child enjoying placement stability is necessarily securely attached.

Sources: Children Looked After in England at March 31 2002, Department of Health, 2003; Making Care Orders Work: A Study of Care Plans and Their Implementation, by Harwin J, Owen M, Locke R, and Forrester D, the Stationery Office, 2001; The Children Act report 2000, Department of Health, 2001

### Children looked after at March 31 2001 by category of need (England)

| Category of need | Number | Percentage |
| --- | --- | --- |
| | Numbers and percentages | |
| Abuse or neglect | 37,100 | 62 |
| Disability | 2,300 | 4 |
| Parental illness or disability | 3,700 | 6 |
| Family in acute stress | 4,100 | 7 |
| Family dysfunction | 6,200 | 10 |
| Socially unacceptable behaviour | 2,000 | 3 |
| Low income | 90 | 0.2 |
| Absent parenting | 4,300 | 7 |
| Total all children[1] | 59,700 | 100 |

[1] Figures for looked after children in this table exclude agreed series of short-term placements

Source: Children Looked After in England at March 31 2002, Department of Health, 2003

| Ethnic origin | Number | Percentage |
|---|---|---|
| White | 48,700 | 82 |
| Mixed | 4,400 | 7 |
| Asian or Asian British | 1,400 | 2 |
| Black or black British | 3,900 | 7 |
| Other ethnic groups | 1,400 | 2 |
| Total of all children[1] | 59,700 | 100 |

Numbers and percentages

[1] Figures for children looked after exclude agreed series of short-term placements and include unaccompanied asylum seeking children.

Source: Children Looked After in England at March 31 2002, Department of Health, 2003

38,400 children were looked after under a care order at March 31 2002, an increase of 800 on a year earlier.

In contrast, the number under voluntary agreements (32%) is down by 4% compared with 1998 (36%).

The number freed for adoption is up by 59% compared with 1998.

The number of interim care orders is up by 40% compared with 1998.

Source: Children Looked After in England 2001-02, Department of Health, Nov 2002

## Numbers of children looked after by legal status at March 31 2002 (England)

| | Numbers | Percentages |
|---|---|---|
| All children[1] | 59,700 | 100 |
| Care orders | 38,400 | 64 |
| Of which: interim | 8,800 | 15 |
| full | 29,600 | 50 |
| Voluntary arrangements under s.20 CA 1989[2] | 19,000 | 32 |
| Freed for adoption | 1,800 | 3 |
| Other[3] | 540 | 1 |

1 Figures for children looked after in this table exclude agreed series of short-term placements.

2 Single placements.

3 Includes children on remand, committed for trial or detained in local authority accommodation under section 38(6) of the Police and Criminal Evidence Act 1984, children subjected to emergency protection orders or police protection, or under child assessment orders.

Source: Children looked after in England at March 31 2002, Department of Health, 2003

# Numbers of children leaving care in England

| Children who ceased to be looked after during the year ending March 31 2002, by age on ceasing[1,2] (England) | |
|---|---|
| | Numbers |
| All children | 25,100 |
| Under 1 | 1,300 |
| 1-4 | 5,100 |
| 5 – 9 | 4,200 |
| 10-15 | 7,800 |
| 16 – 17 | 3,400 |
| 18 & over | 3,300 |

[1] Figures exclude agreed series of short-term placements

[2] Only the latest occasion on which a child ceased to be looked after in the year has been counted

*Source: Children Looked After by Local Authorities Year Ending March 31 2002, Department of Health, 2003*

Most children who ceased to be looked after aged 18 and over ceased on their 18th birthday.

25,100 children ceased to be looked after during 2001-02, virtually the same as last year.

27% of the children who ceased to be looked after were aged 16 or over and this has been fairly constant over the last five years. However, there has been a noticeable change in the age distribution of care leavers. Before 1998-99 the proportion of care leavers aged 16 and 17 was rising (it was 62% in 1998) but since then it has fallen sharply and was 51% in 2001-02.

| Percentage of children age 16 and over ceasing to be looked after during the years ending March 31 1998 to 2002 by age on ceasing (England) | | | | | |
|---|---|---|---|---|---|
| Year ending March 31 | | Percentages | | | |
| Age | 1998 | 1999 | 2000 | 2001 | 2002 |
| 16 & 17 | 62 | 67 | 59 | 53 | 51 |
| 18th birthday | 36 | 32 | 40 | 46 | 48 |

*Source: Children Looked After in England at March 31 2002, Department of Health, 2003*

## Educational qualifications of children who are looked after in England

In 1999 the government established an objective for children's social services in England "to ensure that children who are looked after gain the maximum life chance benefits from educational opportunities, health care and social care". Two specific targets were set in respect of this objective:

- Increase to 50% by 2000-01 the proportion of children leaving care aged 16 and over with a GCSE or GNVQ qualification and to 75% by 2002-03.
- Increase to15% by 2003-04 the proportion of children leaving care aged 16 and over with five GCSEs at grade A*-C, or GNVQ.

During the year ending March 31 2002, 2,600 (41%) of the 6,700 young people leaving care had obtained one or more GCSEs (or GNVQ). In comparison, 95% of year 11 pupils in England as a whole obtained at least one GCSE or GNVQ.

During the same year 300 (or 5%) of young people left care with five or more GCSEs, the same as in the previous year. 50% of all year 11 children attained this level of academic achievement.

Analysis of the statistics shows that children who are looked after for periods of up to three years tend to do better at school the longer they are in care; beyond three years, the improvements are less marked.

*Source: Children Looked After by Local Authorities Year Ending March 31 2002, Department of Health, 2003*

## The education of looked after children: Social Exclusion Unit report

The Social Exclusion Unit's report into the education of looked after children highlights a number of key factors which impact on the educational attainment of children in care:

- Too many young people's lives are characterised by instability in terms of placement moves. Stability is essential to allow children to develop bonds with their carers. If children are unable to develop secure bonds it can have a significant impact on their development and learning.
- Young people in care spend too much time out of school. Around a quarter of children in care of compulsory school age are being educated in non-mainstream settings or at home. Children in care may miss school because they do not have a place, have been excluded or do not attend.

- Children do not have sufficient help with their education if they get behind: support for children in care in early years settings is inconsistent and often limited. Special educational needs among children in care are not always identified and supported. Lack of training for teachers leads some to underestimate the potential of children in care.
- Carers are not expected or equipped to provide sufficient support and encouragement for learning and development.
- Children in care need more help with their emotional, mental or physical health and well being. Children in care face more challenges to their emotional well being as a result of frequent moves, high levels of bullying, and separation from their families. Many have experienced trauma or have recognised mental health problems, and they are more likely than other teenagers to use drugs.

*Source: A Better Education for Children in Care, Social Exclusion Unit, September 2003*

## Being looked after: outcomes

The outcomes relating to having been looked after are almost uniformly poor, although some resilient young people manage to overcome the disadvantage of having a care background and do very well.

The research findings summarised below present a generally gloomy picture, but it is important to note that they relate to studies carried out before some key policy initiatives and legislative changes occurred in respect of looked after children in England, including the introduction of the Quality Protects programme and the passing of the Children (Leaving Care) Act 2000. Things are hopefully now beginning to improve, as the statistics reported above with respect to qualifications suggest.

- Offending: 23% of adult prisoners and 38% of young prisoners have been in care.
- Health: Nearly half the young people in a Save the Children Fund survey found leaving care affected their health, mostly adversely and in terms of their diet and mental health. 42% said they were not eating enough.
- Parenthood: at least one in seven young women leaving care is pregnant or already a mother.
- Poverty: 81% of the care leavers interviewed by Save the Children said their income was not enough to live on. Nearly 80% had faced circumstances where they had no money. The majority were on benefits and unemployed.

*Sources: Too Much Too Young, Action on Aftercare Consortium, 1996; You're On Your Own, Save The Children, 1995; Strategic Planning in Children's Services, Department of Health 1999*

## Adoption

A child is not necessarily being looked after before adoption. Many children are adopted by step parents or relatives. In Great Britain there were 6,500 adoption orders in 2001. Adoption orders give parental responsibility for a child to adoptive parents. Between 1981 and 2001 the number of adoptions fell from 10,400 to 6,500, although the number of adoptions has started to increase in recent years from a low of 4,800 in 1999.

In 2001, 4% of adoptions were for children under one, 44% for children aged between one and four and 31% for children aged five to nine Between 1981 and 2001 there was a decrease in the proportion of adopted children who were under one from 26% to 4% and an increase in the proportion of adoptions of those aged one to four from 20% to 44%.

Sources: Adoptions by Age of Entry on Adoption Register, England and Wales, ONS dataset; Social Trends 33, ONS, the Stationery Office, 2003

## Children adopted from care

3,500 children who were looked after in England were placed for adoption in the year ending March 31 2003, an increase of 3% on the figures for the previous year. This was an increase of 29% on the 1999-2000 figure.

The percentage of looked after children who were adopted has risen each year since 1998; 6% of looked after children were adopted during the year ending March 31 2003, compared with 4% in 1998-99.

The average age of children adopted from care fell from four years 10 months in 1997-98 to four years three months in 2002-03. The most common age group for children adopted from care was between one and four, which in 2002-03 accounted for 59% of all such adoptions. Only 5% of adoptions from care were of children aged 10 and over.

The majority of children adopted from care were aged under one at the time they started to be looked after. In the year ending March 31 2002, only 13% of children adopted from care started their final period of care aged four years or over.

Source: Children Adopted from Care in England: 2002-03, Department for Education and Skills, November 2003

# A profile of adopted children and of their adopters

A statistical study of a sample of 1,801 children drawn from 145 local authorities in England in 1998-99 found:

- 90% of adopted children were white, 7.5% were of mixed parentage.
- Only a fifth had no birth siblings.
- Two-thirds had come into care under the age of one year and half under the age of six months.
- Black and mixed parentage children were younger on coming into care than the average.
- The mean age of placement with adopters was three years one month.
- Cases where foster carers had adopted their foster child amounted to 13% of all the children adopted.
- The vast majority (89%) of adopters were couples where both partners were white.
- 5% of all adopters were single, of whom 92% were female.
- The age of the child when placed was a consideration for 90% of adopters.
- 11% of adopters with a preference sought a child aged under one; 42% sought children aged up to four years and a further 41% would consider children up to the age of nine.

*Source: Surveying Adoption: A Comprehensive Analysis of Local Authority Adoptions 1998-99, British Agencies for Adoption and Fostering (BAAF), 2000*

# Chapter 8

# Children in need

# Children in need: an overview

## By Caroline Abrahams and Jacqui McCluskey

In England and Wales "children in need" are children assessed as being unlikely to achieve or maintain a reasonable standard of health or development without the provision of services by a local authority, under section 17 of the Children Act 1989. This chapter contains facts and figures about three of the groups of children who most frequently receive services because they are "in need" in these terms: children with disabilities, young carers and children who are refugees and asylum seekers.

The children in need census periodically carried out by government on the services delivered by local authorities also includes those provided for children who are looked after and children who are at risk of abuse, each of which is covered by a separate chapter in this book.

## Children with disabilities

The population of children with disabilities has significantly changed in the last 10 years. More children are surviving with complex and severe disabilities because of advances in medical science, leading to an increase in the demand for intensive support services. The numbers of children with autism and attention deficit hyperactivity disorder (ADHD) also seem to be growing.

Children with disabilities are at high risk of poverty. It can be really hard for parents to combine work with their caring responsibilities and their employment levels are much lower than for parents with non-disabled children as a result. Children with disabilities are vulnerable to exclusion: they can face negative attitudes and lack of access to opportunities that others take for granted, such as participation in sports. Minority ethnic children with disabilities and their families may be doubly disadvantaged in all these respects.

The picture is not entirely gloomy however and, in particular, there have been many positive developments in terms of education. Although wide variations in the levels of support for children with special education needs remain, recent legislation such as the Disability Discrimination Act 2001 should gradually lead to children with disabilities being included in the whole life of schools.

Many of last year's green paper proposals should benefit children with disabilities, for example the calls for more family support and for better information sharing. A major focus in the paper is the need for more integrated provision, a concern for many children with disabilities and their families, since they often need to access numerous services. The national service framework for children will set standards to help ensure that health, education and social care services are delivered in an integrated way.

Other policy priorities include the need to ensure that benefit levels take account of the additional costs of caring for a disabled child; a requirement on service providers to listen to their views, with support and training in how to do so; and better care planning for them through children's services and into adult life. Families also need more practical support, particularly more accessible and affordable specialist child care and respite care.

## Young carers

The fact that there are many thousands of children and young people who are caring for sick or disabled relatives across the UK only came prominently to notice about 10 years ago. Arguably policy and practice have been struggling to catch up ever since.

This is one of the practice areas where effective communication between children's and adult social services is particularly important, since staff from both may be supporting different members of the household. The green paper's proposal to create new children's departments, comprising education and children's social services will, if implemented, sever the existing link between children's and adult social services, so new protocols will be needed to ensure effective joint working.

Good links with health services are also crucial to ensuring everyone's well-being in families with young carers, so the extent to which the new structural arrangements in local areas succeed in engaging primary care trusts, GPs, acute hospital trusts and mental health trusts in the planning and delivery of services for children will also be important.

A big issue at present is the fact that most of these children and young people remain unknown to any agency, their caring role hidden from view. All the professionals who work with children, especially teachers, need training to help sensitise them to young carers and their needs. More advice and counselling services for children and young people might also make it easier for young carers to seek help on their own terms. They must be able to do so on a confidential basis, subject to the child protection imperative, once the government's information sharing initiative has been implemented; otherwise they will simply be deterred from coming forward.

Perhaps the most pressing issue of all is the shortage of support services for young carers and their families. Until these unmet needs are addressed, too many young carers and their families will continue to struggle on their own.

## Asylum seeking and refugee children

Asylum seeking and refugee children are among the most vulnerable and disadvantaged children in this country, but they are not given the same protection, care and support as others in the UK. Procedures, legislation and policies are complex, confused and unfair, resulting in what we consider to be the harsh treatment of these children.

Asylum seeking and refugee children in the UK can face poverty and destitution, poor health, social exclusion, racism, forcible dispersal and isolation. The detention of asylum seeking children is set to increase with the development of accommodation centres. In addition, children living in these centres will not be able to access mainstream schools and will instead be educated on site – a policy that we fear will impede community cohesion.

The government is currently proposing further measures that NCH believes to be draconian, including some that could make families destitute when their asylum application has run its course with a negative outcome. There is the prospect of children either having to be taken into care or becoming homeless, until the Home Office can secure an appropriate method of repatriation – sometimes a protracted process.

Unaccompanied asylum seeking children (UASC) currently receive inadequate support, their needs are not fully assessed and too many are left to fend for themselves. They also frequently have to live with the anxiety and uncertainty that they may be removed from the country when they reach the age of 18.

NCH believes that asylum seeking and refugee children are children first and foremost and that they should be granted the same rights and entitlements as other children. The government should withdraw its reservation on the application of the UN Convention on the Rights of the Child with respect to asylum seeking children. The welfare and best interests of the child should be at the heart of a child-centred, efficient and fair asylum process.

NCH opposes the detention of asylum seeking children and families and does not support accommodation centres. We think these children should be educated in mainstream schools. Asylum seeking and refugee families should receive the full level of social security benefits. Under no circumstances should families be left without any means of supporting their children, nor should children be made to suffer as a result of the choices of their parents or their failure to comply with conditions for support. All UASC should receive the level of care and protection to which they are entitled, based on their need, including after care support after they reach 18 years of age.

**Caroline Abrahams** is NCH's director of public policy;
**Jacqui McCluskey** is a senior public policy officer for NCH

# Children with disabilities

## The number of children with disabilities

The most authoritative information comes from a survey carried out by the Office of Population, Censuses and Surveys in 1985. This found that about 3% of children in Great Britain had disabilities.

A more recent analysis was carried out in 1998. Based on mid-year estimates, it found that 393,824 children with disabilities under 16 were living in the UK. 55,200 of them were aged under five and 276,064 were aged between five and 15. More than 100,000 of these children were severely disabled and had at least two different sorts of significant impairment. These figures would again suggest that 3% of children in the UK are disabled. The same methodology showed that 155,976 young people with disabilities aged 16-19 were living in the UK.

*Sources: Quality Protects: Disabled Children, Numbers and Categories, Department of Health, 2000; the Children Act Report 2000, Department of Health, 2001*

| Number of children aged under five with disabilities by severity (UK) | |
|---|---|
| **Severity category** | **Number** |
| I (mild, ill, balance) | 19,872 |
| II (behaviour) | 19,872 |
| III (behaviour, ill, locomotive) | 2,760 |
| IV (intellect, behaviour) | 5,520 |
| V (severe) | 2,760 |
| VI (severe, mainly physical) | 1,656 |
| VII (very severe, life threatening, requires weekly treatment) | 2,760 |
| Total | 55,200 |

*Source: Quality Protects: Disabled Children, Numbers and Categories, Department of Health, 2000*

## Number of children aged five to 15 with disabilities by severity (UK)

| Severity category | Number |
|---|---|
| I (variety, mild) | 38,649 |
| II (behaviour plus other mild) | 71,777 |
| III (behaviour and incontinence) | 22,085 |
| IV (consciousness/behaviour/fits) | 11,043 |
| V (hearing and communication) | 19,324 |
| VI (communication and behaviour) | 38,649 |
| VII (high levels personal care – multiple) | 13,803 |
| VIII (severe learning and behaviour problems) | 13,803 |
| IX (multiple plus severe behaviour) | 22,085 |
| X (multiple plus very severe) | 13,803 |
| XI (multiple including digestion, usually not behaviour) | 11,043 |
| Total | 276,064 |

Source: Quality Protects: Disabled Children, Numbers and Categories, Department of Health, 2000

## Children with visual impairment

At March 31 2000 (the most recent year for which statistics are available) there were 3,860 children aged under 17 who were registered as blind, and 4,270 children in England aged under 17 who were registered as partially sighted. However, registration is not compulsory and these figures are known to be a significant underestimate of the number of visually impaired children: in 1997 the Royal National Institute of the Blind (RNIB) estimated there were about 24,000 children aged under 15 with a registrable visual impairment in the UK.

Sources: Registered blind and partially sighted people, year ending March 31 2000, Department of Health, 2001; RNIB website: www.rnib.org.uk

## Children with hearing impairment

At March 31 2001 (the most recent year for which statistics are available) there were 3,988 children aged under 18 who were registered as deaf and 2,889 children in England aged under 18 who were registered as hard of hearing. However, registration is not compulsory and these statistics are believed to understate the scale of hearing impairment among children.

The National Deaf Children's Society (NDCS) estimates that there are about 20,000 children in the UK aged under 16 who are moderately to profoundly deaf. About 12,000 of these children were born deaf. About one in every 1,000 children is deaf at three years old. This rises to two in every 1,000 children aged nine to 16. An estimated 840 children are born in the UK every year with significant (moderate to profound) deafness.

*Sources: People registered as deaf or hard of hearing year ending March 31 2001, Department of Health, 2002; NDCS website: www.ndcs.org.uk*

## Cerebral palsy

Cerebral palsy describes a physical impairment that affects movement. Movement problems vary from the barely noticeable to the extremely severe. People with cerebral palsy often have difficulty controlling their movement and facial expressions but this does not necessarily mean that their mental abilities are in any way impaired. Some are of higher than average intelligence, others have moderate or severe learning difficulties.

One in every 400 babies born in this country has cerebral palsy, 1,800 children every year. Between a quarter and a third of children and adolescents with cerebral palsy are also affected by epilepsy.

*Source: Scope website: www.scope.org.uk*

## Epilepsy

About one in every 130 people in the UK has epilepsy, making it the second most common neurological condition after migraine. Boys and men are more likely to have epilepsy than girls and women.

In 1997, the British Epilepsy Association (BEA) estimated that at least 50,000 children in the UK suffered from epilepsy and that it affected five in every 1,000 children under 11 years of age. It is the most common neurological disorder encountered by general paediatricians and paediatric neurologists, but is often misdiagnosed in children.

*Sources: BEA website: www.epilepsy.org.uk ; Health committee, second report, the Specific Health Needs of Children and Young People, 1997*

## Autism

Autism is a pervasive developmental disorder arising from a physical dysfunction of the brain, the cause of which is not yet known. It affects four times as many boys as girls. It spans a spectrum ranging from children with extreme behavioural problems and severe communication difficulties to children with above-average IQs and no actual learning disability, but severe social impairment.

In 1997 the National Autistic Society (NAS) estimated that there were some 73,000 children with autism in the UK. There are no reliable statistics, although it has since been suggested that about 91 in every 10,000 people in the UK may be autistic if the most subtle forms of autism are included.

*Sources: Health committee, second report, the Specific Health Needs of Children and Young People, 1997; Notes on the Prevalence of Autistic Spectrum Disorders by Wing L and Potter D, paper produced for the autism99 internet conference, accessible via the NAS website: www.nas.org.uk*

## Down's syndrome

There are more differences between people with Down's syndrome than there are similarities. As well as having some family characteristics, they will have physical features shared by others with Down's syndrome. They will also have a learning disability. However, there is wide variation in mental abilities, behaviour and physical development in individuals with Down's syndrome.

For every 1,000 babies born, one will have Down's syndrome, and about 600 babies are born with Down's syndrome each year.

*Source: Down's Syndrome Association website: www.downs-syndrome.org.uk*

## Childhood disability and poverty and social exclusion

The income distribution for families with disabled children is skewed towards the bottom end compared with the distribution for families with children as a whole.

**Percentage distribution of income for children by whether disabled child in a family, after housing costs, including the self-employed**
(Great Britain)

| Family type | Net equivalent disposable household income | | | | |
|---|---|---|---|---|---|
| | Bottom quintile | 2nd | 3rd | 4th | Top |
| No disabled children | 27 | 23 | 21 | 13 | |
| 1 or more disabled children | 31 | 34 | 20 | 9 | 6 |

*Source: Adapted from Table 4.1 Households below average income statistics, 2001-02; Department for Work and Pensions, 2003*

# Services for disabled children

Provisional figures from the 2003 Children in Need census in England suggest that about 13% of the children in need population are disabled and that they received 15% of gross expenditure on children in need.

The Children in Need census carried out in England in 2000 provided new information about the services provided for children with disabilities. It found that:

- The proportion of disabled children receiving a service compared with all disabled children was small: only one in 13 disabled children did so in an average week.
- Not all the disabled children who were receiving a service were doing so because of their disability: 12% were receiving a service because of abuse or neglect and 9% because of family difficulties.

A more detailed study carried out on service provision for disabled children in 13 authorities within the 2000 Children in Need census found that children were most likely to be looked after if they had behavioural disabilities, visual impairment or learning disabilities, compared with other disabilities. Less than a third of the children who were receiving a service had only one disability and 25% had five or more. The disabled children who were looked after were more likely to be in residential provision than foster care, compared with the population of looked after children as a whole. This was particularly the case for children with multiple disabilities.

*Sources: Children in Need in England: Preliminary results of a survey of activity and expenditure, ONS, Department for Education and Skills, 2003; Children Act report 2000, Department of Health, 2001*

In England in the year ending March 31 2002, 2,300 children were looked after because of their disability. They comprised just under 4% of all children who were looked after that year, a similar proportion to the previous year.

*Source: Children Looked After in England 2001-02, Department of Health, 2002*

# Children who are young carers

The Carers National Association defines a young carer as "anyone under the age 18 whose life is in some way restricted because of the need to take responsibility for the care of a person who is ill, has a disability, is experiencing mental distress or is affected by substance use or HIV/Aids".

## Number of young carers

There are no official national statistics on the number of young carers. Accurate figures are hard to obtain because of the hidden nature of caring. Young carers and their parents are often silent about the extent of caring through fear of separation, guilt, pride and a desire to "keep it in the family". Identification of young carers from black and minority ethnic groups can be even more difficult due to differing racial, cultural and religious needs.

A 1996 ONS survey estimated the total population of young carers to be between 19,000 and 51,000 in England. A recent government report estimated there to be between 20,000 and 50,000 young carers in England. However, in the 2001 census, about 175,000 children and young people were reported as providing unpaid care in their families in the UK so these earlier figures may be serious underestimates.

Sources: Young Carers and Their Families by Walker A, ONS, 1996; Caring About Carers: a National Strategy for Carers, Department of Health, 1999; www.statistics.gov.uk/cci

## Characteristics of young carers

The Carers National Association carried out a major survey of young carers in the UK in 1997. It involved 2,303 young carers who were in contact with 69 projects and also included comparisons with the findings of a similar national survey of young carers from 1995. The survey found:

- The age of young carers ranged from three to 18 years. The average age of young people supported by projects was 12.
- 57% of young carers were girls and 43% were boys.
- 86% of the young carers were white European. The largest minority group were black African and Caribbean carers, accounting for

7% of the total. More carers from minority ethnic communities were caring for members of the extended family (8% compared with 4% of white Europeans).

- Lone parent families were over represented among the families of young carers, although the proportion of young carers in lone parent families had decreased from 60% in 1995 to 54% in 1997.
- As in 1995, the majority of care recipients were mothers (58%), followed by siblings (24%), fathers (13%), and grandparents (4%). There had been a decrease in the incidence of parents as care recipients and an increase in the proportion of siblings receiving care. 12% of young carers were now caring for more than one person - an increase from 10% in 1995. The vast majority of those living in lone parent families were caring for mothers (76%), compared with 53% of those living in two parent families, and were substantially less likely to be caring for siblings. More than a third of young carers living in two parent families were caring for siblings (some could have been caring for other family members as well).
- Most young carers (63%) were caring for people with physical health problems, the most commonly occurring single condition being multiple sclerosis. Over a quarter of young carers (29%) were caring for people with mental health problems. 14% of carers were caring for people with learning difficulties and this was likely to include caring for a sibling with a learning difficulty. 4% were caring for a person with a sensory disability (visual and hearing impairments).
- The majority of young carers were performing domestic tasks like cleaning and meal preparation (72%), over half were doing general tasks (assisting with mobility and giving medications) and a fifth were providing intimate care (washing, showering or toileting), a decrease of only 2% since 1995. 43% provided emotional support. 7% helped to provide childcare for siblings.
- Almost half the young carers and their families were in receipt of social work support, the most common service received. A quarter of the young carers and their families had no outside support services

**Percentage distribution of income for children by whether disabled adult in a family, after housing costs, including the self-employed**
(Great Britain)

| Family type | Net equivalent disposable household income | | | | |
| --- | --- | --- | --- | --- | --- |
| | **Bottom quintile** | **2nd** | **3rd** | **4th** | **Top** |
| No disabled adults | 27 | 23 | 21 | 16 | 13 |
| 1 or more disabled adults | 40 | 27 | 18 | 8 | 7 |

Source: Adapted from Table 4.1 Households below average income statistics, 2001-02; Department for Work and Pensions, 2003

other than their contact with the young carers project. This represented an increase since 1995.
- The likelihood of performing domestic tasks, general and intimate care increased with age. Girls were more likely to be involved in all aspects of care than boys, especially domestic tasks and intimate care.

*Source: Young Carers in the United Kingdom: A Profile, by Dearden C and Becker S, Carers National Association, 1998*

## Poverty

Most young carers live in families in which there are one or more disabled adults. As this table shows, such families are more likely than others to be in the bottom half of the income distribution. Around one in four of children in the UK in low income households (ie with below 60% median income) lives in families containing one or more disabled adults. Children living in families with both a disabled adult and a disabled child are particularly at risk of low income: around three-quarters of this group are in the bottom two quintiles.

## Life chances and well-being

Research published in 2003 found that a third of young carers aged under 16 who took part in a study had suffered educationally as a result of their caring responsibilities. The difficulties they experienced included regular absence, persistent lateness, poor academic performance, tiredness and being victims of bullying. These problems often had a knock-on effect in later life, in relation to career choices and opportunities. The research emphasises that not all young people with caring responsibilities have problems at school and that bullying, for instance, happens to many children. Bullying was often due to prejudices about disability or mental health in families, rather than caring.

*Source: Missed Opportunities, Carers National Association (with Loughborough University), 2003*

A report by the Children's Society asked former young carers to identify the short and longer-term impact of caring. It found:

### Impact on life chances and opportunities
- More than 70% felt their education had been affected by their caring responsibilities. In a number of instances, school was remembered as a painful social experience. Memories involving feelings of isolation, frustration and depression still persisted.
- Some former young carers had returned to education at a later stage in their lives to pursue the qualifications they had been unable to gain, or study for occupational and vocational qualifications.

- In many cases, being a young carer influenced later career choices and aspirations. Almost 50% attributed their chosen career in a caring profession to caring experiences and the acquisition of skills that they felt confident to use.

## Health and well-being

- About 28% of the former carers felt their physical health had suffered as a result of the time they had spent caring. The physical health of a number of former young carers continued to be affected long after direct caring had ceased. Backache caused by lifting, weight loss, allergies and ulcers were among the on-going illnesses and incapacities.
- 40% of the former young carers thought their mental health had been directly affected. Emotional traumas, depression, stress and low self-esteem were not uncommon.
- 70% revealed long-term psychological effects. This was evident especially where the person in need of care had alcohol or mental health problems.
- 50% had (or were still having) some form of counselling, or were considering counselling because the stresses of their caring years had left unresolved needs.

*Source: On Small Shoulders: Learning from the Experiences of Former Young Carers, Frank J et al, the Children's Society, 1999*

---

# Young carers who become looked after

In England, in the year ending March 31 2002, 3,700 children were looked after because of their parents' illness or disability.

*Source: Children Looked After in England 2001-02, Department of Health, 2002*

# Children who are asylum seekers

## Numbers applying for asylum

In 2002 there were 84,130 asylum applications (excluding dependants) in the UK, 18% more than in 2001 (71,025) and 5% more than in 2000 (80,315). The main nationalities of applicants in 2002 were Iraqi (17%), Zimbabwean (9%), Afghan (9%), Somali (8%), and Chinese (4%).

*Source: Asylum Statistics United Kingdom 2002, ONS, 2003*

## Dependants of applicants

The total number of dependants in 2002, accompanying or subsequently joining principal applicants prior to a decision being made was 18,950. Including these dependants the total number of applications in 2002 was 103,080. This equates to an average of just over one dependent for every five principal applicants. Most dependants (80%) in 2002 were aged 20 or under - most of these aged 15 or under; 16% were aged between 21 and 39, and just 4% aged 40 or older. A little under half (43%) of dependants were male.

*Source: Asylum Statistics United Kingdom 2002, ONS, 2003*

## Unaccompanied asylum seeking children

In 2002, 6,200 unaccompanied children, aged 17 or under, applied for asylum in the UK, a 27% increase on 2000 (2,733). Of these 1,240 applications were made at port and 4,955 in country. The main countries of origin were Iraq (21%), Afghanistan (12%), Federal Republic of Yugoslavia[1] (12%) and Somalia (6%).

*Source: Asylum Statistics United Kingdom 2002, ONS, 2003*

[1] Federal Republic of Yugoslavia (FRY) is comprised of Kosovo, Serbia and Montenegro but the majority of FRY applications are thought to be from Kosovars.

## Looked after unaccompanied asylum seeking children

There were 2,200 unaccompanied asylum seeking children (UASC) being looked after by local councils in England at March 31 2002. The overwhelming majority (1,600 or 72%) of these children were in London with a further 410 children (19%) elsewhere in the south-east. 1,700 (78%) of all UASC were boys and only 500 (22%) were girls. 1,100 (48%) were aged 16 or over.

Not all UASC become looked after children. Older UASC – those aged 16 and 17, the majority – are commonly helped under section 17 of the Children Act 1989.

Source: Children Looked After 2001-02, Department of Health, 2003

### Unaccompanied asylum seeking children looked after at March 31 2002 (England)

|  | UASC | | Local children | |
|---|---|---|---|---|
|  | **Number** | **%** | **Number** | **%** |
| All placements | 2,200 | 100 | 57,500 | 100 |
| Foster care | 1,300 | 60 | 37,900 | 66 |
| Children's homes and hostels | 550 | 25 | 6,200 | 11 |
| Placed for adoption | 0 | 0 | 3,600 | 6 |
| Living independently | 250 | 12 | 860 | 1 |
| Other | 70 | 3 | 8,900 | 15 |

Source: Children Looked After 2001-02, Department of Health, 2003

## London

In September 2003 there were 4,231 unaccompanied asylum seeking children (UASC) supported by London authorities: 3,238 16 to17-year-olds and 993 children aged 0 to 15.

The numbers of UASC peaked in November 2002 at 4,872. The figure fluctuated throughout the year, increasing between July and November 2002 and then decreasing from November 2002 to March 2003. But throughout the year April 2002-03, the overall increase only amounted to 34 young people.

Source: London Asylum Seekers Consortium (LASC) Data Services

# Education of asylum seeking children

In schools outside London, the percentage of asylum-seeker pupils on roll ranged from 2% to 26%. The average was around 7%. In London schools, the proportion of asylum seeker pupils was much higher, with the average around 20%.

Source: The Education of Asylum-seeker Pupils, Ofsted, 2003

# Detention of the children of asylum seekers

On April 2 2003, there were 56 children under the age of 18 detained in immigration removal centres.

| Detention of the children of asylum seekers (UK) | |
| --- | --- |
| Immigration service removal centre | Children under 18 years of age in detention at April 2 2003 |
| Dungavel | 21 |
| Harmandsworth | 18 |
| Oakington | 14 |
| Tisley | 3 |
| Total | 56 |

Source: Hansard (House of Commons debates), written answers, Vol. 404, Part No. 88, May 1 2003, Column 523W

# Chapter 9

# Children who offend

# Children who offend: an overview

**By Sharon Moore**

The youth justice system in England and Wales was significantly reformed by the 1998 Crime and Disorder Act, which established the system's purpose as "the prevention of offending". It also created the Youth Justice Board (YJB) for England and Wales to oversee the new system. Under the board's supervision, the youth offending team structure was established, creating multi-disciplinary teams made up of representatives of the police, social services, probation, education and health services, responsible for the delivery of youth justice services to a particular geographical area. These teams are accountable to the chief executive of the local authority area that they serve.

Within the present system, a child can be arrested and charged with an offence from the age of 10. Up until 1998, the principle of doli incapax offered additional protection to children between the ages of 10 and 13 who appeared in court; it required the prosecutor to prove that the child knew that what they were doing was not just naughty but seriously wrong. This protection has been abolished under the auspices of 'getting tough' on crime. Essentially there is no distinction made between children and adults.

The majority of children between the ages of 10 to 17 who are charged with an offence appear before the youth court, a magistrates' court that essentially mirrors the adversarial process for adults. A smaller number of children charged with serious crimes are referred to the crown court for trial and/or sentence.

While the YJB has developed measures to reduce the levels of child custody in England and Wales, the number held has doubled in the last 10 years. The government's recent response to criticisms of the Joint Committee on Human Rights contains an acknowledgement that the figure will probably remain at its current level of approximately 3,000 at any one time. This is hugely disappointing given that we know custody is an expensive, damaging and ineffective way of tackling criminal behaviour.

The lives of children caught up in our criminal justice system are marked by poverty, family breakdown, drug and alcohol abuse, neglect, educational exclusion and poor housing. Our response to them should be as children in need and not as criminals but this latter definition dominates our response to them and largely ignores their welfare.

The Children's Society, along with other children's charities and criminal justice agencies, has recently produced a report, Children in Trouble: Time for Change, which calls for a fundamental review of the current system. The report points out that our current youth justice system is not sufficiently distinct from the adult system, is overly complex, fraught with anomaly and tension and is at odds with children's human rights. The report also highlights how children in the youth justice system are not treated according to the same principles and philosophy that underpin wider children's law and policy and there is a need for harmonisation.

As part of the consultation process around the green paper on children at risk, the Home Office has distributed its own document, Youth Justice – the Next Steps, which lays out the government's vision of the youth justice system for the future. The vision includes a commitment to retaining the present age of criminal responsibility at 10 years and the youth justice system as the best vehicle for maintaining public confidence. No mention is made of the government's obligations to children in trouble with the law in line with the United Nations Convention on the Rights of the Child.

In our submission to the Home Office, the Children's Society calls on the government to use the opportunity presented by the green paper to address the issues it highlights and to resist the creation of additional criminal legislation which will further complicate an already complex system.

**Sharon Moore** is principal policy and practice manager for the Children's Society

# Children who offend: the key facts

## Offences

The overall picture of youth crime is a relatively stable one. The number of offences committed by children and young people who are brought into contact with the youth justice system – either through formal

### National offences (England and Wales)

| | | | | | Age | | | | |
|---|---|---|---|---|---|---|---|---|---|
| | 10 | 11 | 12 | 13 | 14 | 15 | 16 | 17 | Total |
| Arson | 61 | 107 | 207 | 251 | 280 | 248 | 178 | 135 | 1,467 |
| Breach of bail | 13 | 27 | 82 | 211 | 508 | 855 | 1,372 | 1,839 | 4,907 |
| Breach of conditional discharge | 6 | 9 | 35 | 85 | 195 | 295 | 385 | 430 | 1,440 |
| Breach of statutory order | 6 | 21 | 121 | 407 | 777 | 1,545 | 2,417 | 2,962 | 8,256 |
| Criminal damage | 58 | 1,112 | 2,127 | 3,378 | 4,814 | 5,530 | 5,181 | 4,785 | 27,516 |
| Death or injury by reckless driving | 0 | 2 | 2 | 5 | 13 | 21 | 36 | 43 | 122 |
| Domestic burglary | 114 | 192 | 445 | 819 | 1,261 | 1,669 | 1,785 | 1,519 | 7,804 |
| Drugs offences | 10 | 31 | 116 | 402 | 1,137 | 2,501 | 4,169 | 5,048 | 13,414 |
| Fraud & forgery | 14 | 31 | 61 | 128 | 262 | 388 | 749 | 1,406 | 3,039 |
| Motoring offences | 25 | 140 | 379 | 1,239 | 3,801 | 8,780 | 18,810 | 28,560 | 61,734 |
| Non-domestic burglary | 91 | 228 | 367 | 662 | 982 | 1,160 | 1,186 | 938 | 5,614 |
| Public order | 40 | 135 | 400 | 876 | 1,803 | 3,308 | 5,193 | 6,035 | 17,790 |
| Racially aggravated offences | 13 | 24 | 68 | 121 | 226 | 304 | 339 | 265 | 1,360 |
| Robbery | 40 | 96 | 218 | 420 | 747 | 1,047 | 1,142 | 1,027 | 4,737 |
| Sexual offences | 12 | 32 | 101 | 226 | 279 | 377 | 334 | 303 | 1,664 |
| Theft & handling | 617 | 1,495 | 3,129 | 5,529 | 7,994 | 9,485 | 10,045 | 9,598 | 47,892 |
| Vehicle theft | 49 | 170 | 390 | 1,071 | 2,378 | 3,596 | 4,093 | 3,442 | 15,189 |
| Violence against the person | 309 | 798 | 1,939 | 3,428 | 5,854 | 7,808 | 7,766 | 6,994 | 34,896 |
| Other | 53 | 132 | 313 | 538 | 989 | 1,726 | 2,669 | 3,219 | 9,639 |
| Total | 2,062 | 4,782 | 10,500 | 19,796 | 34,300 | 50,643 | 67,849 | 78,548 | 268,480 |

Source: Youth Justice – Annual Statistics 2002-03, Youth Justice Board for England and Wales, 2003.

reprimands and final warnings or though court orders – has remained broadly similar over the last year.

268,480 offences (resulting in disposals) were committed by children and young people aged 10-17 in the financial year 2002-03. Boys committed 226,647 offences compared with 41,833 offences committed by girls.

The most common offences committed by young people brought into contact with the youth justice system fall into the following categories:

- Motoring offences (23%).
- Theft and handling (17.8%).
- Violence against the person (13%).
- Criminal damage (10.2%).
- Public order offences (6.7%).

While overall levels of offences are broadly static, the number of offences of burglary, robbery and vehicle theft committed by young offenders brought to account in the youth justice system was lower in 2002-03 than the previous year.

*Source: Gaining Ground in the Community, annual review 2002-03, Youth Justice Board, 2003*

## Self-reported offending

The Mori youth survey provides information on the types of offences young people say they commit. The most common offences for the 26% of young people in school who say they have offended are:

- Fare dodging (53%).
- Hurting someone that does not lead to them needing medical treatment (41%).
- Damage to property belonging to someone else (33%).
- Graffiti (33%).
- Shoplifting (33%).

The types of offences reported being committed by excluded school age children presents a slightly different picture. The most common offences are:

- Hurting someone in a way that does not leave them needing medical treatment (62%).
- Carrying a knife (62%).
- Dealing in stolen goods (61%).
- Damage/ destroying property (58%).
- Fare dodging (57%).

*Source: Youth Survey 2003, research study for the Youth Justice Board by Mori, Youth Justice Board, 2003*

## Disposals

166,925 children and young people aged 10-17 were issued with pre-court, community or custodial disposals in 2002-03. 81% of these children are male and 19% female.

- 44.2% were issued with a pre-court disposal.
- 35% were issued with a first tier disposal.
- 16.6% were given a community sentence.
- 4.2% were sentenced to custody.

**National disposals** (England and Wales)

| | Age | | | | | | | | |
| | 10 | 11 | 12 | 13 | 14 | 15 | 16 | 17 | Total |
|---|---|---|---|---|---|---|---|---|---|
| **Pre-court** | | | | | | | | | |
| Police reprimand | 1,083 | 2,191 | 4,201 | 6,293 | 8,576 | 9,135 | 8,616 | 7,114 | 47,209 |
| Final warning without intervention | 217 | 192 | 351 | 652 | 1,081 | 1,364 | 1,545 | 1,465 | 6,867 |
| Final warning & intervention | 275 | 641 | 1,245 | 2,330 | 3,410 | 4,421 | 4,235 | 3,109 | 19,666 |
| **First tier** | | | | | | | | | |
| Absolute discharge | 6 | 35 | 69 | 137 | 302 | 505 | 1,060 | 1,810 | 3,924 |
| Bind over | 1 | 9 | 27 | 73 | 171 | 355 | 586 | 748 | 1,970 |
| Compensation order | 12 | 35 | 89 | 212 | 433 | 700 | 938 | 1,208 | 3,627 |
| Conditional discharge | 3 | 45 | 123 | 318 | 712 | 1,255 | 1,839 | 2,540 | 6,835 |
| Fine | 1 | 9 | 32 | 100 | 352 | 934 | 2,830 | 5,978 | 10,236 |
| Referral order | 182 | 446 | 1,066 | 2,195 | 3,835 | 5,531 | 6,498 | 7,603 | 27,356 |
| Reparation order | 8 | 52 | 139 | 332 | 604 | 1,048 | 1,146 | 889 | 4,218 |
| Sentence deferred | 0 | 1 | 3 | 13 | 16 | 41 | 57 | 83 | 214 |
| **Community** | | | | | | | | | |
| Action plan order | 11 | 62 | 187 | 401 | 860 | 1,347 | 1,386 | 1,144 | 5,398 |
| Attendance centre order | 0 | 18 | 61 | 227 | 481 | 793 | 792 | 679 | 3,051 |
| Community punishment & rehabilitation order | 0 | 0 | 0 | 1 | 1 | 44 | 542 | 1,069 | 1,657 |
| Community punishment order | 1 | 1 | 0 | 2 | 6 | 78 | 1,172 | 1,986 | 3,246 |
| Community rehabilitation order | 0 | 0 | 0 | 0 | 2 | 37 | 551 | 1,566 | 2,156 |
| Community rehabilitation order & conditions | 1 | 0 | 0 | 0 | 1 | 6 | 88 | 204 | 300 |
| Curfew order | 6 | 5 | 26 | 60 | 161 | 316 | 352 | 367 | 1,293 |
| Drug treatment & testing order | 0 | 0 | 0 | 1 | 3 | 3 | 10 | 30 | 47 |

Continued overleaf

**National disposals** (England and Wales) - Continued

| | 10 | 11 | 12 | 13 | 14 | 15 | 16 | 17 | Total |
|---|---|---|---|---|---|---|---|---|---|
| Supervision order | 21 | 108 | 290 | 786 | 1,529 | 2,360 | 1,974 | 1,166 | 8,234 |
| Supervision order & conditions | 4 | 13 | 67 | 165 | 374 | 656 | 673 | 508 | 2,460 |
| **Custody** | | | | | | | | | |
| Detention & training Order (4 months) | 0 | 0 | 10 | 71 | 168 | 487 | 668 | 956 | 2,360 |
| Detention & training order ( 4 months to 2 years) | 0 | 1 | 31 | 103 | 301 | 751 | 1,253 | 1,674 | 4,114 |
| Section 90-91 | 5 | 1 | 0 | 15 | 42 | 74 | 137 | 213 | 487 |
| Total | 1,837 | 3,865 | 8,017 | 14,487 | 23,421 | 32,241 | 38,948 | 44,109 | 166,925 |

*Source: Youth Justice – Annual Statistics 2002-03, Youth Justice Board for England and Wales, 2003.*

## Custody

At March 2003 there were 2,874 10 to 17-year-olds in custody within the juvenile secure estate and 452 18 to 19-year-olds.

**Secure estate population – accommodation type** (England and Wales)

| | April 2002 | May 2002 | June 2002 | July 2002 | Aug 2002 | Sept 2002 | Oct 2002 | Nov 2002 | Dec 2002 | Jan 2003 | Feb 2003 | Mar 2003 |
|---|---|---|---|---|---|---|---|---|---|---|---|---|
| **Secure training centre** | | | | | | | | | | | | |
| 10 to 17-year-olds | 122 | 126 | 136 | 152 | 144 | 138 | 145 | 144 | 146 | 155 | 171 | 174 |
| 18 to 19-year-olds | 0 | 0 | 0 | 0 | 0 | 0 | 0 | 0 | 0 | 0 | 0 | 0 |
| **Local authority secure children's home** | | | | | | | | | | | | |
| 10 to 17-year-olds | 323 | 333 | 313 | 315 | 305 | 311 | 303 | 325 | 308 | 286 | 299 | 310 |
| 18 to 19-year-olds | 1 | 1 | 1 | 2 | 0 | 0 | 0 | 1 | 0 | 0 | 0 | 0 |
| **Young offender institutions** | | | | | | | | | | | | |
| 10 to 17-year-olds | 2,588 | 2,665 | 2,618 | 2,730 | 2,648 | 2,677 | 2,740 | 2,682 | 2,479 | 2,423 | 2,404 | 2,390 |
| 18 to 19 year olds | 489 | 531 | 560 | 571 | 486 | 498 | 511 | 505 | 460 | 365 | 395 | 452 |
| **Totals** | | | | | | | | | | | | |
| 10 to 17-year-olds | 3,033 | 3,124 | 3,067 | 3,197 | 3,097 | 3,126 | 3,188 | 3,151 | 2,933 | 2,864 | 2,874 | 2,874 |
| 18 to 19-year-olds | 490 | 532 | 561 | 573 | 486 | 498 | 511 | 506 | 460 | 365 | 395 | 452 |

*Source: Youth Justice – Annual Statistics 2002-03, Youth Justice Board for England and Wales, 2003.*

## Young prisoners

*"Young prisoners" refers to prisoners aged 15 to 20 and some older prisoners, originally received as sentenced young offenders, who have not yet been reclassified as adult prisoners.*

The number of young prisoners in Prison Service custody decreased by 3% from 11,348 in 2002 to 10,984 in April 2003. 8,540 were under sentence, 2,361 on remand and 83 non-criminal prisoners. Young prisoners accounted for 15% of the total prison population of 72,853.

*Source: Prison Population Brief, England and Wales, Home Office, April 2003*

### Males

There were 1,356 receptions of sentenced male young offenders during March 2003, 8% less than one year previously. There were 10,404 young male prisoners in April 2003, 3% less than the 10,708 held at the end of April 2002. There were 2,196 young males on remand. The number of untried young male prisoners dropped by 8% compared with the previous year, from 1,400 to 1,292. The number of convicted unsentenced young male prisoners also decreased by 15% from 1,064 to 904.

In April 2003, there were 8,128 young males under sentence. Of these, three were sentenced for defaulting on a fine. There were also 80 non-criminal prisoners. The number serving sentences of less than six months in April 2003 (820) showed a decrease of 8% from a year earlier. The number serving between six months and less than a year decreased by 15% to 974. The number of young males serving sentences of between one and four years increased by 0.4% to 4,431 and those serving sentences of four years or more increased by 11% to 1,900. The numbers sentenced to prison custody for burglary fell 15% to 1,380 and the largest increase was in the numbers sentenced to custody for robbery (up 239 to 1,957).

*Source: Prison Population Brief, England and Wales, Home Office, April 2003*

### Females

During March 2003, the number of untried young females received into Prison Service establishments was 66, a 19% decrease from a year earlier. During the same period, the number of young sentenced females received decreased by 11% from 118 in March 2002 to 105 in March 2003.

There were 580 young females held in prison at the end of April 2003 - 165 on remand, 412 sentenced and three civil prisoners. This represents 9% less than a year earlier when 162 young females were on remand and 471 were sentenced (and seven civil). Of the 165 young females on remand, 75 were untried prisoners (down 5% from 79 a year earlier) and 90 were convicted unsentenced prisoners (up 8% from 83 a year earlier). There were no young female fine defaulters being held in Prison Service establishments.

At the end of April 2003, young females accounted for 5.3% of the total young prisoner population, 0.3 percentage points lower than the end of April 2002. Young females accounted for 13% of the total female population, 1.5 percentage points lower than in April 2002 (14.5%).

*Source: Prison Population Brief, England and Wales, Home Office, April 2003*

---

# Juveniles

*"Juveniles" refers to sentenced inmates aged from 15 to 17, male remand inmates aged 15 to 17, and female remand inmates aged 17 (15 to 16-year-old female remand inmates are placed in non-Prison Service accommodation).*

Young juvenile prisoners aged 15 to 17 decreased by 9% over the year ending April 2003 to 2,288. There were 290 untried juvenile prisoners, 130 convicted unsentenced juvenile prisoners, and 1,868 sentenced juveniles in April 2003.

There were 768 receptions of juveniles during March 2003, 9% less than during the same period a year earlier.

*Source: Prison Population Brief, England and Wales, Home Office, April 2003*

## Males

There were 283 untried juvenile prisoners at the end of April 2003, a figure which was 16% lower than a year earlier. At the end of April 2003, the number of juvenile males held as convicted unsentenced prisoners was 120, down 38% from a year earlier.

The male sentenced population was 1,804 at the end of April 2003, a decrease of 3% compared with the 1,855 held a year earlier. Juvenile males sentenced to prison for robbery increased by 12%, while theft and handling decreased by 15%.

*Source: Prison Population Brief, England and Wales, Home Office, April 2003*

## Females

The female juvenile sentenced population was 64 in April 2003; a decrease of 38% compared with the 103 held the previous year.

The untried female juvenile population was seven at the end of April 2003. In April 2003, the number of juvenile females held as convicted unsentenced prisoners was 10.

*Source: Prison Population Brief, England and Wales, Home Office, April 2003*

## Population of young prisoners, April 30 2003[1] (England and Wales)

| | All Custody Types | Detention in YOI[2] /DTO[3] | Section 90/ 91 PCC (S)[4] & custody for life | In default of a fine | Untried | Convicted |
|---|---|---|---|---|---|---|
| **Males** | | | | | | |
| 15 | 229 | 164 | 30 | 0 | 21 | 14 |
| 16 | 681 | 472 | 96 | 0 | 83 | 30 |
| 17 | 1,297 | 764 | 278 | 0 | 179 | 76 |
| 18 | 1,925 | 1,036 | 309 | 1 | 279 | 300 |
| 19 | 2,555 | 1,858 | 162 | 1 | 324 | 210 |
| 20 | 2,865 | 2,227 | 72 | 1 | 325 | 240 |
| 21 | 772 | 625 | 32 | 0 | 81 | 34 |
| Total | 10,324 | 7,146 | 979 | 3 | 1,292 | 904 |
| | | | | | | |
| **Females** | | | | | | |
| 15 | 0 | 0 | 0 | 0 | 0 | 0 |
| 16 | 13 | 10 | 3 | 0 | 0 | 0 |
| 17 | 68 | 36 | 15 | 0 | 7 | 10 |
| 18 | 124 | 66 | 20 | 0 | 20 | 18 |
| 19 | 147 | 92 | 8 | 0 | 18 | 29 |
| 20 | 190 | 128 | 3 | 0 | 27 | 32 |
| 21 | 35 | 31 | 0 | 0 | 3 | 1 |
| Total | 577 | 363 | 49 | 0 | 75 | 90 |

Type of custody

[1] Table excludes non-criminal (civil) prisoners.

[2] Young offender institutions

[3] Detention and training orders from April 2000

[4] Powers of Criminal Courts (Sentencing) Act 2000

Source: Prison Population Brief, England and Wales, Home Office, April 2003.

## Children and young people in secure accommodation in England and Wales

Secure units, maintained by local authority Social Services Departments, are not only available for young offenders, whether sentenced or on remand, but for any child or young person being looked after. Specifically, they are provided for children and young people aged up to 18 who:

- Have a history of absconding, are likely to abscond if kept in any other form of local authority accommodation and who are likely to suffer harm if they do abscond; or

- Are likely to injure themselves or others if kept in any other form of accommodation; or
- Have been sentenced for serious offences under Sections 90-92 of the Powers of Criminal Courts (Sentencing) Act 2000 and those under a Detention and Training Order (Crime & Disorder Act 1998) or a juvenile secure remand (section 23(4) Children and Young Persons Act 1969).

As at March 31 2002:

- There were 425 approved places in secure units in England and 20 in Wales.
- 415 children and young people were accommodated in secure units in England and 15 in Wales. There has been an increase of 5% in the number of children accommodated in England and Wales compared with the previous year, continuing the general upward trend since 1995.
- 285 boys (71%) were accommodated in secure units in England compared with 115 girls.
- 46% of children accommodated were aged 14 years or under (compared with 22% in 1992) and 22% were aged 16 and over (compared with 49% in 1992).
- Detention and training orders accounted for 36% of children in secure accommodation, 19% were remanded directly to local authority accommodation under S23(4) CYPA 1969, 18% were detained for grave crimes under Sections 90-92 of the Powers of Criminal Courts (Sentencing) Act 2000, 7% had been remanded under section 25 of the Children Act, 8% were accommodated under section 20 of the Children Act 1989 (where a local authority is looking after the child following a voluntary agreement with the parents), while 10% were looked after under a care order made in  family proceedings.
- 93% of approved places in secure units in England and Wales were occupied, compared with 88% in 2001, representing a 5% increase in the number of children accommodated.
- 235 of the 425 places approved in England (55%) were contracted out for use by the Youth Justice Board.

*Source: Children Accommodated in Secure Units Year Ending March 31 2002, England and Wales, Department of Health Bulletin 2003/01, January 2003*

# International comparisons

With the exception of Germany and Greece, the relative level of child custody in England and Wales is far higher than in other European countries for which data is available.

| Country | Number in custody (date) | | Under-18 population (millions) | Custody per 1,000 under-18 population |
|---|---|---|---|---|
| Germany | 7,556 | (31.08.00) | 15.529 | 0.49 |
| Greece | 574 | (01.09.01) | 2 | 0.28 |
| England/Wales | 3,133 | (30.09.02) | 13.351 | 0.23 |
| Scotland | 160 | (30.06.00) | 1.097 | 0.15 |
| Hungary | 286 | (01.09.00) | 2.056 | 0.14 |
| Austria | 201 | (01.09.98) | 1.634 | 0.12 |
| Czech Republic | 213 | (31.12.01) | 2.084 | 0.1 |
| Portugal | 214 | (31.12.99) | 2.052 | 0.1 |
| Slovakia | 128 | (31.12.00) | 1.317 | 0.1 |
| Slovenia | 28 | (31.12.00) | 0.398 | 0.07 |
| France | 862 | (01.05.02) | 13.456 | 0.06 |
| Belgium | 96 | (01.09.00) | 2.137 | 0.05 |
| Bulgaria | 56 | (01.01.01) | 1.574 | 0.04 |
| Netherlands | 120 | (01.09.00) | 3.455 | 0.034 |
| Albania | 34 | (31.09.01) | 1.11 | 0.03 |
| Spain | 152 | (31.12.00) | 7.341 | 0.02 |
| Norway | 16 | (01.09.00) | 1.042 | 0.015 |
| Denmark | 9 | (01.09.00) | 1.134 | 0.008 |
| Sweden | 12 | (01.10.98) | 1.914 | 0.006 |
| Finland | 2 | (23.10.02) | 1.131 | 0.002 |

[1] Custody figures based on estimates derived from International Centre for Prison Studies website at www.kcl.ac.uk/icps; Population figures from Unicef Statistics: www.unicef.org/statis.

Source: A Failure of Justice, Nacro Policy Report, Nacro, 2003.

## Age, gender and ethnicity of children

The majority of children who offend are in the older age ranges, with 16 and 17-year-olds accounting for more than half of all offences. For 16 and 17-year-olds, motoring offences are most common. For those under 16 years of age, the most common offence category is theft and handling. The ages at which most children started to offend are between 11 and 13 (40%).

The number of offences committed by girls remains broadly the same as 2002, at around 16%.

The ethnic breakdown of all offenders recorded by youth offending teams in 2002-03 is:

- 83.5% white.
- 5.6% black.
- 3% Asian.
- 1% Chinese or other ethnic background.

*Source: Gaining Ground in the Community, annual review 2002-03, Youth Justice Board, 2003*

# Characteristics of children who offend

Boredom, peer pressure and being drunk are the reasons children and young people give to explain their offending behaviour. 16% in school and 26% of excluded children say that they were drunk at the time of the last offence they committed. Children who offend are much more likely to do so with their friends rather than alone or with siblings.

Asset (the individual assessment tool for young offenders used by youth offending teams) provides a picture of the background of children and young people who offend.

- Only 30% of children who offend lived with both their parents.
- 25% had special needs identified (just over 60% of those had a statement of special educational needs).
- 15% were excluded from school at the time.
- 27% had previous permanent exclusions.
- 32% had experienced fixed-term exclusion in the last year.
- 41% were regularly truanting.
- 42% were rated as under-achieving at school.
- 40% were assessed as associating with peers actively involved in criminal activity.
- Nearly 25% were assessed as having friends who were all offenders.
- Over half were recorded as having used cannabis.
- 3% were known to have used class A drugs.
- Nearly three-quarters were considered to be impulsive and to act without thinking.
- Around 20% were considered vulnerable to harm because of the behaviour of other people, specific events or circumstances in their lives.
- 9% were considered to be at risk of self-harm or suicide (15% in the case of females).

*Source: Gaining Ground in the Community, annual review 2002-03, Youth Justice Board, 2003*

## Education

There is a strong link between offending and truancy and school exclusions. Children who truant are more likely to be offenders and the age at which children start playing truant reflects the age at which they start offending.

- The number of mainstream pupils saying they have truanted for a whole day has dropped (from 24% in 2002 to 20% in 2003).
- Excluded pupils are considerably more likely to have truanted from school, with 71% having done so.
- Only 10% of excluded young people have been excluded once, 45% have been excluded five times or more.
- The main reasons for exclusions are disruptive behaviour (71%) and attacking another pupil (54%).

Source: Youth Survey 2003, research study for the Youth Justice Board by Mori, Youth Justice Board, 2003

A Youth Justice Board survey of children and young people who offend found that:

- 27% said they were bullied at school.
- 56% admitted staying away from school without permission.
- 67% said they played truant a lot.
- 76% had been excluded from school at some time.
- 51% said they did not enjoy school.
- 41% said they did not do well there.
- 50% felt their school work was not important.

Of those in young offender institutions:

- 84% had been excluded at least once.
- 60% more than twice.
- Around 50% said they had played truant every day.

When children and young people who offend were asked whether they need help with their reading and writing, 31% said they needed help, although fewer young women said this (19%). Of those surveyed:

- 23% said they had difficulty reading (but not dyslexia).
- 14% had dyslexia.
- 22% had other difficulties in learning.
- 52% had received special help with their education.
- 14% said they needed help and had not received any.
- 54% said the educational help they received was useful or very useful.
- 20% said it was no use at all.

Source: Speaking Out, Youth Justice Board, 2003

# Mental health

The levels of psychosocial and psychiatric problems among children and young people at any stage of the criminal justice system are higher than in the general population. The particular mental health problems experienced by young people who offend are likely to be similar to those of the general adolescent population but more so and include conduct disorder, emotional disturbance, hyperactivity and attentional problems.

- Rates of mental health problems in the general population of adolescents have been estimated at 13% for girls and 10% for boys (11 to 15-year-olds).
- Research suggests that prevalence of mental health problems for young people in contact with the criminal justice system range from 25% to 81%, being highest for those in custody.
- The rates of mental health problems are at least three times as high for those within the criminal justice population as the general population.

Source: The Mental Health of Young Offenders, the Mental Health Foundation, August 2002

A Youth Justice Board survey of children and young people who offend found:

- 48% said they often felt miserable or sad.
- 24% said they often had problems eating or sleeping.
- 10% had deliberately hurt themselves.
- 11% had thought about killing themselves.

In the past two years:

- 20% had seen a counsellor.
- 37% said the help they received for mental health problems was useful or very useful.
- 27% said it was no use at all.

Source: Speaking Out, Youth Justice Board, 2003

# Substance use

There is a strong link between substance use and offending. The combination of substance use with offending may increase the risk of developing substance dependence and/or becoming a persistent offender. A recent Home Office study of young people who were clients of youth offending teams in England and Wales found:

- The group was highly delinquent. Most had committed multiple types of offences, repeatedly. More than 20% reported shoplifting, stealing

goods, taking a car without consent and drug dealing at least 20 times in the previous year.
- Substance use was also very high. More than 85% had used cannabis, alcohol and tobacco. Less than 20% had used heroin or crack cocaine.
- Alcohol, tobacco and cannabis were more strongly related to offending than other drugs. The shift towards the use of heroin and/or cocaine and/or drug injection observed in the 1980s among young people who offend was not evident.
- "Addictive type" drug use (heroin, crack cocaine and valium) was related to shoplifting and "stimulant and poly-drug" use was related to stealing cars and violence.
- Some key factors were related to both substance use and offending: life difficulties and events; disliking and being excluded from school; lack of positive coping mechanisms and expecting to get into trouble again. However, growing up with one parent was not related to offending or drug use.

*Source: Substance Use By Young Offenders, Hammersley R, Marlsand M and Reid M, Findings 192, Home Office, 2003*

When children and young people were asked about drugs and their offending:

- 58% said they sometimes got in fights when they were high on alcohol and drugs.
- 55% said they sometimes smashed or destroyed things when they had been high on alcohol or drugs.
- 52% said they sometimes got so high they didn't care what happened.
- 50% said if they had more money from committing crime they might drink or take drugs more.
- 44% said they sometimes committed crimes to get money for drugs or alcohol.
- 25% said they sometimes took alcohol or drugs to give them courage to commit crimes.
- 60% said they would sometimes use alcohol or drugs to help them cope with stressful events, 23% said they would do this a lot.
- 42% of those on intensive supervision and surveillance programmes said they committed crimes to pay for alcohol and drugs.

In the past two years:

- 24% had visited a specialist drug or alcohol service, although 33% had received help for drug and alcohol problems.
- 6% had needed help and not received any.
- 45% said the help they received with drugs or alcohol was useful or very useful.
- 24% said it was no use at all.

*Source: Speaking Out, Youth Justice Board, 2003*

## Children as victims of crime

There are continuing high levels of fear among children and young people. Excluded children and young people are more likely to be exposed to crime and become a victim of crime than mainstream pupils.

- A third of children and young people feel unsafe in their local area.
- More than 50% of children and young people in school are worried about being physically assaulted or being the victim of theft.
- A third worry about bullying and racism.
- 46% of children and young people in school and 61% of those excluded say they have been a victim of crime in the last year.
- Being threatened by others is the most common offence experienced by children in mainstream schools (26%) and excluded children (41%).
- Two-thirds of children and young people who have been victims of crime say the perpetrator of the offence is another child aged under 18.
- Most children and young people in mainstream education say they were a victim of an offence that took place at school, compared with excluded young people who are more likely to become a victim of crime in their local area.

Source: Youth Survey 2003, research study for the Youth Justice Board by Mori, Youth Justice Board, 2003

## Outcomes of offending

There has been a drop in the proportion of young offenders who are caught by the police since 2001. 21% of offenders in mainstream education and 69% of excluded offenders were caught by the police in 2003, compared with 28% and 71% in 2001.

Excluded children who offend are more likely to be caught by the police than offenders in mainstream education. The consequences of being caught continue to be harsher for excluded young offenders, specifically in terms of having to attend court and being referred to a youth offending team.

While there has been a drop in the proportion of young offenders caught by the police, the likelihood of receiving some form of punishment as a consequence of being caught has increased over the last two years:

- In 2001 22% of mainstream pupils who self-reported committing an offence said nothing happened to them as a result of being caught, compared with just 9% who say nothing happened in 2003.

- Similarly, in 2003 only 3% of excluded offenders said nothing happened as a consequence of being caught, compared with 12% in 2001.

Young people who are caught offending typically receive a final warning as a result (55% of excluded pupils, 42% of those in mainstream schools). More young offenders are having to apologise to victims since 2001 with 27% of offenders who are mainstream pupils and 36% of excluded pupils having to apologise to the victim compared with 20% and 24% respectively in 2001.

There has been a marginal increase in the proportion of young people who re-offend after being caught by the police. In addition, even though they are more likely to be caught and the consequences are often harsher, a higher proportion of excluded young people re-offend, than offenders in mainstream education.

- 44% of mainstream offenders and 39% excluded from school say being caught has impacted on their likelihood of re-offending.
- 57% of those in mainstream schools and 75% of those excluded who have been caught offending say they have re-offended.

Excluded young people are also far less likely to say that the fear of being caught deters them from committing crime than young people in mainstream education (34% and 47% respectively). The reactions of their parents is most likely to deter excluded young people (38%).

*Source: Youth Survey 2003, research study for the Youth Justice Board by Mori, Youth Justice Board, 2003*

# Chapter 10

# Homelessness
# and running away

# Homelessness and running away: an overview

**By Adam Sampson**

Every child deserves the chance of a decent home but this year more than 100,000 children in England will have their lives ruined by the trauma of homelessness. Hundreds of thousands more will be forced to endure overcrowded or substandard housing. Damp and cramped conditions will damage their health. Stress, bullying and missed schooling impairs their education and well-being. For many, including those in so-called temporary accommodation, this is not a short-term problem, but a burden that continues for months or years.

The government has made a commitment to end child poverty and Shelter believes that tackling homelessness and bad housing must be central to the strategy. Big strides have been made in recent years in the effort to tackle homelessness among children and families. A target has been set to end the use of some of the worst accommodation homeless children can find themselves – bed and breakfast hotels – and its use for homeless families will be banned from April. The government's Homelessness Directorate has also stated its intention of improving the standard of temporary accommodation.

The 2002 Homelessness Act will make a big impact in the way children and families are treated. The act not only extends the safety net for 16 and 17-year-olds and children leaving care, it also places a duty on local authorities to develop strategies to tackle and prevent homelessness. Shelter has worked hard over the last 18 months to ensure that all local authorities deliver the most effective strategies possible and there has been a very positive response from councils to this challenge.

We must remember that homelessness does not always end when a family finds a house. They may be left deeply traumatised by the experience. Not just by the loss of their home, but also from the experience of living in temporary accommodation. It can take people a long time to recover before they are able to properly support themselves.

To prevent parents and children from becoming homeless again, they may need long-term practical and emotional support. This may be anything from helping with tasks such as decorating their home to accessing a GP or helping children to settle in a new school. Shelter has already set up several schemes providing such support across the country. These can be funded by the Supporting People programme and it is essential that the support needs of homeless families are taken account of in the allocation of resources.

As I have said, homelessness can damage children's education. There needs to be extra funding to provide support specifically aimed at children in temporary accommodation to prevent their education being adversely affected. Our Manchester education project has been set up to do just that. Woking closely with the city council, support workers help children to continue their education, providing educational support and help with learning at home.

However, we need to ensure that children get all this extra help. Already families are lost by the system and do not get the help they need. Statutory agencies, across local authority boundaries and between council departments, must track and exchange information about children and families in temporary accommodation.

Most importantly, the priority must be given to preventing homelessness and ensuring children do not spend long and damaging periods in temporary housing. The Homelessness Act will go a long way to ensuring that housing advice, advocacy and support services are in place to prevent homelessness, but the severe shortage of decent affordable homes in many parts of the country could hamper the government's efforts.

The lack of affordable housing has been widely accepted to be a major cause of homelessness, most recently in the Barker review into housing supply. I would urge the government to act on the evidence in the report, otherwise much of the good work done so far will be undone by the increasingly severe shortage of affordable housing.

**Adam Sampson** is the director of Shelter

# Homelessness and running away: the key facts

## Homelessness

Homelessness is the most acute indicator of housing shortage. In 2002-03, 129,320 households were recognised as homeless by local authorities in England. This represents an increase of 10% on the previous year's figures, which were themselves a 15% increase on the number accepted as homeless in 1997. This increase is likely to reflect the extensions to the "priority need" categories and therefore to the number of households accepted as homeless. 63% of households accepted as homeless are families with children or families that include a pregnant woman.
*Source: ODPM statistical release June 2003*

This figure is only the tip of the iceberg as there are no comprehensive national statistics on the extent of homelessness among single people and couples without children.

People from minority ethnic groups are over represented among homeless households: in 2002-03, 23% of homeless households in England were from black and minority ethnic groups, although they make up just 9% of the population in England.
*Source: ODPM statistical release June 2003*

In 2002-03, 36% of all households accepted as homeless in England were in this situation because parents, other relatives or friends were no longer able or willing to accommodate them. This is a rise as the proportion has been typically around 29% since the implementation of the 1996 act. A further 22% gave the breakdown of a relationship with a partner as their main reason for the loss of their last settled home; 15% of relationship breakdowns were because of domestic violence.
*Source: ODPM statistical release June 2003*

In 1999, government estimates put the numbers sleeping rough in the UK, on any one night, at 1,850. The target was to reduce this by two-thirds by March 2002. This target was achieved in November 2001, when only 532 people were reported to be sleeping out on any one night, a fall of 71%. The latest figures – June 2003 – found 504 people sleeping rough, the lowest recorded level.

*Source: Homelessness Directorate 2002*

These figures are from counts on a single night or stock figures. There are no national figures on the numbers of people sleeping rough over time. In London, where such figures are collected, 3,031 individuals were identified as sleeping rough in 2000-01, compared with a single night count of around 319 in May 2000-01. If these figures are replicated nationally, then that would suggest that the numbers sleeping rough over a period of a year were around 10 times the number on any one night.

*Source: Helping Rough Sleepers off the Streets, Randall G and Brown S, a report to the Homelessness Directorate, June 2002*

The rough sleeping population has been generally characterised as:

* 90% male.
* Between 25% and 33% have been in local authority care.
* Having a life expectancy of 42 years, compared with a national average of 74 for men and 79 for women.
* 35 times more likely to commit suicide than the general population.

*Source: Addressing the Health Needs of Rough Sleepers, Griffiths S, a paper to the Homelessness Directorate 2002*

## Temporary accommodation

Local authorities have a duty to provide temporary accommodation to homeless households who have a "priority need". At the end of June 2003, local authorities housed 93,480 homeless households in temporary accommodation. Of these, 11,610 were placed in bed and breakfast hotels. In October 2001, the government set up the Bed and Breakfast Unit to tackle the rise in the use of B&Bs and set the target that by March 2004, no homeless family with children should have to live in a B&B hotel.

Since March 2002, the government has collected figures on the number of households with dependent children or expectant mothers in B&Bs. In June 2003, the number decreased to 3,730, a fall of 44% compared with June 2002. The overall number of households in B&Bs has however remained stubbornly close to the 12,000 figure: this is three times the number living in B&Bs when Labour came into power in 1997.

*Source: ODPM statistical release September 2003*

# Youth homelessness

There are no official statistics for youth homelessness; although the government commissioned research to provide a reliable estimate in 1997, this was never published because of methodological difficulties. The best current estimate of youth homelessness in Britain is 32,000 16 to 21-year-olds. The way this figure was computed means it is likely to be a minimum.

*Source: Estimates of Young Single Homelessness, a report to NCH by the London Research Centre, June 1996*

Although we may know little about how many young homeless people there are, we have a much better idea about their characteristics and the problems they face.

Of the young homeless people who receive help from Centrepoint in London:

- 70% have slept rough.
- 40% have no qualifications.
- 32% have run away from home aged 16 or 17.
- 80% have left home due to family conflict, family breakdown, evictions or abuse.
- 21% have been in local authority care.
- 57% are black or of minority ethnic origin (29% of London residents are of minority ethnic origin).

*Source: Centrepoint youth homelessness statistics: www.centrepoint.org.uk, 2003*

It is estimated that approximately a quarter of the people who sleep on the streets in England in the course of a year are aged between 18 and 25.

*Source: Rough Sleeping, Social Exclusion Unit, the Stationery Office, 1998*

The young homeless population is primarily male, by a ratio of around 2:1

*Source: The Mental Health Needs of Homeless Children and Young People, Mental Health Foundation, 2002*

A recent study looking at substance use among young homeless people found that drug taking was high. 43% had taken heroin and 38% crack cocaine. Many were poly-drug users and just over a quarter had injected drugs. Next to leaving home because of conflict or abuse, being asked to leave because of drug or alcohol use was the most common factor given for homelessness.

A survey by the Mental Health Foundation found:

- Homeless young people are almost three times more likely to experience mental health problems, which are more likely to be of a chronic and severe nature.

## Use of drugs among young homeless people compared with 16 to 25-year-olds in the British Crime Survey (BCS 2000)

Percentage who have used drugs in their lifetime

| Drug | Young homeless | BCS 2000 |
| --- | --- | --- |
| Cannabis | 94 | 45 |
| Cocaine | 50 | 10 |
| Crack | 38 | 2 |
| Heroin | 43 | 2 |
| Ecstasy | 64 | 12 |
| LSD | 54 | 11 |
| Amphetamine | 73 | 22 |
| Any | 95 | 51 |

Source: Wincup E, Buckland G, and Bayliss R Youth Homelessness and Substance Use: report to the drugs and alcohol research unit. the Home Office 2003

- A third of homeless young people have attempted suicide.
- Despite the prevalence of mental health problems, only 22% of young people in the survey had any contact with mental health services.

Source: Off to a Bad Start, Mental Health Foundation 1996

There is a link between involvement in street prostitution and homelessness. A recent survey found that 78% of women involved in street prostitution had experience of homelessness and 44% experience of rough sleeping.

Source: Where is She Tonight? Women, Street Prostitution and Homelessness, Base 75, 2000

# Runaways

**Note:** Runaways are under-16s, while the term "homeless young person" refers to those above this age.

## Numbers

An estimated 77,000 (one in nine) run away from home each year, of whom about 11,000 stay away for a week or more. Running away is most common among teenagers with the peak ages being between 13 and 15. However, a quarter (20,000) of all runaways in the UK are under the age of 11. Runaways aged under 11 are more likely to have experienced physical abuse at home.

*Source: Young Runaways, report by the Social Exclusion Unit, November 2002*

## Who runs away and why?

Although runaways are a diverse group research highlights varying patterns between particular groups of young people:

- Girls are slightly more likely to run away than boys. 11.5% of girls and 8.5% of boys are likely to run away once. However, boys are more likely to start running away earlier, to stay away longer and to run repeatedly.
- Black and ethnic minority children are less likely to run away. Rates of lifetime running away have been estimated as more than 10% for white young people, 7.5% for young people of African-Caribbean origin, and 5.5% for young people of Indian, Pakistani or Bangladeshi origin.
- There are similar rates of running away in rural and urban areas.
- Around half of runaways run only once, a further quarter run away twice, while one in eight runaways has run at least three times. Young people who run away at a younger age are more likely to become repeat runaways.
- Most runaways would say they have run away, but 20% say they were forced to leave by parents or carers
- Young people living with lone parents are twice as likely, and those living with a step-parent are three times as likely to run as young people living with both birth parents.

- Nearly half of those who have spent time in local authority care, either residential or foster, have run away, compared with only one in 10 of young people living with families. However, many started running away before they entered care.

Young people who run away are more likely than their peers to have serious problems:

- Occasional runaways were five times more likely and repeat runaways 10 times more likely to say they were having problems with illegal drugs than young people who had not run away.
- Occasional runaways were three times more likely and repeat runaways six times more likely to report problems with alcohol than young people who had not run away.
- Occasional runaways were three times more likely and repeat runaways seven times more likely to say they were in trouble with the police than young people who had not run away.
- Occasional runaways were three times more likely and repeat runaways seven times more likely to say they had truanted repeatedly than young people who had not run away.
- Occasional runaways were seven times more likely and repeat runaways 17 times more likely to say they had been "hit a lot" by their parents than young people who had not run away.

*Source: Young Runaways, report by the Social Exclusion Unit, November 2002*

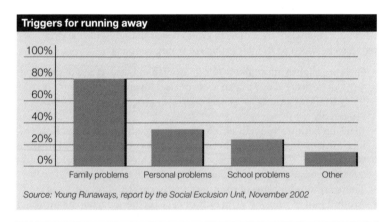

**Triggers for running away**

*Source: Young Runaways, report by the Social Exclusion Unit, November 2002*

## Why does it matter?

Those who run away often put themselves in considerable danger:
Each year one in seven runaways, over 10,000 young people, are physically hurt or sexually assaulted while they are away.
Running away often precedes problems in later life such as drug abuse, homelessness or involvement in crime.

A quarter of runaways report being hungry or thirsty while they are away, while around a third said they had felt frightened or lonely.

*Source: Young Runaways, report by the Social Exclusion Unit, November 2002*

# Chapter 11

# Directory

# Government departments

## The Department of Health
**Address:** Richmond House, 79 Whitehall, London SW1A 2NL
**Tel:** 020 7210 4850
**E-mail:** dhmail@doh.gsi.gov.uk
**Web:** www.doh.gov.uk

**Secretary of State for Health:** John Reid
**Minister of State** (Health): John Hutton
**Minister of State:** Rosie Winterton
**Parliamentary Under Secretary of State** (Lords): Lord Warner
**Parliamentary Under Secretary of State** (Public Health): Melanie Johnson
**Parliamentary Under Secretary of State** (Community): Stephen Ladyman
**Chief Medical Officer** (CMO): Sir Liam Donaldson

Skipton House, 80 London Road, London SE1 6LH
Wellington House, 35-155 Waterloo Road, London SE1 8UG
Quarry House, Quarry Hill, Leeds LS2 7UE

### Wales

**The National Assembly for Wales**
**Address:** Children and Families Division, Cathays Park, Cardiff CF10 3NQ
**Tel:** 029 2082 3676
**Web:** www.wales.gov.uk/subisocialpolicy/ topicindex-e.htm

### Scotland

**The Scottish Executive**
**Address:** Children and Young People's Group, Young People and Looked After Children, Area 2B-S, Victoria Quay, Edinburgh EH6 6QQ
**Tel:** 0131 244 5480
**Web:** www.scotland.gov.uk/socialwork/swsi

### Northern Ireland

**Department of Health, Social Services and Public Safety**
**Address:** Health and Personal Social Services Management Group, Dundonald House, Upper Newtownards Road, Belfast BT4 3SF
**Tel:** 028 9052 4762
**Web:** www.northernireland.gov.uk

*Responsible for community care, public health and children's health; the Department of Health also works closely with inspection bodies on social care policy.*

# Department for Education and Skills

**Address:** Sanctuary Buildings, Great Smith Street, London SW1P 3BT
**Tel:** 0870 000 2288
**Web:** www.dfes.gov.uk

**Secretary of State for Education and Skills:** Rt Hon Charles Clarke MP
**Minister of State for School Standards:** David Miliband MP
**Minister of State for Children:** Rt Hon Margaret Hodge MBE MP
**Minister of State for Lifelong Learning, Further and Higher Education:** Alan Johnson MP
**Parliamentary Under Secretary of State for Sure Start, Early Years and Childcare:**
Baroness Catherine Ashton
**Parliamentary Under Secretary of State for Young People and Adult Skills:** Ivan Lewis MP
**Parliamentary Under Secretary of State for Schools:** Stephen Twigg MP

Department for Education and Skills
Caxton House, Tothill Street, London SW1H 9JN

Department for Education and Skills
Moorfoot, Sheffield S1 4PQ

Department for Education and Skills
Mowden Hall, Staindrop Road, Darlington DL3 9BG

Department for Education and Skills
Castle View House, East Lane, RuncornWA7 2DN

*As well as schools, the department is responsible for early years education, childcare and the Connexions support and advice service for young people. The children's minister, Margaret Hodge, falls within this department and is responsible for many policy areas for children's services – including children's social services, child protection, homelessness and young people at risk.*


# Home Office

**Address:** Home Office, 50, Queen Anne's Gate, London SW1H 9AT
**Tel:** 0870 000 1585
**E-mail:** public.enquiries@homeoffice.gsi.gov.uk
**Web:** www.homeoffice.gov.uk

**Home Secretary:** David Blunkett
**Minister of State** (crime reduction, policing and community safety): Hazel Blears
**Minister of State** (citizenship, immigration, and counter-terrorism): Beverley Hughes
**Minister of State** (criminal justice system and law reform): Baroness Scotland
**Parliamentary Under Secretary** (reducing organised and international crime, anti drugs co- ordination and international and European issues): Caroline Flint
**Parliamentary Under Secretary of State** (correctional services and reducing re-offending): Paul Goggins
**Parliamentary Under Secretary** (race equality, community policy, and civil renewal): Fiona Mactaggart

*Responsible for policy areas including crime and policing, justice and victims and drugs.*

## Office of the Deputy Prime Minister

**Address:** Office of the Deputy Prime Minister, 26 Whitehall, London SW1A 2WH
**Tel:** 020 7944 4400
**Web:** www.odpm.gov.uk

**Deputy Prime Minister:** John Prescott
**Minister of State** (local and regional government): Nick Raynsford
**Minister of State** (housing): Keith Hill
**Minister of State** (regeneration and regional development): Lord Rooker
**Parliamentary Under Secretary:** Yvette Cooper
**Parliamentary Under Secretary:** Phil Hope

*Areas of responsibility include housing, homelessness and social exclusion.*

# Local and regional government

**Local Government Association**
Local Government House,
Smith Square,
London
SW1P 3HZ
020 7664 3131
info@lga.gov.uk
www.lga.gov.uk

**County Councils Network**
020 7664 3011
www.lga.gov.uk/ccn/

**Audit Commission for Local Authorities**
1 Vincent Square, London
SW1P 2PN
020 7396 1494
enquiries@audit-commission.gov.uk
www.audit-commission.gov.uk

**Convention of Scottish Local Authorities**
Rosebery House,
9 Haymarket Terrace,
Edinburgh
EH12 5XZ
0131 474 9200
enquiries@cosla.gov.uk
www.cosla.gov.uk

**Improvement and Development Agency**
Layden House, 76-86 Turnmill Street, London
EC1M 5LG
020 7296 6600
www.idea.gov.uk

**Local government ombudsman**
0845 602 1983
www.lgo.org.uk

**Scotland**
0870 011 5378
www.ombudslgscot.org.uk

**Wales**
01656 661325
www.ombudsman-wales.org

---

# Social services departments

## England

**Barking & Dagenham London Borough**
Social Services Civic Centre
Dagenham
Essex
RM10 7BW
020 8592 4500
www.barking-dagenham.gov.uk

**Barnet London Borough**
The Town Hall
The Burroughs
London
NW4 4BG
020 8359 2000
info.centre@barnet.gov.uk
www.barnet.gov.uk

**Barnsley Met. Borough Council**
Town Hall
Barnsley
S70 2TA
01226 770770
comments@barnsley.gov.uk
www.barnsley.gov.uk

**Bath & North East Somerset Council**
Social and Housing Services
P.O.Box 3343
Bath
BA1 2ZH
01225 477000
janeashman@bathes.gov.uk
www.bathes.gov.uk

**Bedfordshire County Council**
County Hall
Cauldwell Street
Bedford
MK42 9AP
01234 345331
www.bedfordshire.gov.uk

**Bexley London Borough**
Social & Community Services Department
Hill View Drive
Welling, Kent
DA16 3RY
020 8303 7777
info@bexley.gov.uk
www.bexley.gov.uk

## Birmingham City Council

Social Services Department
Louisa Ryland House
44 Newhall Street, Birmingham
B3 3PL
0121 303 2992
assist@birmingham.gov.uk
www.birmingham.gov.uk

## Blackburn with Darwen Borough Council

Jubilee House, Jubilee Street
Blackburn
Lancashire
BB1 1ET
01254 587411
www.blackburn.gov.uk

## Blackpool Borough Council

Social Services Dept
Progress House, Clifton Road
Blackpool
FY4 4US
01253 477500
blackpool@dial.pipex.com
www.blackpool.gov.uk

## Bolton Met. Borough Council

Le Mans Crescent, Civic Centre
Bolton
BL1 1SA
01204 337200
andy.robertson@bolton.gov.uk
www.bolton.gov.uk

## Bournemouth Borough Council

New Century House
24 Christchurch Road
Bournemouth
BH1 3ND
01202 458000
socialservices@bournemouth.
gov.uk
www.bournemouth.gov.uk

## Bracknell Forest Borough Council

Easthampsted House
Town Square
Bracknell
RG12 1AQ
01344 424642
socialservices.housing@bracknell
-forest.gov.uk
www.bracknell-forest.gov.uk

## Bradford City Council

Department of Social Services
Oilcana House Chapel Street
Bradford
BD1 5RE
01274 752900
joanne.barter@bradford.gov.uk
www.bradford.gov.uk

## Brent London Borough

Social Services Department
Mahatma Ghandi House,
34 Wembley Hill Road
Wembley
HA9 8AD
020 8937 1234
jenny.goodall@brent.gov.uk
www.brent.gov.uk

## Brighton & Hove Council

Kings House
Grand Avenue
Hove
BN3 2LS
01273 295030
firstname.surname@brighton-
hove.gov.uk
www.brighton-hove.gov.uk

## Bristol City Council

Social Services & Health
Department
Amelia Court, Pipe Lane
Bristol
BS99 7NB
0117 922 2000
www.bristol.gov.uk

## Bromley London Borough

Social Services Department
Civic Centre, Stockwell Close
Bromley
BR1 3UH
020 8464 3333
www.bromley.gov.uk

## Buckinghamshire County Council

County Hall
Aylesbury
Bucks
HP20 1UA
01296 395000
buckscc.gov.uk
www.buckinghamshire.gov.uk

## Bury Met. Borough Council

Social Services, Health & Housing
Castle Buildings, Market Place
Bury
BL9 0LT
0161 253 5001
m.ahiar@bury.gov.uk
www.bury.gov.uk

## Calderdale Met. Borough Council

Social Services Department
Horsfall House, Skircoat Moor
Road
Halifax
HX3 0HJ
01422 357257
www.calderdale.gov.uk

## Cambridgeshire County Council

Social Services, Box SS1001
Castle Court, Castle Hill
Cambridge
CB3 OAP
01223 717304
eric.robinson@cambridgeshire.gov
.uk
www.cambridgeshire.gov.uk

## Camden London Borough

Social Services Department
79 Camden Road
London
NW1 9ES
020 7974 6637
www.camden.gov.uk

## Cheshire County Council

County Hall
Chester
CH1 1BW
01244 603231
www.cheshire.gov.uk

## Cornwall County Council

Social Services Dept.
County Hall
Truro
TR1 3AY
01872 322000
enquiries@cornwall.gov.uk
www.cornwall.gov.uk

## Coventry City Council

Social Services Dept. Council
House
Earl Street
Coventry
CV1 5RR
024 7683 3333
www,coventry.gov.uk

## Croydon London Borough

Social Services Dept.
Taberner House, Park Lane
Croydon
CR9 2BA
020 8686 4433
corp.info@croydon.gov.uk
www.croydon.gov.uk

## Cumbria County Council

Social Services Dept
The Courts, English Street
Carlisle
CA3 8NA
01228 606060
www.cumbria.gov.uk

**Darlington Borough Council**
Social Services Dept.
Town Hall
Darlington
DL! 5QT
01325 380651
margaret.asquith@darlington.gov
.uk
www.darlington.gov.uk

**Derby City Council**
Social Services Dept.Adult
Services
29 St Mary's Gate
Derby
DE1 3NS
01332 717777
www.derby.gov.uk

**Derby City Council**
Social Services Children & Family
Services
71-73 Rosehill Street
Derby
DE23 8FZ
01332 717777
www.derby.gov.uk

**Derbyshire County Council**
Social Services Department
County Hall
Matlock
DE4 3AG
01629 580000
www.derbyshire.gov.uk

**Devon County Council**
Social Services Dept
County Hall
Topsham Road, Exeter
EX2 4QD
01392 382000
www.devon-cc.gov.uk

**Doncaster Met. Borough
Council**
Social Services Dept.
1st Floor The Council House
College Road, Doncaster
DN1 3DA
01302 737800
www.doncaster.gov.uk

**Dorset County Council**
Social Services Dept
County Hall
Colliton Park, Dorchester
DT1 1XJ
01305 251000
s.j.clements@dorset.gov.uk
www.dorsetcc.gov.uk

**Dudley Met. Borough Council**
Social Services Dept,
Ednam House, St Jame's Road
Dudley
DY1 3JJ
01384 815822
social.services@dudley.gov.uk
www.dudley.gov.uk

**Durham County Council**
Social Services Dept.
County Hall
Durham
DH1 5UF
0191 383 3000
zmail_help@durham.gov.uk
www.durham.gov.uk

**Ealing London Borough**
Social Services Dept
Perceval House,
14-16 Uxbridge Road
London
W5 2HL
020 8825 5000
social.services@ealing.gov.uk
www.ealing.gov.uk

**East Riding of Yorkshire
Council**
County Hall
Beverley
HU9 7BA
01482 396000
tony.hunter@eastriding.gov.uk
www.eastriding.gov.uk

**East Sussex County Council**
Social Services Dept
P.O.Box 5 County Hall
Lewes
BN7 1SW
01273 481266
christian name.surname@
eastsussexcc .gov.uk
www.eastsussexcc.gov.uk

**Enfield London Borough**
Social Services Dept
Civic Centre, Silver Street
Enfield
EN1 3XA
020 8366 6565
www.enfield.gov.uk

**Essex County Council**
Essex Social Services
P.O.Box 297, County Hall
Chelmsford
CM1 1YS
01245 493622
www.essexcc.gov.uk

**Gateshead Met. Borough
Council**
Social Services Dept.
Civic Centre, Gateshead
NE8 1HH
0191 433 3000
www.gateshead.gov.uk

**Gloucestershire County
Council**
Social Services Dept
Shire Hall, Westgate Street
Gloucester
GL1 2TG
01452 425000
gcc@gloscc.gov.uk
www.gloscc.gov.uk

**Greenwich London Borough**
Social Services Dept
Nelson House, Wellington Street
Woolwich
SE18 6PY
020 8921 3059
www.greenwich.gov.uk

**Hackney London Borough**
Social Services Dept
205 Morning Lane
London
E9 9LG
020 8356 5000
www.hackney.gov.uk

**Halton Borough Council**
Social Services Dept.
Municipal Buildings, Kingsway
Widnes
WA8 7QF
0151 424 2061
www.halton.gov.uk

**Hammersmith & Fulham
London Borough**
Social Services Dept
Town Hall, King Street
London
W6 9JU
020 8753 5001
www.lbhf.gov.uk

**Hampshire County Council**
Social Services Dept
Trafalgar House, Trafalgar Street
Winchester
SO23 8UQ
01962 847208
www.hants.gov.uk

**Haringey London Borough**
40 Cumberland Road
Wood Green
London
N22 7SG
020 8489 0000
www.haringey.gov.uk

**Harrow London Borough**
Social Services Dept
P.O.Box 21, Civic Centre
Harrow
HA1 2UJ
020 8863 5611
info@harrow.gov.uk
www.harrowb.demon.co.uk

**Hartlepool Borough Council**
Social Services Dept
Civic Centre
Hartlepool
TS24 8YW
01429 523910
heather.gordan@hartlepool.gov.uk
www.hartlepool.gov.uk

**Havering London Borough**
Community Service Directorate
Town Hall
Romford
RM1 3BD
01708 433001
www.havering.gov.uk

**Herefordshire Council**
Garrick House
Widemarsh Street
Hereford
HR4 9EU
01432 260039
sfiennes@herefordshire.gov.uk
www.herefordshire.gov.uk

**Hertfordshire County Council**
County Hall
Pegs Lane
Hertford
SG13 8DP
01438 737400
hertsdirect@hertscc.gov.uk
www.hertsdirect.org

**Hillingdon London Borough**
Civic Centre
Uxbridge
UB8 1UW
01895 277048
bvenn@hillingdon.gov.uk
www.hillingdon.gov.uk

**Hounslow London Borough**
Social Services Dept.
Civic Centre
Lampton Road, Hounslow
TW3 4DN
020 8583 2000
directors.socialservices@hounslo
w.gov.uk
www.hounslow.gov.uk

**Isle of Wight County Council**
17 Fairlee Road
Newport
Isle of Wight
PO30 2EA
01983 520600
glen.garrod@iow.gov.uk
www.iwight.com

**Isle of Scilly Council**
Town Hall
St Mary's
Isle of Scilly
TR21 OLW
01720 422537
www.scilly.gov.uk

**Islington London Borough**
Social Services Dept
Highbury House, 5 Highbury
Crescent
Islington, London
N5 1RW
020 7527 4293
www.islington.gov.uk

**Kensington & Chelsea
London Borough**
Kensington Town Hall, Hornton
Street
London
W8 7NX
020 7361 2037
social.services@rbkc.gov.uk
www.rbkc.gov.uk

**Kent County Council**
Social Services Dept
Sessions House, County Hall
County Road, Maidstone
ME14 1XQ
01622 671411
social-services@kent.gov.uk
www.kent.gov.uk

**Kingston upon Hull City
Council**
Brunswick House
Strand Close
Hull
HU2 9DB
01482 616000
jan.didrichsen@hullcc.gov.uk
www.hullcc.gov.uk

**Kingston Upon Thames
London Borough**
Community Services Directorate
Guildhall
Kingston Upon Thames
KT1 1EU
020 8546 2121
firstname.surname@rbk.kingston
.gov.uk
www.kingston.gov.uk

**Kirklees Met. Council**
Oldgate House
2 Oldgate
Huddersfield
HD1 6QF
01484 223000
social_services@kirklees.gov.uk
www.kirklees.gov.uk

**Knowsley Met. Borough
Council**
P.O.Box 23 Municipal Buildings
Archway Road
Huyton, Knowsley, Merseyside
L36 9YY
0151 443 3439
christianname.surname.dss@kno
wsley.gov.uk
www.knowsley.gov.uk

**Lambeth London Borough**
Social Services Directorate
Mary Seacole House, 91
Clapham High Street
London
SW4 7TF
020 7926 4788
awebster@lambeth.gov.uk
www.lambeth.gov.uk

**Lancashire County Council**
Social Services Dept.
P.O.Box 162, County Offices
East Cliff, Preston
PR1 3EA
01772 534390
www.lancashire.gov.uk

**Leeds City Council**
Social Services Dept.
Civic Hall
Leeds
LS1 1UR
0113 247 8700
www.leeds.gov.uk

**Leicester City Council**
Social Care and Health Dept
New Walk Centre
Welford Place, Leicester
LE1 6ZG
0116 252 8300
cozeaool@leicester.gov.uk
www.leicester.gov.uk

**Leicestershire County
Council**
Social Services Dept.
County Hall, Glenfield
Leicester
LE3 8RL
0116 232 3232
Social-services@leics.gov.uk
www.leics.gov.uk

**Lewisham London Borough**
Town Hall Chambers
Rushey Green, Catford
London
SE6 4RY
020 8314 6000
www.lewisham.gov.uk

**Lincolnshire County Council**
Lincolnshire Social Services
Orchard House
Lincoln
LN7 7BA
01522 552222
www.lincolnshire.gov.uk

**Liverpool City Council**
Social Services and Housing
Dept
1st Floor, Millennium House
60 Victoria Street, Liverpool
L1 6JQ
0151 233 4612
veronica.jackson@liverpool.gov.uk
www.liverpool.gov.uk

**Luton Borough Council**
Unity House, 111 Stuart Street
Luton
Bedfordshire
LU1 5NP
01582 547500
dunnachieh@luton.gov.uk
www.luton.gov.uk

**Manchester City Council**
P.O.Box 536 Town Hall Extension
Manchester
M60 2AF
0161 234 5000
nspencer@notes.manchester.gov
.uk
www.manchester.gov.uk

**Medway Council**
Municipal Buildings
Canterbury Street
Gillingham
ME7 5LA
01634 306000
www.medway.gov.uk

**Merton London Borough**
Civic Centre
London Road, Morden
Surrey
SM4 5DX
020 8545 3711
rea.mattocks@merton.gov.uk
www.merton.gov.uk

**Middlesbrough Council**
Social Services
P.O.Box 234, Third Floor
Civic Centre, Middlesbrough
TS1 2XH
01642 729501
jan.douglas@middlesbrough.gov.
uk
www.middlesbrough.gov.uk

**Milton Keynes Council**
Neighbourhood Services
Directorate
P.O.Box 110,
Milton Keynes
MK9 2ZS
01908 691691
www.mkweb.co.uk/mkcouncil/
home.asp

**Newcastle Upon Tyne City
Council**
Civic Centre
Newcastle Upon Tyne
NE1 8PA
0191 232 8320
www.newcastle.gov.uk

**Newham London Borough**
Social Services Dept
Broadway House, 322 High
Street
Stratford
EC15 1AJ
020 8430 5250
www.newham.gov.uk

**Norfolk County Council**
Social Services
County Hall, Martineau Lane
Norwich
NR1 2SQ
01603 222141
www.norfolk.gov.uk

**Northamptonshire County
Council**
County Hall
P.O.Box 233
Northampton
NN1 1AZ
01604 236236
www.northamptonshire.gov.uk

**North East Lincolnshire
Council**
Fryston House
Fryston Corner
Grimsby
DN34 5BB
01472 325500
peter.hay@nelincs.gov.uk
www.nelincs.gov.uk

**North Lincolnshire Council**
Social & Housing Services Dept.
The Angel, Market Place
Brigg
DN20 8LD
01724 296402
customerservice@northlincs.gov.uk
www.northlincs.gov.uk

**North Somerset Council**
Social Services & Housing Dept
Town Hall, Walliscote Grove Road
Weston super mare
BS23 1ZY
01934 888888
www.n-somerset.gov.uk

**North Tyneside Borough
Council**
Social Services Dept
Town Hall, High Street
Wallsend
NE28 7RR
0191 200 6565
www.northtyneside.gov.uk

**Northumberland County
Council**
County Hall
Morpeth
Northumberland
NE61 2EF
01670 533000
ghill@northumberland.gov.uk
www.northumberland.gov.uk/
socialservices

**North Yorkshire County
Council**
Social Services Directorate
County Hall, North Allerton
North Yorkshire
DL7 8DD
01609 780780
www.northyorks.gov.uk

**Nottingham City Council**
Social Services Dept
14 Hounds Gate
Nottingham
NG1 7BE
0115 915 5555
www.nottinghamcity.gov.uk

**Nottinghamshire County
Council**
County Hall
West Bridford
Nottingham
NG2 7QP
0115 982 3823
communications.ssd@nottscc.gov
.uk
www.nottsoc.gov.uk

**Oldham Borough Council**
Social Services Dept
Civic Centre, West Street
Oldham
OL1 1UG
0161 911 4750
socs.general.enquiries@oldham.
gov.uk
www.oldham.gov.uk

**Oxfordshire County Council**
Social and Health Care
County Hall, New Road
Oxford
OX1 1ND
01865 792422
www.oxfordshire.gov.uk

**Peterborough City Council**
Bayard Place
Broadway House, 322 High
Street
Peterborough
PE1 1FD
01733 747474
sssb@peterborough.gov.uk
www.peterborough.gov.uk/social
services/ssfront.htm

**Plymouth City Council**
Social Services Dept
Windsor House, Tavistock Road
Plymouth
Pl1 2AA
01752 307343
pullanj@plymouth.gov.uk
www.plymouth.gov.uk

**Poole Borough Council**
Civic Centre
Poole
Dorset
BH15 2RU
01202 633203
f.davies@poole.gov.uk
www.borough.ofpoole.com

**Portsmouth City Council**
Social Services Dept
Civic Offices, Guildhall Square
Portsmouth
PO1 2AL
023 9282 2251
www.portsmouth.gov.uk

**Reading Borough Council**
Civic Centre
Reading
RG1 7TD
0118 939 0900
www.reading.gov.uk

**Redbridge London Borough**
Social Services Dept
Ley Street House, 497-499 Ley
Street
Ilford
IG2 7QX
020 8554 5000
www.redbridge.gov.uk

**Redcar and Cleveland
Borough Council**
Social Services Dept
Seafield House, Kirkleatham
Street
Redcar
TS10 1SP
01642 444000
www.redcar-cleveland.gov.uk

**Richmond upon Thames
London Borough**
Services for Adults Dept.
Fortesque House, Stanley Road
Twickenham
TW2 4PZ
020 8891 1411
www.richmond.gov.uk

**Richmond upon Thames
London Borough**
Services for children & Families
42 York Street
Twickenham
TW1 3BW
020 8891 1411
www.richmond.gov.uk

**Rochdale Met. Borough
Council**
P.O.Box 67 Municipal Offices
Smith Street
Rochdale
OL16 1YQ
01706 647474
council@rochdale.gov.uk
www.rochdale.gov.uk

**Rotheram Met. Borough
Council**
Crinoline House
Effingham Square
Rotheram
S65 1AW
01709 823900
john.gomersall@rotheram.go.vuk
www.rotheram.gov.uk

**Rutland County Council**
Catmose, Oakham
Rutland
LE15 6HP
01572 758322
cfoster@rutland.gov.uk
www.rutnet.co.uk

**Salford City Council**
Crompton House
100 Chorley Road
Swinton
M27 6BP
0161 794 4711
social.services@salford.gov.uk
www.salford.gov.uk

**Sandwell Met. Borough
Council**
Social Inclusion & Health
1st Floor, Kingston House
438 High Street, West Bromwich
B70 9LD
0121 569 5466
angela_saganowska@sandwell.g
ov.uk
www.sandwell.gov.uk/smbc/ssd
home.htm

**Sefton Met. Borough Council**
Social Services Dept
Merton House, Stanley Street
Bootle
L20 3DL
0151 934 3741
www.sefton.gov.uk

**Sheffield City Council**
Social Services Dept
Town Hall
Sheffield
S1 2HH
0114 272 6444
www.sheffield.gov.uk

**Shropshire County Council**
Social Services Dept
The Shirehall, Abbey Foregate
Shrewsbury
SY2 6ND
01743 251000
www.shropshire-cc.gov.uk

**Slough Borough Council**
Town Hall,Bath Road
Slough
SL1 3UQ
01753 875751
dawn.warwick@slough.gov.uk
www.slough.gov.uk

**Solihull Met. Borough
Council**
P.O.Box 32, Council House
Solihull
West Midlands
B91 3QY
0121 704 6728
vicky.jones@solihull.gov.uk
www.solihull.gov.uk

**Somerset County Council**
Social Services
County Hall
Taunton
TA1 4DY
01823 355455
info@somerset.gov.uk
www.somerset.gov.uk

**Southampton City Council**
Civic Centre
Southampton
SO14 7LY
023 8083 2621
j.beer@southampton.gov.uk
www.southampton.gov.uk

**Southend-on-sea Borough Council**
Social Services
Civic Centre
Victoria Avenue,
Southend on sea
SS2 6ER
01702 215000
www.southend.gov.uk

**South Gloucestershire Council**
Social Services Dept
The Council Offices, Castle Street
Thornbury
BS25 1HF
01454 868686
mailbox@southglos.gov.uk
www.southglos.gov.uk

**South Tyneside Met. Borough Council**
Social Care and Health Dept
Kelly House, Campbell Park Road
Hebburn, Tyne and Wear
NE31 2SW
0191 427 1717
www.s-tyneside-mbc.gov.uk

**Southwark London Borough**
Mabel Goldwin House
49 Grange Walk
London
SE1 3DY
020 7525 3838
www.southwark.gov.uk

**Staffordshire County Council**
Social Services Dept
St Chad's Place
Stafford
ST16 2LR
01785 223121
www.staffordshire.gov.uk

**St Helens Met. Borough Council**
The Gamble Building
Victoria Square
St Helens
WA10 1DY
01744 456000
www.sthelens.gov.uk

**Stockport Met. Borough Council**
Ponsonby House
Edward Street
Stockport
SK1 3UR
0161 474 4609
socialservices@stockport.gov.uk
www.stockport.gov.uk

**Stockton on Tees Borough Council**
Social Services Dept
Sun Street, Thornaby
Stockton on Tees
TS17 6HB
01642 393601
www.stockton-bc.gov.uk

**Stoke on Trent City Council**
Social Services Dept
Floor 4, Civic Centre
Glebe St, Stoke on Trent
ST4 1WB
01782 234567
www.stoke.gov.uk

**Suffolk County Council**
Social Care Services
St Paul House Rope Walk
Ipswich
IP4 1LH
01473 583483
anthony.douglas@socserv.suffolk.gov.uk
www.suffolkcc.gov.uk

**Sunderland City Council**
Social Services Dept
50 Fawcett Street
Sunderland
SR1 1RF
0191 553 1000
www.sunderland.gov.uk

**Surrey County Council**
County Hall, Penrhyn Road
Kingston
Surrey
KT1 2DN
020 8541 8500
www.surreycc.gov.uk

**Sutton London Borough**
Civic Offices
St Nicholas Way
Sutton
SM1 1EA
020 8770 5000
www.sutton.gov.uk

**Swindon Borough Council**
Civic Offices
Euclid Street
Swindon
SN1 2JH
01793 463609
jhogg@swindon.gov.uk
www.swindon.gov.uk

**Tameside Met. Borough Council**
Social Services Dept
Council Offices, Wellington Road
Ashton under Lyne
OL6 6DL
0161 342 3361
general@mail.tameside.gov.uk
www.tameside.gov.uk

**Telford & Wrekin Borough Council**
8th Floor, P.O.Box 214
Darby House
Telford
TF3 4LE
01952 202526
john.coughlan@telford.gov.uk
www.telford.gov.uk

**Thurrock Borough Council**
Dept. of Housing & Care
P.O. Box 140, Civic Offices
New Road, Grays, Essex
RM17 6TJ
01375 652675
saclarke@thurrock.gov.uk
www.thurrock.gov.uk

**Torbay Council**
Social Services Dept
Oldway Mansion
Paignton
TQ3 2TS
01803 201201
webmaster@torbay.gov.uk
www.torbay.gov.uk

**Tower Hamlets London Borough**
Social Services Dept.
62 Roman Road
London
E2 OPG
020 7364 5000
www.towerhamlets.gov.uk

**Trafford Met. Borough Council**
Social Services Dept
Trafford Town Hall, Talbot Road,
Stretford, Manchester
M32 0YT
0161 912 1212
mike.cooney@trafford.gov.uk
www.trafford.gov.uk

**Wakefield Met. District Council**
8 St John'sNorth
Wakefield
WF1 3QA
01924 307725
emchale@wakefield.gov.uk
www.wakefield.gov.uk

**Walsall Met. Borough Council**
Civic Centre
Darwall Street,
Walsall
WS1 1RG
01922 650000
sutcliffej@walsall.gov.uk
www.walsall.gov.uk

**Waltham Forest London Borough**
Leyton Municipal Offices,
High Road
Leyton
London
E10 5QJ
020 8496 5382
christine.taylor@lbwf.gov.uk
www.lbwf.gov.uk

**Wandsworth Borough Council**
Social Services Dept
Town Hall, Wandsworth High Street
London
SW18 2PU
020 8871 6000
www.wandsworth.gov.uk

**Warrington Borough Council**
Social Services Dept
Bewsey Old School
Lockton Lane, Bewsey,
Warrington
WA5 5BF
01925 444251
www.warrington.gov.uk

**Warwickshire County Council**
Social Services Dept
Shire Hall, Market Place
Warwick
CV34 4RR
01926 410410
www.warwickshire.gov.uk

**West Berkshire Council**
Avonbank House
West Street
Newbury
RG14 1BZ
01635 42400
info@westberks.gov.uk
www.westberks.gov.uk

**Westminster City Council**
Westminster City Hall
64 Victoria Street
London
SW1E 6QP
020 7641 6000
jjones@westminster.gov.uk
www.westminster.gov.uk

**West Sussex County Council**
West Sussex Social & Caring
Services
The Grange, County Hall,
Tower Street
West Sussex
PO19 1QT
01243 777600
social.services@westsussex.gov.uk
www.westsussex.gov.uk

**Wigan Council**
Civic Centre
Millgate
Wigan
WN 1AZ
01942 244991
b.walker@wiganmbc.gov.uk
www.wiganmbc.gov.uk

**Wiltshire County Council**
Adult and Community Services
Dept.
County Hall, Bythesea Road
Trowbridge
BA14 8LE
01225 713000
claireclarkson@wiltshire.gov.uk
www.wiltshire.gov.uk

**Windsor & Maidenhead Borough Council**
Town Hall, St Ives Road
Maidenhead
Sl6 1RF
01628 798888
morna.sloan@rbwm.gov.uk
www.rbwm.gov.uk

**Wirral Met. Borough Council**
Westminster House
Hamilton Street
Birkinhead, Wirral
CH41 5FN
0151 666 4779/3650
kevinmiller@wirral.gov.uk
www.wirral.gov.uk

**Wokingham District Council**
Community Services Dept
Shute End
Wokingham
RG40 3BN
0118 974 6000
www.wokingham.gov.uk

**Wolverhampton City Council**
Civic Centre,
St Peter's Square
Wolverhampton
WV1 1RT
01902 555300
www.wolverhampton.gov.uk

**Worcestershire County Council**
Social Services Dept.
County Hall
Spetchley Road, Worcester
WR5 2NP
01905 763763
www.worcestershire.gov.uk

**York City Council**
Community Services
10/12 George Hudson Street
York
YO1 6ZE
01904 613161
www.york.gov.uk

---

## Scotland

**Aberdeen City Council**
Neighbourhood Services and
Community Services
Social Work, St Nicholas House
Broad Street, Aberdeen
AB10 1BY
01224 522000
www.aberdeencity.gov.uk

**Aberdeenshire Council**
Housing & Social Work Dept.
Woodhill House, Westburn Road
Aberdeen
AB16 5GB
01467 620981
www.aberdeenshire.gov.uk

**Angus Council**
Social Work Dept.
County Buildings, Market Street
Forfar
DD8 3WS
01307 461460
www.angus.gov.uk

**Argyll & Bute Council**
Tom Johnston House
Civic Way
Kirkintilloch
G66 4TJ
0141 578 8000
www.eastdunbarton.gov.uk

**East Lothian Council**
Social Work & Housing Dept
John Muir House
Haddington
EH41 3HA
01620 827827
www.eastlothian.gov.uk

**East Renfrewshire Council**
Social Work Dept, Council
Headquarters
Eastwood Park, Rouken Glen
Road
Giffnock, Glasgow
G46 6UG
0141 577 3839
george.hunter@eastrenfrewshire.
gov.uk
www.eastrenfrewshire.gov.uk

**Edinburgh City Council**
Shrubhill House,
Leith Walk
Edinburgh
EH7 4PD
0131 554 4301
www.edinburgh.gov.uk

**Falkirk Council**
Social Work Dept.
Fife House, North Street
Glenrothes Fife
KY7 6LT
01592 414141
mike.sawyer@fife.gov.uk
www.fife.gov.uk

**Glasgow City Council**
Nye Bevan House
20 India Street
Glasgow
G2 4PF
0141 287 8853
david.comley@sw.glasgow.gov.uk
www.glasgow.gov.uk

**Highland Council**
Council Offices
Glenurquart Road
Inverness
IV3 5NX
01463 703456
social.work@highland.gov.uk
www.highland.gov.uk

**Inverclyde Council**
Social Work & Housing Dept
Municipal Buildings
Greenock
PA15 1LY
01475 717171
www.inverclyde.gov.uk

**Midlothian Council**
Social Work Dept
Fairfield House
8 Lothian Road, Dalkeith
EH22 3ZH
0131 270 3605
malcolm.mcewan@midlothian.go
v.uk
www.midlothian.gov.uk

**Moray Council**
Community Services Dept
Council Offices, High Street
Elgin
IV30 1BX
01343 543451
hotline@moray.gov.uk
www.moray.gov.uk

**North Ayrshire Council**
Social Work Dept
Elliott House
Irvine
KA12 8TB
01294 317700
www.north-ayrshire.gov.uk

**North Lanarkshire Council**
Scott House
73-77 Merry Street
Motherwell
ML1 1JE
01698 332000
dickiej@northlan.gov.uk
www.northlan.gov.uk

**Orkney Islands Council**
Dept. of Community Social
Services
Council Offices, School Place
Kirkwall, Orkney
KW15 1NY
01856 873535
firstname.surname@orkney.gov.uk
www.orkney.gov.uk

**Perth & Kinross Council**
Moncrieffe Ward
Perth Royal Infirmary
Perth
PH1 1NX
01738 473112
www.pkc.gov.uk

**Renfrewshire Council**
Social Work Dept
North Building
4th Floor, Cotton Street, Paisley
PA1 1TZ
0141 842 5167
david.crawford@renfrewshire.gov
.uk
www.renfrewshire.gov.uk

**Scottish Borders Council**
Council Headquarters
Newton St Bosewells
Melrose
TD6 0SA
01835 825080
social.work@scotborders.gov.uk
www.scottishborders.gov.uk

**Shetland Islands Council**
Social Care Dept
Quendale House, 31 Commercial
Street
Lerwick
ZE1 0AN
01595 744300
www.shetland.gov.uk

**South Ayrshire Council**
County Buildings
Wellington Square
Ayr
KA7 1DR
01292 612419
www.south-ayrshire.gov.uk

**South Lanarkshire Council**
Council Offices, 8th Floor
Almada Street
Hamilton
ML3 0AA
01698 453700
www.southlanarkshire.gov.uk

**Stirling City Council**
Stirling Council
Viewforth
Stirling
FK8 2ET
01786 443322
mcalpinl@stirling.gov.uk
www.stirling.gov.uk

**West Dunbartonshire Council**
Social Work & Housing Dept
Council Offices, Garshake Road
Dunbarton
G82 3PU
01389 737526
www.west-dunbarton.gov.uk

## West Lothian Council
West Lothian House,
Almond Vale Bouvelvard
Livingston, West Lothian
EH54 6QG
01506 777000
grahame.blair@westlothian.gov.uk
www.westlothian.gov.uk

## Wales

### Blaenau Gwent Borough Council
Social Services Dept
Municipal Offices, Civic Centre
Ebow Vale
NP23 6XB
01495 350555
www.blaenau-gwent.gov.uk

### Bridgend County Borough Council
Personal Services Dept
Sunnyside, Sunnyside Road
Bridgend
CF31 4AR
01656 642200
www.bridgend.gov.uk

### Caerphilly County Borough Council
Social Services Dept
Hawtin Park, Gellihaf
Blackwood
NP12 2PZ
01443 864673
info@caerphilly.gov.uk
www.caerphilly.gov.uk

### Cardiff City & Council
County Hall, Atlantic Wharf
Cardiff
CF10 4UW
029 2087 2000
www.cardiff.gov.uk

### Carmarthenshire County Council
3 Spilman Street
Carmarthen
SA31 1SL
01267 234567
socialcarehousing@carmarthens
hire.gov.uk
www.carmarthenshire.gov.uk

### Ceredigion County Council
Social Services Dept
Min-Aeron, Rhiw Goch
Aberaeron, Ceredigion
SA46 ODY
01545 570881
socservs@ceredigion.gov.uk
www.ceredigion.gov.uk

### Conwy County Borough Council
Central Offices, Builder Street
Llandudno
Conwy
LL30 1DA
01492 574065
www.conwy.gov.uk

### Denbighshire County Council
Personal Services Dept
Council Offices, Wynnstay Road
Ruthin
LL15 1AT
01824 706000
www.denbighshire.gov.uk

### Flintshire County Council
County Hall,
Mold
CH7 6NB
01352 752121
www.flintshire.gov.uk

### Gwynedd County Council
Social Services Dept
Council Offices, Shirehall Street
Caemarfon
LL55 1SH
01286 672255
enquiries@gwynedd.gov.uk
www.gwynedd.gov.uk

### Isle of Angelsey County Council
Housing & Social Services Dept.
Swyddfar Sir
Llangefni, Ynys Mon
LL77 7TW
01248 750057
srxss@nysmon.gov.uk
www.ynysmon.gov.uk

### Merthyr Tydfil County Borough Council
Social Services Dept
Tykeir Hardie, Riverside Court
Avenue De Clichy, Merthyr Tydfil
CF47 8XE
01685 725000
socialservices@merthyr.gov.uk
www.merthyr.gov.uk

### Monmouthshire County Council
Social & Housing Services Dept
County Hall
Cwmbran
NP44 2XH
01633 699600
nameofofficer@monmouthshire.g
ov.uk
www.monmouthshire.gov.uk

### Neath Port Talbot County Borough Council
Social Services & Housing Dept
Civic Centre
Port Talbot
SA13 1PJ
01639 763333
social.services@neath-
porttalbot.gov.uk
www.neath-porttalbot.gov.uk

### Newport City Council
Social Wellbeing & Housing
Civic Centre
Newport
NP20 4UR
01633 233104
www.newport.gov.uk

### Pembrokeshire County Council
Social Care & Housing Dept.
County Hall
Haverfordwest
SA61 1TP
01437 764551
enquiries@pembrokeshire.gov.uk
www.pembrokeshire.gov.uk

### Powys County Council
Social Services Dept
County Hall,Llandrindod Wells,
Powys
LD1 5LG
01597 826000
www.powys.gov.uk

### Rhondda Cynon Taff County Borough Council
Community Services Dept.
The Pavillions, Cambrian Park
Clydach Vale, Tonypandy
CF40 2XX
01443 424000
sian.c.hopkins@rhondda-cynon-
taff.gov.uk
www.rhondda-cynon-taff.gov.uk

### Swansea City Council
Social Services Dept
County Hall, Oystermouth Road
Swansea
SA1 3SN
01792 636000
www.swansea.gov.uk

### Torfaen County Borough Council
Social Services Dept.
County Hall
Cwmbran
NP4 6YB
01633 648615
stewart.greenwell@torfaen.gov.uk
www.torfaen.gov.uk

**Vale of Glamorgan Council**
Dock Offices
Subway Road
Barry
CF63 4RT
01446 704776
www.valeofglamorgan.gov.uk

**Wrexham County Borough Council**
Crown Buildings
Wrexham
LL13 8ZE
01978 298010
andrew.figial@wrexham.gov.uk
www.wrexham.gov.uk

# Northern Ireland

## Eastern Health & Social Services Board
Champion House
12-22 Linenhall Street
Belfast
BT2 8BS
028 9032 1313
enquiry@ehssb.n-l-nhs.uk
www.ehssb-n-l-nhs.uk

## Northern Health & Social Services Board
County Hall, 182 Galform Road
Ballymean
Co Antrim
BT43 6NQ
028 2565 3333
chief.executive@nhssb.n-l.nhs.uk
www.nhssb.n-l.nhs.uk

**Southern Health & Social Services Board**
Tower Hill
Armagh
BT61 9DR
028 3741 0041
www.shssb.org

**Western Health & Social Services Board**
15 Gransha Park
Clooney Road
Londonderry
BT47 6FN
028 7186 0086
mgormley@whssb.n-l.nhs.uk
www.whssb.org.uk

# Inspectorates

## National Care Standards Commission

**National Care Standards Commission, Headquarters**
St Nicholas Building, St Nicholas Street
Newcastle Upon Tyne
NE1 1NB
0191 233 3600
enquiries@ncsc.gsi.gov.uk
www.carestandards.org.uk
*The NCSC is the independent regulatory body responsible for inspecting and regulating almost all forms of residential care and other voluntary and private care services in England.*

**The Commission for Social Care Inspection**
csci@doh.gsi.gov.uk
www.doh.gov.uk/csci
*from April 2004, the work of the National Care Standards Commission will be taken over by new organisation the Commission for Social Care Inspection, which will also encompass the government's Social Services Inspectorate, and the joint review team of the SSI and the Audit Commission. CSCI will be a comprehensive independent inspectorate for all social care services - public, private and voluntary.*

### England

### North-east

**NSCS North East Regional Office**
4th Floor, Northgate House
St Augustine's Way
Darlington
DL1 1XA
01325 740630
Enquiries.Northeast@ncsc.gsi.gov.uk

**NCSC South Shields (South of Tyne) Area Office**
Baltic House, Tyne Dock
South Shields
Tyne & Wear
NE34 9PT
0191 497 4220
Enquiries.SouthShields@ncsc.gsi.gov.uk

**NCSC Cramlington (Northumbria) Area Office**
Northumbria House, Manor Walks
Cramlington
Northumbria
NE23 6UR
01670 707900
Enquiries.Cramlington@ncsc.gsi.gov.uk

**NCSC Stockton-on-Tees (Tees Valley) Area Office**
Unit B, Advance, St Mark's Court
Teesdale
Stockton-on-Tees
TS17 6QX
01642 628960
Enquiries.Stockton@ncsc.gsi.gov.uk

**NCSC Darlington Area Office**
No 1 Hopetown Studios
Brinkburn Road
Darlington
DL3 6DS
01325 371720
Enquiries.Darlington@ncsc.gsi.gov.uk

### North-west

**NCSC North West Regional Office**
4th Floor, Unit 1, Tustin Court
Port Way, Preston
Lancs
PR2 2YQ
01772 730100
Enquiries.NorthWest@ncsc.gsi.gov.uk

**NCSC Knowsley (Liverpool North) Area Office**
2nd Floor, Burlington House
Crosby Road North, Waterloo
Liverpool
L22 0LG
0151 949 9540
Enquiries.Knowsley@ncsc.gsi.gov.uk

**NCSC Manchester, Salford, Trafford Area Office**
9th Floor, Oakland House
Talbot Road
Manchester
M16 0PQ
0161 772 1620
Enquiries.Manchester@ncsc.gsi.gov.uk

**NCSC Chorley (South Lancashire) Area Office**
Levens House, Ackhurst
Business Park, Foxhole Road
Chorley
PR7 1NW
01257 236850
Enquiries.Chorley@ncsc.gsi.gov.uk

**NCSC Northwich (Cheshire) Area Office**
Unit D, Off Rudheath Way
Gadbrook Park
Northwich
CW9 7LT
01606 333400
Enquiries.Northwich@ncsc.gsi.gov.uk

**NCSC Bolton, Bury, Rochdale and Wigan Area Office**
Turton Suite, Paragon Business Park
Chorley New Road
Bolton
BL6 6HG
01204 676120
Enquiries.Bolton@ncsc.gsi.gov.uk

**NCSC East Lancashire, Blackburn, Darwen Area Office**
First Floor, Unit 4, Petre Road
Clayton-le-Moors
Accrington
BB5 5JB
01254 306600
Enquiries.Accrington@ncsc.gsi.gov.uk

**NCSC North Lancashire, Blackpool Area Office**
2nd Floor, Unit 1, Tustin Court
Port Way, Preston
Lancs
PR2 2YQ
01772 730100
Enquiries.Preston@ncsc.gsi.gov.uk

**NCSC Ashton-under-Lyne (Oldham, Stockport, Tameside) Area Office**
2nd Floor, Heritage Wharf
Portland Place
Ashton-under-Lyne
OL7 0QD
0161 214 8120
Enquiries.Ashton@ncsc.gsi.gov.uk

**NCSC Penrith (Cumbria) Area Office**
Eamont House, Penrith 40
Business Park
Gillan Way
Penrith
CA11 9BP
01768 214730
Enquiries.Penrith@ncsc.gsi.gov.uk

**NCSC Liverpool/Wirral Area Office**
3rd Floor, Campbell Square
10 Duke Street
Liverpool
L1 5AS
0151 705 2000
Enquiries.Liverpool@ncsc.gsi.gov.uk

## Yorkshire & Humberside

**NCSC Yorkshire & Humberside Regional Office**
4th Floor, Northgate House
St Augustine's Way
Darlington
DL1 1XA
01325 740630
Enquiries.Northeast@ncsc.gsi.gov.uk

**NCSC Hessle (East Riding) Area Office**
Unit 3, Hesslewood Country Office Park, Ferriby Road
Hessle
HU13 0QF
01482 350636
Enquiries.Hessle@ncsc.gsi.gov.uk

**NCSC Leeds Area Office**
Aire House, Town Street
Rodley
LS13 1HP
0113 201 1075
Enquiries.Leeds@ncsc.gsi.gov.uk

**NCSC York Area Office**
Unit 4, Triune Court, Monk's Cross
York
YO32 9GZ
01904 545000
Enquiries.York@ncsc.gsi.gov.uk

**NCSC Brighouse (Wakefield, Kirklees, Calderdale) Area Office**
Park View House
Woodvale Office Park
Woodvale Road
Brighouse
HD6 4AB
01484 404930
Enquiries.Brighouse@ncsc.gsi.gov.uk

**NCSC Scunthorpe (North Lincolnshire) Area Office**
1st Floor, 3 Park Square
Laneham Street, Scunthorpe
North Lincolnshire
DN15 6JH
01724 749040
Enquiries.Scunthorpe@ncsc.gsi.gov.uk

**NCSC Doncaster Area Office**
1st Floor, Barclay Court
Heavens Walk
Doncaster
DN4 5HZ
01302 765350
Enquiries.Doncaster@ncsc.gsi.gov.uk

**NCSC Sheffield Area Office**
Ground Floor, Unit 3
Waterside Court, Bold Street
Sheffield
S9 2LR
0114 256 4530
Enquiries.Sheffield@ncsc.gsi.gov.uk

## East Midlands

**NCSC East Midlands Regional Office**
Unit 7, Interchange 25 Business Park, Bostocks Lane
Nottingham
NG10 5QG
0115 921 0950
Enquiries.Eastmidlands@ncsc.gsi.gov.uk

**NCSC Leicestershire and Rutland Area Office**
The Pavilions, 5 Smith Way
Grove Park, Enderby
Leicester
LE19 1SX
0116 281 5900
Enquiries.Leicester@ncsc.gsi.gov.uk

**NCSC Northamptonshire Area Office**
1st Floor, Newland House
Campbell Square
Northampton
NN1 3EB
01604 887620
Enquiries.Northampton@ncsc.gsi.gov.uk

**NCSC Nottinghamshire Area Office**
Edgeley House, Tottle Road
Riverside Business Park
Nottingham
NG2 1RT
0115 934 0900
Enquiries.Nottingham@ncsc.gsi.gov.uk

**NCSC Derbyshire Area Office**
South Point, Cardinal Square
Nottingham Road
Derby
DE1 3QT
01332 851800
Enquiries.Derby@ncsc.gsi.gov.uk

**NCSC Lincoln Area Office**
Unit A, The Point
Weaver Road (off Whisby Road)
Lincoln
LN6 3QN
01522 699310
Enquiries.Lincoln@ncsc.gsi.gov.uk

## West Midlands

**NCSC West Midlands Regional Office**
1st Floor, Ladywood House
45-56 Stephenson Street
Birmingham
B2 4UZ
0121 600 5720
Enquiries.Westmidlands@ncsc.
gsi.gov.uk

**NCSC Leamington Spa (Warwickshire) Area Office**
Imperial Court, Holly Walk
Leamington Spa
CV32 4YB
01926 436950
Enquiries.LeamingtonSpa@ncsc.
gsi.gov.uk

**NCSC Birmingham Area Office**
1st Floor, Ladywood House
45-56 Stephenson Street
Birmingham
B2 4UZ
0121 600 5711
Enquiries.Birmingham@ncsc.gsi.
gov.uk

**NCSC Wolverhampton Area Office**
2nd Floor, St David's Court
Union Street, Wolverhampton
WV1 3JE
01902 873720
Enquiries.Wolverhampton@ncsc.
gsi.gov.uk

**NCSC Shrewsbury (Shropshire) Area Office**
1st Floor, Chapter House South
Abbey Lawn, Abbey Foregate
Shrewsbury
SY2 5DE
01743 284300
Enquiries.Shrewsbury@ncsc.gsi.
gov.uk

**NCSC Hereford Area Office**
178 Widemarsh Street, Hereford
Herefordshire
HR4 9HN
01432 845700
Enquiries.Hereford@ncsc.gsi.
gov.uk

**NCSC Worcester Area Office**
The Coach House
John Comyn Drive
Perdiswell Park, Droitwich Road
Worcester
WR3 7NW
01905 753910
Enquiries.Worcester@ncsc.gsi.
gov.uk

**NCSC Halesowen (Sandwell & Dudley) Area Office**
Ground Floor, West Point
Mucklow Business Park,
Mucklow Hill, Halesowen
West Midlands
B62 8DA
0121 423 5410
Enquiries.Halesowen@ncsc.gsi.
gov.uk

**NCSC Stafford Area Office**
Unit D, Dyson Court
Staffordshire Technology Park,
Beaconside
Stafford
ST18 0ES
01785 270930
Enquiries.Stafford@ncsc.gsi.
gov.uk

**NCSC Coventry Area Office**
5th Floor, Coventry Point
Market Way
Coventry
CV1 1EB
024 7650 0850
Enquiries.Coventry@ncsc.gsi.
gov.uk

## East

**NCSC Eastern Regional Office**
Compass House, Vision Park
Chivers Way, Histon
Cambridge
CB4 9AD
01223 266130
Enquiries.Eastern@ncsc.gsi.
gov.uk

**NCSC Bedford Area Office**
Clifton House
4a Goldington Road
Bedford
MK40 3NF
01234 220860
Enquiries.Bedford@ncsc.gsi.
gov.uk

**NCSC Colchester (North Essex) Area Office**
Fairfax House
Causton Road
Colchester
CO1 1RJ
01206 715630
Enquiries.Colchester@ncsc.gsi.
gov.uk

**NCSC Hertfordshire (Welwyn Garden City) Area Office**
Wilson Connolly House,
1 Broadwater Road
Welwyn Garden City
Hertfordshire
AL7 3BQ
01707 379370
Enquiries.Hertfordshire@ncsc.
gsi.gov.uk

**NCSC Norwich (Norfolk) Area Office**
3rd Floor, Cavell House
St Crispins Road
Norwich
NR3 1YF
01603 598700
Enquiries.Norwich@ncsc.gsi.
gov.uk

**NCSC Ipswich (Suffolk) Area Office**
5th Floor, St Vincent House
Cutler Street
Ipswich
IP1 1UQ
01473 269050
Enquiries.Ipswich@ncsc.gsi.
gov.uk

**NCSC Cambridge Area Office**
Compass House, Vision Park
Chivers Way, Histon
Cambridge
CB4 9AD
01223 266120
Enquiries.Cambridge@ncsc.gsi.
gov.uk

**NCSC Southend (South Essex) Area Office**
Kingswood House
Baxter Avenue
Southend
SS2 6BG
01702 236010
Enquiries.Southend@ncsc.gsi.
gov.uk

## London

**NCSC London Regional Office**
3rd Floor, Caledonia House
223 Pentonville Road
London
N1 9NG
020 7239 0300
Enquiries.London@ncsc.gsi.
gov.uk

**NCSC Central & South West London (Hammersmith) Area Office**
11th Floor, West Wing
26-28 Hammersmith Grove,
Hammersmith
London
W6 7SE
020 8735 6370
Enquiries.Hammersmith@ncsc.
gsi.gov.uk

**NCSC Brent & Harrow Area Office**
4th Floor, Aspect Gate
166 College Road, Harrow
London
HA1 1BH
020 8420 0100
Enquiries.Harrow@ncsc.gsi.gov.uk

**NCSC West London (Ealing) Area Office**
Ground Floor, 58 Uxbridge Road
Ealing
London
W5 2ST
020 8280 0347
Enquiries.Ealing@ncsc.gsi.gov.uk

**NCSC Ilford (North East) London Area Office**
Ferguson House
109-113 Cranbrook Road
Ilford
IG1 4PU
020 8477 0960
Enquiries.Ilford@ncsc.gsi.gov.uk

**NCSC Camden & Islington Area Office**
Centro 4, 20-23 Mandela Street
Camden Town
London
NW1 0DW
020 7255 9540
Enquiries.Camden@ncsc.gsi.
gov.uk

**NCSC South West London (Wimbledon, Wandsworth, Merton, Kingston, Richmond) Area Office**
Ground Floor, 41-47 Hartfield
Road
Wimbledon
London
SW19 3RG
020 8254 4950
Enquiries.Wimbledon@ncsc.gsi.
gov.uk

**NCSC Stratford (East London) Area Office**
4th Floor, Gredley House
1-11 Broadway, Stratford
London
E15 4BQ
020 8221 3360
Enquiries.Stratford@ncsc.gsi.
gov.uk

**NCSC Southwark Area Office**
Ground Floor, 46 Loman Street
Southwark
London
SE1 0EH
020 7803 4960
Enquiries.Southwark@ncsc.gsi.
gov.uk

**NCSC Croydon & Sutton Area Office**
8th Floor, Grosvenor House
125 High Street
Croydon
CR0 9XP
020 8256 6430
Enquiries.Croydon@ncsc.gsi.
gov.uk

**NCSC South East London (Sidcup) Area Office**
River House, 1 Maidstone Road
Sidcup
DA14 5RH
020 8308 3520
Enquiries.Sidcup@ncsc.gsi.gov.uk

**NCSC North London (Southgate, Enfield, Haringey, Barnet) Area Office**
1st Floor, Solar House
282 Chase Road, Southgate
London
N14 6HA
020 8447 6930
Enquiries.Southgate@ncsc.gsi.
gov.uk

## South-east
**NCSC South East Regional Office**
4th Floor, Caledonia House
223 Pentonville Road
London
N1 9NG
020 7239 0300
Enquiries.Southeast@ncsc.gsi.
gov.uk

**NCSC Eashing (Surrey) Area Office**
The Wharf, Abbey Mill, Eashing
Surrey
GU7 2QN
01483 413540
Enquiries.Eashing@ncsc.gsi.
gov.uk

**NCSC Ashford (Kent East) Area Office**
11th Floor, International House
Dover Place
Ashford
TN23 1HU
01233 619330
Enquiries.Ashford@ncsc.gsi.
gov.uk

**NCSC Aylesbury (Buckinghamshire) Area Office**
Cambridge House, 8 Bell
Business Park, Smeaton Close
Aylesbury
HP19 8JR
01296 737550
Enquiries.Aylesbury@ncsc.gsi.
gov.uk

**NCSC Maidstone (Kent West) Area Office**
Hermitage Court, Hermitage Lane
Maidstone
ME16 9NT
01622 724950
Enquiries.Maidstone@ncsc.gsi.
gov.uk

**NCSC Newport / IOW Area Office**
Ground Floor, Mill Court
The Furrlongs, Newport
IOW
PO30 2AA
01983 824130
Enquiries.Newport@ncsc.gsi.
gov.uk

**NCSC Theale (Berkshire) Area Office**
1015 Arlington Business Park
Theale
RG7 4SA
0118 903 3230
Enquiries.Theale@ncsc.gsi.gov.uk

**NCSC Southampton (Hampshire) Area Office**
4th Floor, Overline House
Blechynden Terrace
Southampton
SO15 1GW
023 8082 1300
Enquiries.Southampton@ncsc.
gsi.gov.uk

### NCSC Oxford Area Office
Burgner House, 4630 Kingsgate,
Cascade Way
Oxford Business Park South,
Cowley
Oxford
OX4 2SU
01865 397750
Enquiries.Oxford@ncsc.gsi.gov.uk

### NCSC Eastbourne (East Sussex) Area Office
Ivy House, 3 Ivy Terrace
Eastbourne
BN21 4QT
01323 636200
Enquiries.Eastbourne@ncsc.gsi.gov.uk

### NCSC Worthing (West Sussex) Area Office
2nd Floor, Ridgeworth House
Liverpool Gardens, Worthing
West Sussex
BN11 1RY
01903 222950
Enquiries.Worthing@ncsc.gsi.gov.uk

## South-west

### NCSC South West Regional Office
Ground Floor, Riverside Chambers
Tangier, Castle Street
Taunton
TA1 4AL
01823 345993
Enquiries.Southwest@ncsc.gsi.gov.uk

### NCSC Gloucester (Gloucestershire) Area Office
Unit 1210 Lansdowne Court,
Gloucester Business Park
Brockworth
Gloucester
GL3 4AB
01452 632750
Enquiries.Gloucester@ncsc.gsi.gov.uk

### NCSC Avon (Bristol North) Area Office
300 Aztec West
Almondsbury
South Gloucestershire
BS32 4RG
01454 454010
Enquiries.Avon@ncsc.gsi.gov.uk

### NCSC Taunton (Somerset) Area Office
Ground Floor, Riverside Chambers
Tangier, Castle Street
Taunton
TA1 4AL
01823 345960
Enquiries.Taunton@ncsc.gsi.gov.uk

### NCSC Ashburton (South Devon) Area Office
Unit D1, Linhay Business Park
Ashburton
Devon
TQ13 7UP
01364 651800
Enquiries.Ashburton@ncsc.gsi.gov.uk

### NCSC Chippenham (Wiltshire & Swindon) Area Office
Suite C, Avonbridge House
Bath Road
Chippenham
SN15 2BB
01249 454550
Enquiries.Chippenham@ncsc.gsi.gov.uk

### NCSC St Austell (Cornwall & Isles of Scilly) Area Office
John Keay House, Tregonissey Road
St Austell
Cornwall
PL25 4AD
01726 624550
Enquiries.Cornwall@ncsc.gsi.gov.uk

### NCSC Exeter (North Devon) Area Office
Suites 1 & 7, Renslade House
Bonhay Road
Exeter
EX4 3AY
01392 474350
Enquiries.Exeter@ncsc.gsi.gov.uk

### NCSC Poole (Dorset) Area Office
Unit 4, New Fields Business Park
Stinsford Road, Poole
Dorset
BH17 0NF
01202 662992
Enquiries.Poole@ncsc.gsi.gov.uk

## Wales

### Care Standards Inspectorate for Wales
National Office, Units 4-5
Charnwood Court, Heol
Billingsley
Parc Nantgarw, Nantgarw
Cardiff
CF15 7QZ
01443 848450
www.wales.gov.uk/subisocialpolicycarestandards/index.htm

### Care Standards Inspectorate for Wales
South East Wales Regional
Office, 6th Floor, Civic Centre
Pontypool
Torfaen
NP4 6YB
01495 766500
CSIW_SE_Wales_Region@Wales.GSI.gov.uk

### Care Standards Inspectorate for Wales
Cardiff Regional Office
1 Alexandra Gate
Ffordd Pengam, Tremorfa
Cardiff
CF24 2SB
029 2047 8600
CSIW_Cardiff_Region@wales.GSI.gov.uk

### Care Standards Inspectorate for Wales
South West Wales Regional
Office, Unit C, Phase 3
Tawe Business Village, Phoenix
Way, Swansea Enterprise Park
Swansea
SA7 9LA
01792 310420
CSIW_SW_Wales_Region@Wales.GSI.gov.uk

### Care Standards Inspectorate for Wales
West Wales Regional Office
Government Buildings, Picton
Terrace
Carmarthen
SA31 3BT
01267 223402
CSIW_West_Wales_Region@Wales.GSI.gov.uk

**Care Standards Inspectorate for Wales**
Mid Wales Regional Office,
Government Buildings
Spa Road East, Llandrindod
Wells
Powys
LD1 5HA
01597 829319
CSIW_Mid_Wales_Region@
wales.GSI.gov.uk

**Care Standards Inspectorate for Wales**
North West Wales Regional
Office, Government Buildings
Penrallt, Caernarfon
Gwynedd
LL55 1EP
01286 662300
CSIW_NW_Wales_Region@
Wales.GSI.gov.uk

**Care Standards Inspectorate for Wales**
North East Wales Regional Office,
Broncoed Business Park
Wrexham Road, Mold
Flintshire
CH7 1HP
01352 707900
CSIW_NE_Wales_Region@
wales.GSI.gov.uk

## Scotland

**Care Commission, Head Office**
Compass House
11 Riverside Drive
Dundee
DD1 4NY
01382 207100 or 0845 603 0890

**Care Commission, North Region Office**
Johnstone House
Rose Street
Aberdeen
AB10 1UD
01224 793870 or 0845 603 0890

**Care Commission, Local Resource Centre**
Unit 4
39-41 Harbour Road
Inverness
IV1 1UA
01463 227630

**Care Commission, Local Resource Centre**
Phoenix House
1 Wards Road
Elgin
IV30 1QL
01343 541734

**Care Commission, Local Resource Centre**
Orkney Islands Council
The Strynd, Kirkwall
Orkney
KW15 1HG
01856 876445

**Care Commission, Local Resource Centre**
Room 205 & 222
Charlotte House, Commercial
Road, Lerwick
Shetland
ZE1 0LX
01595 696661

**Care Commission, Local Resource Centre**
Custom House
Quay House, Stornoway
Isle of Lewis
HS1 2XX
01382 207227

**Care Commission, Central East Regional Office**
Compass House
11 Riverside Drive
Dundee
DD1 4NY
01382 207100 or 0845 603 0890

**Care Commission, Local Resource Centre**
South Suite, Ground Floor
Largo House, Carnegie Campus
Dunfermline
KY11 8PE
01383 841100

**Care Commission, Local Resource Centre**
Springfield House, Laurelhill
Business Park
Kingspark
Stirling
FK7 9JQ
01786 406363

**Care Commission, Central West Regional Office**
4th Floor, No 1 Smithhills Street
Paisley
PA1 1EB
0141 843 4230 or 0845 603 0890

**Care Commission, Local Resource Centre**
Boswell House, Argyll Square
Oban
Argyll
PA34 4BD
01631 564144

**Care Commission, South East Regional Office**
Stuart House
Eskmills
Musselburgh
EH21 7PB
0131 653 4100 or 0845 603 0890

**Care Commission, Local Resource Centre**
Galabank Mill, Wilderhaugh
Industrial Estate
Wilderhaugh
Galashiels
TD1 1PR
01896 664400

**Care Commission, South West Regional Office**
Princes Gate, Castle Street
Hamilton
ML3 6BU
01698 208150 or 0845 603 0890

**Care Commission, Local Resource Centre**
Galloway House, Galloway
Business Centre, The Crichton
Bankend Road
Dumfries
DG1 4ZZ
01382 207195

**Care Commission, Local Resource Centre**
Suite 3, Sovereign House
Academy Road
Irvine
KA12 8RL
01294 323920

# National voluntary organisations

**The Association of Children's Hospices**
Kings House,
14 Orchard Street
Bristol
BS1 5EH
0117 905 5082
info@childhospice.org.uk
www.childhospice.org.uk
*brings together over 40 voluntary sector organisations throughout the UK dedicated to the care of children with life-limiting and life-threatening conditions and their families*

**Barnardo's**
Tanners Lane, Barkingside
Ilford
Essex
IG6 1QG
020 8550 8822
dorothy.howes@barnardos.org.uk
www.barnardos.org.uk

**Northern Ireland**
542-544 Upper Newtownards
Road
Belfast
BT4 3HE
028 9067 2366

**Scotland**
235 Corstrophine Road
Edinburgh
EH12 7AR
0131 334 9893

**Cymru**
11-15 Columbus Walk,
Brigantine Place
Atlantic Wharf
Cardiff
CF10 4BZ
029 2049 3387

**London East Anglia & South-east**
Tanners Lane, Barkingside
Ilford
Essex
IG6 1QG
020 8551 0011

**Midlands**
Brooklands, Great Cornbow
Halesowen
West Midlands
B63 3AB
0121 550 5271/ 6

**South-west**
Unit 19, Easton Business Centre
Felix Road, Easton
Bristol
BS5 0HE
0117 941 5841

**North-west**
7 Lineside Close
Liverpool
L25 2UD
0151 488 1100

**North-east**
Orchard House, Fenwick Terrace
Jesmond
Newcastle Upon Tyne
NE2 2JQ
0191 281 5024

**Yorkshire**
Four Gables, Clarence Road
Horsforth, Leeds
West Yorkshire
LS18 4LB
0113 258 2115

**Childline**
Freepost NATN1111
London
E1 6BR
0800 1111
www.childline.org.uk
*A 24hr Free helpline for children or young people in trouble or danger*

**Children in Need**
PO Box 76
London
W3 6FS
020 8576 7788
www.bbc.co.uk/pudsey

**Northern Ireland**
Broadcasting House,
Ormeau Avenue
Belfast
BT2 8HQ
028 9033 8221

**Scotland**
BBC Edinburgh
Holyrood Road
Edinburgh
EH8 8JF
0131 248 4225

**Wales**
Broadcasting House
Llandaff
Cardiff
CF5 2YQ
029 2032 2383

**North-west (Manchester)**
New Broadcasting House
Oxford Road
Manchester
M60 1SJ
0161 244 3439

**North-east (Leeds)**
Broadcasting Centre
Woodhouse Lane
Leeds
LS2 9PX
0113 224 7155

**Midlands and East (Birmingham)**
BBC Broadcasting Centre
Pebble Mill Road
Birmingham
B5 7QQ
0121 432 8899

**South West (Bristol)**
Broadcasting House
Whiteladies Road
Bristol
BS8 2LR
0117 974 6600

**London and South-east (Elstree)**
Elstree Centre, Clarendon Road
Borehamwood
Hertfordshire
WD6 1JF
020 8228 8275

**The Childrens Society**
Edward Rudolf House
Margery Street
London
WC1X 0JL
0845 300 1128
info@childrenssociety.org.uk
www.childrenssociety.org.uk

**North-east**
Suite O, Walker House
Castle Centre,
Stockton-on-Tees
Cleveland
TS18 1BG
01642 677302

**North-west**
8 Vine Street, Kersal
Salford
Manchester
M7 3PG
0161 792 8885

**Yorkshire and the Humber**
3rd Floor Stamford House
Piccadilly
York
YO1 9PW
01904 627866

**North-east Midlands**
Mayfair Court, North Gate
New Basford
Nottingham
NG7 7GR
0115 942 2974

**West Midlands**
Unit 4, Mitre Court
Lichfield Road,
Sutton Coldfield
West Midlands
0121 362 8600

**East of England**
20-22 White House Road,
Alpha Business Park
Ipswich
Suffolk
IP1 5LT
01473 461911

**London**
91/93 Queens Road
Peckham
London
SE15 2EZ
020 7639 1466

**South-east**
The Annexe, Elsfield Hall
15-17 Elsfield Way
Oxford
OX2 8FQ
01865 514161

**South-west**
Brook House
Pennywell
Bristol
BS5 0TX
0117 941 4333

**National Children's Bureau**
8 Wakley Street
London
EC1V 7QE
020 7843 6000
membership@ncb.org.uk or
library@ncb.org.uk
www.ncb.org.uk

**NCH (formerly known as the National Children's Home)**
85 Highbury Park
London
N5 1UD
020 7704 7000
www.nch.org.uk

**NCH Scotland**
17 Newton Place
Glasgow
G3 7PY
0141 332 7002

**NCH Cymru**
St David's Court
68A Cowbridge Road East
CF11 9DN
029 2022 2127

**NCH Northern Ireland**
45 Malone Road
Belfast
BT9 6RX
028 9068 7785

**National Council of Voluntary Child Care Organisations (NCVCCO)**
Unit 4, Pride Court
80-82 White Lion Street
London
N1 9PF
020 7833 3319
office@ncvcco.org
www.ncvcco.org.uk
*Membership is open to all registered child care and family support charities in England*

**NSPCC**
Weston House, 42 Curtain Road
London
EC2A 3NH
020 7825 2500
NSPCC Child Protection
Helpline: 0808 800 5000
www.nspcc.org.uk

---

## Scotland

**Children in Scotland**
Princes House
5 Shandwick Place
Edinburgh
EH2 4RG
0131 228 8484
info@childreninscotland.org.uk
www.childreninscotland.org.uk
*point of contact for voluntary sector childcare bodies*

---

## Northern Ireland

**Children in Northern Ireland**
216 Belmont Road
Belfast
BT4 2AT
028 9065 2713
info@ci-ni.org.uk
www.ci-ni.org.uk
*point of contact for voluntary sector childcare bodies*

---

## Wales

**Children in Wales**
25 Windsor Place
Cardiff
CF10 3BZ
029 2034 2434
info@childreninwales.org.uk
www.childreninwales.org.uk
*point of contact for voluntary sector childcare bodies*

# Professional associations

**British Association of Social Workers (BASW)**
16 Kent Street
Birmingham
B5 6RD
0121 622 3911
info@basw.co.uk
www.basw.co.uk
*the largest association representing social work and social workers in the UK*

**Association of Child Abuse Lawyers (ACAL)**
PO Box 466, Chorleywood
Rickmansworth
Hertfordshire
WD3 5LG
01923 286888
info@childabuselawyers.com
www.childabuselawyers.com
*committed to the improvement of standards amongst personal injury lawyers*

**Community & Youth Workers Union (CYWU)**
302 the Argent Centre
60 Frederick Street
Birmingham
B1 3HS
0121 244 3344
www.cywu.org.uk

**Social Care Association**
Thornton House, Hook Road
Surbiton
Surrey
KT6 5AN
020 8397 1411
sca@scaed.demon.co.uk
www.socialcareassoc.com
*promotes good professional practice among its members, develops policy, conducts research and offers advice*

**Social Work Students**
sharon@socialwork-students.com
www.socialwork-students.com
*free website for students in social work in the UK and Ireland*

**The Association of Directors of Social Services (ADSS)**
Local Government House
Smith Square
London
SW1P 3HZ
020 7072 7433
team@adss.org.uk
www.adss.org.uk
*represents all the directors of social services in England, Wales and Northern Ireland*

**The National Association of Child Contact Centres**
Minerva House, Spaniel Row
Nottingham
NG1 6EP
0845 450 0280
contact@naccc.org.uk
www.naccc.org.uk
*promotes safe child contact*

## Northern Ireland

**Northern Ireland Social Care Council (NISCC)**
7th Floor, Millennium House
19-25 Great Victoria Street
Belfast
BT2 7AQ
028 9041 7600
info@niscc.n-i.nhs.uk
www.niscc.info
*set up to regulate and register the social care workforce*

# Children's services

## Youth and social care

**The National Youth Agency**
17-23 Albion Street, Leicester,
LE1 6GD
0116 285 3700
nya@nya.org.uk
www.nya.org.uk or
www.youthinformation.com
*funded primarily by the Local Government Association and government departments; provides resources to improve work with young people and its management; create and demonstrate innovation in services and methods; support the leadership of organisations to manage change; influence public perception and policy; and secure standards of education and training for youth work.*

**Social Exclusion Unit**
Office of the Deputy Prime Minister, 7th Floor, Eland House, Bressenden Place
London
SW1E 5DU
020 7944 3344/3319
seuenquiries@odpm.gsi.gov.uk
www.socialexclusionunit.gov.uk
*set up by the prime minister to help improve Government action to reduce social exclusion*

**Care Group Workforce Teams**
Department of Health, Room 2W05, Quarry House, Quarry Hill
Leeds
LS2 7UE
claire.armstrong@doh.gsi.gov.uk
www.doh.gov.uk/cgwt
*aims to support service improvement for children, young people and expectant mothers through integrated workforce planning and development across health, social care and education agencies*

# Government initiatives

## Children's trust trailblazers

*These new organisations, which fall under local authority control, are responsible for planning, commissioning and children's services, with the aim of preventing children from slipping through gaps in the welfare system. Modelled on care trusts, which provide integrated health and social services for older people and/or those with learning disabilities or mental health problems, these are the pilot children's trusts. The government hopes all authorities will have established children's trusts by 2006.*

### North-west

Blackburn with Darwen Borough Council and Primary Care Trust

Bolton Metropolitan Borough Council and Primary Care Trust

Trafford Metropolitan Borough Council and Trafford North and South Primary Care Trust

### North-east

Darlington Borough Council and Primary Care Trust

Gateshead Council

Newcastle City Council and Primary Care Trust

South Tyneside Council, Primary Care Trust and Health Care Trust

### Yorkshire & the Humber

Barnsley Metropolitan Borough Council and Primary Care Trust

Calderdale Council and Primary Care trust

East Riding of Yorkshire Council, local Primary Care Trusts, Hull and East Riding Community Health Trust

North Lincolnshire Council and Primary Care Trust

Sheffield Council, the four Primary Care Trusts in Sheffield and Sheffield Children's NHS Trust

The City of York Council and Selby and York Primary Care Trust

### East Midlands

Leicester City Council, Leicester City West Primary Care Trust and Eastern Leicester Primary care Trust

Nottinghamshire County Council and the seven Primary Care Trusts

### East

Cambridgeshire County Council and Huntingdonshire Primary Care Trust

Essex County Council and Witham, Braintree and Halstead Care Trust

Hertfordshire County Council and North Hertfordshire and Stevenage Primary care Trust

### London

Bexley Council and Primary Care Trust

Croydon Council and Primary Care Trust

Ealing Council and Primary Care Trust

Greenwich Council and Primary Care Trust

Hammersmith & Fulham Council and Primary Care Trust

Redbridge Council and Primary Care Trust

Sutton Council and Sutton and Merton Primary Care Trust

Tower Hamlets Council and Primary Care Trust

### South-east

Brighton and Hove City Council and Primary Care Trust

Hampshire County Council and the seven Primary Care Trusts

Portsmouth City Council and Primary Care Trust

West Sussex County Council and the five West Sussex Primary Care Trusts

Wokingham Council and Primary Care Trust

### South-west

Devon County Council and the six Devon Primary Care Trusts

### West Midlands

Sandwell Council and the three Primary Care Trusts

Solihull Council and Primary Care Trust

Telford and Wrekin Council and Primary Care Trust

# Sure Start

*A cornerstone of the government's drive to eradicate child poverty in 20 years, and to halve it within 10, Sure Start aims to improve children's life opportunities by working with parents and parents-to-be in deprived areas and providing better access to family support, advice on nurturing, health services and early learning.*

## Sure Start Unit

**Address:** Department for Education and Skills and Department for Work and Pensions
Level 2, Caxton House, Tothill Street, London SW1H 9NA
**Tel:** 0870 000 2288
**E-mail:** info.surestart@dfes.gsi.gov.uk
**Web:** www.surestart.gov.uk

### Sure Start Central Team

**Address:** Level 2, Caxton House, Tothill Street, London SW1H 9NA
**E-mail:** firstname.lastname@dfes.gsi.gov.uk

Childminders and Home Childcarers: *Caroline Prichard*
Children's centres: *Richard Neville*
Children's Information Services: *Alan Lott*
Children's Learning: *Tim Afolabi*
Birth to Three Matters: Birth-to-3-Matters.MAILBOX@dfes.gsi.gov.uk
Communications: *Lucy Lloyd*
Community and inclusion: *Sabine Mittag*
Early Excellence Centres: *Linda Duberry*
Extended Schools: *Barbara Scorer*
Neighbourhood Nurseries: *Laurence Blackhall*
Nurseries, playgroups and capital strategy team: 34nurseryeducation.funding@dfes.gsi.gov.uk
Policy on national recruitment campaign: *Sarah Nairne or Alison Oakins*
Policy on recruitment and retention: *Clare Fowler*
Qualifications and Training: qualifications.training@dfes.gsi.gov.uk
Quality assurance: *Jerry O'Connell*
Research and evaluation: *James Haskings*
Standards: *Gerald Peebles-Brown*
School age children and business support: *Dervise Ali-Riza*

---

## East of England

### Sure Start Government Office
**East of England**
01223 372909
ahoulihan.go-east@go-regions.gsi.gov.uk
*Regional Manager: Anne Houlihan*

### Bedfordshire

**Sure Start Cauldwell**
01234 269512
sue.dissent@surestartcauldwell.co.uk
*Programme Manager: Sue Dessent*

## East Midlands

### Sure Start Government Office
**East Midlands**
0115 971 2652
pauline.jones@dfes.gsi.gov.uk
*Regional Manager: Pauline Jones*

### City of Derby

**Sure Start Osmaston/Allenton**
01332 715620
chris.tully@derby.gov.uk
*Programme Manager: Chris Tully*

**Sure Start Rosehill**
01332 717440
donna.brooks@derby.gov.uk
*Programme Manager: Donna Brooks*

**Sure Start Mackworth**
01332 346943
dsulley.surestart@tiscalli.co.uk
*Assistant Director: Debra Sulley*

**Sure Start Austin/Sunnyhill**
01332 718841/2/3
christine.smith-read@derby.gov.uk
*Programme Manager: Christine Smith-Read*

## Derbyshire

**Sure Start Chesterfield**
01246 283030
teresa.cresswell@chesterfieldpct.
nhs.uk
*Locality Health Promotion Co-
ordinator: Teresa Cresswell*

**Sure Start North East
Derbyshire**
01246 852228
rosie.kightley@derbyshire.gov.uk
*Programme Manager: Rosie
Kightley*

**Sure Start East Bolsover**
01623 588320
chriscaley.surestart@derbyshire.
gov.uk
*Acting Programme Manager: Chris
Caley*

**Sure Start Amber Valley**
01773 525099
stephanie.cook@ambervalley-
pct.nhs
*Contact: Stephanie Cook*

**Sure Start Erewash**
0115 909 8200
susanna.williams@derbyshire.
gov.uk
*Programme Manager: Susanna
Williams*

**Sure Start Ilkeston North and
Kirkhalls**
0115 909 8040
ulda.butler@derbyshire.gov.uk
*Service Manager: Ulda Butler*

## Leicester City

**Sure Start Beaumont Leys &
Stocking Farm**
0116 295 4550
surestartbl@lrh-tr.nhs.uk
*Programme Manager: Ann
Marshall*

**Sure Start St Mathews**
0116 242 6370
mel.meggs@surestart.leics.nhs.uk
*Programme Manager: Melanie
Meggs*

Sure Start Saffron
0116 283 2335
saffronsurestart@ukonline.co.uk
*Programme Manager: Lyn Price*

**Sure Start Braunstone**
0116 255 0525
enbss@post.nch.org.uk
*Programme Director: Deirdra
Cusak*

**Sure Start Highfields**
0116 254 8270
sram@nspcc.org.uk
*Programme Manager: Sumerjit Ram*

**Sure Start New Parks**
0116 231 4418
pauline.hinnit@barnardos.org.uk
*Scheme Co-ordinator: Pauline
Hinnit*

## Lincolnshire

**Sure Start Boston**
01205 314588
mary.parkin@boston.gov.uk
*Programme Co-ordinator: Mary
Parkin*

**Sure Start Birchwood**
01522 689991
carrieforrester@surestartbirchwo
od.co.uk
*Programme Manager: Carrie
Forrester*

**Sure Start East Lindsey Coastal
Ribbon**
01507 474411
surestart.elcr@ic24.net
*Programme Manager: Angela
Hickin*

**Sure Start Gainsborough**
01427 617767
debbie.barnes@surestart-
gains.org.uk
*Programme Manager: Debbie
Barnes*

**Sure Start Lincoln City North**
01522 544801
ensslcn@mail.nch.org.uk
*Programme Manager: Viv Siviter*

**Sure Start Lincoln Central**
ellie.hodgeon@westlincs.pct.nhs.uk
*Lead Contact: Ellie Hodgeon*

**Lincoln Mini Sure Start**
01476 406418
p.cameron@skdc.com
*Lead Contact: Paul Cameron*

## Northamptonshire

**Sure Start Corby**
01536 463950
corbysurestartproject@northamp
tonshire.gov.uk
*Project Manager: Bernie Caffrey*

**Sure Start Northampton**
01604 585219
aclouston@northamptonshire.
gov.uk
*Project Officer: Annie Clouston*

**Sure Start Kettering**
01536 311030
enssk@mail.nch.org.uk
*Programme Manager: Frank
McMahon*

**Sure Start Wellingborough**
01933 225587
enannew@mail.nch.org.uk
*Programme Director: Anne
Waterman*

## City of Nottingham

**Sure Start North West
Nottingham**
0115 929 0330
di.kingaby@nch.org.uk
*Programme Director: Di Kingaby*

**Sure Start St Ann's**
0115 934 5613 / 0115 912 1169
jean.pearson@nottinghamcity-
pct.nhs.uk
*Programme Director: Jean Pearson*

**Sure Start Sneinton**
0115 911 2995/2996
liz.lowe@nottinghamcity.gov.uk
*Programme Manager: Liz Lowe*

**Sure Start Aspley/ Bells Lane**
0115 970 6811
enssabl@mail.nch.org.uk
*Programme Manager: Karen Lunt*

**Sure Start Bestwood/ Leen
Valley**
0115 915 9152
lisa.elliker@tiscali.co.uk
*Programme Manager: Lisa Elliker*

**Sure Start Radford/ Hyson
Green**
0115 875 8880
phyllis.brackenbury@nottingham
city.gov.uk
*Programme Manager: Phyllis
Brackenbury*

**Sure Start The Meadows**
0115 915 3844
soniacakmak@nottinghamcity.
gov.uk
*Programme Manager: Sonia
Cakmak*

**Sure Start Bulwell**
0115 927 7992
jgsurestart@freeneasy.net
*Programme Manager: Jennie Garner*

## Nottinghamshire

**Sure Start Ashfield**
01623 723232
surestartash@aol.com
*Programme Manager: Karon Foulkes*

**Sure Start Mansfield Ravensdale**
01623 486982
trish.ross@nottscc.gov.uk
*Programme Manager: Trish Ross*

**Sure Start West Bassetlaw**
01909 735308
sure_start_wb@hotmail.com
*Programme Manager: Elaine McInnes*

**Sure Start Bilsthorpe, Blidworth & Clipstone**
01623 629203
sure.start@education.nottscc.gov.uk
*Programme Manager: Tony Richardson*

**Sure Start Meden Valley (Mansfield)**
01623 648537
jude.burgess@nottscc.gov.uk
*Programme Manager: Jude Burgess*

**Sure Start Gedling**
0115 993 1475
liz.hallam@gedling-pct.nhs.uk
*Programme Manager: Liz Hallam*

**Sure Start Chilwell West & Eastwood (Broxtowe)**
0115 875 4905
david.gilding@broxtowehucknall-pct.nhs.uk
*Community Development Co-ordinator: David Gilding*

**Sure Start West Mansfield**
01623 620700
westmansfield.surestart@virgin.net
*Programme Manager: Jill Shaw*

**Sure Start Sutton Central & Sutton West**
01623 559568
sylvia.wileman@ashfield-pct.nhs.uk
*Strategic Health Partnership Manager: Sylvia Wileman*

---

# London

**Sure Start Government Office London**
020 7217 3249
SureStart.GOL@go-regions.gsi.gov.uk
*Regional Manager: Lonica Vanclay*

## Barking and Dagenham

**Sure Start Thames View**
020 8270 6622
sadaf.mahmood@lbbd.gov.uk
*Programme Manager: Jean Haliday*

**Sure Start Marks Gate**
020 8227 3018
jane@caine.org.uk
*Programme Manager: Jayne Kane*

**Sure Start Abbey**
020 8227 3377
*Programme Manager: Tina Wilkins*

## Bexley

**Sure Start North Bexley**
020 8311 1974
mthompson.nbsurestart@virgin.net
*Programme Manager: Marion Thompson*

## Brent

**Sure Start Central Brent**
020 8451 4180
angelle.sscb@btconnect.com
*Programme Manager: Angelle Bryan*

**Sure Start South Kilburn**
020 7625 1490
jacinthsssk@aol.com
*Director: Jacinth Jeffers*

**Sure Start South Central Roundwood**
020 8214 1464
sure.start@ukonline.co.uk
*Director: Tajinder Nijjar*

## Bromley

**Sure Start Penge**
020 8676 0039
surestartpenge@btopenworld.com
*Programme Manager: Barbara O'Reilly*

## Camden

**Sure Start Euston**
020 7380 0333
laurence.pouliot@camden.gov.uk
*Programme Manager: Laurence Pouillont*

**Sure Start Kilburn Priory**
020 7974 1034
surestart.kilburnpriory@camden.gov.uk
*Programme Manager: Sue Summerbell*

**Sure Start Kentish Town East and West**
020 7974 8961
Ruth.Beecher@camden.gov.uk
*Programme Manager: Ruth Beecher*

**Sure Start Kings Cross & Holborn**
020 7520 0305
gillian@coram.org.uk
*Chief Executive: Gillian Pugh*

## Croydon

**Sure Start Broad Green**
020 8649 8441
surestart@croydonuk.freeserve.co.uk
*Programme Manager: Beverley Noble*

## Ealing

**Sure Start South Northolt**
020 8842 0220
amanda_hancock@btconnect.com
*Sure Start Manager: Kate Saunders*

**Sure Start South Acton & Acton Vale**
020 8993 4049
surestartacton@btconnect.com
*Programme Manager: Gwen Watkins*

## Enfield

**Sure Start Edmonton**
020 8350 5573
laxmi.jamdagni@enfield.gov.uk
www.surestartedmonton.org.uk/home.htm
*Programme Manager: Laxmi Jamdagni*

## Greenwich

**Greenwich Sure Start**
020 8850 6675
greenwichsurestart@compuserve.com
*Programme Manager: Pamela Bowman*

**Sure Start Woolwich Common Neighbourhood**
020 8921 6339
barbara.cannito@greenwich.gov.uk
*Programme Manager: Barbara Cannito*

**Sure Start Riverside & Glyndon**
020 8269 2540
valerie.green@greenwich.gov.uk
*Programme Manager: Valerie Green*

**Sure Start West Greenwich & Abbeywood**
020 8921 6161
julia.phillips@greenwich.gov.uk
*Programme Co-ordinator,*
*Corporate Support Unit: Christine*
*Cobham*

**Sure Start Charlton**
020 8921 2552
christine.cobham@greenwich.
gov.uk
*Temporary Programme Manager:*
*Christine Cobham*

## Hackney

**Sure Start Hackney,**
**Queensbridge & Dalston**
020 7254 7600
audrey@surestartqd.co.uk
*Programme Manager: Richard*
*Dejardins*

**Sure Start Stamford Hill**
020 8510 6502
diane.heywood@chpct.nhs.uk
*Programme Manager: Diane*
*Heywood*

**Sure Start Homerton & Wick**
020 8986 7343
cathy.turner@homerton.nhs.uk
*Programme Co-ordinator: Cathy*
*Turner*

**Sure Start Hoxton**
0800 587 7323
hoxton.surestart@blueyonder.co.uk
*Programme Manager: Anita Grant*

**Sure Start Woodberry Down**
020 8356 7415
tshortla@gw.hackney.gov.uk
*Children's and Women's Service*
*Manager: Lena Cadesse*

**Sure Start South Hackney/**
**Haggerston**
020 7739 6467
kaushika.surestart@virgin.net
*Programme Manager: Kaushika*
*Amin*

## Hammersmith and Fulham

**Sure Start Broadway/**
**Margravine**
020 8753 5774
Lucy.townsend@lbhf.gov.uk
*Programme Manager: Lucy*
*Townsend*

**Sure Start Coningham**
020 8740 2000
john.prentice@nch.org.uk
*Programme Manager: John Prentice*

**Sure Start South**
020 7736 5173
geraldine.finney@btopenworld.com
*Programme Manager: Geraldine*
*Finney*

## Haringey

**Sure Start West Green &**
**Chestnuts**
020 8442 6186 ext 4186
michael.craft@haringey.nhs.uk
*Area Programme Manager:*
*Michael Craft*

**Sure Start Roundway**
020 8885 6196
lingrist@chrysalisconsulting.com
*Programme Manager: Lin Grist*

**Sure Start Noel Park**
020 8489 2751
carol.law2@haringey.gov.uk
*Area Programme Manager: Carol*
*Law*

**Sure Start High Cross**
020 8885 6196
trudi.james@haringey.nhs.uk
*Area Programme Manager: Trudi*
*James*

**Sure Start Park Lane**
020 8885 6196
marion.scott@haringey.nhs.uk
*Temp Area Programme Manager:*
*Marion Scott*

## Havering

**Sure Start Hilldene & Gooshays**
01708 379826
david.woodhull@havering.gov.uk
*Programme Manager: David*
*Woodhull*

## Hillingdon

**Sure Start Townfield**
01895 277914
lpenson@hillingdon.gov.uk
*Programme Manager: Lorraine*
*Penson*

## Hounslow

**Sure Start Hounslow**
020 8570 8156
surestarthounslow@hotmail.com
*Programme Manager: Sharon*
*Walsh*

## Islington

**Sure Start Copenhagen**
020 7833 5832
surestartc.hagen@clara.co.uk
*Programme Manager: Vicki Eves*

**Sure Start Holloway**
020 7700 3402
*Programme Manager: Fiona Oliver*

**Sure Start Mildmay**
020 7527 5921
jan.pearson@islington.gov.uk
*Family Support Development*
*Manager: Jan Pearson*

**Sure Start Highview**
020 7704 0198
nicola@surestartmce.com
*Programme Manager: Garath Platt*

**Sure Start Hillmarton**
020 7527 5704
jenny.rathbone@islington.gov.uk
*Programme Manager: Jenny*
*Rathbone*

## Kensington and Chelsea

**Sure Start North West**
**Kensington**
020 7243 8237
jo.harrison@rbkc.gov.uk
*Programme Manager: Joanne*
*Harrison*

**Sure Start Goldbourne**
020 8960 4936
nandasirker@hotmail.com
*Programme Manager: Nanda*
*Sirker*

## Lambeth

**Sure Start Tulse Hill**
020 7926 9949
tkoci@lambeth.gov.uk
*Programme Manager: Tracy Koci*

**Sure Start Myatt's Field Angell**
**Town**
020 7737 9284
lindy.young@chsltr.sthames.nhs.
uk
*Programme Manager: Lindy Young*

**Sure Start Larkhall**
020 7737 2197
laura.mcfarlane@lambethpct.nhs.
uk
*Programme Manager: Laura*
*McFarlane*

**Sure Start Gipsy Hill**
020 8766 5860
kim.leeds@lambethpct.nhs.uk
*Programme Manager: Kim Leeds*

**Sure Start Stockwell**
020 7737 2197
clare.douglas@lambethpct.nhs.uk
*Programme Director: Clare*
*Douglas*

Sure Start Kennington
020 7735 2385
jondavies.sskennington@btconne
ct.com
*Programme Manager: Jon Davies*

## Lewisham

Sure Start Bellingham and
Grinling Gibbons
020 8698 5205
shirley.mucklow@lewishampct.
nhs.uk
*Programme Manager: Shirley
Mucklow*

Sure Start Honor Oak
020 8314 3873
angela.peart@lewisham.gov.uk
*Programme Manager: Angela Peart*

Evelyn Sure Start
020 8694 6894 ext 235
stell.babudoh@lewishampct.nhs.uk
*Programme Manager: Stella
Babudoh*

Sure Start Downham
020 8314 8530
lyn.may@lewisham.gov.uk
*Head of Early Years: Lyn May*

## Merton

Sure Start Lavender
020 8545 4069
asim.bhattacharyya@merton.gov.
uk
*Programme Manager: Asim
Bhattacharyya*

## Newham

Sure Start North Canning Town
020 7476 9591
naila.qureshi@newham.gov.uk
*Programme Manager: Naila
Qureshi*

Sure Start Little Ilford
020 8553 2346
janine.hunter@newham.gov.uk
*Programme Manager: Janine
Hunter*

Sure Start Carpenters Three
Mills
020 8555 0231
clare.potter@newham.gov.uk
*Programme Manager: Claire Potter*

North Woolwich Sure Start
Centre
020 7473 3728
jaine.stannard@newham.gov.uk
*Programme Manager: Jaine
Stannard*

Sure Start Newtown and Park
020 8555 0231
raymond.wood@newham.gov.uk
*Programme Manager: Raymond
Wood*

Sure Start Plashet (St
Stephens)
020 8503 5217
zahida.lone@newham.gov.uk
*Programme Manager: Zahida Lone*

Sure Start South Canning Town
020 8430 6188
helen.warburton@newham.gov.uk
*Programme Manager: Helen
Warburton*

Sure Start Vicarage
020 8470 3515
*Temporary Programme Manager:
Sarita Badhan*

## Redbridge

Sure Start Loxford
020 8514 3128
roger.truelove@barnardos.org.uk
*Programme Manager: Roger Truelove*

## Southwark

Sure Start Southwark
Aylesbury Plus
020 7771 3967/3978
Kate.Miranda@chsltr.sthames.
nhs.uk
*Programme Director: Kate
Miranda*

Sure Start East Peckham
020 7635 7428
nita.rogers@southwarkpct.nhs.uk
*Programme Director: Nita Rogers*

Sure Start Brunswick
020 7277 3844
*Programme Manager: Leonardo
Greco*

Sure Start West Bermondsey
020 7771 3914
barbara.hills@southwarkpct.nhs.uk
*Programme Manager: Barbara Hills*

Sure Start West Peckham
020 7771 3839
jacqui.mccalla@southwarkpct.nh
s.uk
*Programme Manager: Jacqui
McCalla*

Sure Start Rotherhithe
020 7771 3518
Russell.Garnham@southwarkpct.
nhs.uk
*Programme Manager: Russell
Garnham*

## Tower Hamlets

Sure Start On The Ocean
020 7791 3049/2976
sabes.sugunasabesan@thpct.nh
s.uk
*Programme Co-ordinator: Sabes
Sugunasabesan*

Sure Start Teviot & Chrisp
Street
020 7517 9574
allie.nolan@thpct.nhs.uk
*Programme Manager: Allie Nolan*

Sure Start Weavers and
Spitalfields
020 7247 3430
jo.fisher@thpct.nhs.uk
*Programme Manager: Jo Fisher*

Sure Start Around Poplar
020 7364 6089
geefeng.tan@nhs.net
*Programme Manager: Gee Feng
Tan*

Sure Start Shadwell
020 7702 4196
meena.hoque@nhs.net
*Programme Manager: Meena
Hoque*

Sure Start Collingwood &
Stepney
020 7791 0462
sandra.cater@nhs.net
*Programme Manager: Sandra
Cater*

## Waltham Forest

Sure Start St James
020 8496 2442
Surestart_stjames@hotmail
*Programme Manager: Jay
Hamilton-Taylor*

Sure Start North Leyton
020 8558 8421
graham.cobb@nleytonsurestart.c
o.uk
*Programme Manager: Graham Cobb*

Sure Start Higham High
020 8531 4072
sharon.foster@highamhillsurestar
t.co.uk
www.highamhillsurestart.co.uk
*Programme Manager: Sharon
Foster*

Sure Start Cinch
020 8503 0798
anna.rinaldi@btconnect.com
*Programme Manager: Anna
Rinaldi*

## Wandsworth

### Sure Start Battersea
020 7223 3509
pam.byfield@surestartbattersea.gov.uk
*Programme Co-ordinator: Pam Byfield*

### Sure Start Roehampton
020 8871 8704
sforester@wandsworth.gov.uk
*Programme Manager: Sarah Forester*

## Westminster

### Sure Start Church Street
020 7479 8763
jayne.vertkin@westminster-pct.nhs.uk
*Programme Manager: Jayne Vertkin*

### Sure Start Queens Park
surestartqp@fsu.org.uk
*Interim Programme Manager: Chrissie Kravechenko*

### Sure Start South Westminster
020 7828 4083
rsatchell@westminster.gov.uk
*Programme Manager: Rob Satchell*

---

## North-east

### Sure Start Government Office North East
0191 202 3750
jmoules.gone@go-regions.gsi.gov.uk
*Regional Manager: Jayne Moules*

## Darlington

### Sure Start Central Darlington
01325 487718
pauline.murray@darlington.gov.uk
*Lead Contact: Pauline Murray*

### Together Sure Start Darlington
01325 488176
lynne.henderson@darlington.gov.uk
*Programme Manager: Lynne Henderson*

## Durham County

### Sure Start Peterlee
0191 587 8623/586 8382
Brian.brown@durham.gov.uk
*Programme Manager: Brian Brown*

### Sure Start Stanley
01207 232048
malcolm.pitt@surestartstanley.org.uk
www.surestartstanley.org.uk
*Programme Manager: Malcolm K Pitt*

### Sure Start Ferryhill & Chilton
01740 658080
cdawson@sedgefield.gov.uk
www.durhamweb.org.uk/surestart
*Regeneration Manager: Carol Dawson*

### Sure Start Wear Valley (South Bishop and Auckland)
01388 665665
carol.newsom@durham.gov.uk
www.wear-surestart.org
*Programme Manager: Carol Newsom*

### Sure Start Chester-le-Street
0191 387 5907
surestart@chesterlestreet3.freeserve.co.uk
*Programme Manager: Christine Forrester*

### Sure Start Seaham
0191 513 1590
nesueh@mail.nch.org.uk
*Programme Manager: Sue Howe*

### Sure Start Brandon and Deerness Valley
0191 373 4844
susan.joicey@durham.gov.uk
*Programme Manager: Diane Jones*

### Sure Start Horden & Easington Colliery
0191 586 6681
wendy.robinson@easingtonpct.nhs.uk
*Programme Manager: Wendy Robinson*

### Sure Start Wear Valley East
01388 746740
Jo-ann.turnbull@smtp.sdhc-tr.northy.nhs.uk
*Programme Manager: Fiona Callaghan*

### Sure Start West Derwentside
01207 570396
allison.underwood@durham.gov.uk
*Programme Manager: Allison Underwood*

### Sure Start Teesdale
01833 696506
gillian.quille@durhamdalespct.nhs.uk
*Programme Manager: Gillian Quille*

### Sure Start Shildon and Newton Aycliffe West
01388 777613
jpope@sedgefield.gov.uk
*Programme Manager: Julia Pope*

## Gateshead

### Sure Start Blaydon Winlaton
0191 414 7701
HelenCairns@gateshead.gov.uk
*Programme Manager: Helen Cairns*

### Sure Start Leam Lane
0191 433 6000
Jeanetteharold@Gateshead.Gov.uk
*Programme Manager: Jeanette Harold*

### Sure Start Felling
0191 482 4133 ext 125
carolynjameson@gateshead.gov.uk
*Early Years and Childcare Manager: Carolyn Jameson*

### Sure Start Deckham
0191 482 4133 ext 117
p.stephens@education.gatesheadmbc.gov.uk
*Early Years and Childcare Manager: Pamela Stephens*

## Hartlepool

### Sure Start Hartlepool
01429 292444
linda.bantoft@hartlepool.gov.uk
*Programme Manager: Linda Bantoft*

### Sure Start North Hartlepool
01429 292555
margaret.holdforth@hartlepool.gov.uk
*Programme Manager: Margaret Holdforth*

### Sure Start Hartlepool Central
01429 285137
*Programme Manager: Gill Butler*

## Middlesbrough

### Sure Start Abingdon
01642 249595
bernie_ineichen@middlesbrough.gov.uk
*Temporary Contact: Bernie Ineichen*

### Sure Start Thorntree & Brambles Farm
01642 232809
di.pollitt@middlesborough.gov.uk
*Early Years and Childcare Manager: Di Pollitt*

**Sure Start Berwick Hills, Pallister & Park End**
01642 232261
jacqui_callaghan@middlesbrough.gov.uk
*Programme Manager: Jacqui Callaghan*

**Sure Start Beechwood, Easterside & Grove Hills**
01642 323596
john_keelty@middlesbrough.gov.uk
*Programme Manager: John Keelty*

**Sure Start Hemlington and Newham**
01642 576472
lynn_lang@middlesbrough.gov.uk
*Programme Manager: Lynn Lang*

## Newcastle Upon Tyne

**Sure Start Westgate**
0191 272 7824
lin.simmonds@newcastle.gov.uk
*Programme Manager: Lin Simmonds*

**Sure Start Newcastle East and Fossway**
0191 234 5563/209 1622
Sian.bufton@barnardos.org.uk
*Contact: Sian Bufton*

**Sure Start Cowgate & Blakelaw**
0191 214 2460
neanne@mail.nch.org.uk
*Programme Manager: Ann Armstrong*

**Sure Start Armstrong**
0191 226 0754
all@riversidechp.ssnet.co.uk
*Contact: Sarah Hunter*

**Sure Start Newbiggin Hall**
0191 219 4840
paul.court@ncht.northy.nhs.uk
*Programme Manager: Paul Court*

**Sure Start Blyth & Cramlington**
0191 240 4800
roy.hughes@barnardos.org.uk
*Assistant Director Children's Services: Roy Hughes*

**Sure Start North Moor**
0191 213 4100
julie.dawson@newcastle.gov.uk
*Temporary Co-ordinator: Julie Dawson*

## North Tyneside

**Sure Start Howdon**
0191 200 1333/6666
Janette.Brown@northtyneside.gov.uk
*Programme Manager: Janette Brown*

**Sure Start Shiremoor/Killingworth**
0191 200 8244/8243
jeanette.raper@northtyneside.gov.uk
*Programme Manager: Jeanette Raper*

## Northumberland

**Sure Start Bedlington & Scotland Gate**
01670 822714
pmead@northumberland.gov.uk
*Programme Manager: Paula Mead*

**Sure Start Blyth**
01670 797890
Rpilling@northumberland.gov.uk
*Project Manager: Russell Pilling*

**Sure Start Berwick**
01289 309735
jcasson@northumberland.gov.uk
*Programme Manager: Jan Casson*

**Sure Start Ashington**
01670 819988
nessa@mail.nch.org.uk
*Programme Manager: Gill Physick*

**ABC Sure Start**
01670 735546
surestart.abc@barnardos.org.uk
*Programme Manager: Julie McVeigh*

## Redcar & Cleveland

**Sure Start East Cleveland**
01287 644200
Surestart.ec@ukonline.co.uk
*Programme Manager: Julie Conner*

**Sure Start Redcar & Cleveland**
01642 835055
Grangetownsouthbank_surestart@redcar-cleveland.gov.uk
*Programme Manager: Catherine Pickering*

**Sure Start West Redcar**
01642 485538
westredcar_surestart@redcar-cleveland.gov.uk
*Programme Manager: Vanessa Newlands*

**Sure Start Redcar Coast and Dormanstown**
01642 296498
surestart_redcar_coast@redcar-cleveland.gov.uk
*Programme Manager: Fran White*

## South Tyneside

**Sure Start All Saints and Bede and Rekendyke**
0191 427 4641/4500
jane.deacon@s-tyneside-mbc.gov.uk
*Assistant Programme Manager: Andrea Smith*

**Sure Start Primrose**
0191 427 4615
andrea.hardy@s-tyneside-mbc.gov.uk
*Programme Manager: Andrea Hardy*

**Sure Start Beacon & Bents and Biddick Hall Estate**
0191 427 4716
maureens@s-tyneside-mbc.gov.uk
*Programme Manager: Maureen Sheekey*

## Stockton-on-Tees

**Sure Start Hardwick, Mile House & Roseworth**
01642 393590
Barbara.brookes@stockton.gov.uk
*Programme Manager: Barbara Brookes*

**Sure Start Newtown, Portrack & Tilery**
01642 675552
Janet.seddon@stockton.gov.uk
*Programme Manager: Janet Seddon*

**Sure Start Mandale Village and Stainsby**
01642 675892
laura@familycentre.sagehost.co.uk
*Programme Manager: Laura Provett*

**Sure Start Parkfield & Victoria**
01642 415752
Kim.staff@stockton.gov.uk
*Sure Start Manager: Kim Staff*

**Sure Start Billingham**
01642 3977332
claire.silvers@stockton.gov.uk
*Programme Manager: Claire Silvers*

## Sunderland

**Sure Start North Washington**
0191 219 3995
Rachel.Putz@ssd.sunderland.gov.uk
*Programme Manager: Rachel Putz*

**Sure Start Thorney Close**
0191 553 4127
gillian.patterson@ssd.sunderland
.gov.uk
*Programme Manager: Gillian
Patterson*

**Sure Start Greater Southwick**
0191 549 2631
kate.hinchliffe@ssd.sunderland.
gov.uk
*Programme Manager: Kate
Hinchliffe*

**Sure Start Monument**
0191 382 3087
Phil.hayden@ssd.sunderland.
gov.uk
*Programme Manager: Phil Hayden*

**Sure Start Ford**
0191 553 4001
Janet.Newton@ssd.sunderland.
gov.uk
*Contact: Janet Newton*

**Sure Start Sunderland North
West**
0191 516 4080
geraldine.dowling@ssd.sunderlan
d.gov.uk
*Programme Manager: Geraldine
Dowling*

**Sure Start Hetton/ Houghton**
0191 553 4001
nikki.crowley@ssd.sunderland.
gov.uk
*Programme Manager: Nikki
Crowley*

## North-west

**Sure Start Government Office
North West**
0161 952 4479
kmajid.gonw@go-regions.gsi.
gov.uk
*General queries: Karim Majid*

### Blackburn with Darwen

**Sure Start Sudell and Central;
Blackburn, Mill Hill and
Livesey; Audley & Queen's
Park; Shadsworth and
Whitebirk**
01254 585526
liz.fraser@blackburn.gov.uk
surestart.blackburnworld.com
*Strategic Head: Liz Fraser*

**Sure Start Blackburn West**
01254 263631
christine.dixon@montague-
hc.nhs.uk
*Programme Manager: Christine
Dixon*

### Blackpool

**Sure Start Mereside & Clifton**
01253 694446/470800
ian.currie@blackpool.gov.uk
*Programme Manager: Ian Currie*

**Sure Start Grange Park**
01253 476488
josette.rees@blackpool.gov.uk
*Programme Manager: Josette
Pullan*

**Sure Start Talbot & Brunswick**
01253 473641
carole.sharrock@blackpoolpct.
nhs.uk
*Programme Manager: Jackie
Robinson*

### Bolton

**Sure Start Haliwell**
01204 337090
sylvia.ashworth@bolton.gov.uk
*Programme Manager: Sylvia
Ashworth*

**Sure Start Great Lever**
01204 337090
*Operations Manager: Jayne Brazil*

**Sure Start Greater Farnworth
and Rumworth**
01204 337080
julie.stones@bolton.gov.uk
*Programme Manager: Julie Stones*

### Bury

**Sure Start Redvales**
0161 253 6186
s.a.myers@bury.gov.uk
*Project Manager: Sue Myers*

### Cheshire

**Sure Start Ellesmere Port**
0151 355 2168
turnockr@cheshire.gov.uk
*Programme Manager: Ric Turnock*

**Sure Start Blacon**
01244 398644
paula@surestartblacon.info
www.surestartblacon.info
*Programme Manager: Paula
Worthington*

**Sure Start Crewe**
01270 253431
anna@surestartcrewe.org.uk
www.surestartcrewe.org.uk
*Programme Manager: Wendy
Whittaker*

**Sure Start Winsford (Vale Royal)**
01606 815696
surestartwin@valeroyal.gov.uk
*Programme Manager: Marilyn
Houston*

### Cumbria

**Sure Start Whitehaven**
01946 62681
ann.chambers@howgill-
centre.co.uk
www.howgill-centre.co.uk
*Programme Manager: Ann
Chambers*

**Sure Start Barrow**
01229 871480
selwyn.wright@surestart.barrow.
org.uk
*Programme Co-ordinator: Selwyn
Wright*

**Sure Start West Allerdale**
01900 819190
sswa@btconnect.com
*Programme Manager: Gordon
Henry*

**Carlisle South Sure Start
Programme**
01228 625937
Lyndah@carlisle-city.gov.uk
*Programme Manager: Lynda
Hassall*

**Sure Start Ormsgill & North
Walney**
01229 837160
alison.morgan@mbpct.nhs.uk
*Director: Alison Morgan*

### Halton

**Sure Start Widnes**
0151 420 5482
eileen Stein@halton-borough.
gov.uk
*Programme Co-ordinator: Eileen
Stein*

**Sure Start Runcorn**
01928 573265
rita.ward@halton-borough.gov.uk
*Project Manager: Rita Ward*

**Sure Start Dino Runcorn**
01928 797160
nwssdr@mail.nch.org.uk
*Programme Manager: Kate
McPoland*

**Sure Start New Steps Widnes**
0151 424 7527
barbara.wurburton@halton-
borough.gov.uk
*Programme Co-ordinator: Barbara*
*Warburton*

**Jolly Giraffe (Sure Start)**
nwssjj@mail.nch.org.uk
*Programme Manager: Tracey Dean*

## Knowsley

**Sure Start Knowsley**
0151 489 4908
breeda.mcquillan@barnardos.
org.uk
*Project Manager: Breeda*
*McQuillan*

**Sure Start Knowsley -**
**Northwood**
0151 443 3257
childcare@merseyrail.com
*Programme Manager: Ruth*
*Kennedy*

**Sure Start Halewood**
0151 443 2191
gerry.allen@knowsley.gov.uk
*Programme Manager: Gerry Allen*

**Sure Start Towerhill**
0151 443 5657
towerhill.surestart@knowsley.gov.uk
*Acting Programme Manager:*
*Alistair Scott*

**Sure Start Whiston & Preston**
**East**
0151 426 1576
shirley.jones@knowsley.gov.uk
www.knowsleychildren.org.uk
*Programme Manager: Shirley Jones*

## Lancashire

**Sure Start Bradley & Whitefield**
01282 606333
helen.mountford@ed.lancscc.
gov.uk
*Programme Manager: Helen*
*Mountford*

**Sure Start Daneshouse and**
**Stoneyholme**
01282 714125
surestart@sallykay.fsnet.co.uk
www.surestart-
daneshouse.co.uk
*Programme Manager: Sally Kay*

**Sure Start Bacup and**
**Sacksteads**
01706 871740
surestartbacup@hotmail.com
www.surestartbs.co.uk
*Programme Manager: Michaela*
*Franchioli*

**Sure Start Ribbleton**
01772 655789
shirley.johnson@ed.lancscc.gov.uk
*Programme Manager: Shirley*
*Johnson*

**Sure Start Hyndburn and**
**Accrington South**
01254 387757
surestarthyndburn1@btinternet.
com
*Programme Manager: Ann-Marie*
*Foster*

**Sure Start North Lancaster**
01524 382818
surestartlancaster.lcc@btinternet.
com
*Programme Manager: Elaine*
*Clinton*

**Sure Start Tanhouse & Digmoor**
**- West Lancashire**
01695 716819
alan.johnstone@westlancsdc.
gov.uk
*Programme Manager: Alan*
*Johnstone*

**Sure Start Fishwick & St**
**Matthews**
01772 663130
jane.lloyd@ed.lancscc.gov.uk
*Programme Manager: Jane Lloyd*

**Sure Start Fleetwood**
01253 303130
*Programme Manager: Richard*
*Kerans*

**Sure Start Duke Bar, Burnley**
**Wood**
01282 714186
nwssdbbw@mail.nch.org.uk
*Programme Manager: Terri*
*Hacking*

**Sure Start Preston West**
01772 727032
julie.warburton@ed.lancscc.gov.uk
*Programme Manager: Julie*
*Warburton*

**Sure Start Preston East**
01773 563969
*Programme Manager: Christine*
*Campbell*

**Sure Start Preston Central**
01772 516421
h.walsh@preston.gov.uk
*Programme Manager: Helen Walsh*

**Sure Start South West Burnley**
07734 165641
nwmegand@mail.nch.org.uk
*Programme Manager: Megan*
*Dumpleton*

**Sure Start Brierfield &**
**Walverden**
01282 726004
ann.crichton1@virgin.net
*Programme Manager: Ann*
*Crichton*

## Liverpool

**Sure Start Speke**
0151 425 4028
susan@surestartspeke.org
www.surestartspeke.org
*Programme Manager: Susan*
*Roberts*

**Sure Start West Everton and**
**Breckfield**
0151 233 1969
annette.james@liverpool.gov.uk
www.surestart-web.org.uk
*Programme Manager: Annette*
*James*

**Sure Start Granby**
0151 707 6406
duane.chong2@liverpool.gov.uk
*Project Co-ordinator: Duane Chong*

**Sure Start Kensington**
0151 233 6165
careyl@hope.ac.uk
*Programme Manager: Lyn Carey*

**Sure Start Liverpool East**
0151 906 6806
chambef@hope.ac.uk
*Programme Manager: Fiona*
*Chambers*

**Sure Start Norris Green**
0151 233 4602
sally.croughan@liverpool.gov.uk
*Programme Co-ordinator:*
*Sallyann Croughan*

**Sure Start Picton & Smithdown**
0151 706 6056
alexsorngaard@hotmail.com
*Neighbourhood Services Co-*
*ordinator: Alex Soongaard*

**Sure Start Vauxhall**
0151 298 1544
*Programme Co-ordinator: Marie*
*McGiveron*

Sure Start Netherley Valley
0151 498 4408
nvci.4@virgin.net
*Contact: Diane Severs*

## Manchester

Sure Start Benchill and
Woodhouse Park
0161 998 7280
deborah.rees@barnardos.org.uk
*Programme Manager: Deborah
Rees*

Sure Start Clayton
0161 223 3777
k.wareham@notes.manchester.
gov.uk
*Programme Manager: Kate
Wareham*

Sure Start Longsight
0161 224 1990
surestart@thebiglifecompany.com
*Project Manager: Emma Perry*

Sure Start Lightbowne and
Harpurhey
0161 254 7702
c.allison@notes.manchester.
gov.uk
*Programme Co-ordinator: Cate
Allison*

Sure Start Manchester Central
(Miles and Ancoats)
0161 277 8550
mark@fergusson8.fsnet.co.uk
*Programme Manager: Mark
Ferguson*

Sure Start Cheetham
0161 277 8819
s.benjamins@notes.manchester.
gov.uk
www.surestartcheetham.info
*Programme Manager: Sarah
Benjamins*

Sure Start Moss Side,
Rusholme Fallowfield
0161 232 5487/5480
pcarey@surestart1.freeserve.co.uk
*Programme Manager: Patsy Carey*

Sure Start Newton Heath
0161 205 7402
mcrsecretary@hotmail.com
*Contact: Melanie McGuiness*

Sure Start Hyde Road
0161 272 8055
*Programme Manager: Sheila Bowater*

## Oldham

Sure Start Oldham
0161 633 8417
diane.beacroft@barnardos.org.uk
*Programme Manager: Diane
Beacroft*

Sure Start Westwood and
Coldhurst
0161 626 0536
ecs.paveen.yaqub@oldham.
gov.uk
*Programme Co-ordinator: Paveen
Yaqub*

Sure Start Werneth Freehold &
St Johns
0161 785 0239
alisonj@oldham.nhs.uk
*Programme Co-ordinator: Alison
Jones*

Sure Start Glodwick St Mary's
and Higginshaw
0161 622 6613
andreaf@oldham.nhs.uk
*Programme Manager: Andrea Fallon*

## Rochdale

Sure Start Castlemere,
Deeplish & Newbold
01706 647959
karen.buckley@zen.co.uk
*Project Manager: Karen Buckley*

Sure Start Belfield, Hamer &
Waddleworth
01706 656060
annemarie.bocock@zen.co.uk
*Project Manager: Anne-Marie Bocock*

Sure Start Langley Hollins
0161 653 9526
donna.stockton@zen.co.uk
*Project Manager: Donna Stockton*

Sure Start Kirkholt, Turfhill &
Wellfield
01706 653677
surestart.kirkholt@zen.co.uk
*Project Manager: Kim Brogan*

Sure Start Heywood
01706 622473
surestart.heywood@zen.co.uk
*Progamme Manager: Nasreen
Mennen*

## Salford

Sure Start Seedley, Langworthy
& Precinct Locality
0161 212 4454
tim.littlemore@salford-pct.nhs.uk
*Programme Manager: Tim
Littlemore*

Sure Start Winton and Peel
Green
0161 212 5910
francean.doyle@salford-
pct.nhs.uk
*Programme Manager: Francean
Doyle*

Sure Start Broughton
0161 833 0495 ext 115
dave.fraser@salford-pct.nhs.uk
*Programme Manager: Dave Fraser*

Sure Start Ordsall & Blackfriars
0161 833 0495 ext 115
maureen.lamb@salford-
pct.nhs.uk
*Programme Manager: Maureen
Lamb*

Sure Start Little Hulton
0161 736 8991
*Programme Manager: Paul Walsh*

## Sefton

Sure Start Seaforth & Bootle;
Litherland, Bootle & Dell &
Orrell
0151 920 4389
ceri.daniews@surestartsefton.
org.uk
*Programme Co-ordinator: Ceri
Daniels*

Sure Start Southport
0151 920 0726
seftoncvs@aol.com
*Deputy Chief Executive: Nigel
Bellamy*

Sure Start Netherton
0151 920 0726
claire@seftoncvs.fsnet.co.uk
*Family Support Co-ordinator:
Claire Rogers*

## St Helens

Sure Start Parr
01744 614340
surestartparr@tinyworld.co.uk
*Programme Director: Ruth
Passman*

Sure Start Fourways
01744 678026
surestartfourways@sthelens.
gov.uk
*Senior Inspector/ SEN: Andy
Hough*

Happy Elephants (Sure Start)
01744 813100
sure-start-happy-
elephant@childrensociety.org.uk
*Programme Manager: Ros Polding*

**Sure Start Central Link**
01744 25886
nwjackl@mail.nch.org.uk
*Programme Manager: Jackie Lowe*

**Sure Start Phoenix**
01744 614340
surestartparr@tinyworld.co.uk
*Programme Manager: Gill Eaves*

## Stockport

**Sure Start Adswood & Bridgehall**
0161 482 4906
delia.koczwara@stockport-pct.nhs.uk
*Project Co-ordinator: Delia Koczwara*

## Tameside

**Sure Start Hattersley**
0161 882 9630
geraldine.buckley@surestart.hdt.org.uk
*Programme Manager: Geraldine Buckley*

**Sure Start Ashton**
0161 339 1373
lynn.barber@exchange.tgcps-tr.nrwest.nhs.uk
*Programme Manager: Lynn Barber*

**Sure Start Hyde**
0161 366 5294
vicky.cuddy@tameside.gov.uk
*Programme Manager: Vicky Cuddy*

**Sure Start St Peters**
0161 304 5424
janet_thomas@tamesideandglossop.nhs.uk
*Contact: Janet Thomas*

## Trafford

**Sure Start Partington & Carrington**
0161 777 8437
jenny.chitryn@trafford.gov.uk
*Programme Manager: Jenny Chitryn*

## Warrington

**Westy Sure Start**
01925 637611
lbromley@warrington.gov.uk
*Programme Manager: Lysa Bromley*

**Sure Start North Warrington**
01928 656579
bcadwallader@warrington.gov.uk
*Programme Manager: Bruce Cadwallader*

## Wigan

**Sure Start Hindley/ Hindley Green**
01942 776106
Antonia.Hayes@wiganmbc.gov.uk
*Programme Co-ordinator: Antonia Hayes*

**Sure Start Shakerley/ Tyldesley**
01942 705269
a.winnard@wiganmbc.gov.uk
*Head of Economic Development: Angela Winnard*

## Wirral

**Sure Start Birkenhead North**
0151 651 1190
rosecurtis@wirral.gov.uk
*Programme Manager: Rosemary Curtis*

**Sure Start Ferries**
0151 644 5500
cstewart@surestartferries.org
*Programme Manager: Craig Stewart*

**Sure Start Birkenhead Central**
0151 647 1676
surestart@birkenheadcentral.fsnet.co.uk
*Programme Manager: Kath Shaughnessy*

**Sure Start Wallasey**
0151 291 3291
careym@hope.ac.uk
*Contact: Dr Martin Carey*

---

# South-east

**Sure Start Government Office South East**
01483 882456
sbrivio.gose@go-regions.gsi.gov.uk
*Regional Manager: Stephanie Brivio*

## Brighton & Hove

**Sure Start Central Seafront**
01273 320900
headquarters@surestart-brightonandhove.org.uk
*Programme Manager: Stephen Bell*

**Sure Start Hollingdean**
01273 295225
david.nicholls@brighton-gove.gov.uk
*Programme Manager: David Nicholls*

## East Sussex

**Sure Start Ore Valley**
01424 448143
liz.surestarthastings@virgin.net
*Programme Manager: Liz Abi-Aad*

**Sure Start Hailsham East**
01323 444870
stella.surestart@hailshameast.co.uk
*Programme Manager: Stella Edmonds*

**Sure Start St Leonards**
01424 460112
veronica@nch-se.fsnet.co.uk
*Programme Manager: Veronica Lock*

**Sure Start Bexhill & Sidley**
01424 735635
richard.watson@bar-pct.nhs.uk
*Programme Manager: Richard Watson*

**Sure Start Eastbourne**
01323 732696
carol.roberts@eastbourne.gov.uk
www.eastbourne.surestart.org
*Programme Manager: Carol Roberts*

## Hampshire

**Sure Start Leigh Park**
023 9242 4980
sarah.lamburne@havant.gov.uk
*Programme Manager: Sarah Lamburne*

**Sure Start Rowner**
023 9251 3777
surestartrowner@btconnect.com
*Programme Manager: Barbara Higgins*

## Isle of Wight

**Sure Start Ryde**
01983 568972
surestart_ryde@btinternet.com
*Programme Manager: Sue Erridge*

## Kent

**Sure Start Millmead**
01843 280555
surestart@millmead.freeserve.co.uk
*Programme Manager: Frances Rehal*

**Sure Start Dover**
01304 216293
surestartdover@hotmail.com
*Programme Director: Jayne Meyer*

**Sure Start Folkestone**
01303 298208/ 0800 389 4260
admin@surestartfolkestone.co.uk
*Programme Manager: Sylvia Scott*

**Sure Start Sheerness**
01795 667070
surestart@sssheerness.demon.
co.uk
*Programme Manager: John Fowler*

**Sure Start Ashford**
01223 641156
info@surestart-ashford.co.uk
*Programme Manager: Allan
Collado*

**Sure Start Dartford**
01322 276317
surestartdart@btconnect.com
*Sure Start Director: Sue Gates*

**Sure Start Gravesham**
01474 357569
graveshamsurestart@hotmail.com
*Programme Manager: Hayley
Cann*

**Sure Start Margate**
01843 224119
surestartmargate@tesco.net
*Programme Director: Lynn
Jackson*

**Sure Start Canterbury**
01227 795050
jayne.macdonald@ekentha.nhs.uk
*Primary Care Development
Manager: Jayne MacDonald*

**Medway**

**Sure Start Chatham**
01634 336603
michelle.ford@medway.gov.uk
www.medwayppn.org
*Programme Director: Michelle Ford*

**Milton Keynes**

**Sure Start Milton Keynes**
01908 322970
semkss@mail.nch.org.uk
*Temporary Programme Manager:
Linda Farthing*

**Oxfordshire**

**Sure Start Rose Hill - Littlemore**
01865 716739
tanlea@sure-start.co.uk
*Programme Director: Tan Lea*

**Portsmouth**

**Sure Start Somerstown**
023 9282 1816
jillfitzgerald@portsmouthcc.gov.uk
*Programme Manager: Jill
Fitzgerald*

**ABC Portsmouth (Sure Start)**
023 9289 9742
dbaxendale@portsmouthcc.gov.
uk
*Head of Portsmouth Regeneration:
Dawn Baxendale*

**Reading**

**Sure Start Whitley**
0118 901 5780
steve.green@reading.gov.uk
*Programme Director: Steve Green*

**Slough**

**Sure Start Britwell-
Northborough**
01753 693599
dianne.fletcher@berkshire.nhs.uk
*Programme Director: Dianne
Fletcher*

**Southampton**

**Sure Start Weston**
023 8043 7866
a.kelly@surestartweston.org.uk
*Programme Manager: Amanda
Kelly*

**Sure Start Central**
023 8033 1635
catherine.white@southampton.
gov.uk
*Project Manager (Services): Simon
Dennison*

**Sure Start Millbrook, Redbridge
and Maybush**
023 8052 8526
susan.thompson@southampton.
gov.uk
*Programme Manager: Sue
Thompson*

**West Sussex**
Sure Start Littlehampton
01903 725848
stuart@thewireproject.com
*Programme Manager: Stuart
Fairweather*

**Sure Start Crawley**
01293 895245
Chris.Scanes@westsussex.gov.uk
*Programme Manager: Chris Scanes*

**South-west**

**Sure Start Government Office
South West**
0117 900 1836
cbenjamin.gosw@go-regions.
gsi.gov.uk
*Regional Manager: Cathy Benjamin*

**Bournemouth**

**Sure Start Bournemouth**
01202 593086
swssb@mail.nch.org.uk
*Programme Manager: Phil D'Eath*

**Bristol**

**Sure Start Knowle West**
0117 903 9781
lil_bowers@bristol-city.gov.uk
*Programme Manager: Lil Bowers*

**Sure Start Hartcliffe, Highridge
& Withywood**
0117 903 0460
margaret.boushel@barnardos.
org.uk
*Programme Manager: Margaret
Boushel*

**Sure Start Easton**
0117 941 3400
info@surestarteaston.org.uk
*Programme Manager: Kim Smith*

**Sure Start Kingsweston**
0117 968 3846
surestart.kingsweston@barnardos
.org.uk
*Programme Manager: Susan Russell*

**Cornwall**

**Sure Start Lescudjack**
01736 334856
enquiries@lescudjack.org.uk
*Project Director: Deborah Tredgett*

**Sure Start Trevu**
01209 610123
jscillitoe@cornwall.gov.uk
*Temporary Programme Manager:
Jarvine Scillitoe*

**Sure Start China Clay**
01726 627821
ann.vandyke@centralpct.cornwall
.nhs.uk
*Programme Manager: Ann Van
Dyke*

**Sure Start Pebbles**
01326 213090
jane@surestart-pebbles.org.uk
*Programme Manager: Jane Acton*

**Sure Start Portheyl**
01736 756267
caroline@portheyl.co.uk
*Programme Manager: Caroline
Willis*

**Sure Start North Cornwall**
01840 214214
swssnc@mail.nch.org.uk
*Programme Manager: Alison
Gardner*

**Sure Start Chycarn**
01736 350100
surestartchycarn@btconnect.com
*Programme Manager: Jill Hughes*

## Devon

**Sure Start Ilfracombe, Combe
Martin & Berrynarbor**
01271 865825
swssnd@mail.nch.org.uk
www.surestartnd.org.uk
*Programme Manager: Diane
Pedley*

**Sure Start Exeter**
01392 252341
swess@mail.nch.org.uk
*Programme Manager: Christine
Cottle*

**Sure Start Teignmouth and
Dawish**
01626 879776
swssdt@mail.nch.org.uk
*Programme Manager: Tim Collins*

**Sure Start Bideford**
01237 471784
swssbi@mail.nch.org.uk
*Programme Manager: Tom
Mcculloch*

## Dorset

**Weymouth & Portland Sure
Start**
01305 786367
carol.pitman@sswandp.org
*Programme Manager: Carol
Pitman*

## Gloucestershire

**Sure Start Barton, Tredworth &
White City**
01452 550059
melanie.dopson@gloucestershire
.gov.uk
www.surestartgloucester.org.uk
*Programme Manager: Melanie
Dopson*

**Sure Start Cheltenham**
01242 582822
surestart@hwnp.org.uk
*Programme Manager: Tracy Elwin*

## North Somerset

**Sure Start Factory**
01934 645131
info.surestart@n-somerset.gov.uk
*Programme Manager: Fiona Castle*

## City of Plymouth

**Sure Start North Prospect
LARK Project**
01752 313293
surestart.plymouth@virgin.net
*Programme Manager: Steve
Canning*

**Sure Start North West
Plymouth**
01752 366795
swsspl@mail.nch.org.uk
*Programme Manager: Heather
Reid*

**Sure Start Tamar FOLK**
01752 516080
bbcat@lineone.net
*Programme Manager: Maria
Ashurst*

**Sure Start Keystone**
01752 208345
wendy_projectdeveloper@hotmail.
com
*Programme Manager: Wendy
Johnson*

## Somerset

**Sure Start Bridgwater,
Somerset**
01278 433416
julia@surestart-bridgwater.co.uk
*Programme Manager: Julia Setter*

**Sure Start West Somerset**
01984 635354
fevesham@somerset.gov.uk
Programme Manager: Frances
Evesham

**Sure Start Taunton Deane**
01823 322124
jonbazley@surestarttaunton.fsnet
.co.uk
*Programme Manager: Jon Bazley*

## Swindon

**Sure Start Pinehurst & Penhill**
01793 651828
liz.evans@swindon-pct.nhs.uk
*Programme Manager: Liz Evans*

## Torbay

**Sure Start Paignton**
01803 556081
Jaynebirbeck.surestart@torbay.
gov.uk
*Programme Manager: Jayne
Birbeck*

**Sure Start Torquay**
01803 299356
swssbi@mail.nch.org.uk
*Torbay Early Years Co-ordinator:
Jane Osburn*

---

# West Midlands

**Sure Start Government Office
West Midlands**
0121 212 5449
rwiseman.gowm@go-regions.
gsi.gov.uk
Regional Manager: Rita Wiseman

## Birmingham

**Sure Start Billesley**
0121 464 4772
*Programme Manager: Khairum
Butt*

**Sure Start Balsall Heath**
0121 464 6349
Alison.corns@stpaulscom.co.uk
*Programme Manager: Alison Corns*

**Sure Start Ladywood**
0121 410 5500
andyquinn@surestartladywood.c
o.uk
*Programme Manager: Andrew
Quinn*

**Sure Start Saltley**
0121 464 4532
farahsher@hotmail.com
*Programme Manager: Hazel
Stewart Davies*

**Sure Start Handsworth &
Winson Green**
0121 622 8240
*Programme Manager: Rajinder
Ghatora*

**Sure Start Lozells & Duddeston**
0121 248 3000
alison.morgan@mbpct.nhs.uk
*Programme Manager: Louise
Huckelby*

**Sure Start Birmingham East**
0121 789 9779
*Programme Manager: Lee Richards*

**Sure Start Sparkbrook**
0121 766 6541
karenpearson@surestartsparkbrook.co.uk
*Programme Manager: Karen Pearson*

**Sure Start South West Birmingham**
0121 428 4187
andllj@blueyonder.co.uk
*Programme Manager: Andy Jenkins*

**Sure Start Small Heath**
0121 622 8255
azora.hurd@southbirminghampct.nhs.uk
*Programme Manager: Azora Hurd*

**Sure Start Heathfield**
0121 622 8257
elaineaustin@yahoo.co.uk
*Programme Manager: Elaine Veronica Austin*

**Sure Start Kingstanding**
0121 332 1954
paola.pedrelli@northbirminghampct.nhs.uk
*Programme Manager: Paola Pedrelli*

### Coventry

**Sure Start Coventry South East**
024 7663 6926
webster.sue@talk21.com
*Programme Manager: Sue Webster*

**Sure Start Coventry West**
024 7647 0039
surestart.coventry-west@virgin.net
*Programme Manager: Latif Ahmed*

**Sure Start Foleshill**
024 7666 1631
viva.cummins@coventry.gov.uk
Programme Manager: Viva Cummins

**Sure Start Coventry North East**
024 7683 2345
margaret.brassington@coventry.gov.uk
*Programme Manager: Margaret Brassington*

### Dudley

**Sure Start Brierley Hill**
01384 813322
mdpaulw@mail.nch.org.uk
*Programme Manager: Paul Watling*

**Sure Start Kates Hill and Sledmere**
01384 239421
wmsuep@mail.nch.org.uk
*Programme Manager: Sue Payne*

**Sure Start Lye, Rufford and Wollescote**
01384 813954
*Programme Manager: Chris Gittings*

### Herefordshire

**Sure Start Leominster and Kingston**
01432 383340
leominster/kingtonsurestart@herefordshire.gov.uk
*Programme Manager: Ros Adams*

### Sandwell

**Sure Start Rowley Regis**
0121 559 9916
jim_anderson@sandwell.gov.uk
*Programme Manager: Jim Anderson*

**Sure Start Smethwick**
0121 555 6756
surestartsmethwick@hotmail.com
*Programme Manager: Bhavna Solanki*

**Sure Start Friar Park, Mesty Croft & Woods**
0121 556 5405
info@surestartfpmcw.org.uk
www.surestartfpmcw.org.uk
*Programme Manager: Sandra Fitzpatrick*

**Sure Start Tipton**
0121 557 4341
carol.thompson@barnardos.org.uk
*Programme Manager: Carol Thompson*

**Sure Start Burnt Tree**
0121 521 2390
katherine@surestarttividale.org.uk
*Programme Manager: Katherine Stinson*

**Sure Start Rood End, Oldbury & Beeches**
0121 552 9248
pauline.lewars@barnardos.org.uk
*Programme Manager: Pauline Lewars*

**Sure Start Cradley Heath**
01384 567091
*Programme Manager: Lucy Loveless*

**Sure Start Smethwick, Londonderry & Uplands**
0121 569 3740
peter_forth@sandwell.gov.uk
*Project Manager: Peter Forth*

### Shropshire

**Sure Start Oswestry**
01691 656513
michael.jarrett@surestartoswestry.co.uk
*Programme Manager: Michael Jarrett*

**Sure Start Shrewsbury**
01743 254605
ted.eames@shropshire-cc.gov.uk
*Programme Manager: Ted Eames*

### Solihull

**Sure Start Chelmsley Wood**
0121 779 7624
sue.barnett@nch.org.uk
*Programme Manager: Sue Barnett*

### Staffordshire

**Sure Start Cannock Chase**
01543 506535
sarah.rivers@staffordshire.gov.uk
*Programme Manager: Sarah Rivers*

**Sure Start Newcastle-Under-Lyme**
01782 296229
shirleytorrens@knutton-infants.staffs.sch.uk
*Programme Manager: Shirley Torrens*

**Sure Start Moorlands**
01298 687163
louis.hughes@staffordshire.gov.uk
*Programme Manager: Louis Hughes*

**Sure Start Tamworth**
01827 261360
anne.cummins@staffordshire.gov.uk
*Programme Manager: Anne Cummins*

**Sure Start East Staffs Inner Burton**
01283 562217
kay.jaques@staffordshire.gov.uk
*Programme Manager: Kay Jaques*

### Stoke-on-Trent

**Sure Start Stoke-on-Trent North**
01782 232977
barbara.banks@swann.stoke.gov.uk
*Programme Manager: Barbara Banks*

**Sure Start Blurton**
01782 344910
fiona@surestart-blurton.org
*Programme Manager: Fiona Green*

**Sure Start Longton South**
01782 425501
kirsty.crank@northstoke-pct.nhs.uk
*Programme Manager: Kirsty Crank*

**Sure Start Shelton Cobridge**
01782 425003
*Programme Manager: Pat Price*

**Sure Start Abbey Bucknall**
01782 209096
michael.durell@northstoke-pct.nhs.uk
*Programme Manager: Michael Durrell*

**Sure Start Bentille & Berryhill**
01782 233670
vince.owen@swann.stoke.gov.uk
*Contact: Vince Owen*

### Telford and Wrekin

**Sure Start Lawley and Overdale**
01952 247926
Mark.Ferguson@telford.gov.uk
*Programme Manager: Mark Ferguson*

**Sure Start Jubilee**
01952 202296
jane.clark@telford.gov.uk
*Programme Manager: Jane Clark*

### Walsall

**Sure Start Blakenall**
01922 476698
smithd@walsall.gov.uk
www.surestartblakenall.co.uk
*Programme Manager: Carol Ferron-Smith*

**Sure Start Palfrey**
01922 642382
team@surestartpalfrey.co.uk
*Programme Manager: Mick Davies*

**Sure Start Birchills**
01922 646574
hastingsh@walsall.gov.uk
*Programme Manager: Hilary Hastings*

**Sure Start Alumwell Pleck**
01922 637794
Chanel.Lawrence@walsall.nhs.uk
*Programme Manager: John Hood*

**Sure Start Darlaston South**
07968 212962
clarkeangie@walsall.gov.uk
Programme Manager: Angie Clarke

### Warwickshire

**Sure Start Nuneaton**
024 7637 8600
mdssn@nch.org.uk
*Programme Director: Julie Doyle*

**Sure Start Warwick District**
01926 337506
wmolwynd@;post.nch.org.uk
*Programme Manager: Olwyn Ditchburne*

### Wolverhampton

**Sure Start Bilston and Ettingshall**
01902 556937
contacts@bess.uk.net
*Programme Manager: Jan Barlow*

**Sure Start Whitmore Reans & Dunstall**
01902 556585
*Programme Manager: Kali Lewis*

**Sure Start Eight Village**
01902 553945
heathtownemb@compuserve.com
*Programme Manager: Ersuline Whittle*

**Sure Start Low Hill & the Scotlands**
01902 556348
rohit.mistry@wolvespct.nhs.uk
*Programme Manager: Rohit Mistry*

**Sure Start Eastfield, East Park & Portobello**
01902 555894
sue.coleman@wolverhampton.gov.uk
*Programme Manager: Mary Bentley*

### Worcestershire

**Sure Start Redditch**
01527 534149
judith.willis@redditchbc.gov.uk
*Programme Manager: Judith Willis*

**Sure Start Wyre Forest Oldington**
01562 514980
wmphiliph@post.nch.org.uk
*Programme Manager: Philip Hoare*

**Sure Start Worcester**
01905 611976
icraigan@cityofworcester.gov.uk
*Programme Manager: Ian Craigan*

## Yorkshire and Humberside

**Sure Start Government Office Yorkshire & Humber**
0113 283 5237
agraham@dfes.gsi.gov.uk
*Regional Manager: Anne-Marie Graham*

### Barnsley

**Sure Start Kendray and Worsbrough**
01226 298459
robert.skidmore@barnsley.org.uk
*Programme Manager: Robert Skidmore*

**Sure Start Athersley, New Lodge & Smithies**
01226 321666
annehuntersurestart@ukonline.co.uk
*Programme Manager: Anne Hunter*

**Sure Start Thurnscoe**
01709 894538
thurnscoe.consortium@ukonline.co.uk
*Programme Manager: Jenny Foulstone*

**Sure Start Hoyland & Jump**
01226 747082
*Programme Manager: Neil Spencer*

**Sure Start Bolton and Golthorpe**
01423 524286
juliew@nch.org.uk
*Assistant Director of Children's Services: Julie Ward*

### Bradford

**Sure Start Barkerend**
01274 321830
kalnawaz@ssbarkerend.fsnet.co.uk
*Programme Manager: Kal Nawaz*

**Sure Start Keighley**
01535 604687
chrisr.surestartkeighley@blueyonder.co.uk
*Interim Programme Manager: Chris Rollings*

**Sure Start West Bowling**
01274 777033/5
sonia@sswbowling.plus.com
*Programme Manager: Sonia*
*Sandbach*

**Sure Start Shipley**
01274 597717
nigel@surestartshipley.co.uk
*Programme Manager: Nigel Taylor*

**Sure Start Holmewood Bierley**
**& Tyersal**
01274 322339
sarahprocter@surestartbht.org.uk
*Programme Manager: Sarah*
*Proctor*

**Sure Start Manningham**
01274 223203
kulbir@surestartmanningham.
org.uk
*Programme Manager: Kulbir Bura*

**Sure Start Canterbury**
01274 523462
angelasurestart@hotmail.com
*Programme Manager: Angela T*
*Wiggan*

**Sure Start North East Bradford**
01274 668573
ann.kendal@childrensociety.org.uk
*Programme Manager: Ann Kendal*

## Calderdale

**Sure Start Elland**
01422 373133
mark.nicholas@surestartelland.
org.uk
*Programme Manager: Mark*
*Nicholas*

**Sure Start Halifax West Central**
01422 342552
lisa@surestartwch.org.uk
www.surestartwch.org.uk
*Programme Manager: Lisa Cahill*

**Sure Start North Halifax**
01422 251091
steve@surestartnorthhalifax.org.uk
*Programme Manager: Steve*
*Woodhead*

## Doncaster

**Sure Start Denaby Main &**
**Coinsborough**
01709 770099
julie.warren@doncasterwestpct.n
hs.uk
*Programme Manager: Julie*
*Warren*

**Sure Start Moorends & The**
**Willows**
01405 818158
nessmwt@mail.nch.org.uk
*Programme Manager: Tracie Dodds*

**Sure Start Bentley Central &**
**Adwick**
01302 875398
*Programme Manager: Helen*
*Brumwell*

**Sure Start Intake & Wheatley**
01302 761755
nessibv@mail.nch.org.uk
*Programme Manager: Ailsa*
*Johnson*

**Sure Start Mexborough**
01709 589017
jane.Stanley@doncasterwestpct.
nhs.uk
*Programme Manager: Jane Stanley*

**Spa Spiders (Sure Start)**
01302 709376
pam.ley@doncasterwestpct.
nhs.uk
*Programme Manager: Pam Ley*

## East Riding

**Sure Start Bridlington**
01262 409596
Alison.cummings@eastridingcolle
ge.ac.uk
*Programme Managers: Wendy*
*Wilson/ Alison Cummings*

## Kingston Upon Hull

**Sure Start Marfleet**
01482 705333
angela.hancock@hullcc.gov.uk
*Programme Manager: Angela*
*Hancock*

**Sure Start Northern Hull**
01482 803978
sam.bell@herch-tr.nhs.uk
*Programme Manager: Samantha*
*Bell*

**Sure Start Noddle Hill**
01482 828901
NoddleHill.Surestart@hullcc.gov.uk
*Programme Manager: Pam Crane*

**Sure Start Myton & St Andrews**
01482 587550
dsewell@goodwin-centre.org
*Programme Manager: Diane Sewell*

**Sure Start Longhill**
01482 708953
judith.haldenby@hullcc.gov.uk
*Programme Manager: Chris*
*Campbell*

**Sure Start Newington &**
**Gipsyville**
01482 616972
geoff@surestart.karoo.co.uk
*Programme Manager: Geoff*
*Martindale*

**Sure Start Newland and**
**Avenues**
01482 313866
KWoodall@goodwin-centre.org
*Programme Manager: Jackie*
*Wright*

## Kirklees

**Sure Start Thornhill**
01924 325334
ian.bond@kirkleesmc.gov.uk
*Programme Manager: Ian Bond*

**Sure Start Dewsbury Moor**
01924 516778
nessdmsh@mail.nch.org.uk
*Joint Programme Managers:*
*Amanda Taylor/ Ros Stansfield*

**Sure Start Deighton and East**
**Fartown**
01484 544984
dcsurestartdef@btopenworld.com
*Programme Manager: Denise*
*Campbell*

**Sure Start Walpole/ Thornton**
**Lodge**
01484 223547
Amanda.Jackson@kirklees.gov.uk
*Programme Manager: Amanda*
*Jackson*

**Sure Start Batley**
01484 225290
jan.wallis@kirklees.gov.uk
*Contact: Jan Wallis*

## Leeds

**Sure Start Bramley**
0113 217 2200
info@surestartbramley.co.uk
*Programme Manager: Kathryn*
*Shaw*

**Sure Start Middleton**
0113 276 2386
surestartmiddleton@i12.com
*Programme Manager: Cathryn*
*Gurney*

**Sure Start Seacroft**
0113 224 3461
seacroft.surestart@lycos.co.uk
www.surestart.freeuk.com
*Programme Manager: Bernard*
*McMahon*

**Sure Start Chapeltown**
0113 295 1796
dawnlewis@i12.com
*Programme Manager: Dawn Lewis*

**Sure Start Beeston Hill**
0113 270 2288
sally.ben@fsu.org.uk
*Programme Manager: Sally Ben*

**Sure Start Burley**
0113 289 9807
BurleySureStart@aol.com
*Programme Manager: John Ashton*

**Sure Start Harehills**
0113 295 1598
surestart01@btconnect.com
*Programme Manager: Judy Morgan*

**Sure Start Little London, Woodhouse and Meanwood**
0113 245 8480
Sure-Start-Little-London@childrenssociety.org.uk
*Programme Manager: Paul Gathercole*

**North East Lincolnshire**
Sure Start Nunsthorpe and Bradley Park
01472 326600
charlotte.ramsey@nelincs.gov.uk
*Programme Manager: Charlotte Ramsey*

**Sure Start East Marsh**
01472 360776
nessem@mail.nch.org.uk
*Programme Manager: Caroline Bowditch*

**Sure Start Grimsby - West Marsh/Yarborough**
01472 242831
nesswmy@mail.nch.org.uk
*Programme Manager: Sue Rawlings*

**Sure Start Northern Cleethorpes**
01472 290202
nesscn@mail.nch.org.uk
*Programme Manager: Helen Norris*

**Sure Start Grange, Western & Central Grimsby**
01472 241115
*Programme Manager: Sharon Clark*

**North Lincolnshire**

**Sure Start Scunthorpe and Cloverleaf**
01724 277812
Margaret.hornsby@northlincs.gov.uk
*Programme Manager: Margaret Hornsby*

**North Yorkshire**

**Sure Start Scarborough**
01723 503677
susan.richings@surestartscarborough.co.uk
*Programme Manager: Mrs Susan Richings*

**Sure Start Selby District**
01757 291111
selbyavs@hotmail.com
*AVS Co-ordinator: Gill Cashmore*

**Rotherham**

**Sure Start Rawmarsh**
01709 336899
maggie.whitfield@rotherham.gov.uk
*Programme Manager: Maggie Whitfield*

**Sure Start Maltby**
01709 816946
penny.verity@rotherham.gov.uk
*Acting Programme Manager: Sally Buck*

**Sure Start Rotherham Central**
01709 835499
barbara.nellist@rotherham.gov.uk
www.surestartrotherhamcentral.cjb.net
*Programme Manager: Barbara Nellist*

**Sheffield**

**Foxhill & Parson Cross Sure Start**
0114 231 3509/2512
nelindaf@post.nch.org.uk
www.shef.ac.uk/surestart
*Programme Manager: Linda Fox*

**Sure Start Burngreave & Firvale**
0114 244 3887
sure-start@burngreave-firvale-surestart.co.uk
*Programme Manager: Resh Spafford*

**Sure Start Sharrow**
0114 278 7104
anne.davies@sharrowsurestart.org.uk
*Programme Manager: Anne Davis*

**Sure Start Tinsley**
0114 261 8181
surestarts9@btconnect.com
*Programme Manager: Sally Fellows*

**Sure Start Gleadless Valley**
0114 254 4810
nepaulaw@mail.nch.org.uk
*Programme Manager: Paula Williams*

**Sure Start Firth Park & Shiregreen**
0114 240 3134
*Programme Manager: Gwyn Fields*

**Sure Start Woodthorpe & Wybourn**
0114 265 1188
info@wwsurestart.f9.co.uk
*Programme Co-ordinator: Jean Kinder*

**Sure Start Southey Green and Shirecliffe**
0114 231 3509
nessfpc@mail.nch.org.uk
*Assistant Director: Julie Ward*

**Wakefield**

**Sure Start Wakefield**
01924 304258
ikalischer@wakefield.gov.uk
*Programme Manager: Ingrid Kalischer*

**Sure Start Ferry Fryston and Airedale**
01977 724044
susan.richardson@ewpct.nhs.uk
*Programme Manager: Shaheen Khawaja*

**Sure Start Hemsworth, Kinsley & Fitzwilliam**
01977 625277
surestarthkf@btconnect.com
*Programme Manager: Gail Faulkner*

**Sure Start Wakefield East**
01924 306280
afarrell@wakefield.gov.uk
*Head of Early Education and Childcare: Anita J Farrell*

**City of York**

**Sure Start York**
01904 793640
Alison.walls@york.gov.uk
*Programme Manager: Alison Walls*

# Connexions

*Connexions is an all-encompassing youth service, launched by the government in April 2001 to replace the careers service and other statutory youth services. Aimed at giving 13 to 19 year-olds "the best transition to adulthood". It involves personal advisers going into schools, colleges and communities to steer young people towards goals and guide them to relevant services.*

## Connexions Service National Unit
**Address:** Department for Education and Skills, Moorfoot, Sheffield S1 4PQ
**E-mail:** info@dfes.gsi.gov.uk
**Web:** www.connexions.gov.uk

### Connexions Direct
**Tel:** 0808 001 3219;
**Text:** 077664 13219
*Confidential advice, support and information via telephone, e-mail, webchat for everyone aged between 13 and 19*

## Connexions regional government office contacts

### North-east

Eric Bannister
Government Office North East
Wellbar House, Gallowgate
Newcastle
NE1 4TD
0191 202 3559
ebannister.gone@go-regions.gsi.
gov.uk

### North-west

Tony McGee
Government Office North West
16th Floor, Sunley Tower,
Piccadilly Plaza
Manchester
M1 4BE
0151 224 2912
tmcgee.gonw@go-regions.gsi.
gov.uk

### Yorkshire and the Humber

Derek Ireland
Government Office Yorkshire and
the Humber
516 City House, New Station
Street
Leeds
LS1 4JD
0113 283 5259/5260
direland.goyh@go-regions.gsi.
gov.uk

### West Midlands

John Robertson
Government Office West
Midlands
Floor 3, Chamberlain House,
Queensway
Birmingham
B1 2DT
0121 212 5441
jrobertson.gowm@go-regions.gsi.
gov.uk

### East Midlands

Peter Ward
Government Office East Midlands
Belgrave Centre, Talbot Street
Nottingham
NG1 5GG
0115 971 2631
pward.goem@go-regions.gsi.gov.uk

### East of England

Roger Allen
Government Office for the East of
England
Eastbrook, Shaftesbury Road
Cambridge
CB2 2DF
01223 372504
rallen.go-east@go-regions.gsi.
gov.uk

### London

Clive Senior
Government Office London
Riverwalk House, 157-161
Millbank
London
SW1P 4RR
020 7217 3116
csenior.gol@go-regions.gsi.
gov.uk

### South-east

Di Morrish
Government Office South East,
Bridge House
1 Walnut Tree Close
Guildford
GU1 4GA
01483 882277
dmorrish.gose@go-regions.gsi.
gov.uk

### South-west

Nita Murphy
Government Office South West
2 Rivergate, Temple Quay
Bristol
BS1 6ED
0117 900 1932
nmurphy.gosw@go-regions.gsi.
gov.uk

# regional centres

## North-east

### Durham County
Connexions County Durham
0191 383 1777; 0800 783 3578
info@connexions-durham.org
www.connexions-durham.org

Consett Connexions Centre
01207 502795

Stanley Connexions Centre
01207 232033

Chester-le-Street Connexions
Centre
0191 388 3019

Durham City Connexions
Centre
0191 384 9766

Seaham Connexions Centre
0191 581 2487

Peterlee Connexions Centre
0191 586 7551

Crook Connexions Centre
01388 646500

Bishop Auckland Connexions
Centre
01388 603468

Spennymoor Connexions
Centre
01388 816888

Sedgefield Connexions Centre
01388 724100

Newton Aycliffe Connexions
Centre
01325 316054

### Northumberland
Connexions Northumberland
01670 798180
info@connexions-
northumberland.org.uk
www.connexions-
northumberland.org.uk

### Tees Valley
Connexions Tees Valley
01642 601600
enquiries@connexionsteesvalley.
co.uk
www.connexionsteesvalley.co.uk

Hartlepool One Stop Shop
01429 275501

Stockton One Stop Shop
01642 677600

Darlington One Stop Shop
01325 480055

Redcar One Stop Shop
01642 490870

Middlesbrough One Stop Shop
01642 240081

### Tyne & Wear
Connexions Tyne & Wear
0191 490 1717; 0800 073 8700
helpline@connexions-tw.co.uk
www.connexions-tw.co.uk

## North-west

### Cheshire and Warrington
Connexions Cheshire and
Warrington
0800 980 9877
info@connexions-cw.co.uk
www.connexions-cw.co.uk

Connexions Centre
01244 389200

Connexions Centre
01260 276116

Connexions Centre
01270 251002

Connexions Centre
0151 355 7135

Connexions Centre
01625 424026

Connexions Centre
01606 331515

Connexions Centre
01925 416611

Connexions Centre
01606 862213

### Cumbria
Connexions Partnership Office
Cumbria
01931 711300; 0800 435709
info@connexionscumbria.co.uk
www.connexionscumbria.co.uk

Connexions Carlisle
01228 596272

Connexions Penrith
01768 865296

Connexions Barrow
01229 824052

Connexions Kendal
01539 730045

Connexions Kendal
01539 734820

Connexions Ulverston
01229 583466

Connexions Workington
01900 604674

Connexions Whitehaven
01946 695541

Connexions Maryport
01900 815928

Connexions Millom
01229 773246

### Greater Manchester
Connexions Greater
Manchester Head Office
0161 227 7000; 0800 032 2727
reception@connexions-
gmcr.org.uk
www.gmconnexions.com

Connexions Bolton
0800 052 5559
www.connexions-bolton.com

Connexions Bolton
0800 195 8526

Connexions Bury
0161 763 5884
www.connexions-bury.com

Connexions Salford
0161 743 0163
info@connexions-salford.com
www.connexions-
manchester.com

Connexions Manchester
Central
0161 248 7684
info@connexions-
manchester.com

Connexions Manchester North
0161 205 1644

Connexions Manchester South
0161 437 4288

Connexions Manchester -
Didsbury
0161 434 6582

Connexions Manchester -
Moss Side
0161 226 8609

Connexions Manchester -
Cheetham Hill
0161 205 1944

Connexions Manchester -
Newton Heath
0161 205 1944

Connexions Crossley House
East Manchester
0161 231 2700

Connexions Manchester -
Clayton
0161 231 2700

Connexions Tameside - Ashton
0161 330 1528
info@connexions-tameside.com

Connexions Tameside - Hyde
0161 330 1528

Connexions Rochdale
01706 759515
reception@connexions-gmcr.org.uk
www.connexions-rochdale.org.uk

Connexions Middleton
0161 643 3125

Connexions Heywood
01706 622770

Connexions Oldham
0161 911 4296
www.connexions-oldham.com

Connexions Wigan
0800 953 0109
positivefuturesinfo@wbp.org.uk
www.positivefutures-wigan.org.uk

Connexions Leigh
0800 953 0109

Connexions Trafford
0161 911 8600
contactus@connexions-
trafford.co.uk
www.connexions-trafford.org.uk

Connexions Stockport
0161 475 7700
www.connexions-stockport.com

### Lancashire

Lancashire Connexions Centre
01254 685120

Accrington Connexions Centre
01254 393316

Blackburn Connexions Centre
01254 610662

Preston Connexions Centre
01772 554459

Blackpool Connexions Centre
01253 293161

Burnley Connexions Centre
01282 478600

Chorley Connexions Centre
01257 248900

Fleetwood Connexions Centre
01253 775050

Lancaster Connexions Centre
01524 387600

Morecambe Connexions
Centre
01524 413229

Leyland Connexions Centre
01772 450800

Nelson Connexions Centre
01282 613067

Skelmersdale Connexions
Centre
01695 724557

### Greater Merseyside

Connexions Greater
Merseyside
0151 703 7400; 0808 001 3219
hq@connexions-
gmerseyside.co.uk
www.connexions-
gmerseyside.co.uk

Bebington Connexions Centre
0151 472 4600
bebington@connexions-
gmerseyside.co.uk

Birkenhead Connexions Centre
0151 666 4385
birkenhead@connexions-
gmerseyside.co.uk

Bootle Connexions Centre
0151 955 6300
bootle@connnexions-
gmerseyside.co.uk

Huyton Connexions Centre
0151 949 5700
huyton@connexions-
gmerseyside.co.uk

Kirkby Connexions Centre
0151 545 5400
kirkby@connexions-
gmerseyside.co.uk

Liverpool City Connexions
Centre
0151 709 5400
city@connexions-
gmerseyside.co.uk

Liverpool East Connexions
Centre
0151 228 2285
east@connexions-
gmerseyside.co.uk

Liverpool North Connexions
Centre
0151 270 2246
north@connexions-
gmerseyside.co.uk

Liverpool South Connexions
Centre
0151 336 9400
south@connexions-
gmerseyside.co.uk

Newton Le Willows Connexions
Centre
01744 623757
st.helens@connexions-
gmerseyside.co.uk

Runcorn Connexions Centre
01928 580220
runcorn@connexions.gmerseysid
e.co.uk

Southport Connexions Centre
01704 504500
southport@connexions-
gmerseyside.co.uk

St Helens Connexions Centre
01744 29882
st.helens@connexions-
gmerseyside.co.uk

Wallasey Connexions Centre
0151 638 5625
wallasey@connexions.
gmerseyside.co.uk

West Kirby Connexions Centre
0151 471 6020
west.kirkby@connexions.
gmerseyside.co.uk

Widnes Connexions Centre
0151 422 9120
widnes@connexions-
gmerseyside.co.uk

## Yorkshire and the Humber

### Humber
Connexions Humber
01482 350150; 0808 180 4636
cburgess@connexionshumber.
co.uk
www.connexionshumber.co.uk

### Hull
Connexions
01482 223081

Connexions
01482 835780

Connexions
01482 611818

Connexions
01482 224337

Connexions
01482 331000

Connexions
01482 331461

Connexions
01482 218115

Connexions
01482 568647

Connexions
01482 331505

### East Riding and Lincolnshire

Connexions
01482 862741

Connexions
01405 764558

Connexions
01262 678943

Connexions
01482 647127

Connexions
01472 355303

Connexions
01469 572986

Connexions New Start
01472 323247

Connexions
01472 323301

Connexions
01472 323210

Connexions
01472 355303

Connexions
01742 282200

### South Yorkshire

Connexions South Yorkshire
0114 261 9393;
Barnsley, Doncaster or
Rotherham: 0800 169 9338;
Sheffield: 0800 652 9900
info@connexions-sy.org.uk
www.connexionssy.org.uk

### West Yorkshire

Connexions West Yorkshire
01484 727500

enquiries@connexionswestyorks
hire.co.uk
www.connexionswestyorkshire.
co.uk

Connexions Centre
01274 829429

Connexions Centre
0800 106699

Connexions Centre
01422 330033

Connexions Centre
01484 226800

Connexions Centre
01924 371579

### York and North Yorkshire

Connexions York and North
Yorkshire
01904 799937; 0800 032 3272
info@connexionsyny.org.uk
www.connexionsyorkandnorthyork
shire.org.uk

---

## West Midlands

### Black Country

Connexions Black Country
0121 502 7400; 0808 100 1980
info@blackcountryconnexions.
co.uk
www.blackcountryconnexions.
co.uk

### Birmingham and Solihull

Connexions Birmingham and
Solihull
0121 248 8004/5;
0845 145 0845
info@connexions-bs.co.uk
www.connexions-bs.co.uk

Aston Connexions Centre
0121 248 7955
aston-enquiry@connexions-bs.
co.uk

Chelmsley Wood Connexions
Centre
0121 770 1861
chelmsley-enquiry@connexions-
bs.co.uk
jim.bartholomew@britishcouncil.org
*Contact: Jim Bartholomew*

Erdington Connexions Centre
0121 248 8700
erdington-enquiry@connexions-
bs.co.uk
bsweeney@youthcouncil-
ni.org.uk
*Contact: Bernice Sweeney*

Handsworth Connexions
Centre
0121 248 8250
handsworth-
enquiry@connexions-bs.co.uk
mail@ rywu.org.uk
*Contact: Leon Mexter*

Kingshurst Connexions Centre
0121 770 5372
jan@teambase.fsnet.co.uk
sharon@nwrysu.demon.co.uk
*Contact: Sharon Moore*

Kingstanding Connexions
Centre
0121 464 5559
lisacarter@birmingham.gov.uk
theunit@rywu-yandh.co.uk
*Contact: Miriam Jackson/ Lisa
Bristow*

Kings Heath Connexions
Centre
0121 248 7177
kingsheath-enquiry@connexions-
bs.co.uk
katie.antippas@wya.org.uk
*Contact: Katie Antippas*

Lee Bank Connexions Centre
0121 622 4570
ermason@bigfoot.com
connectyouth.wm@staffordshire.
gov.uk and
yc.moorlands@staffordshire.gov.uk
*Contact: Kate Lawton*

Maypole Connexions Centre
0121 464 6181
emrywu@emrywu.freeserve.co.uk
*Contact: Clare Meakin*

Northfield Connexions Centre
0121 464 1964
ncx@birmingham.gov.uk
kdodson@essexcc.gov.uk
*Contact: Krysia Dodson*

Connexions South West Team
0121 248 8150
gill_millar@swafet.org.uk
*Contact: Gill Millar*

**Selly Oak Connexions Centre**
0121 248 3800
sellyoak-enquiry@connexions-
bs.co.uk
tina.saunders@westsussex.gov.uk
*Contact: Tina Saunders, County
Youth and Community Officer*

**Shirley Connexions Centre**
0121 251 1800
shirley-enquiry@connexions-
bs.co.uk
n.carter@richmond.gov.uk
*Contact: Nicci Carter*

**Stechford Connexions Centre**
0121 783 1772
*youthis@hotmail.com*

**Sutton Coldfield Connexions
Centre**
0121 248 8600
sutton-enquiry@connexions-
bs.co.uk

**Yardley Connexions Centre**
0121 248 8200
yardley-enquiry@connexions-
bs.co.uk

## Coventry and Warwickshire

**Connexions Coventry and
Warwickshire**
024 7670 7400
advice@cswpconnexions.org.uk
www.connexions-
covandwarks.org.uk

**Coventry One Stop Shop**
024 7660 7900

**Nuneaton One Stop Shop**
024 7632 4620

**Warwick Connexions Office**
01926 401300

**Atherstone Connexions Office**
01827 712482

**Bedworth Connexions Office**
024 7631 2846

**Coleshill Connexions Office**
01675 462245

**Kenilworth Connexions Office**
01926 856823

**Leamington Spa Connexions
Office**
01926 334241

**Nuneaton Connexions Office**
024 7634 7677

**Rugby Connexions Office**
01788 337901

**Rugby One Stop Shop**
01788 577154

**Stratford Upon Avon
Connexions Office**
01789 266841

## Herefordshire and
Worcestershire

**Connexions Herefordshire and
Worcestershire**
01905 765428
msanders@connexions-
hw.org.uk
www.connexions-hw.org.uk

**Connexions Bromsgrove**
01527 575855
bromsgrove@connexions-
hw.org.uk

**Connexions Droitwich**
01905 796700

**Connexions Evesham**
01386 444220
evesham@connexions-hw.org.uk

**Connexions Hereford**
01432 269404
hereford@connexions-hw.org.uk

**Connexions Kidderminster**
01562 820110
kidderminster@connexions-
hw.org.uk

**Connexions Ledbury**
01531 614949

**Connexions Leominster**
01568 612548

**Connexions Malvern**
01684 892518
malvern@connexions-hw.org.uk

**Connexions Pershore**
01386 565000

**Connexions Redditch**
01527 66525
redditch@connexions-hw.org.uk

**Connexions Ross-On-Wye**
01989 563037

**Connexions Worcester**
01905 738900
worcester@connexions-
hw.org.uk

## Shropshire, Telford
and Wrekin

**Connexions Shropshire, Telford
and Wrekin**
0800 252972
enquiry@connexionsstw.org.uk
www.connexionsstw.org.uk

**Oswestry Connexions Branch**
01691 659111

**Market Drayton Connexions
Branch**
01630 654138

**Madeley Connexions Branch**
01952 684289

**Wellington Connexions Branch**
01952 643070

**Bridgnorth Connexions Branch**
01746 765001

**Ludlow Connexions Branch**
01584 873725

## Staffordshire

**Connexions Staffordshire Head
Office**
01785 355700; 0808 100 0434
info@cxstaffs.co.uk
www.cxstaffs.co.uk

**Biddulph Connexions Centre**
01782 297865

**Burton Connexions Centre**
01283 239400

**Cannock Connexions Centre**
01543 510270

**Cheadle Connexions Centre**
01538 483870

**Hanley Connexions Centre**
01782 295300

**Leek Connexions Centre**
01538 483169

**Lichfield Connexions Centre**
01543 510683

**Longton Connexions Centre**
01782 591000

**Newcastle Connexions Centre**
01782 297383

**Rugeley Connexions Centre**
01889 256190

**Stafford Connexions Centre**
01785 356656

**Tamworth Connexions Centre**
01827 475580

Tunstall Connexions Centre
01782 825681

Uttoxeter Connexions Centre
01889 256426

---

# East Midlands

## Derbyshire

Connexions Derbyshire
01773 570939
jane.godfrey@dcpltd.org
www.connexions-derbyshire.org

Alfreton Connexions
01773 832935

Buxton Connexions Centre
01298 22322

Chesterfield Connexions
Centre
01246 201581

Derby Connexions Centre
01332 200033

Glossop Connexions Centre
01457 864641

Ilkeston Connexions Centre
0115 930 2636

Long Eaton Connexions Centre
0115 973 2806

Matlock Connexions Centre
01629 760403

Ripley Connexions Centre
01773 745921

Swadlincote Connexions Centre
01283 229709

## Leicestershire

Connexions Leicestershire
0116 287 7033
info@connexions-leics.org
www.connexions-leics.org

Coalville Connexions Centre
01530 812231
coalville@connexions-leics.org

Hinckley Connexions Centre
01455 632719
hinckley@connexions-leics.org

Leicester Connexions Centre
0116 262 7254
leicester@connexions-leics.org

Connexions Youth Info Shop
0116 254 6722
youthinfoshop@connexions-
leics.org

Loughborough Connexions
Centre
01509 214002
loughborough@connexions-
leics.org

Market Harborough
Connexions Centre
01858 462309
marketharborough@connexions-
leics.org

Melton Mowbray Connexions
Centre
01664 569966
melton@connexions-leics.org

## Northamptonshire

Northamptonshire Connexions
Head Office
01604 630033
info@4you2.org.uk or
info@northamptonshire-
connexions.org.uk
www.4you2.org.uk or
www.connexions-
northamptonshire.org.uk

Connexions Corby
01536 202917

Connexions Daventry
01327 705831

Connexions Kettering
01536 513862

Connexions Northampton
01604 631400

Connexions Rushden
01933 353553

Connexions Towcester
01327 359080

Connexions Wellingborough
01933 222626

## Nottinghamshire

Connexions Nottinghamshire
0115 912 6611; young persons
helpline 0800 052 9977
info@cnxnotts.co.uk
www.sortitonline.com or
www.cnxnotts.co.uk

Retford Connexions Centre
0845 600 2234
retford@cnxnotts.co.uk

Worksop Connexions Centre
01909 473165
worksop@cnxnotts.co.uk

Mansfield Connexions Centre
01623 632000
westnotts@cnxnotts.co.uk

The Acre Connexions Centre
01623 727470
kirkby@cnxnotts.co.uk

Newark Connexions Centre
0845 600 2234
newark@cnxnotts.co.uk

Hucknall Connexions Centre
0115 840 2067
hucknall@cnxnotts.co.uk

Eastwood Connexions Centre
01773 713449
eastwood@cnxnotts.co.uk

## Nottingham

Nottingham Connexions Centre
0115 948 4484
fls@cnxnotts.co.uk

City Team East
0115 992 6014
eastteam@cnxnotts.co.uk

City Team North
0115 992 6044
northteam@cnxnotts.co.uk

City Team South
0115 992 6027
southteam@cnxnotts.co.uk

City Team West
0115 992 6041
westteam@cnxnotts.co.uk

Gedling
0115 924 7251
gedling@cnxnotts.co.uk

Rushcliffe (inc. West Bridgford)
0115 992 6110
rushcliffe@cnxnotts.co.uk

South Broxtowe (inc. Beeston,
Chilwell, Stapleford, Toton,
Bramcote, Attenborough)
0115 992 6088
southbroxtowe@cnxnotts.co.uk

## Lincolnshire and Rutland

Connexions Lincolnshire and
Rutland
01522 875000; 0800 163026
admin@connexionslr.co.uk
www.connexions-
lincsandrutland.co.uk

Boston Connexions Centre
01205 310800
boston@connexionslr.co.uk

Gainsborough Connexions
Centre
01427 612096
gainsborough@connexionslr.co.uk

**Grantham Connexions Centre**
01476 404060
grantham@connexionslr.co.uk

**Lincoln Connexions Centre**
01522 875454
lincoln@connexionslr.co.uk

**Louth Connexions Centre**
01507 603377
louth@connexionslr.co.uk

**Oakham Connexions Centre**
01572 756655
oakham@connexionslr.co.uk

**Skegness Connexions Centre**
01754 762595
skegness@connexionslr.co.uk

**Sleaford Connexions Centre**
01529 303707
sleaford@connexionslr.co.uk

**Spalding Connexions Centre**
01775 766151
spalding@connexionslr.co.uk

**Stamford Connexions Centre**
01780 762238
stamford@connexionslr.co.uk

## East of England

### Bedfordshire and Luton

**Connexions Bedfordshire and Luton**
01582 727184; 0800 032 1319
info@connx.org.uk
www.connx.org.uk

**First Stop Shop**
01582 477445

**First Stop Shop**
01525 631900

**First Stop Shop**
01234 6364454

**First Stop Shop**
01582 579714

**First Stop Shop**
01582 654445

**First Stop Shop**
01582 566607

**First Stop Shop**
01582 519500

**First Stop Shop**
01582 736812

**First Stop Shop**
01582 696355

### Cambridgeshire and Peterborough

**Connexions Cambridgeshire and Peterborough**
01480 376000; 0800 561 3219
stives@connexionscp.co.uk
www.purplepigeon.net or
www.connexionscp.co.uk

**Connexions Cambridge**
01223 712800
cambridge@connexionscp.co.uk

**Connexions Ely**
01353 616990
ely@connexionscp.co.uk

**Connexions Huntingdon**
01480 376800
huntingdon@connexionscp.co.uk

**Connexions March**
01354 651703
march@connexionscp.co.uk

**Connexions Peterborough**
01733 703400
peterborough@connexionscp.co.uk

**Connexions St Neots**
01480 376013
stneots@connexionscp.co.uk

**Connexions Wisbech**
01945 585128
wisbech@connexionscp.co.uk

### Hertfordshire

**Connexions Hertfordshire**
01992 556320

**Hertfordshire Connexions One Stop Shop**
01707 266223

### Essex, Southend and Thurrock

**Connexions Essex, Southend and Thurrock**
01376 518998
enquiries@estconnexions.co.uk
www.estconnexions.co.uk

**Basildon Connexions Centre**
01268 501300
basildon@estconnexions.co.uk

**Braintree Connexions Centre**
01376 557400
braintree@estconnexions.co.uk

**Brentwood Connexions Centre**
01277 693300
brentwood@estconnexions.co.uk

**Canvey Island Connexions Centre**
01268 683067
canvey@estconnexions.co.uk

**Chelmsford Connexions Centre**
01245 706806
chelmsford@estconnexions.co.uk

**Clacton Connexions Centre**
01255 254300
clacton@estconnexions.co.uk

**Colchester Connexions Centre**
01206 717100
colchester@estconnexions.co.uk

**Corringham Connexions Centre**
01375 643912

**Harlow Connexions Centre**
01279 625300
harlow@estconnexions.co.uk

**Loughton Connexions Centre**
020 8532 5120
loughton@estconnexions.co.uk

**Maldon Connexions Centre**
01621 853552

**Rayleigh Connexions Centre**
01268 749600
rayleigh@estconnexions.co.uk

**Southend Connexions Centre**
01702 272300
southend@estconnexions.co.uk

**Thurrock Connexions Centre**
01375 413735
thurrock@estconnexions.co.uk

**Witham Connexions Centre**
01376 520776

### Norfolk

**Connexions Norfolk**
01603 764370
enquiries@connexions-norfolk.co.uk
www.cnxsnfk.co.uk or
www.connexions-norfolk.co.uk

**Norwich Connexions Centre**
01603 766994

**Great Yarmouth Connexions Centre**
01493 845400

**Kings Lynn Connexions Centre**
01553 666500

**North Walsham Connexions Centre**
01692 408200

Thetford Connexions Youth Venue
01842 855800

**Suffolk**

Connexions Suffolk
01473 261900; 0800 085 4448
enquiries@connexionssuffolk.org.uk
www.thesource.me.uk

Bury and Sudbury Connexions Team
01284 768493

Ipswich Connexions Team
01473 581449/50

North Suffolk Connexions Team
01502 508680

# London

## Central

Connexions Central London
020 7938 8080
info@centrallondonconnexions.org.uk
www.centrallondonconnexions.org.uk

Connexions
020 7482 3996
www.capitalcareers.ltd.uk

Connexions
020 7388 6007
www.centrallondonconnexions.org.uk/connexions
www.westeustonpartnership.co.uk/onestopshop

Connexions
020 7527 7030

The Connexions Centre
020 8355 5200

The Connexions Centre
020 8355 5150

The Connexions Centre
020 7326 8700

Connexions
020 7487 9315

Connexions @ Stowe
020 7266 7074

## East

Connexions East London
020 8536 3630
info@LondonEastConnexions.co.uk

## North

Connexions North London
020 8347 2380
feedback@connexions-northlondon.co.uk
www.connexions-northlondon.co.uk

## South

Connexions South London
0800 511111
www.connexions-southlondon.org.uk

Bromley Connexions
020 8461 7572
paulking@connexions-southlondon.org.uk

Croydon Connexions
020 8760 5848
johncairns@connexions-southlondon.org.uk

Kingston Upon Thames Connexions
020 8547 5816
juliacopping@connexions-southlondon.org.uk

Merton Connexions
020 8640 7226
mariewright@connexions-southlondon.org.uk

Richmond Upon Thames
020 8831 6149
deleryder@connexions-southlondon.org.uk

Sutton Connexions Centre
020 8642 6600
kerenmiller@connexions-southlondon.org.uk

## West

Connexions London West
020 8453 5000
enquiries@connexions-londonwest.com
www.connexions-londonwest.com

# South-east

## Berkshire

Connexions Berkshire
0118 987 0040
info@connexions-berkshire.org.uk
www.connexions-berkshire.org.uk

Connexions Bracknell
01344 454151

Connexions Maidenhead
01628 622481

Connexions Newbury
01635 41722

Connexions Reading
0118 952 3800

Connexions Slough
01753 576136

Connexions Windsor
01753 576136

Connexions Wokingham
0118 978 6845

## Kent and Medway

Connexions Kent and Medway
01622 683155
website@connexionskentandmedway.co.uk
www.connexionskentandmedway.co.uk

Connexions Milton Keynes
01908 232808
miltonkeynescareers@vtis.com

Connexions Aylesbury
01296 397738
aylesburycareers@vtis.com

Connexions High Wycombe
01494 551800
highwycombecareers@vtis.com

## Milton Keynes, Oxfordshire and Buckinghamshire

Connexions Milton Keynes, Oxfordshire and Buckinghamshire
01296 392424
info@connexions-mob.org
www.connexionsmkob.org or
www.connexionsmkob.com

# South Central

Connexions South Central
01489 566990
www.connexions-southcentral.org

## Surrey

Connexions Surrey
01372 746500; 0808 001 3219
info@connexionssurrey.co.uk
www.connexionssurrey.co.uk

Camberley Connexions Centre
01276 27172

Epsom Connexions Centre
01372 722291

Guildford Connexions Centre
01483 576121

Redhill Connexions Centre
01737 773801

Staines Connexions Centre
01784 455081

Woking Connexions Centre
01483 760041

## Sussex

Connexions Sussex
01273 783648/783624
admin@connexions-sussex.org.uk
www.connexions-sussex.org.uk

---

# South-west

## Bournemouth, Dorset and Poole

Connexions Bournemouth, Dorset and Poole
0800 358 3888
headoffice@connexions-bdp.co.uk
www.connexions-bdp.co.uk

Blandford Connexions Shop
01258 454454

Bournemouth Connexions Shop
01202 315331

Gillingham Connexions Shop
01747 826358

Poole Connexions Shop
01202 677557

Weymouth Connexions Shop
01305 782180

## Cornwall and Devon

Connexions Cornwall and Devon
0800 975 5111
partnership@connexions-cd.org.uk
www.connexions-cd.org.uk

Barnstaple Connexions Information and Advice Centre
01271 378585
barnstaple@connexions-cd.org.uk

Bodmin Connexions Information and Advice Centre
01208 77999
bodmin@connexions-cd.org.uk

Exeter Connexions Information and Advice Centre
01392 203603
exeter@connexions-cd.org.uk

Pool Connexions Information and Advice Centre
01209 315171
pool@connexions-cd.org.uk

Newton Abbot Connexions Information and Advice Centre
01626 367579
newtonabbot@connexions-cd.org.uk

Plymouth Connexions Information and Advice Centre
01752 207700
plymouth@connexions-cd.org.uk

Torquay Connexions Information and Advice Centre
01803 200202
torquay@connexions-cd.org.uk

Truro Connexions Information and Advice Centre
01872 277993
truro@connexions-cd.org.uk

## Somerset

Connexions Somerset
01823 423450
webmaster@connexions-somerset.org.uk
www.connexions-somerset.org.uk

Bridgwater Connexions Centre
01278 423788
bridgwater@connexions-somerset.org.uk

Frome Connexions Centre
01373 465302
frome@connexions-somerset.org.uk

Street Connexions Centre
01458 443051
street@connexions-somerset.org.uk

Taunton Connexions Centre
01823 321212
taunton@connexions-somerset.org.uk

Yeovil Connexions Centre
01935 381800
yeovil@connexions-somerset.org.uk

Minehead Connexions Centre
01643 701900
webmaster@connexions-somerset.org.uk

## Gloucestershire

Connexions Gloucestershire
01452 833600
info: 01452 524800
info@connexionsglos.org.uk
www.connexionsglos.co.uk

Connexions First Stop Shop
01452 426900

Connexions First Stop Shop
01453 757133

Connexions First Stop Shop
01242 250317

## Wiltshire and Swindon

Connexions Wiltshire and Swindon
01249 448855

---

# West of England

Connexions West of England
0117 987 3700; 0800 923 0323
enquiries@connexionswest.org.uk
www.connexionswest.org.uk

Connexions Bath & NE Somerset
01225 461501

Connexions Filton, South Gloucestershire
0117 969 8101

Connexions Kingswood, South Gloucestershire
0117 961 2760

Connexions North Somerset
01934 644443

# Adoption and fostering

## Records and government offices

### England & Wales

**The Family Records Centre**
1 Myddleton Street
London
EC1R 1UW
020 8392 5300
enquiry@pro.gov.uk
www.familyrecords.gov.uk/frc

**A2A Public Record Office**
Kew
Richmond
Surrey
TW9 4DU
020 8487 9211
a2a@pro.gov.uk
www.a2a.pro.gov.uk
*contains catalogues describing archives held throughout England and dating from the 900s to the present day*

**General Register Office (GRO)**
Smedley Hydro, Trafalgar Road
Southport
PR8 2HH
0870 243 7788
certificate.services@ons.gov.uk
www.statistics.gov.uk/nsbase/registration/
*responsible for ensuring the registration of all births, marriages and deaths that have occurred in England and Wales since 1837 and for maintaining a central archive*

**Adoption Records**
0151 471 4830
adoptions@ons.gov.uk
www.statistics.gov.uk/registration/
Adoptions.asp

**Overseas Records**
0151 471 4801
overseas.gro@ons.gov.uk
www.statistics.gov.uk/registration/CertOverse
as/OverseasListRecords.asp

**Placement, Permanence & Children's Trusts Branch (including Intercountry Section)**
Wellington House
133-55 Waterloo Road
London
SE1 8UG
weekdays 9-1pm 020 7972 4014
dhmail@doh.gsi.gov.uk
*inter-country section processes applications to adopt children from overseas; provides factsheets and advice regarding inter-country adoption law*

**The Adoption Register**
PO Box 33629
London
N16 0XA
020 8800 3332
admin@adoptionregister.net
www.adoptionregister.net
*holds details about all children in England and Wales awaiting adoption and all approved adopters*

**Home Office - Immigration and Nationality Directorate**
Section 1, Room 1101
Apollo House, 36 Wellesley Road
Croydon
CR9 3RR
*for enquiries from British citizens who are resident overseas and wish to bring a child adopted in that country into the UK*

## Northern Ireland

### General Register Office
### for Northern Ireland
Oxford House, 49/55 Chichester Street
Belfast
BT1 4HL
028 9025 2000
www.groni.gov.uk

### Birth, Death, Marriage Certificate Queries
gro.nisra@dfpni.gov.uk

### Marriage, Re-registration and Adoptions
groreg.nisra@dfpni.gov.uk

### Statistics Queries
grostats.nisra@dfpni.gov.uk

## Scotland

### General Register Office for Scotland
Scotland's People, c/o Scotland On Line
Gateway East, Technology Park
Dundee
DD2 1SW
0870 777 9495 Mon-Thu 9-5.30pm,
Fri 9-5pm
scotlandspeople@scotlandonline.co.uk
www.gro-scotland.gov.uk

### Adoptions & Parental orders
0131 314 4444
adoption@gro-scotland.gov.uk
*Contact: Miss L Anderson*

### Re-registrations of Births
0131 314 4444
reregistration@gro-scotland.gov.uk
*Contact: Miss L Anderson*

### Changes of name
0131 314 4444
namechange@gro-scotland.gov.uk
*Contact: Miss L Anderson*

### General enquiries relating to false
### information (Bigamy, still-births etc)
0131 314 4452
gru_support@gro-scotland.gov.uk
*Contact: Mrs Y Ravizza*

### Archives & public records, family research
0131 314 4433
records@gro-scotland.gov.uk
*Contact: Mrs H Ewing*

### Publications and Statistics for Births,
### Deaths, Marriages & Population
0131 314 4243
customer@gro-scotland.gov.uk
*Contact: Ms C Welch*

### Adoption Unit
New Register House
Edinburgh
EH1 3YT
0131 334 0380
adoption@gro-scotland.gov.uk
*can provide extracts of original birth entries*

### Birth Link
c/o Family Care Adoption Society
21 Castle Street
Edinburgh
EH2 3DN
0131 225 6441
mail@birthlink.org.uk
www.birthlink.org.uk
*register for Scotland offering the opportunity
to provide details for tracing; open to parents,
children and birth relatives*

# Independent adoption and fostering agencies

## Barnardo's

### Kent

**APEX Project**
128 London Road, Southborough
Tunbridge Wells
Kent
TN4 0PL
01892 510650
apex@barnardos.org.uk
services.barnardos.org.uk/apex/
*a varied fostering service including full-
time, holiday and short break placements
for children and young people with severe to
moderate learning difficulties and
emotional and behavioural problems*

### East London

**Jigsaw**
12 Church Hill
Walthamstow
London
E17 3AG
020 8521 0033
jigsaw@barnardos.org.uk
services.barnardos.org.uk/jigsaw/
*adoption, bridge fostering and permanent
fostering*

### Colchester

**New Families Colchester**
54 Head Street
Colchester
Essex
CO1 1PB
01206 562438
jane.horne@barnardos.org.uk
services.barnardos.org.uk/newfamilies
colchester
*permanent placements, Onto Independence
programme and short bridge foster
placements*

### South London

**Kusadiki**
020 8291 9200
kusadiki@barnardos.org.uk
*Foster placements for Lewisham young
people aged 10-15 years*

### Dudley

**8 to 18 project**
01384 253652
8to18@barnardos.org.uk
*Permanent & long term placements to
children between 8 and 18 years*

**Breakaway Project**
01384 458585
breakaway@barnardos.org.uk
*permanent & long term placements to
children with severe disabilities*

### West Midlands

**Midlands New Families**
0121 550 4737
nick.dunster@barnardos.org.uk

### Midlands

**Albion Court Project**
024 7635 6052
albion.court@barnardos.org.uk
*foster placements for young people on bail
aged 10 to 16 years providing family based
accommodation as an alternative to
custody*

### East Midlands

**East Midlands Family Placement Project**
01332 544711
eastmidlands.fpc@barnardos.org.uk
*long term foster placements*

### North Wales

**New Families Mold**
01352 751510
newfamilies.mold@barnardos.org.uk

### Rest of Wales

**Derwen Family Placement Services**
029 2043 6200
cymru.derwen@barnardos.org.uk

### North East

**New Families North East**
0191 240 4814
ne.newfamilies@barnardos.org.uk

**Family Placement Project**
0191 240 4811
ne.familyplacement@barnardos.org.uk

**Genesis**
0191 240 4836
ne.genesis@barnardos.org.uk

## Durham

**Shared Care**
0191 378 4800

## North West

**North West Fostering Service Project**
0151 488 0822

## Merseyside

**FAIM (Fostering Adolescents in Merseyside)**
5 Lineside Close
Liverpool
L25 2UD
0151 488 1105 or
0151 488 1124 (24hr answer phone)
Peter.tomlin@barnardos.org.uk
services.barnardos.org.uk/faim/
*a fostering service for young people aged
8-18 years across Merseyside*

## Bradford

**New Families Yorkshire**
01274 532852
newfamiliesyorkshire@barnardos.org.uk

## Edinburgh

**Family Placement Services (FPS)**
6 Torphichen Street
Edinburgh
EH3 8JQ
0131 228 4121
fps.scotland@barnardos.org.uk
services.barnardos.org.uk/familyplacement
edinburgh/
*specialises in finding families for children
considered 'hard to place'*

## Belfast

**Professional Fostercare**
028 9065 2288
*fostering service for children with complex
needs and/or disabilities*

---

## England

**Adoption Matters**
14 Liverpool Road
Chester
CH2 1AE
01244 390938
info@adoptionmatters.org
www.adoptionmatters.org
*voluntary adoption agency; operational area
includes Cheshire, Halton and Warrington,
Wirral, South Manchester - including Tameside,
Stockport and Trafford - and north-east Wales*

**Alliance Foster Care**
Moulton Park Business Centre, Unit G2
Redhouse Road, Moulton Park
Northampton
NN3 6AQ
0870 240 2395
www.alliancefostercare.co.uk
*an independant fostering agency covering
Northamptonshire, Peterborough,
Cambridgeshire, Lincolnshire, Bedfordshire,
Luton, Hertfordshire, Buckinghamshire and
Milton Keynes*

**Boys and Girls Welfare Society (BGWS)**
The BGWS Centre, Schools Hill
Cheadle
Cheshire
SK8 1JE
0161 283 4848
enquiries@bgws.org.uk
www.bgws.org.uk
*fostering and adoption*

**Care Today/ Parallel Parents**
Suite 6, New Mansion House
173 Wellington Road South
Stockport
SK1 3UA
0161 477 5830
admin@caretoday.co.uk
www.caretoday.co.uk
*long and short-term placements to all ages of
young people and sibling groups*

---

**Car-Es (UK)**
The Old Hall
Byers Green
County Durham
DL16 7PS
01388 458888
socialwork@cares.co.uk
www.cares.co.uk
*specialist services in child care, residential,*
*crisis intervention, fostering, social work*
*escort service with nationwide coverage*

**Catholic Care (Diocese of Leeds)**
Adoption Yorkshire, 11 North Grange Road
Headingley
Leeds
LS6 2BR
0113 388 5400
adoption@catholic-care.org.uk
www.adoption-yorkshire.org.uk
*a charitable organisation working on behalf*
*of the Diocese of Leeds arranging adoptions in*
*Yorkshire*

**Childlink Adoption Society**
10 Lion Yard
Tremadoc Road
London
SW4 7NQ
020 7501 1700
enquiries@adoptchildlink.org.uk
www.adoptchildlink.org.uk
*voluntary adoption agency, formerly The*
*Church Adoption Society*

**The Children's Family Trust**
MKA House, 4-6 Andrews Road
Droitwich
Worcester
WR9 8DN
01905 798229
cft.headoffice@btinternet.com
*long-term care including voluntary registered*
*homes and foster care*

**Coram Family Adoption Service**
Coram Community Campus
49 Mecklenburgh Square
London
WC1N 2QA
020 7520 0384
adoption@coram.org.uk
www.coram.org.uk
*a family placement service adoption service of*
*the children's charity, Coram Family,*
*formerly the Thomas Coram Foundation for*
*Children*

**Credo Care**
PO Box 29
Romney Marsh
TN29 9ZN
0870 241 4285
enquiries@credocare.co.uk
www.credocare.co.uk
*an intensive foster care option for children*
*and young people with disabilities and*
*complex medical needs*

**Ethelbert Specialist Homes Ltd**
Cheesemans Farmhouse, Alland Grange Lane
Manston
Kent
CT12 5BZ
01843 823762
headoffice@ethelberthomes.co.uk
www.ethelberthomes.co.uk
*cater for a diverse range of problems and*
*difficulties exhibited by vulnerable children*

**Families Are Best**
0115 955 8811
enquiries@ccsnotts.co.uk
www.families-are-best.co.uk
*the adoption service of the Catholic Children's*
*Society, Nottingham*

**Families for All**
The Catholic Children's Society (Westminster)
73 St Charles Square
London
W10 6EJ
020 8969 5305
stevel@athchild.org.uk
www.cathchild.org.uk
*Recruits, prepares and provides adoptive*
*families for local authorities for children aged*
*0-12 years*

**Families That Last**
After Adoption
12-14 Chapel Street
Manchester
M3 7NH
0161 819 3108
familiesthatlast@afteradoption.org.uk
www.afteradoption.org.uk
*a family finding project for hard to place*
*children in the north-west, run by the charity*
*After Adoption*

## Father Hudson Society
Coventry Road
Coleshill
Birmingham
B46 3EB
01675 434000
enquiries@fatherhudsons.org.uk
www.fatherhudsons.org.uk
*3 services: Families through Adoption, a
registered adoption agency, New Routes, a
registered fostering project for older children
and Origins, a service provided to people who
were formerly in the care of Father Hudson's
Homes, child migrants and people who were
involved in adoptions*

## Five Rivers
0800 389 8708
www.five-rivers.org
*offers a wide range of placements including
permanency, parent and child, bridge and
independence, short and long term
placements; accomodates children who have
experienced multiple placements, abuse,
educational and learning difficulties*

**Republic of Ireland**  00 353 634 5063

**Salisbury/ South West**  01722 421142

**London**  020 8599 5251

**Midlands**  01332 638036

**Devon & Cornwall**  01392 276959

**Cheltenham**  01242 514194

## Foster Care Associates
0800 085 2225
contactus@thefca.co.uk
www.fostercareassociates.co.uk
*providing family placements for 'difficult to
place' children*

## The Foster Care Co-operative
203-205 West Malvern Road
Worcestershire
WR14 4BB
01684 892380
enquiries@fostercarecooperative.co.uk
www.fostercarecooperative.co.uk
*offers assessment, short-term and permanent
placements*

## The Fostering Agency
211 Piccadilly
London
W1J 9HF
020 7917 2947
www.londonfostering.net
*provides foster care resources for Local
Authorities in and around London*

The Fostering Agency (Anglia)
Owl House Ground Floor Offices
Battery Green, Lowestoft
Suffolk
NR32 1DH
01502 588349

The Fostering Agency (London South)
Unit 2, Eurolink Business Centre
49 Effra Road
London
SW2 1BZ
020 7771 6970

The Fostering Agency (London West)
Uxbridge House, 464 Uxbridge Road
Hayes
Middlesex
UB4 0SD
020 8848 7878

## FosterPlus
11 Doolittle Mill, Ampthill
Bedfordshire
MK45 2ND
01525 841803
info@fosterplus.co.uk
www.fosterplus.com
*offers a wide range of care solutions and
advice*

FosterPlus (Eastern Region)
Latton Bush Business Centre
Southern Way,
Harlow
Essex
CM18 7BH
01279 836283

FosterPlus (Midlands)
9 Millstone Lane
Leicester
LE1 5JN
0116 262 6123

## Futures for Children
Head Office, 69 College Road
Maidstone
Kent
ME15 6SX
01622 673555
contact@futures-for-children.org
www.futures-for-children.org.uk
*fostering agency*

Futures for Children
Royce House, 630-634 London Road
Westcliff-on-Sea
Essex
SS0 9HW
01702 335932

Futures for Children
19 Canon Harnett Court, Warren Farm
Wolverton Mill
Milton Keynes
MK12 5NF
01908 313222

Futures for Children
Cedarmount House, 90a Owlsmoor Road
Owlsmoor, Sandhurst
Berkshire
GU47 0SS
01344 777521

## Heath Farm Family Services
Heath Farm, Charing Heath
Nr Ashford
Kent
TN27 0AX
01233 712030
www.heathfarm.org
*independent fostering agency*

## Hillcrest Care
Metro House, Northgate
Chichester
West Sussex
PO19 1BE
01243 531277
jane.barker@hillcrestcare.co.uk
www.hillcrestcare.co.uk
*Fostering & Supported Lodgings Service*

## Independent Adoption Service
121-123 Camberwell Road
London
SE5 0HB
020 7703 1088
admin@i-a-s.org.uk
www.i-a-s.org.uk
*an adoption agency and registered charity*

## Independent Fostering Ltd
3 Clarence Street
Nottingham
NG3 2ET
0115 947 3328
placements@independentfostering.com
www.independentfostering.com
*foster agency*

## Jigsaw (North West) IFA
The Old Courthouse
Chapel Street
Dukinfield
SK16 4DT
0161 609 1282
theteam@jigsaw-nw.org.uk
www.jigsaw-nw.org.uk
*a not for profit foster agency*

## Kindercare Fostering
Kelsey House, 77 High Street
Beckenham
Kent
BR3 1AN
020 8663 6327
kindercare@netsite.co.uk
www.kindercare.co.uk
*an independent fostering agency that
provides specialist fostering services to
compliment existing statutory provision*

## Lifeways Community Care
118 Garratt Lane
Wandsworth
London
SW18 4DJ
020 8877 1338
head-office@lifeways.co.uk
www.lifeways.co.uk
*a not for profit company offering transitional
care, supported living services, respite and
family breaks, residential care and
therapeutic or specialised foster care*

## Lifeways Community Care, Ayr
2 Newmarket Street
Ayr
South Ayrshire
KA7 1LH
01292 880220
ayr@lifeways.co.uk

## Lifeways Community Care, East Midlands
The Manse, 2 Third Avenue
Sherwood Rise
Nottingham
NG7 6JH
0115 962 0666
eastmidlands@lifeways.co.uk

**Lifeways Community Care, Greater Glasgow**
Suite 6-E-3, Templeton Business Centre
Templeton Street
Glasgow
G40 1DA
0141 556 5930
glasgow@lifeways.co.uk

**Lifeways Community Care, North & East Devon**
Portland House, Longbrook Street
Exeter
Devon
EX4 6AB
01392 491897
exeter@lifeways.co.uk

**Lifeways Community Care, North & East London**
27 Station Road, New Barnet
Hertfordshire
EN5 1PW
020 8441 7757
n.london@lifeways.co.uk

**Lifeways Community Care, Northwest**
Dallam Court, Dallam Lane
Warrington
Cheshire
WA2 7LT
01925 652438
northwest@lifeways.co.uk

**Lifeways Community Care, South & West Devon**
Unit A, Kingsley Close
Eastway, Ivybridge
Devon
PL21 9LL
01752 691122
ivybridge@lifeways.co.uk

**Lifeways Community Care, South & West London**
Unit J, Garratt Court
Furmage Street, Wandsworth
London
SW18 4DF
020 8877 3448
s.london@lifeways.co.uk

**The Manchester Adoption Society**
47 Bury New Road, Sedgley Park, Prestwich
Manchester
M25 9JY
0161 773 0973
bc@manadopt.u-net.com
www.manadopt.u-net.com
*small voluntary adoption agency*

**The Muslim Fostering Society UK**
116a Stoke Newington High Street
London
N16 7NY
020 7923 3333
info@Muslimfostering.co.uk
www.muslimfostering.co.uk
*an independent fostering agency*

**Norwood Jewish Adoption Society (NJAS)**
Broadway House
80-82 The Broadway, Stanmore
Middlesex
HA7 4HB
020 8954 4555
norwood@norwood.org.uk
www.nwrw.org
*five Service Divisions: Ravenswood Village,*
*Learning Disability Services, Children &*
*Family Services, Special Education Services*
*and Fostering & Adoption Services*

**The Orange Grove Foster Care Agency**
Orange Grove House,
203-205 West Malvern Road
West Malvern
Worcestershire
WR14 4BB
01684 567724
enquiries@theorangegrove.co.uk
www.theorangegrove.co.uk
*independent fostering agency*

**East Riding/ Hull Region**
33a Highgate
Beverley
East Yorkshire
HU17 0DN
01482 888816
jayne.ford@theorangegrove.co.uk

**Parents for Children**
41 Southgate Road
London
N1 3JP
020 7359 7530; 0845 307 6653
info@parentsforchildren.co.uk
www.parentsforchildren.org.uk
*established to find families for children*
*considered hard to place*

**Pathway Care**
Unit 10, Ty Nant Court
Morganstown
Cardiff
CF15 8LW
029 2081 1173
mail@pathwaycare.org.uk
www.pathwaycare.com
*foster agency aiming to provide family
placements for difficult to place children*

**Pathway Care Bristol**
Unit 1, Vincent Court
89-93 Soundwell Road, Staple Hill
Bristol
BS16 4QR
0117 957 3533
mail@pathwaycarebristol.org.uk

**Pathway Care Midlands**
3 Morgans Close, New Arley
Nr Coventry
CV7 8PR
01676 549174
pathwaycare@freeola.com

**Pathway Care West Wales**
Capel Dewi Hall, Capel Dewi
Carmarthen
Carmarthenshire
SA32 8AD
01267 290033
mail@pathwaycarecarmarthen.org.uk

**The Rose Road Association**
Rose Road
Southampton
Hampshire
SO14 6TE
023 8022 9017
ask@roseroad.co.uk
www.roseroad.co.uk
*services for young people with profound and
multiple disabilities; residential short breaks
and short family respite placements*

**SACCS Shropshire**
Mytton Mill
Montford Bridge
Shropshire
SY4 1HA
01743 850015; fostering service, Find Us
Keep Us: 01743 850086
saccs@saccs.co.uk
www.saccs.co.uk
*provides recovery facilities for severely
traumatised children and young people
between the ages of 4 and 12 (on admission)*

**SACCS Staffordshire**
Building 300, Relay Point
Relay Drive, Tamworth
Staffordshire
B77 5PA
01827 287487

**Seafields Fostering**
29-31 Malvern Road
Hornchurch
Essex
RM11 1BG
01708 733735
www.seafields.com
*provides a range of foster placements
including: emergency, respite, short term,
sibling placements, bridging placements,
mother and baby placements and long term
provision; covers London, the south-east and
East Anglia*

**Sedgemoor**
Ashwell Park
Ilminster
Somerset
TA19 9DX
0845 070 0513
referral@sedgemoor.net
www.sedgemoor.net
*a single sex specialist care provision
providing residential facilities and education
for young people and children, including
those with hearing impairment and learning
difficulties*

**SSAFA Forces Help**
19 Queen Elizabeth Street
London
SE1 2LP
020 7403 8783
info@ssafa.org.uk
www.ssafa.org.uk
*adoption and post adoption services for those
in the serving military community*

**St Cuthbert's Care**
Head Office, St Cuthbert's House
West Road
Newcastle upon Tyne
NE15 7PY
0191 228 0111
www.stcuthbertscare.org.uk
*foster agency with specialist residential foster
preparation unit*

**St Francis' Children's Society**
Collis House, 48 Newport Road
Woolstone
Milton Keynes
MK15 0AA
01908 572700
enquires@sfcs.org.uk
www.sfcs.org.uk
*Bedfordshire, Northamptonshire,
Buckinghamshire and the Slough area of
Berkshire*

**SWIIS Foster Care**
19 Portland Place
London
W1B 1PX
020 7307 8383
info@swiis.com
www.swiis.co.uk/foster_care.shtml
national independent fostering agency

**TACT (The Adolescent & Children's Trust)**
London - South
020 8695 8111
enquiries@tactfostercare.org.uk
*teams of foster carers covering all of Greater
London, the Midlands and Wales*

**London - North**
020 8200 2363

**Birmingham, East Midlands / Anglia**
01832 731734

**TACT Cymru**
01639 622320

**Bristol / West**
01454 203657

**Liverpool**
0151 707 9968

**Team Fostering North East**
Howdon Terminal, Willington Quay
Wallsend
NE28 6UL
0191 262 8855
www.teamfostering.co.uk
*a not for profit, voluntary fostering agency*

**Team Fostering Yorkshire**
The Business Centre, Bowbridge Close
Bradmarsh Business Park
Rotherham
S60 1BY
01709 782361

## Northern Ireland

**The Church of Ireland Social and Family
Welfare Association (N.I.) and Adoption
Society**
Church of Ireland House
61-67 Donegall Street
Belfast
BT1 2QH
028 9023 3885
admin@cofiadopt.org.uk
www.cofiadopt.org.uk
*voluntary adoption agency*

## Scotland

**FosterPlus**
Unit 0, Kirton Business Centre
Kirk Land, Livingston Village
Livingston
EH54 7AY
01506 420610
info@fosterplus.co.uk
www.fosterplus.com
*offers a wide range of care solutions and
advice*

**FosterPlus**
Room 121, St James Business Centre
Linwood Road
Paisley
PA3 3AT
0141 889 8481

**Scottish Adoption Association Ltd**
2 Commercial Street, Leith
Edinburgh
EH6 6JA
0131 553 5060

**St Andrews Childrens Society Ltd**
7 St John's Place
Edinburgh
EH6 7EL
0131 454 3370
info@standrews-children.org.uk
*Adoption services, Foster care, Adoptee
counselling and Pregnancy counselling*

**St Margaret of Scotland Children
& Family Care Society**
274 Bath Street
Glasgow
G2 4JR
0141 332 8371
adopt@stmargarets8.fsnet.co.uk

# Post adoption services, associations and charities

**British Agencies for Adoption and Fostering (BAAF)**
Skyline House
200 Union Street
London
SE1 0LX
020 7593 2000
mail@baaf.org.uk; fundraising@baaf.org.uk; press@baaf.org.uk; pub.sales@baaf.org.uk
www.baaf.org.uk
*a national registered charity which promotes best practice in adoption and fostering services; operates a family-finding service; supports professionals and adoptive parents and foster carers; lobbies for legislative improvements; runs courses, seminars, consultancy and conferences around the UK for people involved in childcare; produces thousands of books, guides and leaflets for professionals and those with a general interest in adoption and fostering. Membership includes almost all local authorities and voluntary adoption agencies in the UK, as well as more than 50 independent fostering agencies*

**Central England**
Midlands Office, Dolphin House
54 Coventry Road
Birmingham
B10 0RX
0121 753 2001;
Advice Line (9-1) 0870 241 0663
midlands@baaf.org.uk

**Cymru/Wales**
Cardiff Office
7 Cleeve House, Lambourne Crescent
Cardiff
CF14 5GP
029 2076 1155
cymru@baaf.org.uk

**Cymru/Wales**
Rhyl Office
19 Bedford Street, Rhyl/ Y Rhyl
Denbighshire
LL18 1SY
01745 336336
cymru.rhyl@baaf.org.uk

**Cymru/Wales**
Carmarthen Office
1st Floor, 3 Red Street
Carmarthen
SA31 1QL
01267 221000
carmarthen@baaf.org.uk

**Northern England**
Leeds Office
Grove Villa, 82 Cardigan Road
Headingley, Leeds
LS6 3BJ
0113 274 4797;
Advice Line (9-1) 0870 241 0663
leeds@baaf.org.uk

**Northern England**
Newcastle Office
MEA House, Ellison Place
Newcastle upon Tyne
NE1 8XS
0191 261 6600;
Advice Line (9-1) 0870 241 0663
newcastle@baaf.org.uk

**Scotland**
40 Shandwick Place
Edinburgh
EH2 4RT
0131 220 4749
scotland@baaf.org.uk

**Southern England**
Southern Office
Skyline House, 200 Union Street
London
SE1 0LX
020 7593 2041/42
southern@baaf.org.uk

## Adoption and Fostering Information Line

193 Market Street
Hyde
Cheshire
SK14 1HF
0800 783 4086 (everyday 9am - 9pm)
www.adoption.org.uk
*internet site offering advice and information*

## Adoption LINK UK

99 Claremont Avenue, Maghull
Merseyside
L31 8AH
0151 527 2218
info@adoptionlink.co.uk
www.adoptionlink.co.uk
*undertakes post adoptive tracing enquiries*

## Adoption UK

Manor Farm
Appletree Road, Chipping Warden
Banbury
OX17 1LH
01295 660121
helpdesk@adoptionuk.org.uk
www.adoptionuk.com
*a national self help group run by adoptive parents*

## Adoption-net

c/o Northcliffe Electronic Publishing, East Point
Cardinal Square, 10 Nottingham Road
Derby
DE1 3QT
0116 227 3123
mbailey@nep.co.uk
www.adoption-net.co.uk
*a national website dedicated to adoption and fostering*

## Adoptions Reunited

180 Bridge Road
Sarisbury Green
Southampton
SO31 7EH
www.adoptionsreunited.com
*free post adoption reunion registry and help pages*

## After Adoption

Head Office, 12-14 Chapel Street
Manchester
M3 7NH
Head Office: 0161 839 4932;
Actionline: 0800 056 8578 (mon, wed, thurs 10-6pm; tues 10-8pm; fri 10-4pm);
Talkadoption (for callers under 26):
0808 808 1234 (hours as before)
information@afteradoption.org.uk or
helpline@talkadoption.org.uk
www.afteradoption.org.uk
*charity providing independent adoption support services*

### Lancashire, Blackpool & Blackburn

01772 258893
preston@afteradoption.org.uk

### London

020 7628 3443
london@afteradoption.org.uk

### Merseyside, Wirral & Cheshire

0151 707 4322
merseyside@afteradoption.org.uk

### North East & Cumbria

0191 230 0088
northeast@afteradoption.org.uk

### Wales

029 2066 6597
southwales@afteradoption.org.uk

## Barnardo's Family Connections

Cottage No. 1, Tanners Lane
Barkingside, Ilford
Essex
IG6 1QG
020 8550 2688
family.connections@barnardos.org.uk
services.barnardos.org.uk/familyconnections/
*post adoption services*

## The Fostering Network

### England

87 Blackfriars Road
London
SE1 8HA
020 7620 6400
www.thefostering.net
*charity for all those involved in foster care*

**Scotland**
Ingram House, 2nd Floor
227 Ingram Street
Glasgow
G1 1DA
0141 204 1400

**Northern Ireland**
216 Belmont Road
Belfast
BT4 2AT
028 9067 3441

**Wales**
Suite 11, 2nd Floor
Bay Chambers, West Bute Street
Cardiff Bay
CF10 5BB
029 2044 0940

## International Foster Care Organisation
Anna Paulownastraat 103
2518 BC The Hague
The Netherlands
00 31 70 346 2153
denhaagoffice@ifco.info
www.internationalfostering.org
*a voluntary organisation committed to the
improvement of the quality of service given to
children and young people in care and the
development of standards for organisations
and individual carers*

## NORCAP
112 Church Road
Wheatley
Oxfordshire
OX33 1LU
01865 875000 (weekdays 10-4pm)
enquiries@norcap.org
www.norcap.org.uk
*a support group for adults affected by
adoption; offers a telephone helpline, contact
register, research service, intermediary service
and specialised advice*

## North East Post Adoption Service (NEPAS)
Royal Quays Community Centre, Prince
Consort Way
Royal Quays, North Shields
Tyne and Wear
NE29 6XB
0191 296 6064
nepas@nepas.org
www.nepas.org
*charity providing independent adoption
support services*

## NPN (Natural Parents Network)
Garden Suburb
Oldham
Lancashire
OL8 3AY
helpline: 0161 287 8737; office: 01273
307597
administrator@n-p-n.fsnet.co.uk
www.n-p-n.fsnet.co.uk
*self help charity which provides helpline for
natural parents and relatives who have lost
children to adoption*

## Parents and Children Together (PACT)
7A Southern Court
South Street
Reading
RG1 4QS
0118 938 7600
postadoption@pactcharity.org
*post adoption services*

## Post Adoption Centre
5 Torriano Mews
Torriano Avenue
London
NW5 2RZ
020 7284 0555; advice line: 020 7485 2931
advice@postadoptioncentre.org.uk
www.postadoptioncentre.org.uk
*offers advice, short term counselling, a list of
recommended psychotherapists and
counsellors, mediation services and training*

## TIGER website
www.tiger.gov.uk/adoption/
*provides advice on rights and responsibilities
around leave and pay for adoptive parents*

# Children in care and leaving care

## Carelaw
www.carelaw.org.uk
*an information site for children and young people in care in England & Wales; it covers many topics from your rights in care to what happens when you leave care; CareZone is The Who Cares? Trust's new set of secure online services for children in public care*

## The Careleavers Association
PO Box 179
Shipley
BD18 3WX
01274 581124
www.careleavers.org
*a union of care leavers who actively advocate and support radical change within the care system; acts to protect, promote and strengthen rights for care leavers and to empower members through support, education and training*

## Careleavers Reunited
www.careleaversreunited.com
*puts care leavers in touch with those they grew up with*

## The Line
0800 884444
*ChildLine's special helpline aimed at children and young people in residential or foster care, at boarding school, in secure units and those who have to stay in hospital for long periods; open on weekdays between 3.30pm and 9.30pm and on Saturdays and Sundays from 2pm until 8pm*

## National Youth Advocacy Service
99-105 Argyle Street
Birkenhead
Wirral
CH41 6AD
0151 342 7852; freephone: 0800 616101
help@nyas.net
www.nyas.net
*a 'not for profit' children's charity which offers socio-legal advocacy services to children, young people, parents, carers and professionals; has an Advocacy Service for children in care; lines are open 3.30pm - 9.30pm every week day and 2pm to 8pm on Saturdays and Sundays*

## Voice for the Child in Care
Unit 4, Pride Court
80-82 White Lion Street
London
N1 6PF
020 7833 5792
info@vcc-uk.org; blueprint@vcc-uk.org
www.vcc-uk.org
*help for children in care including visiting and advocacy services; also manages the blueprint project with backing from the National Children's Bureau. This project is due to finish in March 2004 and involves the development of proposals for change in the care system*

## The Who Cares? Trust
Kemp House, 152-160 City Road
London
EC1V 2NP
020 7251 3117; freephone: 0500 564570
mailbox@thewhocarestrust.org.uk
www.thewhocarestrust.org.uk
*a major on-line resource for people in the care sector. The site has a database of all UK approved social work courses, extensive policy and law references, a sector specific care jobs service, daily news, features on professional practice, over 1400 links to other sites, discussion areas and guides to finding the right training courses*

## Wales

### The Bryn Melyn Group Foundation
PO Box 202
Bala
LL23 7ZB
01678 540598
enquiries@brynmelyngroupfoundation.org
www.brynmelyngroupfoundation.org
*a charity which conducts research into ways
of minimising the negative impact of care,
and administers a trust fund for young
adults vulnerable to social exclusion as a
result of their care experiences*

## Ireland

### Irish Association of Young People In Care
4 Christ Church Square, Dublin 8, Ireland
00 353 1 453 0355
IAYPIC@Barnardos.ie
homepage.tinet.ie/~iaypic/
*a forum in the Republic of Ireland, to
represent the interests of young people in care*

## Scotland

### The Scottish Throughcare & Aftercare Forum
2nd Floor, 37 Otago Street
Glasgow
G12 8JJ
0141 357 4124
enquiries@scottishthroughcare.org.uk
www.scottishthroughcare.org.uk
*a voluntary organisation whose aim is to
improve support for young people leaving
residential or foster care in Scotland*

# Children at risk

## Government agencies

### Protection of Children Act Tribunal
**Address:** 6th Floor, St Christopher House, 90-114 Southwark Street, London SE1 0TE
**Tel:** 020 7921 1629
**E-mail:** pocat@gtnet.gov.uk
**Web:** www.pocat.gov.uk

*The Tribunal was established by Parliament in the Protection of Children Act 1999 and started work on 2 October 2000; it provides an independent appeal procedure for child care workers who have been put on the statutory list of people forbidden to work with children because they are unsuitable to do so and for teachers who have been banned from working in schools or further education colleges or whose right to do so has been restricted; its members are appointed by the Lord Chancellor; the Tribunal makes no charge for conducting appeals, and public funding may be available to help those who apply.*

### Department of Health - Area Child Protection Committees
**E-mail:** acpc@doh.gsi.gov.uk
**Web:** www.acpc.gov.uk

### London boroughs

**Barking and Dagenham ACPC**
Civic Centre, Social Services
Department
Dagenham
Essex
RM10 7BW
020 8227 2233
out of hours: 020 8594 8356
cathryn.williams@lbbd.gov.uk

**Barnet ACPC**
The Old Town Hall, Barnet House
1255 High Road, Friern Barnet Lane
London
N20 0EJ
020 8359 3149
paul.fallon@barnet.gov.uk

**Bexley ACPC**
Hill View, Hill View Drive
Welling
Kent
DA16 3RY
020 8303 7777 ext 6428
out of hours: 020 8303 7777
sheila.murphy@bexley.gov.uk

**Brent ACPC**
Mahatma Ghandi House, 6th
Floor
34 Wembley Hill Road, Wembley
Middlesex
HA9 8AD
020 8937 4237
mick.anderson@brent.gov.uk

**Bromley ACPC**
Social Services and Housing
Department, Bromley Civic
Centre
Stockwell Close
Bromley
BR1 3UH
020 8313 4612
out of hours: 020 8464 4848
terry.rich@bromley.gov.uk

**Camden ACPC**
79 Camden Road
London
NW1 9ES
020 7974 6641
out of hours: 020 7974 6666
catherine.doran@camden.gov.uk

**Croydon ACPC**
Social Services Department,
Taberner House
Park Lane, Croydon
Surrey
CR9 2BA
020 8686 4433 ext 2125
joan.semeonoff@croydon.gov.uk

**Ealing ACPC**
Perceval House
14-16 Uxbridge Road
London
W5 2HL
020 8825 7106
out of hours: 020 8825 5000
finlayj@ealing.gov.uk

**Enfield ACPC**
PO Box 59, Civic Centre
Silver Street
Enfield
EN1 3XL
020 8379 4541
out of hours: 020 8366 6565
andrew.fraser@enfield.gov.uk

**Greenwich ACPC**
Nelson House
50 Wellington Street
London
SE18 6PY
020 8854 8888 ext 3000

**Hackney & City ACPC**
205 Morning Lane
London
E9 6JX
020 8356 4523
Emergency Duty Team: 020 8356 5527
jkwhali@gw.hackney.gov.uk

**Hammersmith & Fulham ACPC**
4th Floor, 145 King Street
Hammersmith
London
W6 9XY
020 8753 5002/ 020 8748 3020 ext 5002
a.christie@inet.ibhf.gov.uk

**Haringey ACPC**
c/o Civic Centre
High Road
Wood Green
N22 7SG
020 8489 0000
ruth.gisbon@haringey.gov.uk

**Harrow ACPC**
PO Box 7, Civic Centre
Harrow
Middlesex
HA1 2UL
020 8424 1365
amy.weir@harrow.gov.uk

**Havering ACPC**
The Town Hall
Main Road
Romford
RM1 3BD
01708 433001
anthony.douglas@havering.gov.uk

**Hillingdon ACPC**
Civic Centre
Uxbridge
UB8 1UW
01895 250393
out of hours: 01895 250111
jwilson@hillingdon.gov.uk

**Hounslow ACPC**
Children & Families, The Civic Centre
Lampton Road, Hounslow
Middlesex
TW3 4DN
020 8583 3002
out of hours: 020 8583 2222
cecilia.hitchen@hounslow.gov.uk

**Islington ACPC**
Highbury House, Room 305, 5/6
Highbury Crescent
Islington
London
N5 1RN
020 7527 4265
david.worlock@islington.gov.uk

**Kensington & Chelsea ACPC**
Town Hall Room 140
Hornton Street, Kensington
London
W8 7NX
020 7361 2354
alastair.pettigrew@rbkc.gov.uk

**Kingston ACPC**
Royal Borough of Kingston upon Thames, Guildhall 1
St James Road, Kingston Upon Thames
Surrey
KT1 1EU
020 8547 6056
out of hours: 020 7613 6950
margie.rooke@rbk.kingston.gov.uk

**Lambeth ACPC**
Mary Seacole House
91 Clapham High Street
London
SW4 7TF
020 7926 4787
out of hours: 020 7926 1000
phowes@lambeth.gov.uk

**Lewisham ACPC**
Laurence House
1 Catford Road
London
SE6 4RU
020 8314 8678
out of hours/ voice mail: 020 8314 8678 or 0774 082 5218
mark.wheeler@lewisham.gov.uk

**Merton ACPC**
Merton Civic Centre, London Road
Morden
Surrey
SM4 5DX
020 8545 3711
out of hours: 020 8770 5000
Rea.mattocks@merton.gov.uk

**Newham ACPC**
Broadway House, Social Services Department
322 High Street, Stratford
London
E15 1AJ
020 8430 5250
out of hours: 020 8430 2000
kathryn.hudson@newham.gov.uk

**Redbridge ACPC**
Children & Families, Ley Street House
497-499 Ley Street, Ilford
Essex
IG2 7QX
020 8708 5752
patrick.power@redbridge.gov.uk

**Richmond Upon Thames ACPC**
Services for Children and Families
42 York Street
Twickenham
TW1 3BW
020 8891 7360 or 7601
out of hours: 020 8744 2442
j.jerome@richmond.gov.uk

**Southwark ACPC**
Mable Goldwin House
49 Grange Walk
London
SE1 3DY
020 7525 3846
out of hours: 020 7525 5000
romi.bowen@southwark.gov.uk

**Sutton ACPC**
London Borough of Sutton Civic Offices
St Nicholas Way
Sutton
SM1 1EA
020 8770 5000
david.warlock@sutton.gov.uk

**Tower Hamlets ACPC**
Social Services Directorate HQ
62 Roman Road, Bethnal Green
London
E2 0QJ
020 7364 2213

**Waltham Forest ACPC**
Leyton Municipal Offices, High
Road
Leyton
London
E10 5QJ
020 8496 5113
out of hours: 020 8496 3000
hugh.valentine@soc.lbwf.gov.uk

**Wandsworth ACPC**
Fairfield Annexe
Fairfield Street
London
SW18 2PU
020 8871 6291
out of hours: 020 8871 6000
mrundle@wandsworth.gov.uk

**Westminster ACPC**
Child Protection Unit, 7th Floor,
City Hall
64 Victoria Street
London
SW1E 6QP
020 7641 2679
out of hours: 020 7641 6000
strench@westminster.gov.uk

---

# England

**Barnsley ACPC**
Wellington House
36 Wellington Street
Barnsley
S70 2DU
01226 772301
grahamgatehouse@barnsley.gov.
uk

**Bath & North East Somerset
ACPC**
7 North Parade Buildings
Bath
BA1 1NY
01225 396289
out of hours: 07977 228427
maurie_lindsay@bathnes.gov.uk

**Bedfordshire ACPC**
Children's Services, Bedfordshire
Social Services Department
County Hall, Cauldwell Street
Bedford
MK42 9AP
01234 363222
Mattail@bedfordshire.sccd.gov.uk

**Luton ACPC**
Luton Social Services, Unity
House
111 Stuart Street
Luton
LU1 5TD
01582 547502
out of hours: 01582 280366
cuellw@luton.gov.uk

**Birmingham ACPC**
Louisa Ryland House, Level 5,
Social Service Department
44 Newhall Street
Birmingham
B3 3PL
0121 303 4861
andrea.hickman@birmingham.go
v.uk

**Blackburn with Darwen ACPC**
Jubilee House
Jubilee Street
Blackburn
BB1 1ET
01254 587592
out of hours: 01254 587547
stephen.sloss@blackburn.gov.uk

**Blackpool ACPC**
Progress House, Clifton Road
Marton
Blackpool
FY4 4US
01253 477601
sheila.sutherland@blackpool.gov.uk

**Bolton ACPC**
Children & Families Division
Le Mans Crescent
Bolton
BL1 1SA
01204 337203
Lynne.jones@bolton.gov.uk

**Bournemouth ACPC**
New Century House, 3rd Floor
24 Christchurch Road,
Bournemouth
Dorset
BH1 3ND
01202 458721
out of hours: 01202 668123
kevin.jones@bournemouth.gov.uk

**Bracknell Forest ACPC**
Bracknell Forest Borough
Council, Times Square
Market Street, Bracknell
Berkshire
RG12 1JD
01344 424642
out of hours: 01344 786543
daphne.obang@bracknell-
forest.gov.uk

**Bradford ACPC**
City of Bradford Social Services
Department, Children's Services
5th Floor, Olicana House, Chapel
Street
Bradford
BD1 5RE
01274 432904
out of hours: 01274 530434
kath.tunstall@bradford.gov.uk

**Brighton & Hove ACPC**
Medway Martine Hospital NHS
Trust
Windmill Road, Gillingham
Kent
ME7 5NY
01634 833944
andrew.horne@medway-
tr.sthames.nhs.uk

**Bristol ACPC**
Social Services & Health, PO Box
30, Amelia Court
Pipe Lane
Bristol
BS99 7NB
0117 903 7946
tony_willetts@bristol-city.gov.uk

**Buckinghamshire ACPC**
Buckinghamshire County
Council, Room 50, Old County
Offices
Walton Street, Aylesbury
Bucks
HP20 1UA
01296 383692
out of hours: 0794 1278708
subutt@buckscc.gov.uk

**Bury ACPC**
Castle Buildings
Market Place
Bury
BL9 0LT
0161 253 5662
a.cogswell@bury.gov.uk

**Calderdale ACPC**
Health & Social Care Directorate,
Social Services Department
1 Park Road, Halifax
West Yorkshire
HX1 2TU
01422 393561
Emergency Duty Team: 01422
365106
CP.Admin@calderdale.gov.uk

**Cambridgeshire ACPC**
Cambridgeshire County Council,
c/o SS1007, Castle Court
Castle Hill
Cambridge
CB3 0AP
01223 717369
out of hours: 07967 374658
sara.glennie@cambridgeshire.
gov.uk

**Cheshire ACPC**
Cheshire County Council, County
Hall
Castle Drive
Chester
CH1 1BW
01244 603201
out of hours: 07802 582712
Webba@cheshire.gov.uk

**Cornwall & Isles of Scilly ACPC**
Old County Hall, Station Road
Truro
TR1 3RY
01720 422148
j.gould@cornwall.gov.uk or
Hcharnock@scilly.gov.uk

**Coventry ACPC**
Coventry Council, Civic Centre
1 Little Park Street
Coventry
CV1 5RS
02476 833405
out of hours: 024 7683 2222
john.bolton@coventry.gov.uk

**Cumbria ACPC**
NSPCC
7 Chatsworth Square
Carlisle
CA1 1HB
01228 521829
out of hours: 07711 190544
gbrooks@nspcc.org.uk

**Darlington ACPC**
Darlington Social Services,
Central House
Gladstone House
Darlington
DL3 6JX
01325 346200
Elaine.clarke@nspcc.org.uk

**Derby City ACPC**
Social Services Department,
Middleton House
27 St Mary's Gate
Derby
DE1 3NS
01332 718860
out of hours: 01332 523928
rachel.dickinson@derby.gov.uk

**Derbyshire ACPC**
Derbyshire County Council
County Hall
Matlock
DE4 3AG
01629 772005
out of hours: 01773 728222
ian.johnson@derbyshire.gov.uk

**Devonshire ACPC**
The Annexe, Topsham Road
County Hall
Exeter
EX2 4QR
01392 383480 or 01392 866657
awhiteley@devon.gov.uk or
Cdimmelo@devon.gov.uk

**Doncaster ACPC**
PO Box 251, The Council House
College Road, Doncaster
South Yorkshire
DN1 3DA
01302 737780
out of hours: 01302 530367
jim.stewart@doncaster.gov.uk

**Dorset ACPC**
Dorset County Council, County
Hall
Colliton Park, Dorchester
Dorset
DT1 1XJ
01305 225089
out of hours: 01202 668123
j.last@dorset-cc.gov.uk

**Dudley ACPC**
Dudley Metropolitan Borough
Council, Ednam House
St James Road
Dudley
DY1 3JJ
01384 815807
out of hours: 01384 456111
pauline.sharratt@dudley.gov.uk

**Durham ACPC**
Durham County Council
County Hall
Durham
DH1 5UG
0191 383 3322
out of hours: 0845 850 5010
debbie.jones@durham.gov.uk

**East Sussex ACPC**
County Hall, St Anne's Crescent
Lewes
East Sussex
BN7 1SW
01273 481238
david.archibald@eastsussexcc.
gov.uk

**Essex ACPC**
PO Box 11, County Hall
Chelmsford
Essex
CM1 1YS
01245 430307
Sue.park@essexcc.gov.uk

**Gateshead ACPC**
Civic Centre, Regents Street
Gateshead
Tyne & Wear
NE8 1HH
0191 433 2352
out of hours: 0191 477 0844
simonhart@gateshead.gov.uk

**Gloucestershire ACPC**
Bearland Wing, Shire Hall
Westgate
Gloucestershire
GL1 2TR
01452 425186
out of hours: 01367 860096
mswann@gloscc.gov.uk

**Halton ACPC**
Grosvenor House
Halton Lea
Runcorn
WA7 2ED
0151 471 7539
out of hours: 0160 676611
Kath.o'dwyer@halton-
borough.gov.uk

**Hampshire ACPC**
Hampshire County Council
The Castle
Winchester
SO23 8UQ
01483 782881
out of hours: 01252 325469
johng_g.h@virgin.net

**Hartlepool ACPC**
Hartlepool Borough Council,
Civic Centre
Victoria Road
Hartlepool
TS24 8YW
01429 523884
peter.seller@hartlepool.gov.uk

**Herefordshire ACPC**
Social Care & Strategic Housing,
Garrick House
Widemarsh Street
Hereford
HR4 9EU
01432 260000
out of hours: 01905 358116
hlewis@herefordshire.gov.uk

**Hertfordshire ACPC**
Hertfordshire County Council,
Children, Schools and Families
(CSF)
County Hall, Pegs Lane, Hertford
Herts
SG13 8DF
01992 555755
urmila.gohil@hertscc.gov.uk

**Isle of Wight ACPC**
Isle of Wight County Council,
Social Services HQ
Fairlee House, 17 Fairlee Road
Newport
PO30 2EA
01983 520600
Jimmy.doyle@iow.gov.uk

**Kent ACPC**
Kent County Council
Sessions House, County Hall
Maidstone
ME14 1XQ
01622 694888
out of hours: 0845 762 6777
peter.gilroy@kent.gov.uk

**Kingston upon Hull & East
Riding ACPC**
Aneurin Bevan Lodge
140 Hotham Road North
Hull
HU5 5RJ
01482 846082
kathy.rowe@hullcc.gov.uk

**Kirklees ACPC**
Kirklees Metropolitan Council,
Oldgate House, 2 Oldgate
Huddersfield
HD1 6QF
01484 225331
out of hours: 07980 312864
paul.johnson@kirklees.gov.uk

**Knowsley ACPC**
Knowsley SSD,
Municipal Buildings
PO Box 23, Archway Road
Huyton
L36 9YY
0151 443 3440
out of hours: 0151 221 2741;
pager: 8295
Jan.coulter@knowsley.gov.uk

**Lancashire ACPC**
Social Services Directorate,
PO Box 162
East Cliff County Offices
Preston
PR1 3EA
01772 264237
out of hours: 0845 602 1043
gill.rigg@socserv.lancscc.gov.uk

**Leeds ACPC**
Leeds City Council, Social
Services Department
Merrion House, 110 Merrion
Centre
Leeds
LS2 8QB
0113 247 8597
ruth.woodhead@leeds.gov.uk

**Leicester City ACPC**
Child Protection & Independent
Review Service, Leicester City
Social Care and Health
Room 230, Town Hall, Town Hall
Square
Leicester
LE1 9BQ
0116 225 4752
matts004@leicester.gov.uk

**Leicestershire & Rutland ACPC**
Child Protection & Review Unit,
Leicestershire County Council
SSD
County Hall, Glenfield
Leicester
LE3 8RL
0116 265 7407
matts004@leicester.gov.uk

**Lincolnshire ACPC**
Lincolnshire NHS Trust, Rauceby
Hospital
Orchard House, Orchard Street
Near Sleaford
NJ34 8PP
01529 416094
out of hours: 07778 786860
caroline.blundell@linessouthwest
-pct

**Liverpool ACPC**
1st Floor, Millennium House
60 Victoria Street
Liverpool
L1 6JQ
0151 233 4250/4213
out of hours: 07753 812085
peter.duxbury@liverpool.gov.uk

**Manchester ACPC**
Q.A.P.M. Unit, 3rd Floor
Victoria Mill, 10 Lower Vickers,
Streetmiles Platting
Manchester
M40 7EL
0161 234 3803
out of hours: 0161 255 8250
eliskaschofield@notes.manchester
.gov.uk

**Medway ACPC**
Medway Towns Council,
Municipal Building
Canterbury Street
Gillingham
ME7 5LA
01634 331291
out of hours: 0845 762 6777
ann.windiate@medway.gov.uk

**Milton Keynes ACPC**
Milton Keynes Council, Saxon
Court, 502 Avebury Boulevard
Central Milton Keynes
MK9 3HS
01908 253324
out of hours: 07932 693079
paul.sutton@milton-keynes.gov.uk

**Newcastle ACPC**
Newcastle-Upon-Tyne City Council
Civic Centre, Barras Bridge
Newcastle-Upon-Tyne
NE1 8PA
0191 232 8520
out of hours: 0191 232 8520
ruth.rogan@newcastle.gov.uk

**Norfolk ACPC**
Room 617, County Hall
Martineau Lane
Norwich
NR1 2DL
01603 223409
paul.shreeve.socs@norfolk.gov.uk

**Northamptonshire ACPC**
NRCS, Robert Street
Northampton
NN1 3AR
01604 259200
scruickshank@northamptonshire.
gov.uk

**North Lincolnshire ACPC**
NCH, 892 Holderness Road
Hull
HU9 4AA
01482 799526
petera@nch.org.uk

**North East Lincolnshire ACPC**
Fryston House, Fryston Corner
Bargate
Grimsby
DN34 5BB
01472 325499
Philip.watters@nelincs.gov.uk

**North Somerset ACPC**
North Somerset Council Housing
& Social Services Department
PO Box 52, Town Hall
Weston Super Mare
BS23 1ZY
01934 634803

**North Tyneside ACPC**
Camden House, Camden Street
North Shields
Tyne & Wear
NE30 1NW
0191 200 5519
juilehogg@northtyneside.gov.uk

**Northumberland ACPC**
c/o Northumberland SSD
163 Langdale Drive
Cramlington
NE23 8EH
01670 593645
efinlay@northumberland.gov.uk

**North Yorkshire ACPC**
North Yorkshire County Council,
County Hall, Racecourse Lane
Northallerton
DL7 8DD
01609 780780
out of hours: 01904 762314
rosemary.archer@northyorks.gov.uk

**Nottingham City ACPC**
14 Hounds Gate, 3rd Floor
Nottingham
NG1 7BE
0115 915 7000
paul.snell@nottinghamcity.gov.uk

**Nottinghamshire County ACPC**
Social Services County Hall
West Bridgford
Nottingham
NG2 7QP
0115 977 3303
jill.pedley@nottscc.gov.uk

**Oldham ACPC**
Oldham Metropolitan Borough
Council
Oldham Civic Centre, West Street
Oldham
OL1 1XL
0161 622 6606
out of hours: 07970 848324
Alanh@oldham.nhs.uk

**Oxfordshire ACPC**
Oxfordshire County Council,
County Hall, New Road
Oxford
OX1 1ND
01865 815833
out of hours: 0800 833408
phil.hodgson@oxfordshire.gov.uk

**Peterborough ACPC**
Peterborough City Council,
Education & Children 2nd Floor
Bayard Place, Broadway
Peterborough
PE1 1FD
01733 746054
judy.jones@peterborough.gov.uk

**Plymouth ACPC**
Windsor House
Tavistock Road
Plymouth
PL1 2AA
01752 307329
out of hours: 01548 856889
lesley.reid@plymouth.gov.uk

**Poole ACPC**
Paediatric Hospital NHS Trust,
Poole General Hospital
Longfleet Road
Poole
BH15 2JB
01202 442382
richard.coppen@poole.nhs.uk

**Portsmouth ACPC**
Civic Office
Guildhall Square
Portsmouth
PO1 2EP
023 9282 2251
out of hours: 0845 600 4555
steve.hayes@portsmouthcc.gov.
uk

**Reading ACPC**
Floor 7, Fountain House
PO Box 2624, Civic Centre
Reading
RG1 7WB
0118 939 0351
out of hours: 01344 488495
bridget.harnett@reading.gov.uk

**Rochdale ACPC**
Childcare Service, Municipal
Offices, PO Box 67
Smith Street
Rochdale
OL16 1YQ
01706 865203
steve.titcombe@rochdale.gov.uk

**Rotherham ACPC**
Social Services Department,
Crinoline House
Effingham Square
Rotherham
S65 1AW
01904 641110
roger.thompson4@btinternet.com

**Salford ACPC**
Salford Community and Social
Services Directorate,
Crompton House
100 Chorley Road, Swinton
Salford
M27 6BP
0161 793 2243
out of hours: 0161 794 8888
paul.woltman@salford.gov.uk

**Sandwell ACPC**
Sandwell Council House,
PO Box 2374
Oldbury
West Midlands
B69 3DE
0121 607 3471
out of hours: 0121 449 1324
david.low@swdh.nhs.uk

**Sefton ACPC**
Sefton Social Services
Department, Merton House
Stanley Road, Bootle
Liverpool
L20 3UU
0151 934 3735
charlie.barker@social-
services.sefton.gov.uk

**Sheffield ACPC**
Child Protection Unit, Floor 3,
Palatine Chambers
Pinstone Street
Sheffield
S1 2HN
0114 273 4934

**Shropshire ACPC**
Social Services Department,
Shirehall, Abbey Foregate
Shrewsbury
SY2 6ND
01743 253823
out of hours: 01743 244197
terry.jones@shropshire-cc.gov.uk

**Slough ACPC**
Social Services Department,
Town Hall
Bath Road
Slough
SL1 3UQ
01753 875754
out of hours: 01344 786543
ann.domeney@slough.gov.uk

**Solihull ACPC**
Education & Children's Services,
Council House
PO Box 20, Solihull
West Midlands
B91 3QU
0121 704 6734
aplummer@solihull.gov.uk

**Somerset ACPC**
Somerset County Council,
County Hall
Taunton
TA1 4DY
01823 355455 ext 6901
out of hours: 01458 253241
DJTaylor@somerset.gov.uk

## Southampton ACPC
Children and Families Services,
Southampton City Council
14 Cumberland Place
Southampton
SO15 2BG
023 8083 3260
carol.tozer@southampton.gov.uk

## Southend-On-Sea ACPC
PO Box 6, Civic Centre
Victoria Avenue,
Southend on Sea
Essex
SS2 6ER
01702 534610
out of hours: 07775 506608
meeraspillett@southend.gov.uk

## South Gloucestershire ACPC
South Gloucestershire Council,
Emersons Green Lane
Emersons Green
BS16 7AL
01454 865902
ruby_parry@southglos.gov.uk

## Southtees, Redcar & Cleveland & Middlesbrough
Tees Health Shared Services,
Poole House
Stokesley Road, Nunthorpe
Middlesbrough
TS7 0NJ
01642 320000
Alex.Giles@email.tees-
ha.northy.nhs.uk

## South Tyneside ACPC
Social Care and Health
Directorate, Kelly House
Campbell Park Road, Hebburn
Tyne & Wear
NE31 2SW
0191 427 1717
out of hours: 0191 456 2093
trevor.doughty@s-tyneside-
mbc.gov.uk or
mick.mccracken@s-tyneside-
mbc.gov.uk

## Staffordshire ACPC
Staffordshire County Council
St Chad's Place
Stafford
ST16 2LR
01785 277000
out of hours: 01785 354030
robert.lake@staffordshire.gov.uk
or
greg.williams@staffordshire.gov.uk

## St Helens ACPC
St Helens Metropolitan Council,
Gamble Building, 2nd Floor
Victoria Square, St Helens
Merseyside
WA10 1DY
01744 456318
patriciamoore@sthelens.gov.uk

## Stockport ACPC
Social Services, Stockport
Metropolitan Council, Ponsonby
House, Edward Street
Stockport
SK1 3XE
0161 474 4600
out of hours: 0161 718 2118
cpu@stockport.gov.uk

## Stockton-On-Tees ACPC
Health and Social Care Directorate
Alma House, 6 Alma Street
Stockton-on-Tees
TS18 2AP
01642 393317
jane.humphreys@stockton.gov.uk

## Stoke-on-Trent ACPC
Social Services Department,
Civic Centre
Glebe Street
Stoke-on-Trent
ST4 1RT
01782 235902
emergency duty team: 01782
342995
helen.oakley@stoke.gov.uk

## Suffolk ACPC
Suffolk County Council, Social
Care Services
St Paul House, Rope Walk
Ipswich
IP4 1LH
01473 583453
shirley.coleman@socserv.suffolkc
c.gov.uk

## Sunderland ACPC
Sunderland Social Services
Department
50 Fawcett Street
Sunderland
SR1 1RF
0191 553 7174
out of hours: 0191 553 1991
barbara.williams@ssd.sunderland
.gov.uk

## Surrey ACPC
Beaufort House
Mayford Green, Woking
Surrey
GU22 0PG
01483 728022
felicity.budgen@surreycc.gov.uk

## Swindon ACPC
Social Services & Housing
Department, Civic Offices
Euclid Street
Swindon
SN1 2JH
01793 465855
out of hours: 01793 465853
Tscragg@swindon.gov.uk

## Tameside ACPC
Conference and Review Section
Quality Assurance Unit
Union Street
Hyde
SK14 1ND
0161 342 4343
out of hours: 0161 342 2222
annie.dodd@tameside.gov.uk or
acpc@tameside.gov.uk

## Telford & Wrekin ACPC
Borough of Telford & Wrekin,
Darby House, PO Box 214
Telford
TF3 4LE
01952 202040
out of hours: 01952 202958
barbara.evans@wrekin.gov.uk

## Thurrock ACPC
Thurrock Council Housing &
Social Care
PO Box 140, Civic Offices,
New Road, Grays, Thurrock
Essex
RM17 6TJ
01375 652419
out of hours: 01375 372468
mgurrey@thurrock.gov.uk

## Torbay ACPC
Social Services Department,
Oldway Mansion
Torquay Road, Paignton
Devon
TQ3 2TS
01803 208400
Jain.wood@torbay.gov.uk

## Trafford ACPC
Trafford Town Hall, PO Box 77
Talbot Road, Stretford
Manchester
ME2 0YT
0161 912 4009
out of hours: 0161 912 2020
mike.cooney@trafford.gov.uk

## Wakefield ACPC
Housing and Social Care
Department, 8 St John's North
Wakefield
WF1 3QA
01924 307734
kferris@wakefield.gov.uk

**Walsall ACPC**
Walsall Primary Care Tust,
Lichfield House
27-31 Lichfield Street
Walsall
WS1 1TE
01922 720255
out of hours: 07970 948664
Jane.m.evans@walsall.nhs.uk

**Warrington ACPC**
Social Services Department
Children and Families Division
Bewsey Old School, Lockton
Lane, Warrington
Cheshire
WA5 5BF
01925 444097
jdunkerley@warrington.gov.uk

**Warwickshire ACPC**
Warwickshire County Council,
PO Box 48, Shire Hall
Warwick
CV34 4RD
01926 412394
out of hours: 01926 745685
simonlord@warwickshire.gov.uk

**West Berkshire ACPC**
Avonbank House, West Street
Newbury
Berkshire
RG14 1BZ
01635 519735
out of hours: 01344 786543
acouldrick@westberks.gov.uk

**West Sussex ACPC**
The Grange, Tower Street
Chichester
West Sussex
PO19 1QT
01243 777660
out of hours: 01903 694422
John.dixon@westsussex.gov.uk

**Wigan ACPC**
Wigan Metropolitan Borough
Council, Civic Centre
Millgate
Wigan
WN1 1AZ
01942 827793
out of hours: 0161 834 2436
g.meehan@wiganmbc.gov.uk

**Wiltshire ACPC**
Children, Education & Libraries
Department, County Hall
Trowbridge
Wiltshire
BA14 8LE
01225 713944
out of hours: 0845 607 0888
anniehudson@wiltshire.gov.uk

**Windsor & Maidenhead ACPC**
4 Marlow Road
Maidenhead
Berkshire
SL6 7YR
01628 683177
heather-andrews@rbwm.gov.uk

**Wirral ACPC**
Westminster House, Hamilton
Street
Birkenhead
Wirral
CH41 5FN
0151 666 3650
out of hours: 0151 652 4991
kevinmiller@wirral.gov.uk

**Wokingham ACPC**
Wokingham District Council,
Community Services Department
PO Box 154, Shute End
Wokingham
RG40 1WN
0118 974 6775
Mark.Molly@wokingham.gov.uk

**Wolverhampton ACPC**
Children's Services Directorate,
Beldray Building
66 Mount Pleasant, Bilston
West Midlands
WV14 7PR
01902 553033
slane.wolverhampton.ssd@dial.pipex.com

**Worcestershire ACPC**
Worcestershire County Council,
Social Services Department
PO Box 372
Worcester
WR5 2XE
01905 766911
areader@worcestershire.gov.uk

**York ACPC**
City of York Council Community
Services
PO Box 402, George Hudson
Street
York
YO1 6ZE
01904 554006
out of hours: 01904 762314
pete.dwyer@york.gov.uk

# Wales

**Ynys Mons/ Anglesey ACPC**
Children's Services, Council
Offices
Llangefni
Ynys Mon
LL77 7TW
01248 752706
tgjss@anglesey.gov.uk

**Blaenau Gwent /
Monmouthshire ACPC**
Social Services Housing
Department, Monmouthshire
County Council
County Hall
Cwmbran
NP44 2XH
01633 644571
johnwaters@monmouthshire.gov.uk

**Bridgend County Borough
ACPC**
Children's Services Division,
Personal Services Directorate
Sunnyside
Bridgend
CF31 4AR
01656 642314
out of hours: 01443 204010
streebm@bridgend.gov.uk

**Caerphilly ACPC**
Caerphilly CBC, Hawtin Park
Gellihaf, Pontllanfraith
Blackwood
NP12 2PZ
01443 864512
milled@caerphilly.gov.uk

**City & County of Cardiff ACPC**
County Hall
Atlantic Wharf
Cardiff
CF10 5UW
029 2087 2000

Carmarthenshire ACPC
3 Spilman Street
Carmarthen
SA31 1LE
01267 228903
out of hours: 01267 222288
AnnWilliams@carmarthenshire.gov.uk

**Ceredigion ACPC**
Min Aeron, Vicarage Hill
Aberaeron
SA46 0DY
01545 572601

## Conwy County Borough Council ACPC
Children & Families Services,
Social Services Department
Civic Centre Annex
Colwnbay
LL29 8AR
01492 575158
out of hours: 01492 515777
sue.maskell@conwy.gov.uk

## Denbighshire ACPC
Royal Alexandra Hospital
Marine Drive
Rhyl
LL18 3AS
01745 443000

## Flintshire ACPC
Flintshire County Hall Education
Department, County Hall
Mold
CH7 6ND
01352 702504
out of hours: 01352 753403
karen_reilly@flintshire.gov.uk

## Gwynedd ACPC
Cyneor Gwynedd, Swydofa'r
Cyngor, Stryd Y Jel, Caernarfon
Gwynedd
LL55 1BN
01286 679742
out of hours: 01286 675502
catrinwilliams@gwynedd.gov.uk

## Merthyr Tydfil ACPC
Social Services Department, Ty
Keir Hardie, Riverside Court,
Avenue De Clichy
Merthyr Tydfil
CF47 8XE
01685 724694
out of hours: 01443 204010
childrenandfamilies@merthyr.
gov.uk

## Neath Port Talbot ACPC
Port Talbot Civic Centre
Port Talbot
SA13 1PJ
01639 763357
out of hours: 01639 895455
l.pearce@neath-portalbort.gov.uk

## Newport ACPC
Social Wellbeing & Housing,
Newport City Council
Civic Centre
Newport
NP20 4UR
01633 233297
out of hours: 01633 244999

## Pembrokeshire ACPC
Social Care & Housing,
Pembrokeshire County Council
County Hall
Haverfordwest
SA61 1TP
01437 775350
out of hours: 0845 601 5522
david.halse@pembrokeshire.gov.uk

## Powys ACPC
Children & Families Learning,
County Hall
Llandrindod Wells
Powys
LD1 5LG
01597 826123/ 465
out of hours: 0845 757 3818
ruthforr@powys.gov.uk

## Rhondda Cynon Taff County Borough Council ACPC
Education & Children's Services,
Ty Trevithick
Abercynon
Mountain Ash
CF45 4UQ
01443 744003
out of hours: 07799 132088
sally.m.halls@rhondda-cynon-
taff.gov.uk

## Swansea ACPC
County Hall
Oystermouth Road
Swansea
SA1 3SN
01792 636248
out of hours: 01792 548823
mark.roszkowski@swansea.
gov.uk

## Torfaen ACPC
Torfaen Social Services
Department, County Hall
Cwmbran
Torfaen
NP44 2WN
01633 648571
out of hours: 01443 838940
peter.langley@torfaen.gov.uk

## Vale of Glamorgan ACPC
Vale of Glamorgan Council
Community Services
Haydock House, 1 Holton Road
Barry
CF63 4HA
01446 725202

## Wrexham ACPC
Social Services Department
2nd Floor, Crown Buildings, 31
Chester Street
Wrexham
01978 267020

# National voluntary associations

## England

### NSPCC
Weston House
42 Curtain Road
London
EC2A 3NH
020 7825 2500; NSPCC Child
Protection Helpline: 0808 800
5000
www.nspcc.org.uk

## Scotland

### CHILDREN 1ST
The Royal Scottish Society for
Prevention of Cruelty to
Children
83 Whitehouse Loan
Edinburgh
EH9 1AT
0131 446 2300
www.children1st.org.uk

## Ireland

### The Irish Society for the Prevention of Cruelty to Children (ISPCC)
Head Office, 20 Molesworth
Street
Dublin 2
00 353 1 679 4944
ispcc@ispcc.ie
www.ispcc.ie

# Other useful contacts

**The Ann Craft Trust Centre for Social Work (ACT)**
University of Nottingham
University Park
Nottingham
NG7 2RD
0115 951 5400
ann-craft-
trust@nottingham.ac.uk
www.nottingham.ac.uk/sociolo
gy/ACT
*dedicated to the protection of adults and children with learning disabilities from abuse*

**BASPCAN (the British Association for the Study and Prevention of Child Abuse and Neglect)**
10 Priory Street
York
YO1 6EZ
01904 613605
baspcan@baspcan.org.uk
www.baspcan.org.uk

**Bullying Online**
help@bullying.co.uk
www.bullying.co.uk/
*advice for pupils and parents*

**Childline**
Freepost NATN1111
London
E1 6BR
0800 1111
www.childline.org.uk/
*A 24hr free helpline for children or young people in trouble or danger*

**The Children are unbeatable! Alliance**
020 7713 0569
info@endcorporalpunishment.
org
www.childrenareunbeatable.
org.uk
*national campaign to end physical punishment of children by promoting positive, non-violent discipline and legal reform*

**Kidscape**
2 Grosvenor Gardens
London
SW1W 0DH
020 7730 3300
contact@kidscape.org.uk
www.kidscape.org.uk/
*a registered charity committed to keeping children safe from harm or abuse*

**One in Four**
219 Bromley Road
Bellingham
London
SE6 2PG
020 8697 2112
admin@oneinfour.org.uk
www.oneinfour.org.uk/
*offers counselling, peer support groups, and one day workshops for people who have experienced sexual abuse; also provides training for professionals*

**Pupiline.net**
Westgate House, Museum Street
Ipswich
IP1 1HQ
01473 400100
oli.watts@pupiline.net
www.pupiline.net
*a website written, designed, edited and managed by young people for young people; topics covered: addictions, bullying, dating, exam stress, food, health, money, self harm and sex*

**RESPOND**
Third Floor
24-32 Stephenson Way
London
NW1 2HP
0845 606 1503
services@respond.org.uk
www.respond.org.uk/
*provides a range of services to victims and perpetrators of sexual abuse who have learning disabilities and training and support to those working with them, including psychotherapy*

**SACCAA (Sexually Abused Children's Counselling and Advocacy Agency)**
Sparrows House 1a,
Bushey Lane
Bushey
Hertfordshire
WD2 3JP
020 8950 7855
saccaa@horsfieldwatford.demon
.co.uk

**Sexual Abuse Child Consultancy Service**
Mytton Mill
Montford Bridge
Shropshire
SY4 1HA
01743 850015
*provides individual therapeutic work with children and young people, group work, consultation, conferences and training workshops*

**UK Missing Kids website**
www.missingkids.co.uk/

**VOICE UK**
The College Business Centre
Uttoxeter New Road
Derby
DE22 3WZ
01332 202555
voiceuk@clara.net
*provides advice and practical help on legal matters related to survivors with learning difficulties*

# Diversity

---

## Race

**Britkid**
www.britkid.org
*a educational website about race, racism and life*

**Commission for Racial Equality**
St Dunstan's House
201-211 Borough High Street
London
SE1 1GZ
020 7939 0000
info@cre.gov.uk
www.cre.gov.uk
*provides information and advice to people who think they have suffered racial discrimination or harassment*

**CRE Birmingham**
3rd Floor, Lancaster House
67 Newhall Street
Birmingham
B3 1NA
0121 710 3000

**CRE Leeds**
1st Floor, Yorkshire Bank Chambers
Infirmary Street
Leeds
LS1 2JP
0113 389 3600

**CRE Manchester**
5th Floor, Maybrook House
40 Blackfriars Street
Manchester
M3 2EG
0161 835 5500

---

### Scotland

**CRE Scotland (Edinburgh)**
The Tun, 12 Jackson's Entry
off Holyrood Road
Edinburgh
EH8 8PJ
0131 524 2000
scotland@cre.gov.uk

### Wales

**CRE Wales (Cardiff)**
3rd Floor, Capital Tower
Greyfriars Road
Cardiff
CF10 3AG
029 2072 9200

---

### Northern Ireland

**Northern Ireland Council for Ethnic Minorities (NICEM)**
3rd Floor, Ascot House
24-31 Shaftesbury Square
Belfast
BT2 7DB
028 9023 8645/ 9031 9666
www.nicem.org.uk
*represents the interests of ethnic minority communities in Northern Ireland*

---

## Gay and lesbian

**Families and Friends of Lesbians and Gays (FFLAG)**
PO Box 84
Exeter
EX4 4AN
01454 852418
info@fflag.org.uk
www.fflag.org.uk
*dedicated to supporting parents and their gay, lesbian and bisexual sons and daughters*

**Gay Youth UK**
info@gayyouthuk.co.uk
www.gayyouthuk.co.uk
*information and support for young gay people in the UK*

**Lesbian Information Service**
PO Box 8
Todmorden
Lancashire
OL14 5TZ
01706 817235
lis@lesbianinformationservice.org
www.lesbianinformationservice.org
*conducts research, develops publications and offers training programmes for professionals*

**Outzone**
PACE Youth Work
34 Hartham Road
London
N7 9JL
020 8348 1785

info@outzone.org
www.outzone.org
*for all lesbians, bisexuals, gay men and those questioning their sexuality, who are under 25*

**The Queer Youth Alliance**
Article 12 Offices
94 White Lion Street
London
N1 9PF
info@queeryouth.org.uk
www.queeryouth.org.uk
*a website run by LGBT young people, for LGBT young people.*

---

# Migration and asylum

**Home Office - Immigration and Nationality Directorate**
IND Block C, Whitgift Centre
Wellesley Road
Croydon
CR9 1AT
0870 606 7766
www.ind.homeoffice.gov.uk
*to enquire about the provisions in the Immigration Rules & individual cases*

**Home Office - Immigration and Nationality Directorate**
Section 1, Room 1101
Apollo House, 36 Wellesley Road
Croydon
CR9 3RR
*for enquiries from British citizens who are resident overseas and wish to bring a child adopted in that country into the UK*

**Home Office - Immigration and Nationality Directorate**
Nationality Enquiries, 3rd Floor
India Buildings, Water Street
Liverpool
L2 0QN
0151 237 5326
*for enquiries regarding nationality and citizenship*

**Home Office Immigration and Nationality Directorate**
Lunar House
40 Wellesley Road
Croydon
CR9 2BY
0870 606 7766
www.ind.homeoffice.gov.uk
*responsible for immigration control at air and sea ports throughout the UK; also considers applications for permission to stay, citizenship and asylum*

**Asylum Aid**
28 Commercial Street
London
E1 6LS
020 7377 5123
info@asylumaid.org.uk
www.asylumaid.org.uk
*an independent, national charity assisting refugees in the UK*

**AsylumSupport.info**
27 Old Gloucester Street
Bloomsbury
London
WC1N 3XX
info@asylumsupport.info
www.asylumsupport.info
*provides information regarding matters that concern people seeking asylum including: asylum and refugees, conflict, country data, court cases. deportation, detention, discrimination, funding, gender, government, human rights, human trafficking, law, media, migration, policy and studies*

**Citizens Advice**
The National Association of Citizens Advice Bureaux
Myddelton House,
115-123 Pentonville Road
London
N1 9LZ
www.adviceguide.org.uk
*website provides information in English, Welsh, Bengali, Punjabi, Gujarati, Urdu and Chinese; covers financial needs, family issues and rights*

## The Immigration Advisory Service
3rd Floor, County House
190 Great Dover Street
London
SE1 4YB
020 7357 7511
advice@iasuk.org
www.iasuk.org
*community legal advice &
representation for immigrants &
asylum seekers*

## Immigration Law Practitioners' Association
Lindsey House
40-42 Charterhouse Street
London
EC1M 6JN
020 7251 8383
info@ilpa.org.uk
www.ilpa.org.uk
*aims to promote and improve the
advising and representation of
immigrants and provide
information to members on domestic
and European immigration, refugee
and nationality law*

## Joint Council for the Welfare of Immigrants
115 Old Street
London
EC1V 9RT
020 7251 8708
info@jcwi.org.uk
www.jcwi.org.uk
*an independent national voluntary
organisation, campaigning for
justice and combating racism in
immigration and asylum law and
policy; provides free advice and
casework, training courses, and a
range of publications*

## Migrant Helpline
The Rendezvous Building, Freight
Services Approach Road
Eastern Docks
Dover
CT16 1JA
01304 203977
dover@migranthelpline.org
www.migranthelpline.org.uk
*an independent charity committed
to providing a reception and advice
service to asylum seekers and
refugees in Kent and East Sussex*

## The North of England Refugee Service (NERS)
2 Jesmond Rd West
Newcastle Upon Tyne
NE2 4PQ
0191 245 7311
info@refugee.org.uk
www.refugee.org.uk
*an independent and charitable
organisation which exists to meet
the needs and promote the interests
of asylum seekers and refugees who
have arrived or have settled in the
North of England*

19 Bigg Market
Newcastle Upon Tyne
NE1 1UN
0191 222 0406
biggmarket@refugee.org.uk

3rd Floor, Forum House
The Forum, Wallsend
North Tyneside
NE28 8LX
0191 200 1199
wallsend@refugee.org.uk

19 Villiers Street
Sunderland
SR1 1EJ
0191 510 8685
sunderland@refugee.org.uk

27 Borough Road
Middlesbrough
TS1 4AD
01642 217447
teesvalley@refugee.org.uk

## Refugee Action
The Old Fire Station, 150
Waterloo Road
London
SE1 8SB
020 7654 7700
www.refugee-action.org.uk
*an independent national charity
that provides practical advice and
assistance for newly arrived asylum
seekers and long-term commitment
to their settlement through
community development work*

The Wardlow Road Centre
Wardlow Road
Birmingham
B7 4JH
0121 464 3548

Senate House
36 Stokes Croft
Bristol
BS1 3QD
0117 989 2100

34 Princes Road
Liverpool
L8 1TH
0151 702 6300

Centenary House
59 North Street
Leeds
LS2 8JS
0113 244 5345

Muslim Community Resource
Centre
Melbourne Centre, Melbourne
Road
Leicester
LE2 0GU
0116 261 4830

4th Floor, Dale House
35 Dale Street
Manchester
M1 2HF
0161 233 1200

Albion House, 3rd Floor
5-13 Canal Street
Nottingham
NG1 7EG
0115 941 8552

Virginia House
40 Looe Street
Plymouth
PL4 0EB
01752 519860

50 Oxford Street
Southampton
SO14 3DP
023 8024 8130

240a Clapham Road
London
SW9 0PZ
020 7735 5361

## Refugee Arrivals Project
41b Cross Lances Road
Hounslow
Middlesex
TW3 2AD
020 8607 6888
*an independent charity that assists
newly arrived asylum seekers and
refugees*

**The Refugee Council**
3 Bondway
London
SW8 1SJ
020 7820 3000;
advice line: 020 7346 6777
info@refugeecouncil.org.uk
www.refugeecouncil.org.uk
*the largest organisation in the UK*
*working with asylum seekers and*
*refugees*

**Yorkshire & Humberside
Region Office**
Ground Floor, Hurley House,
1 Dewsbury Road
Leeds
LS11 5DQ
0113 244 9404

**Eastern Region Office**
First Floor, 4-8 Museum Street
Ipswich
IP1 1HT
01473 297900

**West Midlands Region Office**
First Floor, Smithfield House,
Digbeth
Birmingham
B5 6BS
0121 622 1515

**The Refugee Legal Centre
(RLC)**
153-157 Commercial Road
London
E1 2DA
020 7780 3200
RLC@Refugee-Legal-
Centre.org.uk
www.refugee-legal-centre.org.uk
*Provides legal advice and*
*representation for those seeking*
*protection under international and*
*national Human Rights Asylum*
*law; delivers training and other*
*support to those giving advice and*
*representation in such cases*

## Scotland

**Scottish Asylum Seekers
Consortium**
Wheatley House
25 Cochrane Street
Glasgow
G1 1LH
0141 287 3623
carolanne.joyce@gch.glasgow.
gov.uk
www.asylumscotland.org.uk
*set up to manage and monitor the*
*commissioning and provision of*
*accommodation and other services*
*for asylum seekers*

**Scottish Refugee Council**
5 Cadogan Square
(170 Blythswood Court)
Glasgow
G2 7PH
0141 248 9799; Freephone
number for advice: 0800 085 6087
www.scottishrefugeecouncil.org.uk
*provides advice, information and*
*assistance to asylum seekers and*
*refugees in Scotland*

# Education

## National agencies

**Ofsted**
Alexandra House
33 Kingsway
London
WC2B 6SE
020 7421 6800
geninfo@ofsted.gov.uk
www.ofsted.gov.uk

**The Qualifications and Curriculum Authority (QCA)**
Customer Relations
83 Piccadilly
London
W1J 8QA
020 7509 5555;
enquiry line: 020 7509 5556
info@qca.org.uk
www.qca.org.uk

**The Association of Teachers and Lecturers (ATL)**
7 Northumberland Street
London
WC2N 5RD
020 7930 6441
info@atl.org.uk
www.atl.org.uk
*a professional association and trade union representing over 160,000 teachers, lecturers and education support staff in England, Wales and Northern Ireland*

**The General Teaching Council for England**
0870 001 0308
Info@gtce.org.uk
www.gtce.org.uk

**GTC Birmingham Office**
3rd Floor, Cannon House
24 The Priory Queensway
Birmingham
B4 6BS

**GTC London Office**
344-354 Gray's Inn Road
London
WC1X 8BP

**National Association of Head Teachers (NAHT)**
1 Heath Square
Boltro Road, Haywards Heath
West Sussex
RH16 1BL
01444 472472
info@naht.org.uk
www.naht.org.uk

**NASUWT**
Hillscourt Education Centre,
Rose Hill
Rednal
Birmingham
B45 8RS
0121 453 6150
nasuwt@mail.nasuwt.org.uk
www.teachersunion.org.uk
*the only TUC affiliated teachers' union representing teachers in all parts of the UK. NASUWT has over 212,000 members in all sectors from early years to further education*

**National Union of Teachers**
Hamilton House
Mabledon Place
London
WC1H 9BD
020 7388 6191
www.teachers.org.uk
*Membership of the Union is open to all with qualified teacher status, including headteachers and deputy headteachers*

**The Professional Association of Teachers (PAT)**
2 St James' Court
Friar Gate
Derby
DE1 1BT
01332 372337
hq@pat.org.uk
www.pat.org.uk
*an independent trade union and professional association for teachers, head teachers, lecturers; education support staff (Professionals Allied to Teaching (PAtT)) and nursery nurses, nannies and other childcarers (Professional Association of Nursery Nurses (PANN))*

**Secondary Heads Association (SHA)**
130 Regent Road
Leicester
LE1 7PG
0116 299 1122
info@sha.org.uk
www.sha.org.uk
**the professional association for leaders of secondary schools and colleges**

**Teacher Support Network**
Hamilton House
Mabledon Place
London
WC1H 9BE
020 7554 5200
enquiries@teachersupport.info
www.teachersupport.info
*national charity that provides practical and emotional support to teachers and lecturers (both serving and retired) and their families*

## Northern Ireland

### Department of Education
Rathgael House
43 Balloo Road, Bangor
Co Down
BT19 7PR
028 9127 9279
mail@deni.gov.uk
www.deni.gov.uk

### The Council for the Curriculum, Examinations and Assessment (CCEA)
29 Clarendon Road
Clarendon Dock
Belfast
BT1 3BG
028 9026 1200
info@ccea.org.uk
www.ccea.org.uk

### ATL Northern Ireland
397a Holywood Road
Belfast
BT4 2LY
028 9047 1412
erodgers@n-ireland.atl.org.uk

### The General Teaching Council for Northern Ireland (GTCNI)
4th Floor, Albany House
73-75 Great Victoria Street
Belfast
BT2 7AF
028 9033 3390
info@gtcni.org.uk
www.gtcni.org.uk

### NASUWT Northern Ireland
Ben Madigan House, Edgewater
Office Park
Edgewater Road
Belfast
BT3 9JQ
028 9078 4480
rc-nireland@mail.nasuwt.org.uk

### PAT Northern Ireland
northernireland@pat.org.uk

### Teacher Support Northern Ireland
44 Grange Road
Bangor
BT20 3QQ
028 9127 5929
paddy.hanna@teachersupport.info

## Scotland

### HM Inspectorate of Education (HMIE)
G Spur, Saughton House
Broomhouse Drive
Edinburgh
EH11 3XD
www.hmie.gov.uk

### The Scottish Qualifications Authority (SQA)
Hanover House
24 Douglas Street
Glasgow
G2 7NQ
0141 242 2214
customer@sqa.org.uk
www.sqa.org.uk

### The Scottish Qualifications Authority (SQA)
Ironmills Road
Dalkeith
Midlothian
EH22 1LE

### The General Teaching Council for Scotland
Clerwood House, 96 Clermiston
Road
Edinburgh
EH12 6UT
0131 314 6000; general
enquiries: 0131 314 6080
gtcs@gtcs.org.uk
www.gtcs.org.uk

### Learning and Teaching Scotland
74 Victoria Crescent Road
Glasgow
G12 9JN
0141 337 5000; 0870 010 0297
enquiries@LTScotland.org.uk
www.ltscotland.org.uk
*a national public body which
provides support, resources and
staff development for early years
and school education*

### Learning and Teaching Scotland
Gardyne Road
Dundee
DD5 1NY
01382 443600; 0870 010 0297

### NASUWT Scotland
6 Waterloo Place
Edinburgh
EH1 3BG
0131 523 1110
rc-scotland@mail.nasuwt.org.uk

### PAT Scotland
scotland@pat.org.uk

### Teacher Support Scotland
5 Afton Terrace
Edinburgh
EH5 3NG
0131 551 4784
Mike.Finlayson@teachersupport.info

## Wales

### Estyn
Anchor Court
Keen Road
Cardiff
CF24 5JW
029 2044 6446
enquiries@estyn.gsi.gov.uk
www.estyn.gov.uk
*the office of Her Majesty's Chief
Inspector of Education and
Training in Wales*

### Qualifications Curriculum and Assessment Authority for Wales (ACCAC)
Castle Buildings
Womanby Street
Cardiff
CF10 1SX
029 2037 5400
info@accac.org.uk
www.accac.org.uk

### ATL Wales
1st Floor, Empire House
Mount Stuart Square
Cardiff
CF10 5FN
029 2046 5000
cymru@atl.org.uk

### The General Teaching Council for Wales
4th Floor, Southgate House
Wood Street
Cardiff
CF10 1EW
029 2055 0350
information@gtcw.org.uk
www.gtcw.org.uk

### Learning Wales
www.learning.wales.gov.uk
the Welsh Assembly
Government's Training and
Education website

**NASUWT Wales**
Greenwood Close
Cardiff Gate Business Park
Cardiff
CF23 8RD
029 2054 6080
rc-wales-
cymru@mail.nasuwt.org.uk

**PAT Wales**
wales@pat.org.uk

**Teacher Support Cymru**
Sandringham House
Australian Terrace
Cardiff
CF31 1LY
01656 766287
cymru@teachersupport.info

# International

## Connect Youth International
www.connectyouthinternational.com
*a department of the Education and Training Group of the British Council that runs programmes that give young people an international experience. These programmes range from group exchanges to individual voluntary service. They also provide funding to help all those working in the youth field develop skills and establish contacts necessary to do their work better. Activities are supported by funds from the Foreign and Commonwealth Office, the Department for Education and Skills, and the European Commission (Education and Culture).*

## North

**Regional Youth Work Unit**
Design Works, William Street
Felling, Gateshead
Tyne & Wear
NE10 0JP
0191 423 6200
mail@rywu.org.uk
*Contact: Leon Mexter*

## North West

**North-West RYSU**
Derbyshire Hill Youth Centre,
Derbyshire Hill Road
Parr
St Helens
WA9 2LN
01744 453800
sharon@nwrysu.demon.co.uk
*Contact: Sharon Moore*

## Yorkshire and the Humber

**Regional Youth Work Unit**
Belle Isle Open Access Centre,
Enterprise Way
Middleton Road, Belle Isle
Leeds
LS10 3DZ
0113 270 3595
theunit@rywu-yandh.co.uk
*Contact: Miriam Jackson/ Lisa Bristow*

## West Midlands

**District Youth and Education Office**
County Services Building,
Fountain Street
Leek
Staffordshire
ST13 6JR
01538 483267
connectyouth.wm@staffordshire.
gov.uk and
yc.moorlands@staffordshire.gov.uk
*Contact: Kate Lawton*

## East Midlands

**East Midlands Regional Youth Work Unit**
Room 5, Queen's Walk,
Community Centre
Queens Walk, The Meadows
Nottingham
NG2 2DF
0115 840 2012
emrywu@emrywu.freeserve.co.uk
*Contact: Clare Meakin*

## East

**Connect Youth Eastern Region**
International Department, Essex
County Council, County Hall
Chelmsford
Essex
CM1 1QH
01245 437314
kdodson@essexcc.gov.uk
*Contact: Krysia Dodson*

## South West

**South-West Association for Further Education & Training**
Bishops Hull House, Bishops Hull
Taunton
Somerset
TA1 5EP
01823 365441
gill_millar@swafet.org.uk
*Contact: Gill Millar*

## South

**Education Department**
County Hall
Chichester
West Sussex
PO19 1RF
01243 777066
tina.saunders@westsussex.gov.uk
*Contact: Tina Saunders, County Youth and Community Officer*

## London

**The Youth Office**
Education Department, London
Borough of Richmond
Regal House, London Road
Twickenham
TW1 3QB
020 8891 7502
n.carter@richmond.gov.uk
*Contact: Nicci Carter*

## Scotland

**British Council Scotland**
The Tun, 4 Jackson's Entry
Holyrood Road
Edinburgh
EH8 9PJ
0131 524 5728
jim.bartholomew@britishcouncil.org
*Contact: Jim Bartholomew*

## Northern Ireland

**Youth Council for Northern Ireland**
Forestview
Purdy's Lane
Belfast
BT8 7AR
028 9064 3882
bsweeney@youthcouncil-ni.org.uk
*Contact: Bernice Sweeney*

## Wales

Wales Youth Agency
Leslie Court
Lon-y-Llyn
Caerphilly
CF83 1BQ
029 2085 5714
katie.antippas@wya.org.uk
*Contact: Katie Antippas*

# Early years

**The British Association for Early Childhood Education**
136 Cavell Street
London
E1 2JA
020 7539 5400
office@early-education.org.uk
www.early-education.org.uk
*national voluntary organisation which provides support, advice and information on best practice for everyone concerned with the education and care of young children from birth to eight*

**Daycare Trust**
21 St George's Road
London
SE1 6ES
childcare hotline: 020 7840 3350
info@daycaretrust.org.uk
www.daycaretrust.org.uk
*national childcare charity*

**Kids' Club Network**
Bellerive House
3 Muirfield Crescent
London
E14 9SZ
020 7512 2112
information.office@kidsclubs.org.uk
*national organisation for out of school childcare*

**The National Childminding Association (NCMA)**
8 Masons Hill
Bromley
Kent
BR2 9EY
020 8464 6164; 0800 169 4486
(10am - 4pm Monday to Friday)
info@ncma.org.uk
www.ncma.org.uk
*national charity and membership organisation that speaks on behalf of registered childminders in England and Wales*

**The Pre-school Learning Alliance**
Unit 213-216
30 Great Guildford Street
London
SE1 0HS
020 7620 0550
www.pre-school.org.uk
*an educational charity representing and supporting community pre-schools in England*

**Under5s**
PO Box 137
Ilkley
West Yorkshire
LS29 7AH
07929 769493
mail@underfives.co.uk
www.underfives.co.uk
*provides free learning resources, practical information and help on all aspects of education for the under fives*

# Primary education

**The National Association for Primary Education**
University of Leicester,
Moulton College, Moulton
Northampton
NN3 7RR
01604 647646
nationaloffice@nape.org.uk
www.nape.org.uk
*promotes high quality primary education for every child; membership includes parents, teachers, school governors, inspectors, education officers and entire school communities*

**MAPE**
Cilgeraint Farm, St Ann's
Nr Bethesda
Gwynedd
LL57 4AX
www.mape.org.uk
*produces publications, software, reviews, events and a website regarding the use of ICT in primary education*

**The Centre for Literacy in Primary Education**
Webber Street
London
SE1 8QW
020 7401 3382/3 or 020 7633 0840
info@clpe.co.uk
www.clpe.co.uk
*an educational centre focusing on the fields of language, literacy and assessment*

# Special needs and learning difficulties

**Afasic**
2nd Floor
50-52 Great Sutton Street
London
EC1V 0DJ
020 7490 9410; helpline: 0845
355 5577
info@afasic.org.uk
www.afasic.org.uk
*a parent-led organisation to help
children and young people with
speech and language impairments
and their families*

**The British Dyslexia
Association**
98 London Road
Reading
RG1 5AU
0118 966 2677; helpline: 0118
966 8271
info@dyslexiahelp-
bda.demon.co.uk
www.bda-dyslexia.org.uk

**The British Institute of
Learning Disabilities (BILD)**
Campion House, Green Street
Kidderminster
Worcestershire
DY10 1JL
01562 723010
enquiries@bild.org.uk
www.bild.org.uk
*provides information, publications
and training and consultancy
services for organisations and
individuals*

**Centre for Studies on
Inclusive Education (CSIE)**
New Redland, Frenchay Campus
Coldharbour Lane
Bristol
BS16 1QU
0117 344 4007
inclusion.uwe.ac.uk/csie/csieho
me.htm
*an independent centre working in
the UK and overseas to promote
inclusion and end segregation*

**CHANGE**
Unity Business Centre,
Units 19 & 20
26 Roundhay Road
Leeds
LS7 1AB
0113 243 0202
changepeople@btconnect.com
www.changepeople.co.uk
*fights for the rights of learning
disabled people especially people
with learning disabilities who are
deaf or blind*

**DfES Centre for Special
Educational Needs (SEN)**
Sanctuary Buildings
Great Smith Street
London
SW1P 3BT
0870 000 2288
info@dfes.gsi.gov.uk
www.dfes.gov.uk/sen/
*provides a wide range of advice and
materials for teachers, parents and
others interested in or working with
children with special educational
needs*

**Dyslexia in Scotland**
Stirling Business Centre
Wellgreen
Stirling
FK8 2DZ
01786 446650
info@dyslexia-in-scotland.org
www.dyslexia.scotland.dial.pipex
.com

**The Dyspraxia Foundation**
8 West Alley
Hitchin
Hertfordshire
SG5 1EG
admin@dyspraxiafoundation.org.uk
www.dyspraxiafoundation.org.uk

**The Foundation for People
with Learning Disabilities**
83 Victoria Street
London
SW1H 0HW
020 7802 0300
fpld@fpld.org.uk
www.learningdisabilities.org.uk
*part of the Mental Health
Foundation which uses research
and projects to promote the rights of
people with learning disabilities
and their families*

**The Independent Panel for
Special Education Advice
(IPSEA)**
6 Carlow Mews
Woodbridge
Suffolk
IP12 1EA
England and Wales:
0800 018 4016;
Northern Ireland: 01232 705654
www.ipsea.org.uk
*a voluntary organisation which
provides free independent advice,
representation and information*

**Learning Disabilities UK**
www.learningdisabilitiesuk.org.uk
*aims to be the most informative
and up to date learning disability
related site in the UK*

**Learning Disability Website**
info@learningdisability.co.uk
www.learningdisability.co.uk
*primarily aimed at providing
education information for people
with learning disabilities, their
carers, advocates, friends,
professional carers, social and
health care workers, students and
those who have an active interest in
promoting equality of opportunity
for people with learning disabilities*

**Mencap**
123 Golden Lane
London
EC1Y 0RT
020 7454 0454
information@mencap.org.uk
www.mencap.org.uk
*learning disability charity working
with people with a learning disability
and their families and carers*

**Mencap Northern Ireland**
Segal House
4 Annadale Avenue
Belfast
BT7 3JH
028 9069 1351
mencapni@mencap.org.uk

**Mencap Wales**
31 Lambourne Crescent
Cardiff Business Park, Llanishen
Cardiff
CF14 5GF
029 2074 7588
information.wales@mencap.org.uk

## The National Association for Gifted Children

Suite 14, Challenge House
Sherwood Drive, Bletchley
Milton Keynes
MK3 6DP
0870 770 3217
amazingchildren@nagcbritain.org.uk
www.nagcbritain.org.uk

## The National Association for Special Educational Needs (NASEN)

NASEN House, 4/5 Amber
Business Village
Amber Close, Arnington
Tamworth
B77 4RP
01827 311500
welcome@nasen.org.uk
www.nasen.org.uk
*aims to promote the education, training, advancement and development of all those with special educational needs*

## National Development Team (NDT)

Albion Wharf
Albion Street
Manchester
M1 5LN
0161 228 7055
office@ndt.org.uk
www.ndt.org.uk
*an independent not for profit development agency that wants new opportunities and inclusion in ordinary life for all people with learning disabilities*

## The National electronic Library for Learning Disabilities (NeLLD)

www.minervation.com/ld/
*aims to provide access to best current knowledge in relation to the development and delivery of services for people with a learning disability*

# Resources

## The Advisory Centre for Education (ACE)

1c Aberdeen Studios, 22
Highbury Grove
London
N5 2DQ
0808 800 5793 (2-5pm Monday-Friday)
www.ace-ed.org.uk
*an independent national advice centre for parents*

## The Times Educational Supplement

Admiral House
66-68 East Smithfield
London
E1W 1BX
020 7782 3000
www.tes.co.uk

## EducationGuardian.co.uk

3-7 Ray Street
London
EC1R 3DR
020 7278 2332
education.editor@guardianunlimited.co.uk
education.guardian.co.uk

## @School

www.atschool.co.uk
*website offering choice of links, resources, information and interactive activities on the Internet for children aged 4 to 13*

## LearningChannel.org

www.learningchannel.org
*a portal that seeks to facilitate experience sharing between organisations and individuals working in education*

## National Curriculum online

www.nc.uk.net
*website which links every National Curriculum programme of study requirement to resources on the Curriculum Online*

## Schoolsnet

www.schoolsnet.com
*website offering lesson ideas, revision strategies and a broad range of information regarding school supplies, tests, fundraising and equipment; also contains search facilities for finding schools and jobs*

## TeacherNet

www.teachernet.gov.uk
*developed by the Department for Education and Skills as a resource to support the education profession*

## The National Grid for Learning

www.ngfl.gov.uk
*provides a network of selected links to websites that offer high quality content and information*

## UK Online

www.ukonline.gov.uk
*government info and services online*

## Virtual Teacher Centre (VTC)

www.vtc.ngfl.gov.uk
*a service for schools professionals providing news, support for professional development and the facility to search quality-badged resources across the National Grid for Learning*

# Housing

## Centrepoint
Neil House
7 Whitechapel Road
London
E1 1DU
020 7426 5300
www.centrepoint.org.uk or
www.street-level.org.uk
*charity helping homeless and socially
excluded young people to rebuild their lives*

### Main Southern Office
c/o OCHA
244 Barns Road
Oxford
OX4 3RW
01865 782561

### Main Northern Office
Miners Hall
Red Hill
Durham
DH1 4BB
0191 384 403

## Shelter
24 hour helpline: 0808 800 4444
info@shelter.org.uk
www.shelter.org.uk
*a national organisation with local
solutions working to improve the lives
of homeless and badly housed people*

### Shelter Scotland
4th Floor, Scotiabank House
6 South Charlotte Street
Edinburgh
EH2 4AW
0131 473 7170
shelterscot@shelter.org.uk

### Shelter Cymru
25 Walter Road
Swansea
SA1 5NN
01792 469400

## The Foyer Federation
3rd Floor, 5-9 Hatton Wall
London
EC1N 8HX
020 7430 2212
federation@foyer.net
www.foyer.net
*one of the UK's largest
providers of youth housing;
integrates training and job
search, personal support
and motivation with a place
to live*

## Homeless Link
First Floor, 10-13 Rushworth
Street
London
SE1 0RB
020 7960 3010
www.homeless.org.uk
*membership organisation
supporting and representing
more than 700 agencies
working with homeless
people across England and
Wales*

## Homeless Pages
www.homelesspages.org.uk
*source of information about
publications and training
on homelessness*

## Housing Options
78a High Street
Witney
Oxfordshire
OX28 6HL
01993 776318 or 0845 456
1497
enquiries@housingoptions.
org.uk
www.housingoptions.org.uk
*an independent, advisory
service for people with
learning disabilities, their
relatives and housing and
care providers*

# 11.14

# Family information and support

## Childcare options

**ChildcareLink Service**
Trust Court, Vision Park
Histon
Cambridge
CB4 9PW
0800 096 0296
childcarelink@opp-links.org.uk
www.childcarelink.gov.uk
*funded by the Department for Education and Skills and the Scottish Executive; provides advice and information on all aspects of childcare*

### North-west Scotland

**Orkney Childcare Information Service**
01856 876445

**Western Isles Childcare Information Service**
01851 707462

**Highland Council Childcare Information Service**
0845 601 1345

**Argyll & Bute Childcare Information Service**
01369 708504

### North-east Scotland

**Moray Childcare Information Service**
01343 557233

**Aberdeenshire Childcare Information Service**
0800 298 3330

**Aberdeen City Childrens Information Service**
01224 649172

**Angus Childcare Information Service**
01307 473303/3229

**Perth and Kinross Childcare Information Service**
0845 601 4477

**Dundee City Childcare Information Service**
01382 433900

**Fife Childcare Information Service**
01592 414838

### Central and Lothians

**Stirling Children's Information Service**
01786 442626

**Clackmannanshire Pre-School & Childcare Information Service**
01259 452453

**Falkirk Childcare Information Service**
01324 506632

**West Lothian Childcare Information Service**
01506 776660

**City of Edinburgh Childcare Information Service**
0800 032 0323

**Midlothian Childcare Information Service**
0131 271 3754

**Childcare Choices in East Lothian**
0800 028 8629

### West Scotland

**Inverclyde Childcare Information Service**
0800 052 9126

**Childcare in Renfrewshire Information Service**
0141 840 3853

**West Dunbartonshire Childcare Information Service**
0800 980 4683

Glasgow City Childcare
Information Service
  0141 287 8307

East Dunbartonshire
Childcare Information
Service
  0141 570 0091

East Renfrewshire Childcare
Information Service
  0141 577 3990

North Lanarkshire Childcare
Information Service
  01236 812281

South Lanarkshire Childcare
Information Service
  01698 527154

Ayrshire Childcare
Information Service
  0845 351 3000

## South Scotland

Scottish Borders Children's
Information Service
  01896 758186

Dumfries and Galloway
Childcare Information
Service
  0845 601 0191

## North-east

Northumberland Childcare
Information Service
  01670 534440

Newcastle Children's
Information Service
  0191 277 4133

Children's Information
Service - North Tyneside
  0191 200 1417

South Tyneside CIS
  0800 783 4645

Children's Information
Service in Gateshead
  0191 491 5979

Children's Information
Service Sunderland
  0191 553 5678

Durham County Council
Childcare Information
Service
  0845 602 4469

Children's Information
Service Hartlepool
  01429 284284

Stockton CIS
  01642 391329

Redcar and Cleveland CIS
  01642 771173

Childcare Plus (Teeside and
Darlington)
  0845 601 1984

## North-west

Cumbria Children's
Information Service
  0845 712 5737

Blackburn with Darwen
Childcare Information
Service
  01254 667877

Lancashire Childcare
Information Service
  0800 195 0137

Bury Children's Information
Service
  0800 731 4611

Rochdale Childcare
Information Service
  01706 719900

Oldham Children's
Information Service
  0800 731 1518

Manchester CIS
  0161 234 7111

Salford CIS
  0161 778 0321

Tameside CIS
  0161 339 6705

Trafford CIS
  0161 962 4296

Family Info Link Stockport
  0808 800 0606

Childcare Direct (Cheshire)
  0800 085 2863

Warrington Children's
Information Service
  01925 443131

Halton Childcare Information
Service
  01928 704306

Sefton Children's Information
Service (Merseyside)
  0800 316 4351

St Helens CIS (Merseyside)
  0800 073 0526

Knowsley CIS (Merseyside)
  0800 953 0244

Liverpool CIS (Merseyside)
  0151 233 3000

Wirral CIS (Merseyside)
  0800 085 8743

Wigan Children's Information
Service
  01942 827826

Bolton Childcare Information
Service
  01204 386030

Blackpool Childcare
Information Service
  0800 092 2332

## Yorkshire and the Humber

North Yorkshire CIS
  0845 601 1630

York Children's Information
Service
  01904 554628

East Riding Children's
Information Service
  01482 396469

Kingston-Upon-Hull
Children's Information
Service
  0800 915 5144

North East Lincolnshire
Children's Information
Service
  01472 323250

North Lincolnshire CIS
(Kidslincs)
  01724 296629

**Doncaster CIS**
0800 138 4568

**Rotherham Children's Information Service**
0800 073 0230

**Children's Information Service (Sheffield)**
0114 275 6699

**Childcare Information Service Ltd (Barnsley)**
0800 034 5340

**Wakefield Children's Information Service**
01924 306290

**Kirklees Children's Information Service**
01484 223041

**Calderdale Children's Information Service**
01422 253053

**Bradford Children's Information Link**
01274 437503

**Leeds CIS**
0113 247 4386


## East Midlands

**Nottinghamshire Children's Information**
0800 781 2168

**Nottingham City CIS**
0115 915 0773

**Children's Choices in Lincolnshire**
0800 195 1635

**Derbyshire Early Years and Childcare Partnership**
01629 585585

**Derby City Council**
01332 716381

**Leicestershire Children's Information Service**
0116 265 6545

**Leicester Children's Information Service**
0116 225 4890

**Rutland Children's Information Service**
01572 758495

**Jigsaw Northamptonshire**
01604 828400


## West Midlands

**Stoke on Trent (CIS)**
0800 015 1120

**Staffordshire (CIS)**
0845 650 9876

**Wolverhampton Children's Information Service**
0800 294 9939

**Walsall Children's Information Service**
01922 653383

**Childcare Information Bureau Birmingham**
0121 303 3521

**Solihull Childcare Information Service**
0121 788 4288

**Coventry (CIS)**
024 7683 4373

**Sandwell Childcare Information Service**
0121 569 4914

**Warwickshire Childcare Information Service**
0845 090 8044

**Dudley CIS**
01384 814398

**Worcestershire Children's Information Service**
01905 790560

**Herefordshire CIS**
01432 261681

**Childcare Outlook (Shropshire)**
01743 254400

**Telford & Wrekin CIS**
01952 202088


## North Wales

**Anglesey CIS**
01248 752920

**Conwy CIS**
01492 532221

**Denbighshire CIS**
01824 708220

**Flintshire CIS**
01244 547017

**Wrexham CIS**
01978 292094

**Gwynedd CIS**
01286 675570


## West Wales

**Ceredigion CIS**
01545 572636

**Pembrokeshire CIS**
01437 763344

**Carmarthenshire CIS**
01267 224224


## East Wales

**Powys CIS**
0845 1303637;
Welsh: 0845 130 3839


## South Wales

**Torfaen CIS**
01633 648175

**Blaenau Gwent CIS**
0800 032 3339

**Caerphilly CIS**
01443 863232

**Merthyr Tydfil CIS**
01685 724632

**Rhondda-Cynon-Taff CIS**
01443 744000

**Swansea CIS**
01792 612155

**Neath Port Talbot CIS**
01792 865914

**Bridgend CIS**
01656 727164

**Vale of Glamorgan CIS**
01446 704738

**Cardiff CIS**
029 2087 2713

**Newport CIS**
01633 233264

**Monmouthshire CIS**
01633 644461

## East of England

**Norfolk Childcare Information Service**
01603 622292

**Cambridgeshire and Peterborough Childcare Information Services**
0800 298 9121

**Suffolk Childcare Information Service**
01473 581493

**Bedfordshire Childrens Information Service**
01234 228229

**Young in Herts Children's Information Service**
01438 737502

**Luton Children's Information Service**
01582 548888

**Essex Children's Information Service**
01245 440400

**Thurrock Children's Information Service**
01375 652801

**Southend in Sea's Children's Information Service**
01702 392468

## South-west

**Children's Information Service Swindon**
01793 541786

**Families' & Children's Information Service, Gloucestershire**
01452 336100

**Wiltshire Childcare Information Service**
0845 758 5072

**South Gloucestershire Children's Information Service**
01454 868666

**Bristol Children's Information Service**
0845 129 7217

**North Somerset Childcare Service**
01275 888778

**Family Information Service, Bath & North East Somerset**
01225 395343

**Somerset Childrens Information Service**
0845 600 7171

**Devon Information on Services for Children**
0800 056 3666

**Children's Information Service, Cornwall**
0800 587 8191

**Isles of Scilly CIS**
01720 423680

**Plymouth Children's Information Service**
0800 783 4259

**Dorset Children's Information Service**
0845 355 2099

**Poole Children's Information Service**
01202 261999

**Bournemouth Children's Information Service**
01202 456222

## South-east

**Oxfordshire Children's Information Service**
01993 886933

**Wokingham Children's Information Service**
0118 935 2255

**Children's Information Centre, Berkshire**
0800 328 9148

**Hampshire CIS**
0845 602 1125

**Southampton CIS**
0800 169 8833

**FIZ (Family Information Zone), Isle of Wight**
01983 821999

**Portsmouth CHAT (Childcare Advice and Training)**
023 9269 5000

**West Sussex Childcare Information Service**
01243 777807

**Brighton & Hove Children's Information Service**
01273 293545

**KITES Childcare Information Service, East Sussex**
0845 601 0777

**Kent Children's Information Service**
0800 032 3230

**Medway Children's Information Service**
01634 335566

**Surrey Childrens Information Service**
0845 601 1777

**Slough CIS**
01628 660098

**Windsor and Maidenhead CIS**
01753 869100

**Buckinghamshire Children's Information Service**
0800 328 3317

**Milton Keynes Childcare Information Service**
01908 253918

## London

**Ealing CIS**
020 8825 5588

**Hillingdon CIS**
01895 277194

**Hounslow CIS**
0800 783 1696

**Kingston-Upon-Thames CIS**
020 8547 6582

**Merton CIS**
020 8646 5401

| | | |
|---|---|---|
| **Richmond-Upon-Thames CIS**<br>020 8831 6298 | **Newham CIS**<br>0800 074 1017 | **City of London CIS**<br>020 7332 1002 |
| **Wandsworth CIS**<br>020 8871 7899 | **Redbridge CIS**<br>0800 587 7500 | **Hackney CIS**<br>020 8356 7583 |
| **Bexley CIS**<br>020 8856 5398 | **Tower Hamlets CIS**<br>020 7364 6495 | **Hammersmith & Fulham CIS**<br>020 8735 5868 |
| **Bromley CIS**<br>020 8464 0276 | **Waltham Forest CIS**<br>020 8539 0870 | **Islington CIS**<br>020 7527 5959 |
| **Croydon CIS**<br>0845 111 1100 | **Barnet CIS**<br>0800 389 8312 | **Kensington & Chelsea CIS**<br>020 7361 3302 |
| **Greenwich CIS**<br>020 8921 6921 | **Brent CIS**<br>020 8937 3001 | **Lambeth CIS**<br>0845 601 5317 |
| **Lewisham CIS**<br>0800 085 0606 | **Enfield CIS**<br>020 8482 1066 | **Southwark CIS**<br>020 7525 5189 |
| **Sutton CIS**<br>020 8770 6000 | **Haringey CIS**<br>020 8801 1234 | **Westminster CIS**<br>020 7641 7929 |
| **Barking and Dagenham CIS**<br>020 8227 2338 | **Harrow CIS**<br>020 8861 5609 | |
| **Havering CIS**<br>01708 371991 | **Camden CIS**<br>020 7974 1679 | |

# Resources for carers

**Association of Children's Hospices**
Kings House
14 Orchard Street
Bristol
BS1 5EH
0117 905 5082
info@childhospice.org.uk
www.childhospice.org.uk

**Carers UK**
20/25 Glasshouse Yard
London
EC1A 4JT
020 7490 8818
info@ukcarers.org
www.carersonline.org.uk
*provides carers, those supporting them and others with national and local information*

**Carers North of England**
23 New Mount Street
Manchester
M4 4DE
0161 953 4233

**Carers Northern Ireland**
58 Howard Street
Belfast
BT1 6PJ
028 9043 9843
info@carersni.demon.co.uk

**Carers Scotland**
91 Mitchell Street
Glasgow
G1 3LN
0141 221 9141
information@carerscotland.org

**Carers Wales**
River House, Ynysbridge Court
Gwaelod y Garth
Cardiff
CF15 9SS
029 2081 1370
info@carerswales.demon.co.uk

**CarersNet**
www.carers.net
*offers information about carers and carer organisations in Scotland*

**Contact A Family**
209-211 City Road
London
EC1V 1JN
020 7608 8700; helpline: 0808 808 3555
info@cafamily.org.uk
www.cafamily.org.uk
*a UK-wide charity providing support, advice and information for families with disabled children*

**Contact A Family Northern Ireland**
Bridge Community Centre
50 Railway Street
Lisburn
BT28 1XP
028 9262 7552
nireland@cafamily.org.uk

**Contact A Family Scotland**
Norton Park
57 Albion Road
Edinburgh
EH7 5QY
0131 475 2608
scotland@cafamily.org.uk

**Contact A Family Cymru**
Room 153 S, 1st Floor
The Exchange Building,
Mount Stuart Square
Cardiff
CF10 5EB
029 2049 8001
wales@cafamily.org.uk

**Contact A Family North East England**
The Dene Centre,
Castle Farm Road
Newcastle upon Tyne
NE3 1PH
0191 213 6300
northeast@cafamily.org.uk

**Contact A Family North West England**
6th Floor, St James House
Pendleton Way
Salford
M6 5FW
0161 743 0700
northwest@cafamily.org.uk

**Contact A Family West Midlands**
Somerville House,
20/22 Harborne Road
Edgbaston
Birmingham
B15 3AA
0121 455 0655
westmids@cafamily.org.uk

**Crossroads Association**
10 Regent Place
Rugby
Warwickshire
CV21 2PN
0845 450 0350
communications@crossroads.
org.uk
www.crossroads.org.uk
*provides in-home services to give
carers a break*

**The Princess Royal Trust for Carers**
London Office
142 Minories
London
EC3N 1LB
020 7480 7788
help@carers.org
www.carers.org
*provides information, support and
practical help to carers*

**Glasgow Office**
Campbell House,
215 West Campbell Street
Glasgow
G2 4TT
0141 221 5066
infoscotland@carers.org

**Northern Office**
Suite 4, Oak House, High Street
Chorley
PR7 1DW
01257 234070
infochorley@carers.org

**Ring Around Carers**
www.bbc.co.uk/ringaroundcarers
*a 'meeting place on the phone' for
carers*

**The Young Carers Initiative**
Unit 2, Wessex Business Park
Wessex Way, Colden Common
Hants
SO21 1WP
01962 711511
young-carers-initiative@
childrenssociety.org.uk
www.childrenssociety.org.uk
youngcarers/initiative.htm
*part of The Children's
Society.working to create a
national focus for people that
work to support young carers and
their families across England
and the UK*

# Money

## Associations

| The National Association for Child Support Action (NACSA) PO Box 2977 Kingswinford West Midlands DY6 9YS | Child Poverty Action Group (CPAG) 94 White Lion Street London N1 9PF 020 7837 7979 staff@cpag.org.uk www.cpag.org.uk *promotes action for the relief, directly or indirectly, of poverty among children and families with children* | CPAG in Scotland Unit 09 Ladywell 94 Duke Street Glasgow G4 0UW general: 0141 552 3303; advice: 0141 552 0552 staff@cpagscotland.org.uk |

## Support agencies

**The Department for Work and Pensions (DWP)**
Correspondence Unit
Room 540
The Adelphi
1-11 John Adam Street
London
WC2N 6HT
020 7712 2171
www.dwp.gov.uk

**National Child Support Agency**
PO Box 55
Brierley Hill
West Midlands
DY5 1YL
0845 713 3133
Mon-Fri 8am-8pm,
Sat 8.30am-5pm
www.csa.gov.uk

**Scotland and North-east**

**Falkirk Child Support Agency Centre**
Parklands
Callendar Business Park
Callendar Road
Falkirk
FK1 1XT
0845 609 0042
*Area Director: Gerry Rooney*

**Northern Ireland and East**

**Belfast Child Support Agency Centre**
Great Northern Tower
17 Great Victoria Street
Belfast
BT2 7AD
0845 609 0092
*Area Director: John Canavan*

**South-east**

**Hastings Child Support Agency Centre**
Ashdown House
Sedlescombe Road North
St Leonards on Sea
East Sussex
TN37 7NL
0845 609 0052
*Area Director: Chris Forster*

## South-west

**Plymouth Child Support Agency Centre**
Clearbrook House, Towerfield Drive
Bickleigh Down Business Park
Plymouth
PL6 7TN
0845 609 0072
Area Director: Jean Brown

**Post Handling Department for Dudley and Birkenhead CSA Centre**
2 Weston Road
Crewe
CW8 1DD

## Midlands

**Dudley Child Support Agency Centre**
Pedmore House, The Waterfront
Brierley Hill, Dudley
West Midlands
DY5 1XA
0845 609 0062
*Area Director: Bill Hearn*

## Wales and North-west

**Birkenhead Child Support Agency Centre**
Great Western House, Woodside
Ferry Approach
Birkenhead
Merseyside
CH41 6RG
0845 609 0082; Welsh language line: 0845 713 8091
*Area Director: Margaret John*

# Gambling

**Gamblers Anonymous**
PO Box 88
London
SW10 0EU
0870 050 8880
www.gamblersanonymous.org.uk

**London**
020 7384 3040

**Sheffield**
0114 262 0026

**Manchester**
0161 976 5000

**Birmingham**
0121 233 1335

**Glasgow**
0141 630 1033

**Belfast**
028 7135 1329

**Gam-Anon**
0870 050 8880
contact@gamanon.org.uk
www.gamanon.org.uk
*for those affected by someone else's gambling*

**GamCare**
2 & 3 Baden Place
Crosby Row
London
SE1 1YW
020 7378 5200;
helpline: 0845 600 0133
info@gamcare.org.uk
www.gamcare.org.uk
*promotes responsible attitudes to gambling and works for the provision of proper care for those who have been harmed by gambling dependency*

# 11.16

# Law

## Government agencies

### The Court Service

**Address:** Southside, 105 Victoria Street, London SW1E 6QT
**Tel:** 020 7210 2266
**E-mail:** cust.ser.cs@gtnet.gov.uk
**Web:** www.courtservice.gov.uk
*an executive agency of the Department for Constitutional Affairs; responsible for the running of most of the courts and tribunals in England & Wales ie Crown, County, Appeals, and provides the necessary services to the judiciary and court users to ensure its impartial and efficient operation*

### Protection of Children Act Tribunal

**Address:** 6th Floor, St Christopher House, 90-114 Southwark Street, London SE1 0TE
**Tel:** 020 7921 1629
**E-mail:** pocat@gtnet.gov.uk
**Web:** www.pocat.gov.uk
*the Tribunal was established by parliament in the Protection of Children Act 1999 and started work on October 2 2000; it provides an independent appeal procedure for child care workers who have been put on the statutory list of people forbidden to work with children because they are unsuitable to do so and for teachers who have been banned from working in schools or further education colleges or whose right to do so has been restricted; its members are appointed by the Lord Chancellor; the Tribunal makes no charge for conducting appeals, and public funding may be available to help those who apply.*

### The Youth Justice Board for England and Wales

**Address:** 11 Carteret Street, London SW1H 9DL
**Tel:** 020 7271 3033
**E-mail:** enquiries@yjb.gsi.gov.uk
**Web:** www.youth-justice-board.gov.uk
*a non-departmental public body which aims to prevent offending by children and young people*

### Children and Family Court Advisory and Support Services for England and Wales (CAFCASS)

**Address:** 13th & 14th Floors, Archway Tower, 2 Junction Road, London N19 5HQ
**Tel:** 020 7210 4400
**E-mail:** cafcass@cafcass.gov.uk
**Web:** www.cafcass.gov.uk
*a national non-departmental public body for England and Wales that looks after the interests of children involved in family proceedings*

## East Midlands

### Derbyshire
CAFCASS
New Enterprise House, St
Helen's Street
Derby
Derbyshire
DE1 3GY
01332 866480

CAFCASS
12 The Strand
Derby
Derbyshire
DE1 1BA
01332 290214

CAFCASS
5-7 Brimington Road
Chesterfield
Derbyshire
S41 7UG
01246 221082

### Leicestershire
CAFCASS
Riverside House
49 Western Boulevard
Leicester
Leicestershire
LE2 7HN
0116 249 5600

### Lincolnshire
CAFCASS
Grange House, 46 Union Street
Grantham
Lincolnshire
NG31 6NZ
01522 554838

CAFCASS
Lincoln County Court, 360 High
Street
Lincoln
Lincolnshire
LN5 7RL
01522 510435

CAFCASS
The Annexe, County Hall
Boston
Lincolnshire
PE21 6LX
01205 310010

CAFCASS
14 Upgate
Louth
Lincolnshire
LN11 9ET
01507 604427

CAFCASS
Broadgate House
Westlode Street
Spalding
Lincolnshire
PE11 2AF
01775 722078

CAFCASS
2nd Floor, Hamilton House
1-3 Clasketgate, Lincoln
Lincolnshire
LN2 1JG
01522 580750

### Northampton
CAFCASS
Newlands House
Campbell Square
Northampton
Northamptonshire
NN1 3EB
01604 608000

### Nottinghamshire
CAFCASS
Clumber House, 7 Clumber Street
Mansfield
Nottinghamshire
NG18 1NU
01623 466880

CAFCASS
2A Castlebridge, Office Village,
Castle Marina Road
Nottingham
Nottinghamshire
NG7 1TP
0115 853 2500

## Eastern

### Bedfordshire
CAFCASS
Southway, 290 London Road
Bedford
Bedfordshire
MK42 0PY
01234 269274

CAFCASS
1st Floor, Cresta House
Alma Street, Luton
Bedfordshire
LU1 2PU
01582 735265

### Cambridgeshire
CAFCASS
Bridge House, Bridge Street
Cambridge
Cambridgeshire
CB2 1UA
01733 312159

CAFCASS
71 London Road
Peterborough
Cambridgeshire
PE2 9BB
01733 312159

### Essex
CAFCASS
St Mary's House,
90 Victoria Road
Chelmsford
Essex
CM1 1RD
01245 255660

CAFCASS
7 St Peter's Court
Middleborough
Colchester
Essex
CO1 1WD
01206 540885

### Norfolk
CAFCASS
Suite A, St Clements House
St Clements Alley
2-16 Colegate, Norwich
Norfolk
NR3 1BQ
01603 226600

### Suffolk
CAFCASS
6 Merchant's Court
74 Foundation Street
Ipswich
Suffolk
IP4 1BN
private law: 01473 408120;
public law: 01473 408122

## Greater London

### Central
CAFCASS
1st Floor
59-65 Wells Street
London
W1A 3AE
020 7255 1555

CAFCASS
5th Floor
First Avenue House
42-49 High Holborn
London
WC1V 6NP
020 7947 6054

**Croydon**
CAFCASS
3rd Floor, Carolyn House
22-26 Dingwall Road, Croydon
Surrey
CR0 9XF
020 8603 2620

**Archway**
CAFCASS
13th Floor, Archway Tower
2 Junction Road
London
N19 5HQ
020 7210 4100

**Ilford**
CAFCASS
2nd Floor, Charter House
450 High Road, Ilford
Essex
IG1 1QF
020 8553 0535

**Bromley**
CAFCASS
5 Upper Park Road
Bromley
Kent
BR1 3HN
020 8460 4606

**Kingston**
CAFCASS
125 Richmond Road
Kingston Upon Thames
Surrey
KT2 5BX
020 8541 0233

**Uxbridge**
CAFCASS
Academy House, 75 High Street
Uxbridge
Middlesex
UB8 1JR
01895 251398

---

## North-east

**County Durham**
CAFCASS
Alport House, 35 Old Elvet
Durham
County Durham
DH1 3HN
0191 386 9426

CAFCASS
38 Saddler Street
Durham
County Durham
DH1 3NU
0191 383 9279

**Middlesbrough**
CAFCASS
2nd Floor, Prudential House
31/33 Albert Road
Middlesbrough
TS1 1PE
01642 251555

**Northumberland**
CAFCASS
Units 5-7, Dudley Court
Manor Walks Shopping Centre,
Cramlington
Northumberland
NE23 8QW
01670 591940

**South Tyneside**
CAFCASS
Campbell Park Road. Hebburn
South Tyneside
NE31 2SS
private law: 0191 428 6356;
public law: 0191 483 4611

**Hebburn**
CAFCASS
3rd Floor, Park View House
Front Street, Benton
Newcastle
NE7 7TZ
0191 270 1897

---

## North-west

**Cheshire**
CAFCASS
55 Hoole Road
Chester
Cheshire
CH2 3NJ
01244 348201

CAFCASS
Quattro Tower,
Buttermarket Street
Warrington
Cheshire
WA1 2LS
01925 428900

CAFCASS
10 Congleton Road
Sandbach
Cheshire
CW11 1WJ
01270 760658

CAFCASS
1st/2nd Floor, Edward House
Edward Street, Stockport
Cheshire
SK1 3DQ
0161 480 5450

**Cumbria**
CAFCASS
Capital Building, Hilltop Heights
Carlisle
Cumbria
CA1 2NS
01228 549130

CAFCASS
Meadow Bank, Shap Road
Kendal
Cumbria
LA9 6NY
01539 739417

CAFCASS
The Court House,
Catherine Street
Whitehaven
Cumbria
CA28 7PA
01946 62031

**Greater Manchester**
CAFCASS
3 Great Moor Street
Bolton
Greater Manchester
BL1 1NS
01204 370831

CAFCASS
4 Candleford Road, Withington
Manchester
M20 3JH
0161 445 8221

CAFCASS
7 Great Moor Street
Bolton
Greater Manchester
BL1 1NS
01204 548200

CAFCASS
6th Floor, Byrom House,
Quay Street
Manchester
M3 3JD
regional law: 0161 830 5720;
public law: 0161 830 5701

**Lancashire**
CAFCASS
87-89 Manchester Road
Rochdale
Lancashire
OL11 4JG
01706 341529

CAFCASS
Broadfield House,
91 Manchester Road
Rochdale
Lancashire
OL11 4JG
01706 525774

CAFCASS
241 Church Street
Blackpool
Lancashire
FY1 3PB
01253 294780

CAFCASS
1st Floor
Darwen Health Centre
Union Street
Darwen
Lancashire
BB3 0DA
01254 771321

CAFCASS
18 Winckley Square
Preston
Lancashire
PR1 3TU
01772 203999

CAFCASS
711 Cameron House,
White Cross
South Road
Lancaster
Lancashire
LA1 4XQ
01524 586300

**Merseyside**
CAFCASS
3rd Floor, State House
22 Dale Street
Liverpool
Merseyside
L2 4TR
0151 286 6464

CAFCASS
PO Box 234
Albert Dock
Liverpool
Merseyside
L69 4PB
0151 708 7906

CAFCASS
21-31 Barrow Street
St Helens
Merseyside
WA10 1RX
01744 630245

CAFCASS
PO Box 348
24 Lathom Road
Southport
Merseyside
PR9 0YZ
01704 513880

# South-east

**Berkshire**
CAFCASS
Glasson Centre
319 Oxford Road, Reading
Berkshire
RG3 1AU
0118 956 6322

CAFCASS (interview facility)
77 London Road
Newbury
Berkshire
RG14 1JN
01635 550108

**Buckinghamshire**
CAFCASS
Bridge House, Bridge Street
High Wycombe
Buckinghamshire
HP11 2EL
01494 436622

CAFCASS
Clyde House
10 Milburn Avenue
Oldbrook, Milton Keynes
Buckinghamshire
MK6 2WA
01908 359420

**East Sussex**
CAFCASS
12 Old Steine
Brighton
East Sussex
BN1 1EJ
01273 666960

CAFCASS
Map House
34-36 St Leonard's Road
Eastbourne
East Sussex
BN21 3QA
01323 433100

**Hampshire**
CAFCASS
35 Guildhall Walk
Portsmouth
Hampshire
PO1 2RY
023 9261 1061

CAFCASS
7 Meridian's Cross, Ocean Village
Southampton
Hampshire
SO14 3TJ
023 8063 0996

CAFCASS
1st Floor, Grosvenor House
Basing View, Basingstoke
Hampshire
RG21 4HG
01256 392770

CAFCASS (interview facility)
63 Christchurch Road
Ringwood
Hampshire
BH24 1PH
01425 472055

**Isle of Wight**
CAFCASS
30 Quay Street
Newport
Isle of Wight
PO30 5BA
01983 528867

**Kent**
CAFCASS
Lesser Knowlesthorpe
Barton Mill Road, Canterbury
Kent
CT1 1BP
01227 763263

CAFCASS
9 New Road Avenue
Chatham
Kent
ME4 6BB
01634 815855

CAFCASS
Rooms 3.43 - 3.51
Sessions House
County Road, Maidstone
Kent
ME14 1XQ
01622 694476/ 284

**Oxford**
CAFCASS
1st Floor, 2 Cambridge Terrace
Oxford
Oxfordshire
OX1 1TP
01865 728421

**Surrey**
CAFCASS
2nd Floor, Blenheim House
1 Bridge Street, Guildford
Surrey
GU1 4RY
01483 543300

## West Sussex

CAFCASS
38 Southgate
Chichester
West Sussex
PO19 1DP
private law: 01243 531764;
public law: 01243 839036

CAFCASS
The Law Courts, Hurst Road
Horsham
West Sussex
RH12 2DE
01403 265445

## South-west

**Avon**
CAFCASS
The Old Convent, 35 Pulteney
Road
Bath
Avon
BA2 4JE
01225 460673

CAFCASS
Unit 9, York Court
Wilder Street, Bristol
Avon
BS2 8QH
0117 923 2070

**Cornwall**
CAFCASS
22 Lemon Street
Truro
Cornwall
TR1 2LS
01872 265767

CAFCASS
62 Fore Street
Bodmin
Cornwall
PL31 2HR
01208 269192

**Devon**
CAFCASS
8 Ford Park Lane, Mutley
Plymouth
Devon
PL4 6RR
01752 229124

CAFCASS
Minerva House, Pynes Hill
Exeter
Devon
EX2 5JL
01392 354600

**Dorset**
CAFCASS
The Courts of Justice, Deansleigh
Road
Bournemouth
Dorset
BH7 7DS
01202 430616

CAFCASS
The Law Courts, Westwey Road
Weymouth
Dorset
DT4 8SU
01305 771864

CAFCASS
The Law Courts, Hanham Road
Wimborne
Dorset
BH21 1AS
01202 881416

**Gloucester**
CAFCASS
Northgate House, 19 London
Road
Gloucester
Gloucestershire
GL1 3HB
01452 311888

**Somerset**
CAFCASS
6 Mendip House, High Street
Taunton
Somerset
TA1 3SX
Regional law: 01823 340224;
private law: 01823 330202

**Wiltshire**
CAFCASS
The Boulter Centre, Avon
Approach
Salisbury
Wiltshire
SP1 3SL
01722 410357

CAFCASS
East House, 9 East Street
Swindon

**Wiltshire**
SN1 5BU
private law: 01793 612299;
public law: 01225 444339

CAFCASS
2 Prospect Place
Trowbridge
Wiltshire
BA14 8QA
01225 774414

## West Midlands

**Birmingham**
CAFCASS
1 Printing House Street
Birmingham
B4 6DE
0121 248 6285

CAFCASS
1st Floor, The Citadel
190 Corporation Street
Birmingham
B4 6QD
0121 248 6270

**Coventry**
CAFCASS
Greyfriars House
2 Greyfriars Road
Coventry
CV1 3RY
024 7655 3601

**Dudley**
CAFCASS
109 Dixons Green Road
Dudley
DY2 7DJ
01384 455123

**Staffordshire**
CAFCASS
13 Hartshill Road, Stoke
Stoke On Trent
Staffordshire
ST4 7QT
01782 747127

CAFCASS
Horninglow Street
Burton upon Trent
Staffordshire
DE14 1PH
01283 500503

CAFCASS
Moor Street
Tamworth
Staffordshire
B79 7QZ
01827 53066

CAFCASS
Marsh Court, Tillington Street
Stafford
Staffordshire
ST16 2RE
01782 785816

**Telford**
CAFCASS
Flora Dugdale House, 27
Wrockwardine Road
Wellington, Telford
Shropshire
TF1 3DA
01952 240172

**Walsall**
CAFCASS
Midland Road
Walsall
WS1 3QE
01922 720665

**Wolverhampton**
CAFCASS
Gough Street
Wolverhampton
WV1 3LG
01902 576076

**Worcester**
CAFCASS
Virginia House, The Butts
Worcester
Worcestershire
WR1 3PA
01905 723601

## York & Humberside

**Humberside**
CAFCASS
21 Dudley Street
Grimsby
DN31 2AW
01472 251999

CAFCASS
20 The Weir
Hessle
HU13 0MS
01482 640228

CAFCASS
90 Finkle Street
Cottingham
Hull
HU16 4AU
01482 842153

CAFCASS
96 Oswald Road
Scunthorpe
DN15 7PA
01724 271033

**North Yorkshire**
CAFCASS
5-7 Haywra Crescent
Harrogate
HG1 5BG
01423 566764

CAFCASS
1 Westbourne Grove
Scarborough
YO11 2DJ
01723 341083

CAFCASS
37 Fishergate
York
YO10 4AP
01904 641448

**South Yorkshire**
CAFCASS
32 Park Street
Wombwell
Barnsley
S73 0HF
01226 754646

CAFCASS
Orsborn House
1/2 Highfield, Doncaster Road
Rotherham
S65 1EA
private law: 01709 839090;
public law: 01709 786200

CAFCASS
3 Dragoon Court,
Hillsborough Barracks
Penistone Road
Sheffield
S6 2GZ
0114 231 6119

CAFCASS
Kings Mews
Frances Street
Doncaster
DN1 1JB
01302 327202

**West Yorkshire**
CAFCASS
West House, Hanover Street
Batley
WF17 5DZ
01924 479006

CAFCASS
PO Box 92, Kenburgh House
28A Manor Row
Bradford
BD1 4WR
01274 386100

CAFCASS
1 Park Cross Mews
Park Cross Street
Leeds
LS1 2QS
general: 0113 394 7400;
regional: 0113 394 7474

CAFCASS
3rd Floor, Bull Ring House
23 Northgate
Wakefield
WF1 3BJ
01924 204410

## Wales

**Aberystwyth**
CAFCASS
Swyddfa'r Ysqubor
Alexandra Road, Aberystwyth
Ceredigion
SY23 1PT
01970 623390

**Bridgend**
CAFCASS
Level 2, Brackla House
Brackla Street
Bridgend
CF31 1BZ
01656 647272

**Cardiff**
CAFCASS Main Office South
Llys y Delyn
107-111 Cowbridge Road East
Cardiff
CF11 9AG
main office: 029 2064 7979;
private & public law: 029 2064
7900

**Carmarthen**
CAFCASS
33 Quay Street
Carmarthen
Carmarthenshire
SA31 3JT
01267 235904

**Conwy**
CAFCASS
Heulwen, Glyn y Marl Road
Llandudno Junction
Borough of Conwy
LL31 9NS
01492 581975

**Haverfordwest**
CAFCASS
Penffynnon, Hawthorn Rise
Haverfordwest
Pembrokeshire
SA61 2AZ
01437 761960

**Newport**
CAFCASS
35 Godfrey Road, Newport
Newport County Borough Council
NP20 4PE
01633 264265

**Newtown**
CAFCASS
Merchant's House
High Street
Newtown
SY16 2NR
01686 627891

**Swansea**
CAFCASS
76A Walter Road
Swansea
SA1 4QA
01792 460179

CAFCASS
3rd Floor, 37 The Kingsway
Swansea
SA1 5LF
01792 645535

**Tredegar**
CAFCASS
Tredegar Magistrates' Court
Spencer Square
Tredegar
NP22 3XR
01495 725555

**Wrexham**
CAFCASS Main Office North
Grosvenor Lodge
Grosvenor Road

**Wrexham**
LL11 1DB
main office: 01978 368479;
private & public law: 01978
368450

## Scotland

### Scottish Executive Education Department
Children's Hearings Branch,
Area 2-B (S) Victoria Quay
Edinburgh
EH6 6QQ
0131 244 5483
childrens.hearings@scotland.gsi.gov.uk
www.childrens-hearings.co.uk
*Children's Hearings deal with children and young people under 16 who commit offences or are in need of care or protection. All referrals must be made to the reporter. The reporter is an*

*official employed by the Scottish Children's Reporter Administration. They must then make an initial investigation before deciding what action, if any, is necessary in the child's interests. The reporter must consider whether the evidence is sufficient to support the grounds for referral and then decide whether compulsory measures of supervision may be required*

### Scottish Children's Reporter Administration
Ochil House
Springkerse Business Park
Stirling
FK7 7XE
01786 459500
www.childrens-reporter.org

---

# Professional associations

### Association of Child Abuse Lawyers (ACAL)
PO Box 466, Chorleywood
Rickmansworth
Hertfordshire
WD3 5LG
01923 286888
info@childabuselawyers.com
www.childabuselawyers.com

### NAGALRO
PO Box 264
Esher
Surrey
KT10 0WA
01372 818504
nagalro@globalnet.co.uk
www.nagalro.com
*the professional association for childrens guardians and children and family reporters*

### NAPO
4 Chivalry Road
London
SW11 1HT
020 7223 4887
info@napo.org.uk?Subject=Fee dback from Napo website
www.napo.org.uk
*the trade union and professional association for family court and probation staff*

### UNISON
1 Mabledon Place
London
WC1H 9AJ
0845 355 0845
www.unison.org.uk
*the union for people delivering public services*

### PCS
160 Falcon Road
London
SW11 2LN
020 7924 2727
www.pcs.org.uk
*represents members working in government departments, agencies and private sector companies that deliver government services*

### The Solicitors Family Law Association (SFLA)
PO Box 302
Orpington
Kent
BR6 8QX
01689 850227; 0345 585671
www.sfla.co.uk
*an association of over 5000 family law solicitors; It sets high standards of good practice in family law and runs an accreditation scheme for specialist family lawyers; also keeps an up-to-date list of children's panel solicitors*

# Courts

## Crown courts

Central Criminal Court
- Old Bailey
020 7248 3277

Aylesbury
01296 434401

Barnstaple
01271 373286

Barrow-in-Furness
01772 832300

Basildon Combined Court
01268 458000

Birmingham
0121 681 3300

Blackfriars
020 7922 5800

Bolton Combined Court
Centre
01204 392881

Bournemouth
01202 502800

Bradford Combined Court
Centre
01274 840274

Bristol
0117 976 3030

Burnley Combined Court
Centre
01282 416899

Bury St Edmonds
01284 762676

Caernarfon
01286 675200

Cambridge
01223 224666

Canterbury Combined Court
Centre
01227 819200

Cardiff
029 2041 4400

Carlisle Combined Court
Centre
01228 520619

Carmarthen
01267 236071

Chelmsford
01245 603000

Chester
01244 317606

Chichester Combined Court
Centre
01243 520742

Coventry Combined Court
Centre
024 7653 6166

Croydon Combined Court
Centre
020 8410 4700

Derby Combined Court
Centre
01332 622600

Dolgellau
01286 675200

Doncaster
01302 322211

Dorchester
01305 778684

Durham
0191 386 6714

Exeter Combined Court
Centre
01392 210655

Gloucester
01452 529351

Great Grimsby Combined
Court Centre
01472 311811

Guildford
01483 468500

Harrow
020 8424 2294

Haverfordwest
01437 764782

Hereford
01432 276118

Inner London
020 7234 3100

Ipswich
01473 220750

Isleworth
020 8380 4500

Kingston-upon-Hull
Combined Court Centre
01482 586161

Kingston-upon-Thames
020 8240 2500

Knutsford 01685 388307

Leeds Combined Court
Centre
0113 283 0040

Lewes Combined Court
Centre
01273 480400

Lincoln
01522 525222

Liverpool Combined Court
Centre
0151 473 7373

Luton
01582 522000

Maidstone
01622 202000

Manchester (Crown Square)
0161 954 1702

Manchester at Minshull St
0161 954 7500

Merthyr Tydfil Combined
Court Centre
01685 358222

Middlesex Guildhall
020 7202 0370

Mold
01244 356709

Newcastle-upon-Tyne
Combined Court Centre
0191 201 2000

Newport (South Wales)
01633 266211

Newport, I.O.W.
01983 821569

Northampton Combined
Court
01604 470400

Norwich Combined Court
Centre
01603 728200

Nottingham
0115 910 3551

Oxford Combined Court
Centre
01865 264200

Peterborough Combined
Court Centre
01733 349161

Plymouth Combined Court
01752 677400

Portsmouth Combined Court
Centre
023 9289 3000

Preston Combined Court
Centre
01772 832300

Reading
0118 967 4400

Salisbury Combined Court
Centre
01722 325444

Sheffield Combined Court
Centre
0114 281 2400

Shrewsbury
01743 355775

Snaresbrook
020 8530 0000

Southampton Combined
Court Centre
023 8021 3200

Southwark
020 7522 7200

St. Albans
01727 753220

Stafford Combined Court
Centre
01785 610730

Stoke-on-Trent Combined
Court
01782 854000

Swansea
01792 510200

Swindon Combined Court
01793 690514

Taunton
01823 326685

Teesside Combined Court
Centre
01642 340000

Truro Combined Court
Centre
01872 222340

Warrington Combined Court
Centre
01925 256700

Warwick Combined Court
Centre
01926 495428

Welshpool
01938 553144

Weymouth and Dorchester
Combined Court Centre
01305 788684

Winchester Combined Court
Centre
01962 841212

Wolverhampton Combined
Court Centre
01902 48100

Wood Green
020 8881 1400

Woolwich
020 8312 7000

Worcester Combined Court
Centre
01905 730800

York
01904 645121

# Northern Ireland courts

**Court Service,
Northern Ireland**
028 9032 8594
www.courtsni.gov.uk

Antrim
028 9446 2661

Armagh
028 3572 2816

Ballymena
028 2564 9416

Belfast
028 9024 2099

Craigavon
028 3834 1324

Downpatrick
028 4461 4621

Enniskillen
028 6632 2356

Londonderry
028 7136 3448

Newry
028 4062 3622

Omagh
028 8224 2056

# Sheriff courts, Scotland

## Scottish Courts Administration
0131 226 9200
www.scotcourts.gov.uk

Aberdeen
01224 657200

Airdrie
01236 751121

Alloa
01259 722734

Arbroath
01241 876600

Ayr
01292 268474

Banff
01261 812140

Campbelltown
01586 552503

Cupar
01334 652121

Dingwall
01349 863153

Dornoch
01862 810224

Dumbarton
01389 763266

Dumfries
01387 262334

Dundee
01382 229961

Dunfermline
01383 724666

Dunoon
01369 704166

Duns
01361 883719

Edinburgh
0131 225 2525

Elgin
01343 542505

Falkirk
01324 620822

Forfar
01307 462186

Fort William
01397 702087

Glasgow
0141 429 8888

Greenock
01475 787073

Hamilton
01698 282957

Inverness
01463 230782

Jedburgh
01835 863231

Kilmarnock
01563 520211

Kirkcudbright
01557 330574

Kirkwall
01856 872110

Lanark
01555 661531

Lerwick
01595 693914

Linlithgow
01506 842922

Lochmaddy
01876 500340

Oban
01631 562414

Paisley
0141 887 5291

Peebles
01721 720204

Perth
01738 620546

Peterhead
01779 476676

Portree
01478 612191

Rothesay
01700 502982

Stirling
01786 462191

Stonehaven
01569 762758

Stornoway
01851 702231

Stranraer
01776 702138

Tain
01862 892518

Wick
01955 602846

# County courts

Aberdare
01685 874779

Aberystwyth
01970 636370

Accrington
01254 237490

Aldershot & Farnham
01252 321639

Altrincham
0161 975 4760

Ashford
01233 632464

Aylesbury
01296 393498

Banbury
01295 265799

Barnet
020 8343 4272

Barnsley
01226 203471

Barnstaple
01271 372252

Barrow-In-Furness
01229 820046

Basildon Combined Court
01268 458000

Basingstoke
01256 318200

Bath
01225 310282

Bedford
01234 760400

Birkenhead
0151 647 8826

Birmingham Civil Justice
Centre
0121 681 4441

Bishop Auckland
01388 602423

Blackburn
01254 680640

Blackpool
01253 293178

Blackwood
01495 223197

Bodmin
01208 74224

Bolton Combined Court
01204 392881

Boston 01205 366080

Bournemouth
01202 502800

Bow
020 8536 5200

Bradford Combined Court
Centre
01274 840274

Brecknock
01874 622671

Brentford
020 8580 7300

Bridgend
01656 768881

Brighton
01273 674421

Bristol
0117 929 4414

Bromley
020 8464 9727

Burnley Combined Court
01282 416899

Bury
0161 764 1344

Bury St Edmunds
01284 753254

Burton upon Trent
01283 568241

Buxton
01298 23734

Caernarfon
01286 678911

Cambridge
01223 224500

Canterbury Combined Court
01227 819200

Cardiff Civil Justice Centre
029 2037 6400

Carlisle Combined Court
Centre
01228 520619

Carmarthen
01267 228010

Central London
020 7917 5000

Cheltenham
01242 519983

Chelmsford
01245 264670

Chester Civil Justice Centre
01244 404200

Chesterfield
01246 501200

Chichester
01243 520700

Chorley
01257 262778

Clerkenwell
020 7359 7347

Colchester
01206 572743

Consett
01207 502854

Conwy & Colwyn
01492 530807

Coventry Combined Court
Centre
01203 536 166

Crewe

01270 212255

Croydon Combined Court
020 8410 4700

Darlington
01325 463224

Dartford
01322 629820

Derby Combined Court
01332 622600

Dewsbury
01924 466135

Doncaster
01302 365400

Dudley
01384 480799

Durham
0191 3865941

Eastbourne
01323 735195

Edmonton
020 8807 1666

Epsom
01372 721801

Evesham
01386 442287

Exeter Combined Court
01392 210655

Gateshead
0191 477 2445

Gloucester Crown &
01452 529351

Grantham
01476 563638

Gravesend
01474 321771

Great Grimsby Combined
Court
01472 311811

Guildford
01483 595200

Halifax
01422 344700

Harlow
01279 443291

| | | |
|---|---|---|
| Harrogate<br>01423 503921 | Kingston upon Hull<br>01482 586161 | Melton Mowbray<br>01664 568336 |
| Hartlepool<br>01429 268198 | Kingston-upon-Thames<br>020 8546 8843 | Merthyr Tydfil Combined<br>Court<br>01685 358200 |
| Hastings<br>01424 435128 | Lambeth<br>020 7091 4410 | Milton Keynes<br>01908 668855 |
| Haverfordwest<br>01437 772060 | Lancaster<br>01524 68112 | Mold<br>01352 700313 |
| Haywards Heath<br>01444 456326 | Leeds<br>0113 283 0040 | Morpeth & Berwick<br>01670 512221 |
| Hertford<br>01992 503954 | Leicester<br>0116 222 2323 | Neath and Port Talbot<br>01639 642267 |
| Hereford<br>01432 357233 | Leigh<br>01942 673639 | Nelson<br>01282 601177 |
| High Wycombe<br>01494 436374 | Lewes Combined Court<br>01273 480400 | Newark<br>01636 703607 |
| Hitchin<br>01462 450011 | Lichfield<br>01543 262137 | Newcastle Combined Court<br>0191 201 2000 |
| Holywell<br>01352 711027 | Lincoln Combined Court<br>01522 883000 | Newbury<br>01635 40928 |
| Horsham<br>01403 252474 | Liverpool Combined Court<br>0151 473 7373 | Newport<br>01633 227150 |
| Hove Court Centre<br>01273 770643 | Llanelli<br>01554 757171 | Newport (Isle Of Wight)<br>01983 526821 |
| Hove Trial Centre<br>01273 770643 | Llangefni<br>01248 750225 | North Shields<br>0191 257 5866 |
| Huddersfield<br>01484 421043 | Lowestoft<br>01502 586047 | Northampton (County Court<br>Bulk Centre)<br>01604 601636 |
| Huntingdon<br>01480 450932 | Ludlow<br>01584 872091 | Northampton Combined<br>Court<br>01604 470452 |
| Ilford<br>020 8478 1132 | Luton<br>01582 506700 | Northwich<br>01606 42554 |
| Ipswich<br>01473 214256 | Macclesfield<br>01625 422872 | Norwich Combined Court<br>01603 728200 |
| Keighley<br>01535 602803 | Maidstone Combined Court<br>01622 202000 | Nottingham<br>0115 910 3500 |
| Kendal<br>01539 721218 | Manchester<br>0161 954 1800 | Nuneaton<br>01203 386134 |
| Kettering<br>01536 512471 | Mansfield<br>01623 656406 | Oldham<br>0161 290 4200 |
| Kidderminster<br>01562 822480 | Mayor's & City Of London<br>Court<br>020 7796 5400 | Oswestry<br>01691 652127 |
| King's Lynn<br>01553 772067 | Medway<br>01634 402881 | |

Oxford Combined Court
Centre
01865 264200

Penrith
01768 862535

Penzance
01736 362987

Peterborough Combined
Court
01733 349161

Plymouth Combined Court
01752 208284

Pontefract
01977 702357

Pontypool
01495 762248

Pontypridd
01443 402471

Poole
01202 741150

Portsmouth Combined Court
023 9289 3000

Preston Combined Court
01772 832300

Rawtenstall
01706 214614

Reading
0118 987 0500

Redditch
01527 67822

Reigate
01737 763637

Rhyl
01745 330216

Romford
01708 750677

Rotherham
01709 364786

Rugby
01788 542543

Runcorn
01928 716533

Salford
0161 745 7511

Salisbury

01722 325444

Scarborough
01723 366361

Scunthorpe
01724 289111

Sheffield Combined Court
0114 281 2400

Shoreditch
020 7253 0956

Shrewsbury
01743 289069

Skegness
01754 762429

Skipton
01756 793315

Slough
01753 690300

South Shields
0191 456 3343

Southampton Combined
Court
023 8021 3200

Southend
01702 601991

Southport
01704 531541

St Albans
01727 856925

St Helens
01744 27544

Stafford
01785 610730

Staines
01784 459175

Stockport
01614 747707

Stoke On Trent Combined
Court
01782 854000

Stourbridge
01384 394232

Stratford upon Avon
01789 293056

Sunderland
0191 568 0750

Swansea Civil Justice Centre
01792 510350

Swindon Combined Court
01793 690500

Tameside
0161 339 1711

Tamworth
01827 62664

Taunton
01823 335972

Teesside Combined Court
01642 340000

Telford
01952 291045

Thanet
01843 228771

Torquay & Newton Abbot
01803 616791

Trowbridge
01225 752101

Truro Combined Court
01872 222340

Tunbridge Wells
01892 515515

Uxbridge
020 8561 8562

Wakefield
01924 370268

Walsall
0845 351 3513

Wandsworth
020 8333 4351

Warrington Combined Court
01925 256700

Warwick Combined Court
Centre
01926 495428

Watford
01923 249666

Wellingborough
01933 226168

Welshpool And Newtown
01938 552004

West London
020 7602 8444

Weston Super Mare
01934 626967

Weymouth & Dorchester
01305 778684

Whitehaven
01946 67788

Wigan
01942 246481

Winchester Combined Court
01962 841212

Willesden
020 8963 8200

Wolverhampton Combined
Court
01902 481000

Woolwich
020 8854 2127

Worcester Combined Court
01905 730807

Worksop
01909 472358

Worthing
01903 206721

Wrexham
01978 351738

Yeovil
01935 474133

York
01904 629935

# Appeal courts

**Court of Appeal**
020 7947 6000
www.courtservice.gov.uk/cms
/supremecourt.htm

**High Court**
020 7947 6000
www.courtservice.gov.uk/cms
/supremecourt.htm

High Court, Scotland
0131 225 2595

High Court of Justiciary,

Scotland
0131 240 6906

Court of Session, Scotland
0131 240 6743

Supreme Court of
Judicature, N Ireland
028 9023 5111

Judicial Committee of the
Privy Council
020 7270 0483

House of Lords Appellate
Committee
020 7219 3000

# Court, legal and prison services

Appeals Service
020 7712 2640
www.appeals-service.gov.uk

Court Service
020 7210 2266
www.courtservice.gov.uk

Court Service, Northern
Ireland
028 9032 8594
www.courtsni.gov.uk

Crown Prosecution Service
020 7796 8000
www.cps.gov.uk

Scottish Courts
Administration
0131 226 9200
www.scotcourts.gov.uk

Magistrates Court Service
Inspectorate
020 7217 4344
www.mcsi.gov.uk

Prison Service
020 7217 6633
www.hmprisonservice.gov.uk
Press 020 7273 4545, victim
helpline 0845 758 5112

Scottish Prison Service
0131 244 8745
www.sps.gov.uk
Chief executive: 0131 244
8522

N Ireland Prison Service
028 9052 5065
www.niprisonservice.gov.uk

# Law centres

**Law Centres Federation**
020 7387 8570
www.lawcentres.org.uk

Avon & Bristol
0117 924 8662

Barnet
020 8203 4141

Battersea
020 7585 0716

Bradford
01274 306617

Brent Community
020 8451 1122

Bury
0161 272 0666

Camden Community
020 7284 6510

Cardiff
029 2049 8117

Carlisle
01228 515129

Central London
020 7839 2998

Chesterfield
01246 550674

Coventry
024 7622 3053

Derby
01332 344557

Devon
01752 519794

| | | |
|---|---|---|
| Gateshead<br>0191 478 2847 | Leicester<br>0116 255 3781 | South Manchester<br>0161 225 5111 |
| Gloucester<br>01452 423492 | Lewisham<br>020 8692 5355 | Southwark<br>020 7732 2008 |
| Greenwich Community<br>020 8305 3350 | Liverpool<br>0151 709 7222 | Springfield<br>020 8767 6884 |
| Hackney Community<br>020 8985 8364 | Luton<br>01582 481000 | Stockport<br>0161 476 6336 |
| Hammersmith & Fulham<br>020 8741 4021 | Newcastle<br>0191 230 4777 | Thamesmead<br>020 8311 0555 |
| Harehills & Chapeltown<br>0113 249 1100 | North Kensington<br>020 8969 7473 | Tottenham<br>020 8800 5354 |
| Hillingdon<br>020 8561 9400 | North Manchester<br>0161 205 9031 | Tower Hamlets<br>020 7247 8998 |
| Hounslow<br>020 8570 9505 | Nottingham<br>0115 978 7813 | Vauxhall Law and<br>Information Centre<br>0151 330 0239 |
| Humberside<br>01482 211180 | Oldham<br>0161 627 0925 | Wandsworth & Merton<br>020 8767 2777 |
| Islington<br>020 7607 2461 | Paddington<br>020 8960 3155 | Warrington Community<br>01925 651104 |
| Lambeth<br>020 7737 9780 | Plumstead Community<br>020 8855 9817 | Wiltshire<br>01793 486926 |
| Northern Ireland: Belfast<br>028 9024 4401 | Rochdale<br>01706 657766 | Wythenshawe<br>0161 498 0905 |
| Northern Ireland: western<br>area<br>028 7126 2433 | Saltley & Nechells<br>0121 328 2307 | |
| | Sheffield<br>0114 273 1888 | |

# Prisons

## National agencies

**Prison Service**
020 7217 6633
www.hmprisonservice.gov.uk
victim helpline 0845 758 5112

**Scottish Prison Service**
0131 244 8745
www.sps.gov.uk
Chief executive: 0131 244 8522

**N Ireland Prison Service**
028 9052 5065
www.niprisonservice.gov.uk

**Parole Board for England
and Wales**
020 7217 5314
www.paroleboard.gov.uk

**Prisons Ombudsman for
England and Wales**
020 7276 2876

**Scottish Parole Board**
0131 244 8755

**Scottish Prisons
Inspectorate**
0131 244 8481

**Chief Inspector of Prisons**
0870 267 4298
www.homeoffice.gov.uk/justice/
prisons/inspprisons

# Professional bodies

**Prison Governors Association**
020 7217 8591
www.prisongovernors.org.uk

**Prison Officers Association**
020 8803 0255
www.poauk.org.uk

**National Association of Prison Visitors**
01234 359763

**National Association of Probation Officers**
020 7223 4887

# Youth Offending Teams

## North-west

**Blackburn YOT**
Bryan Peake, YOT Manager
Bank House
44 Wellington Street
St John's, Blackburn
Lancashire
BB1 8AF
01254 299800
Bryan.peake@blackburn.gov.uk

**Blackpool YOT**
Steve Cook, YOT Manager
Stanley Buildings
1-3 Caunce Street
Blackpool
FY1 3DN
01253 478686
steve.cook@blackpool.gov.uk

**Bolton YOT**
Stephen Agger, YOT Manager
Bolton YOT
Le Mans Cresent
Bolton
BL1 1SA
01204 331263
steve.agger@bolton.gov.uk

**Bury YOT**
Graham Smyth, YOT Manager
Seedfield Resource Centre
Parkinson Street
Bury
BL9 6NY
0161 253 6862
G.M.Smyth@Bury.gov.uk

**Cheshire YOT**
Aileen Shepherd, YOT Manager
St Thomas House, Whitby Road
Ellesmere Port
Cheshire
CH65 6TU
01244 615500
shepherda@cheshire.gov.uk

**Cumbria YOT**
Yvonne Lake, YOT Manager
5 Brunswick Street
Carlisle
Cumbria
CA1 1PB
01228 607380
cumbria.yot@btinternet.com

**Halton/ Warrington YOT**
Rhona Bradley, Head of Youth
Offending Services
Warrington Police Station
Arpley Street
Warrington
WA1 1LQ
01925 445006
rhona.bradley@halton.borough.
gov.uk

**Knowsley YOT**
Richard Ford, YOT Manager
10 Derby Street, Prescot
Knowsley
Merseyside
L34 3LG
0151 443 3872
richard.ford.ce@knowsley.gov.uk

**Lancashire YOT**
Catherine Witt, YOT
ManagerSocial Services
Directorate, PO Box 162
E Cliff County Offices
Preston
PR1 3EA
01772 261305
catherine.witt@yot.lancscc.gov.uk

**Liverpool YOT**
Sue Cook, YOT Manager
Management Suite, 1st Floor
Millennium House
Liverpool
L1 6JQ
0151 233 4651
sue.cook@liverpool.gov.uk

**Manchester YOT**
Phil Lloyd, YOT Manager
Grey Mare Lane Police Station,
Bell Crescent
Beswick
Manchester
M11 3BA
0161 856 3604
p.lloyd2@notes.manchester.gov.uk

**Oldham YOT**
Allan Broadbent, YOT Manager
Youth Offending Team
Marion Walker House
Frederick Street
Oldham
OL8 1SW
0161 620 7546
yot@oebgs.org

**Rochdale YOT**
Rodger Massiah, YOT Manager
Dunsterville House
Manchester Road
Rochdale
L11 3RB
01706 643327
Yot@Rochdale.gov.uk

**Salford YOT**
Tom Healy, YOT Manager
City of Salford
10-12 Encombe Place
Salford
Manchester
M3 6FJ
0161 832 5382
tom.healy2@salford.gov.uk

**Sefton YOT**
Steve Eyre, YOT Manager
Police Station, Marsh Lane
Bootle
Merseyside
L20 5HJ
0151 934 2770
steve.eyre@sefton.gov.uk

**St Helens YOT**
Alan Critchley, YOT Manager
5a Bickerstaffe Street
St Helens
Merseyside
WA10 1DH
01744 25171
alancritchley@sthelens.gov.uk

**Stockport YOT**
Geoff Walley, YOT Manager
1st Floor, Owls House
56-61 Great Underbank
Stockport
SK1 1NE
0161 476 2876
geoff.walley.yot@stockport.gov.uk

**Tameside YOT**
John Whittle, YOT Manager
Francis Thompson Drive
Ashton-Under-Lyne
OL6 7AJ
0161 330 3012
john.whittle@nxcorp1.tameside.g
ov.uk

**Trafford YOT**
Helen McFarlane, YOT Manager
4th Floor, Arndale House
Chester Road, Stretford
Greater Manchester
M32 9XY
0161 912 3424
helen.mcfarlane@trafford.gov.uk

**Wigan YOT**
Sharon Bond, YOT Manager
91 Victoria Road
Platt Bridge
Wigan
WN2 5DN
01942 776886
s.bond@wiganmbc.gov.uk

**Wirral YOT**
Steve Pimblett, YOT Manager
3rd Floor, 76 Hamilton Street
Birkenhead
Wirral
CH41 5EN
0151 666 3629
stevepimblett@wirral.gov.uk

# West Midlands

**Birmingham YOT**
Graham Fletcher, YOT Manager
Kingsmere.18 Gravelly Hill North
Birmingham
B23 6BQ
0121 464 0600
Graham.Fletcher@birmingham.g
ov.uk

**Coventry YOT**
Andy Pepper, YOT Manager
c/o Police Station
Little Park Street
Coventry
CV1 2JX
024 7683 4297
andy.pepper@coventry.gov.uk

**Dudley YOT**
Mike Galikowski, YOT Manager
Brindley, Hall Street
Dudley
West Midlands
DY2 7DT
01384 813060
team.yot@dudley.gov.uk

**Sandwell YOT**
Keith Barham, YOT Manager
SGS House, Johns Lane
Tipton Road, Tividale
Oldbury
B69 3HX
0121 557 8804
keith_barham@sandwell.gov.uk

**Shropshire & Telford/Wrekin**
Willie Goodwillie, YOT Manager
24 Victoria Road, Wellington
Telford
Shropshire
TF1 1LG
01952 257477
willie.goodwillie@wrekin.gov.uk

**Solihull YOT**
Adrian Quinn, YOT Manager
Craig Croft Centre, 8 Craig Croft
Chelmsley Wood
Solihull
B37 7TR
0121 779 1750
aquinn@solihull.gov.uk

**Staffordshire YOT**
Sally Rees, YOT Manager
Stafford Fire Station Complex,
Beaconside
Stafford
Staffordshire
ST18 0DD
01785 358310
sally.rees@staffordshire.gov.uk

**Stoke-on-Trent YOT**
John Tate, YOT Manager
Unit C, Metro Business Park
Clough Street, Hanley
Stoke-on-Trent
ST1 4AF
01782 235957
john.tate.@stoke.gov.uk

**Walsall YOT**
Ged Campion, YOT Manager
104 Essington Road
New Invention
Willenhall
West Midlands
WV12 5DT
01922 493006
CampionG@walsall.gov.uk

**Warwickshire YOT**
Diane Johnson, YOT Manager
Sterling House
21 Hamilton Terrace
Hollywalk, Leamington Spa
Warwickshire
CV32 4LY
01926 736204
dianejohnson@warwickshire.
gov.uk

**Wolverhampton YOT**
Sally Nash, YOT Manager
Beckminster House, Birches
Barn Road
Wolverhampton
WV3 7BJ
01902 553722
sally.nash@wolverhampton.gov.uk

**Worcestershire & Herefordshire
YOT**
Dina Holder, YOT Manager
Central Admin Office
Tolladine Road
Worcestershire
WR4 9NB
01905 732215

# South-west

**Bath & NE Somerset YOT**
Sally Churchyard, YOT Manager
180 Frome Road
Combe Down
Bath
BA2 5RF
01225 396966
Sally_churchyard@bathnes.gov.uk

**Bournemouth & Poole YOT**
Pauline Batstone, YOT Manager
5 Hyde Road
Bournemouth
Dorset
BH10 5JJ
01202 575945
pauline.batstone@bournemouth.
gov.uk

**Bristol YOT**
Paul Burton, YOT Manager
Kenham House
Wilder Street
Bristol
BS2 8PD
0117 903 6480
paul_burton@bristol-city.gov.uk

**Cornwall & the Isles of Scilly YOT**
John Cousins, YOT Manager
Chiltern House, City Road
Truro
Cornwall
TR1 2JL
01872 274567
jcousins@cornwall.gov.uk

**Devon YOT**
Martin Spragg, YOT Manager
Ivybank
45 St David's Hill
Exeter
EX4 4DN
01392 384963
mspragg@devon.gov.uk

**Dorset YOT**
Clive Hawkins, YOT Manager
Youth Justice Centre,
Southwinds
11 Cranford Avenue, Weymouth
Dorset
DT4 7TL
01305 760336
c.r.hawkins@dorset-cc.gov.uk

**Gloucestershire YOT**
Phil Kendrick, YOT Manager
Windsor House, 40 Brunswick
Road
Gloucester
Gloucestershire
GL1 1HG
01452 547540
yot@gloscc.gov.uk

**North Somerset YOT**
Mike Rees, YOT Manager
c/o The Police Station, Walliscote
Road
Weston-Super-Mare
North Somerset
BS23 1UU
01934 638206
mike.rees@n-somerset.gov.uk

**Plymouth YOT**
Steve Moore, YOT Manager
3rd Floor, Midland House
Notte Street
Plymouth
PL1 2EJ
01752 306999
steve.moore@plymouth.gov.uk

**Somerset YOT**
Linda Barnett, YOT Manager
5-7 West End
Street
Somerset
BA16 0LG
01458 440820
LHBarnett@somerset.gov.uk

**South Gloucestershire YOT**
Steve Waters, YOT Manager
48-50 Elm Park
Filton
South Gloucestershire
BS34 7PH
01454 868561
steve_waters@southglos.gov.uk

**Swindon YOT**
Karen McKeown, YOT Manager
The Limes, 21 Green Road
Upper Stratton
Swindon
SN2 7JA
01793 823153
kmckeown@swindon.gov.uk

**Torbay YOT**
Fred Pethard, YOT Manager
3rd Floor, Commerce House
97-101 Abber Road, Torquay
Devon
TQ2 5PJ
01803 201655
fred.pethard@torbay.gov.uk

**Wiltshire YOT**
Mike Hitchings, YOT Manager
The Martins, 56a Spa Road
Melksham
Wiltshire
SN12 7NY
01225 793616
mikehitchings@wiltshire.gov.uk

## South

**Bracknell Forest YOT**
Paul Sutton, YOT Manager
76 Binfield Road
Bracknell
Berkshire
RG42 2AR
01344 354300
paul.sutton@bracknell-
forest.gov.uk

**Brighton & Hove YOT**
Nigel Lewis, YOT Manager
22 Ship Street
Brighton
East Sussex
BN1 1AD
01273 296156
nigel.lewis@brighton-hove.gov.uk

**Buckinghamshire YOT**
Pauline Camilleri: YOT Manager
Walton House, Walton Street
Aylesbury
Bucks
HP21 7QQ
01296 434624
pcamilleri@buckscc.gov.uk

**East Sussex YOT**
John Hawkins, YOT Manager
Ridgewood Rise Centre,
Highview Lane
Uckfield
East Sussex
TN22 5SY
01825 768297
john.hawkins@eastsussexcc.
gov.uk

**Kent YOT**
Kumar Mehta, YOT Manager
Kent County Council, Sessions
House
County Hall
Maidstone
ME12 1XQ
01622 694773
kumar.mehta@kent.gov.uk

**Medway YOT**
Ian Sparling, YOT Manager
The Family and Adolescent
Centre, 67 Balfour Road
Chatham
Kent
ME4 6QU
01634 336237
ian.sparling@medway.gov.uk

**Milton Keynes YOT**
Lee Westlake, YOT Manager
Manor Road Centre, Oakwood
Drive
Bletchley
Milton Keynes
MK2 2JG
01908 391000
lee.westlake@milton-
keynes.gov.uk

**Oxfordshire YOT**
Mike Simm, YOT Manager
43 Westgate
Oxford
OX1 1PF
01865 202218
mike.simm@oxfordshire.gov.uk

**Reading & Wokingham YOT**
Philip Hutchins, YOT Manager
34-36 Crown Street
Reading
Berkshire
RG1 2SE
0118 939 0298
phil.hutchins@reading.gov.uk

**Slough YOT**
Shelley LaRose-Jones, YOT
Manager
Partnership House, Chalvey Park
Slough
Berkshire
SL1 2HT
01753 522702
shelley.larosejones@slough.gov.uk

**Surrey YOT**
Toby Wells, YOT Manager
Churchill House, Mayford Green
Woking
Surrey
GU22 0PW
01483 723922
toby.wells@surreycc.gov.uk

**Wessex YOT**
Phil Sutton, YOT Manager
2nd Floor, 85 High Street
Winchester
Hampshire
SO23 9BL
01962 876100
phil.sutton@hants.gov.uk

**West Berkshire YOT**
Davy Pearson, YOT Manager
The Portacabin,
c/o Police Station
20 Mill Lane
Newbury
RG14 5QU
01635 264800
adpearson@westberks.gov.uk

**West Sussex YOT**
Terry Bishop, YOT Manager
County Buildings, East Street
Littlehampton
West Sussex
BN17 6AP
01903 718739
terry.bishop@westsussex.gov.uk

**Windsor & Maidenhead YOT**
Dennis Pete, YOT Manager
Maidenhead Project Centre,
Reform Road
Maidenhead
Berkshire
SL6 8BY
01628 683295
pete.dennis@rbwm.gov.uk

## Eastern

**Bedfordshire YOT**
Sue Corbett, YOT Manager
Bedfordshire County Council,
County Hall
Cauldwell Street
Bedford
MK42 9AP
01234 316405
corbets@sccd.bedfordshire.gov.
uk

**Cambridgeshire YOT**
Tom Jefford, YOT Manager
Unit 100, Rustat House
Clifton Road
Cambridgeshire
CB1 7EG
01223 718223
tom.jefford@cambridgeshire.gov.
uk

**Essex YOT**
Tanya Gillett, YOT Manager
Suite 2, Empire House
Victoria Road
Chelmsford
CM1 1PE
01245 265151
Tanya.Gillett.yot@essexcc.gov.uk

**Hertfordshire YOT**
Tom Rees, YOT Manager
County Hall
Pegs Lane
Hertford
SG13 8DP
01992 556337
tom.rees@hertscc.gov.uk

**Luton YOT**
Mike Thomas, YOT Manager
16 Rothesay Road
Luton
Bedfordshire
LU1 1QX
01582 547900
thomasm@luton.gov.uk

**Norfolk YOT**
Sue Massey, YOT Manager
45 Netherwood Green
Norwich
Norfolk
NR1 2JF
01603 223615
sue.Massey.yot@norfolk.gov.uk

**Peterborough YOT**
Bob Footer, YOT Manager
13-15 Cavell Court
Lincoln Road
Peterborough
PE1 2RH
01733 746540/1
bob.footer@peterborough.gov.uk

**Southend YOT**
Derek Eyres, YOT Manager
West Wing 7th Floor, Baryta
House
29 Victoria Avenue
Southend
SS2 6AZ
01702 608500
derekeyre@southend.gov.uk

**Suffolk YOT**
Julia Stephens-Row,
YOT Manager
Alexandra House
Rope Walk
Ipswich
IP4 1LR
01473 583389
julia.stephens-
row@yots.suffolkcc.gov.uk

**Thurrock YOT**
Peter Kay, YOT Manager
Five Wells, West Street
Grays
Essex
RM17 6XR
01375 413900
pkay@thurrock.gov.uk

## East Midlands

### Derby City YOT
Sharon Squires, YOT Manager
55 Ashbourne Road
Derby
DE22 3FS
01332 717525
sharon.squires@derby.gov.uk

### Derbyshire YOT
Bob Smith, YOT Manager
County Hall
Matlock
Derbyshire
DE4 3AG
01629 772164
youthoffendingservice@derbyshire
. gov.uk

### Leicester City YOT
Mary Campagnac, YOT Manager
Eagle House
11 Friar Lane
Leicester
LE1 5RB
0116 299 5830
campm003@leicester.gov.uk

### Leicestershire YOT
Philip Hawkins, YOT Manager
Leicestershire County Council
3rd Floor, County Hall
Glenfield
LE3 8RL
0116 265 6780
phawkins@leics.gov.uk

### Lincolnshire YOT
John Simkins, YOT Manager
Development House
64 Newland
Lincoln
LN1 1YA
01522 554554
simkij@lincolnshire.gov.uk

### Northamptonshire YOT
Sandy Pragnell, YOT Manager
53 Billing Road
Northampton
NN1 5DB
01604 602400
Spragnell@northamptonshire.gov
.uk

### Nottingham City YOT
Helen Jones, YOT Manager
2 Isabella Street
Nottingham
NG1 6AT
0115 841 3008
Helen.Jones@nottinghamcity.gov
.uk

### Nottinghamshire YOT
Philip Arnold, YOT Manager
15 West Hill Avenue
Mansfield
NG18 1PQ
01623 476611
philip.arnold@nottscc.gov.uk

## Yorkshire & Humberside

### Barnsley YOT
Colin Barnes, YOT Manager
Phase 1 & 2
County Way
Barnsley
S70 2DT
01226 774977
colinbarnes@barnsley.gov.uk

### Bradford YOT
Paul O'Hara, YOT Manager
Fraternal House
45 Cheapside
Bradford
BD1 4HP
01274 703760
paul.ohara@bradford.gov.uk

### Calderdale YOT
Steven Toye, YOT Manager
3 Trinity Place
Halifax
West Yorkshire
HX1 2BD
01422 368279
steven.toye@calderdale.gov.uk

### Doncaster YOT
Mark Summers, YOT Manager
Rosemead, May Avenue
Balby
Doncaster
DN4 9AE
01302 736119
Mark.Summers@doncaster.gov.uk

### East Riding of Yorkshire YOT
Darren O'Neill, YOT Manager
Council Office, Main Road
Skirlaugh
East Riding of Yorkshire
HU11 5HN
01482 885924
darren.oneill@east-riding-of-
yorkshire.gov.uk.

### Hull YOT
Neil Colthup, YOT Manager
Myton Centre
Porter Street
Kingston-upon-Hull
HU1 2RE
01482 609991
Neil.Colthup@hullcc.gov.uk

### Kirklees YOT
Richard Smith, YOT Manager
2nd Floor, Somerset Building
10 Church Street
Huddersfield
HD1 1LS
01484 226935
richard.smith@kirkleesmc.gov.uk

### Leeds YOT
Edwina Harrison, YOT Manager
Social Services, Merrion House
110 Merrion Centre
Leeds
LS2 8QB
0113 247 7483
Edwina.Harrison@leeds.gov.uk

### North East Lincolnshire YOT
Mike Brightmore, YOT Manager
44 Heneage Road
Grimsby
North East Lincolnshire
DN32 9ES
01472 325252
youth.justice@nelincs.gov.uk

### North Lincolnshire YOT
John Waters, YOT Manager
Shelford House, Shelford Street
Scunthorpe
North Lincolnshire
DN15 6NU
01724 274188
yot@ic24.net

### North Yorkshire YOT
Peter Foulsham, YOT Manager
4 Hawkhills Drive, The Hawkhills
Easingwold
North Yorkshire
YO61 3EG
01347 823177/084
peter.Foulsham@btinternet.com

### Rotherham YOT
Simon Perry, YOT Manager
4-6 Moorgate Road
Rotherham
South Yorkshire
S60 2EN
01709 516999
simon.perry@Rotherham.gov.uk

### Sheffield YOT
Malcolm Potter, YOT Manager
7 St Peters Close
Sheffield
S1 2EJ
0114 228 8577
Malcolm.Potter@Sheffield.gov.uk

**Wakefield YOT**
Steven Lawrenson, YOT Manager
5 West Parade
Wakefield
West Yorkshire
WF1 1LT
01924 304155
slawrenson@wakefield.gov.uk

**York YOT**
David Poole, YOT Manager
PO Box 246, Mill House
North Street
York
YO1 9YX
01904 554565
david.poole@york.gov.uk

## North-east

**Darlington YOT**
David Haddick, YOT Manager
Central House, Gladstone Street
Darlington
DL3 6JX
01325 346226
david.haddick@darlington.gov.uk

**Durham YOT**
Christina Blythe, YOT Manager
County Hall
Durham
DH1 5UG
0191 383 3982
christina.blythe@durham.gov.uk

**Gateshead YOT**
Brian Langley, YOT Manager
Former Felling Police Station,
Sunderland Road
Gateshead
Tyne and Wear
NE10 9NJ
0191 440 0500
b.langley@socialservices.gatesheadmbc.gov.uk

**Hartlepool YOT**
Danny Dunleavy, YOT Manager
Aneurin Bevan House
35 Avenue Road
Hartlepool
TS24 8HD
01429 523962
danny.dunleavy@hartlepool.gov.uk

**Newcastle-upon-Tyne YOT**
Rod Stapley, YOT Manager
Block D, 4th Floor
Jesmond Quadrant,
3 Archbold Terrace
Sandyford
NE2 1BZ
0191 277 7377
Rod.stapley@Newcastle.gov.uk

**North Tyneside YOT**
Jen Harrison, YOT Manager
Youth Court Services Team,
153 Tynemouth Road
North Shields
Tyne & Wear
NE30 1ED
0191 200 5897/6001
jen.harrison@northtyneside.gov.uk

**Northumberland YOT**
Carol Long, YOT Manager
Chief Executives Dept.,
County Hall
Morpeth
Northumberland
NE23 6SJ
01670 533931
CLong@northumberland.gov.uk

**South Tees YOT**
Colin Wilson, YOT Manager
14 Farndale Road
Middlesbrough
TS4 2PL
01642 501500
colin_wilson@middlesbrough.gov.uk

**South Tyneside YOT**
Phil Bennett, YOT Manager
30 Commercial Road
South Shields
Tyne & Wear
NE33 1RW
0191 427 2850
phil.bennett@s-tyneside-mbc.gov.uk

**Stockton-on-Tees YOT**
Tony Hodgson, YOT Manager
52-54 Hartington Road
Stockton-on-Tees
TS18 1HE
01642 393390
tony.hodgson@stockton.gov.uk

**Sunderland YOT**
Helen Watson, YOT Manager
11 John Street
Sunderland
SR1 1HT
0191 553 7370
helenj.watson@ssd.sunderland.gov.uk

## London & South-east

**Barking and Dagenham YOT**
Robin Tuddenham, YOT Manager
5a Parsloes Avenue
Dagenham
Essex
RM9 5PA
020 8270 6462
rtuddenham@barking-dagenham.gov.uk

**Barnet YOT**
Kate Malleson, YOT Manager
Churchfield House, 45-51
Woodhouse Road
North Finchley
London
N12 9ET
020 8446 9996
kate.malleson@barnet.gov.uk

**Bexley YOT**
Hazel Simmonds, YOT Manager
2 Nuxley Road
Belvedere
Kent
DA17 5JF
020 8284 5555
Hazel.simmonds@bexleyyot.org

**Brent YOT**
Peter Sutlieff, YOT Manager
1 Craven Park
Harlesden
London
NW10
020 8965 6020
peter.sutlieff@brent.gov.uk

**Bromley YOT**
Jeremy Shatford, YOT Manager
B28 St Blaise, Bromley Civic
Centre
Stockwell Close
Bromley
BR1 3UH
020 8313 4318
jeremy.shatford@bromley.gov.uk

**Camden YOT**
Peggy Schaffter, YOT Manager
LB Camden, Social Services
115 Wellesley Road
London
NW5 4PA
020 7974 6762
peggy.schaffter@camden.gov.uk

**Croydon YOT**
Ray McGuire, YOT Manager
Youth Justice Team, 14
Whitehorse Road
Croydon
Surrey
CR0 2JA
020 8404 5800
ray_maquire@croydon.gov.uk

**Ealing YOT**
Ed Shaylor, YOT Manager
2b Cheltenham Place
Acton
London
W3 8JS
020 8993 9555

**Enfield YOT**
Keith Napthine, YOT Manager
St George's Chambers,
23 South Mall
Edmonton
London
N9 0TS
020 8345 5557
Keith.Napthine@enfield.gov.uk

**Greenwich YOT**
Ray Seabrook, YOT Manager
The Well Hall Project, Tudor
Parade
Well Hall Road
London
SE9 6SU
020 8859 4492
ray.seabrook@greenwich.gov.uk

**Hackney YOT**
Lisa Matthews, YOT Manager
55 Daubeney Road
London
E5 0EE
020 8533 7070

**Hammersmith & Fulham YOT**
Larry Wright, YOT Manager
56a Bloemfontein Road
London
W12 7DH
020 8753 6200
Larry.Wright@lbhf.gov.uk

**Haringey YOT**
Jean Croot, YOT Manager
2-6 Middle Lane
Hornsey
London
N8 8PL
020 8489 1574
jean.croot@haringey.gov.uk

**Harrow YOT**
Richard Segalov, YOT Manager
Social Services Department, PO
Box 7
Civic Centre
Harrow
HA1 2UL
020 8420 9680
richard.segalov@harrow.gov.uk

**Havering YOT**
David Stonehouse, YOT Manager
Portman House,
16-20 Victoria Road
Romford
Essex
RM1 2JH
01708 436220
david.stonehouse@havering.gov.uk

**Hillingdon YOT**
Lynn Hawes, YOT Manager
Darren House
65 High Street
Uxbridge
UB8 1JP
01895 812279
lhawes@hillingdon.gov.uk

**Hounslow YOT**
Christine Pangbourne,
YOT Manager
Redlees Centre
Twickenham Road
Isleworth
TW7 7EF
020 8847 8000
christine.pangbourne-lbh@hounslow.gov.uk

**Islington YOT**
Sally Gran, YOT Manager
27 Dingley Place
Islington
London
EC1V 8BR
020 7527 7050/60
sally.gran@islington.gov.uk

**Kensington & Chelsea YOT**
Brendan O'Keefe, YOT Manager
36 Oxford Gardens
London
W10 5UQ
020 7598 4700
brendan.o'keefe@rbkc.gov.uk

**Kingston-Upon-Thames YOT**
Phillip Harris, YOT Manager
Eagle Chambers, 18 Eden Street
Kingston-upon-Thames
Surrey
KT1 1BB
020 8547 6920
phil.harris@rbk.kingston.gov.uk

**Lambeth YOT**
Lambert Allman, YOT Manager
1-9 Acre Lane
Brixton
London
SW2 5SD
020 7926 2644
LAllman@lambeth.gov.uk

**Lewisham YOT**
Ann McDermott, YOT Manager
23 Mercia Grove
Lewisham
London
SE13 6BJ
020 8314 7474
ann.mcdermott@lewisham.gov.uk

**Merton YOT**
Geoff Lowry, YOT Manager
1st Floor, Athena House
86-88 London Road
Morden
SM4 5AZ
020 8274 4949
geoff.lowry@merton.gov.uk

**Newham YOT**
Peter Nicholson, YOT Manager
Stratford Police Station, 18 West
Ham Lane
Stratford
London
E15 4SG
020 8217 5042
peter.nicholson@newham.gov.uk

**Redbridge YOT**
Kathy Nixon, YOT Manager
Oakside, Fencepiece Road
Fullwell Cross
Barkingside
IG6 2JS
020 8708 9300
kathy.nixon@redbridge.gov.uk

**Richmond-Upon-Thames YOT**
Robert Henderson,
YOT Manager
65 Strathmore Road
Teddington
TW11 8UH
020 8943 3353
r.henderson@richmond.gov.uk

## Southwark YOT
Chris Domeney, YOT Manager
1 Bradenham Close
Walworth
London
SE17 2QA
020 7525 7875
chris.domeney@southwark.gov.uk

## Sutton YOT
Sandra McGinley, YOT Manager
Level 3, Central Library
St Nicholas Way
Surrey
SM1 1EH
020 8337 0095
sandra.mcginley@sutton.gov.uk

## Tower Hamlets & City of London YOT
Stuart Johnson, YOT Manager
St Mary's Church Hall, Kitcat Terrace
Bow
London
E3 2SA
020 7364 1144
stuartj@dial.pipex.com

## Waltham Forest YOT
Ronke Martins, YOT Manager
604 High Road
Leyton
London
E10 6RN
020 8496 2121
ronke.martins@soc.lbwf.gov.uk

## Wandsworth YOT
Sean Dunkling, YOT Manager
177 Blackshaw Road
London
SW17 0DJ
020 8672 7074
sdunkling@wandsworth.gov.uk

## Westminster YOT
Eamon Brennan, YOT Manager
6a Crompton Street
London
W2 1ND
020 7641 7799
ebrennan@westminster.gov.uk

## Wales

## Bridgend YOT
Mal Gay, YOT Manager
Suite 2, Phase 1
Tremains Business Park,
Tremains Road
Brigdend
CF31 1TZ
01656 657243
gaym@bridgend.gov.uk

## Caerphilly & Blaenau Gwent YOT
Gillian O'Donovan, YOT Manager
Libanus House
260 High Street
Blackwood
NP12 1FA
01495 235652
odonog@caerphilly.gov.uk

## Cardiff YOT
Ingrid Masmeyer, YOT Manager
The Rise
Penhill Road
Cardiff
CF11 9PR
029 2056 0839
Imasmeyer@cardiff.gov.uk

## Carmarthenshire YOT
Richard Summers, YOT Manager
1 Westend
Llanelli
Carmarthenshire
SA15 3DN
01554 740120
RSummers@Carmarthenshire.gov.uk

## Conwy & Denbighshire YOT
Nia Elis-Willliams, YOT Manager
68 Conwy Road, Colwyn Bay
Llandudno
Wales
LL29 7LD
01492 523500

## Flintshire YOT
Eric Phillips, YOT Manager
6th Floor, County Hall
Mold
Flintshire
CH7 5BD
01352 701125
eric.phillips@flintshire.gov.uk

## Gwynedd & Ynyn Mon YOT
Gareth Hughes-Jones,
YOT Manager
Menai Office, Beach Road
Felinheli
Gwynedd
LL56 4RQ
01248 679183
TheresaAdshead@gwynedd.gov.uk

## Merthyr Tydfil YOT
Alan Elmer, YOT Manager
Merthyr CBC Youth Justice,
47-48 Pontmorlais Centre
Merthyr Tydfil
Wales
CF47 8UN
01685 389304
alanelmer@merthyryot.freeserve.co.uk

## Mid Wales Powys & Ceredigion YOT
Bernard Steer, YOT Manager
The Park
Newtown
Powys
SY16 2PL
01686 627006
bernards@powys.gov.uk

## Neath Port Talbot YOT
Mike Goldman, YOT Manager
Cramic Way
Port Talbot
SA13 1RU
01639 885050
m.goldman@neath-porttalbot.gov.uk

## Newport YOT
Andrew Wallsgrove,
YOT Manager
Helyg Centre
Ringland Circle
Newport
NP19 9PJ
01633 292900
andrew.wallsgrove@newport.gov.uk

## Pembrokeshire YOT
Paul Brecknell, YOT Manager
Social Services Department,
Woodbine Terrace
Riverside (Old Block)
Pembroke
SA71 4PL
01646 683571
paul.brecknell@pembrokeshire.gov.uk

## Rhondda Cynon Taff YOT
Andrew Gwynn, YOT Manager
Cottage 5, Garth Olwg
Church Village
Pontypridd
CF38 1BT
01443 219400
andrew.v.gwynn@rhondda-cynon-taff.gov.uk

**Swansea YOT**
Eddy Isles, YOT Manager
Llwyncelyn Campus
Cocket Road, Cocket
Swansea
SA2 0FJ
01792 522815
eddie.isles@swansea.gov.uk

**Torfaen & Monmouthshire YOT**
Steve Williams, YOT Manager
Mamhilad House, Mamhilad Park
Estate
Pontypool
Torfaen
NP4 0YT
01495 768310
stevejwilliams@monmouthshire.
gov.uk

**Vale of Glamorgan YOT**
Jane Hoey, YOT Manager
91 Salisbury Road
Barry
Wales
CF62 6PD
01446 745820
jehoey@valeofglamorgan.gov.uk

**Wrexham YOT**
Darren Johnson, YOT Manager
Unit 2G, Redwither Tower
Redwither Business Park
Wrexham
LL13 9XT
01978 667303
darren.johnson@wrexham.gov.uk

# Young Offenders Institutions

P = privately operated

**HMP/ YOI Ashfield (P)**
Shortwood Road
Pucklechurch
Bristol
BS16 9QJ
0117 303 8000

**HMP/ YOI Askham Grange**
Askham Richard
York
YO23 3FT
01904 772000

**HMYOI Aylesbury**
Bierton Road
Aylesbury
Bucks
HP20 1EH
01296 444000

**HMYOI Brinsford**
New Road
Featherstone
Wolverhampton
WV10 7PY
01902 532450

**HMP/ YOI Brockhill**
Redditch
Worcs.
B97 6RD
01527 552650

**HMP/ YOI Bullwood Hall**
High Road
Hockley
Essex
SS5 4TE
01702 562800

**HMP/ YOI Castington**
Morpeth
Northumberland
NE65 9XG
01670 762100

**HMP/ YOI Chelmsford**
200 Springfield Road
Chelmsford
Essex
CM2 6LQ
01245 272000

**HMYOI Deerbolt**
Bowes Road
Barnard Castle
County Durham
DL12 9BG
01833 633200

**HMP/ YOI Doncaster (P)**
Off North Bridge, Marshgate
Doncaster
South Yorkshire
DN5 8UX
01302 760870

**HMP/ YOI Drake Hall**
Eccleshall
Staffordshire
ST21 6LQ
01785 858100

**HMP/ YOI East Sutton Park**
Sutton Valence
Maidstone
Kent
ME17 3DF
01622 845000

**HMP/ YOI Eastwood Park**
Falfield
Wotton-Under-Edge
Gloucestershire
GL12 8DB
01454 382100

**HMP/ YOI Exeter**
New North Road
Exeter
Devon
EX4 4EX
01392 415650

**HMP/ YOI Feltham**
Bedfont Road
Feltham
Middlesex
TW13 4ND
020 8844 5000

**HMP/ YOI Forest Bank (P)**
Agecroft Road
Pendlebury
Manchester
M27 8FB
0161 925 7000

**HMYOI/ RC Glen Parva**
Tigers Road
Wigston
Leicester
LE8 4TN
0116 264 3100

**HMP/ YOI Gloucester**
Barrack Square
Gloucester
GL1 2JN
01452 453000

**HMP/ YOI Guys Marsh**
Shaftesbury
Dorset
SP7 0AH
01747 856400

**HMYOI Hindley**
Gibson Street, Bickershaw
Wigan
Lancashire
WN2 5TH
01942 855000

**HMP/ YOI Holloway**
Parkhurst Road
London
N7 0NU
020 7979 4400

**HMYOI Huntercombe**
Huntercombe Place
Nuffield, Henley-on-Thames
Oxfordshire
RG9 5SB
01491 643100

**HMP/ YOI Lancaster Farms**
Far Moor Lane, Stone Row Head
off Quernmore Road
Lancaster
LA1 3QZ
01524 563450

**HMP/ YOI Lewes**
Brighton Road
Lewes
East Sussex
BN7 1EA
01273 405100

**HMYOI Low Newton**
Brasside
Durham
DH1 3YA
0191 376 4000

**HMP/ YOI Moorland Open
(formerly HMP/ YOI Hatfield)**
Thorne Road, Hatfield
Doncaster
South Yorkshire
DN7 6EL
01405 746500

**HMP/ YOI Moorland Closed**
Bawtry Road, Hatfield
Woodhouse
Doncaster
South Yorkshire
DN7 6BW
01302 523000

**HMP/ YOI New Hall**
Dial Wood, Flockton
Wakefield
West Yorkshire
WF4 4AX
01924 844200

**HMYOI Northallerton**
15A East Road
Northallerton
North Yorkshire
DL6 1NW
01609 785100

**HMP/ YOI Norwich**
Mousehold
Norwich
Norfolk
NR1 4LU
01603 708600

**HMYOI Onley**
Willoughby
Rugby
Warwickshire
CV23 8AP
01788 523400

**HMP/ YOI Parc (P)**
Heol Hopcyn John
Bridgend
Mid-Glamorgan
CF35 6AP
01656 300200

**HMYOI Portland**
Easton
Portland
Dorset
DT5 1DF
01305 825600

**HMP/ YOI Prescoed**
Coed-y-Paen
Pontypool
Gwent
NP14 0TD
01291 672231

**HMYOI/ RC Reading**
Forbury Road
Reading
Berks
RG1 3HY
0118 908 5000

**HMYOI Stoke Heath**
Stoke Heath
Market Drayton
Shropshire
TF9 2JL
01630 636000

**HMP/ YOI Styal**
Styal
Wilmslow
Cheshire
SK9 4HR
01625 553000

**HMYOI Swinfen Hall**
Swinfen
Lichfield
Staffordshire
WS14 9QS
01543 484000

**HMYOI Thorn Cross**
Arley Road, Appleton Thorn
Warrington
Cheshire
WA4 4RL
01925 605100

**HMYOI Warren Hill**
Woodbridge
Suffolk
IP12 3JW
01394 412400

**HMYOI Werrington**
Werrington
Stoke-on-Trent
Staffordshire
ST9 0DX
01782 463300

**HMYOI Wetherby**
York Road
Wetherby
West Yorkshire
LS22 5ED
01937 544200

# Secure units

## Aldine House Secure Children's Unit
75 Limb Lane
Dore
Sheffield
S17 3E
0114 262 1160

## Atkinson Secure Unit
Northbrook
Beacon Lane
Exeter
EX4 8NA
01392 251449

## Aycliffe Young People's Centre
Copelaw Aycliffe
Newton Aycliffe
County Durham
DL5 6JB
01325 300101

## Barton Moss Secure Care Centre
Barton Moss Road
Eccles
Manchester
M30 7RL
0161 707 2402

## Beechfield Observation and Assessment Unit
Effingham Road
Copthorne
West Sussex
RH10 3HZ
01342 712309

## Brunel Unit
125C Market Street
Clay Cross
Chesterfield
S45 9LX
01246 348734

## Clare Lodge / Salters
104 Welmore Road
Glinton
Peterborough
PE6 8LF
01733 253246

## Clayfields House Secure Unit
18-20 Moorbridge Lane
Stapleford
Nottingham
NG9 8GU
0115 917 0010

## Dales House
Normoss Road
Blackpool
Lancs
FY3 6BE
01253 884412

## Earlswood Secure Unit
Gravelly Hill North
Erdington
Birmingham
B23 6BQ
0121 382 5121

## Eastmoor Children's Secure Unit
Tile Lane
Adel
Leeds
LS16 8BT
0113 267 3459

## Dyson Hall
Higher Lane
Fazakerley
Liverpool
L9
0151 284 3000

## Glenthorne Youth Treatment Centre
Kingsbury Road
Erdington
Birmingham
B24 9SA
0121 623 1700

## Kyloe House
Netherton Park
Stannington
near Morpeth
NE61 6DE
01607 785900

## Nugent Care: St Catherine's Community Home
Blackbrook House,
Blackbrook Road
St Helens
Lancs
01744 606119

## Lansdowne Children's Centre
Hawks Farm Road
Hailsham
East Sussex
BN27 1NP
01323 843771

## Leverton Hall Secure Unit
Dark Lane
Great Warley
Brentwood
CM14 5LL
01277 233588

## Lincolnshire Secure Unit
Rookery Ave
Sleaford
Lincolnshire
NG32 7TY
01529 414300

## Neath Hillside Secure Unit
Off Burnside
Cimla, Neath
South Wales
SA11 1UL
01639 641648

## Redsands Children's Centre
Crewe Rd, Willaston
Nantwich
Cheshire
CW5 6NE
01270 664116

## Briars Hey Community Home
5A Briars Hey, Mill Lane
Rainhill, Prescot
Merseyside
L35 6NE
0151 43077

## Orchard Lodge
William Booth Road
Anerley Hill
London
SE20 8BG
020 8402 9696

## Stamford House
25 Cathnor Road
Shepherds Bush
London
W12 9PA
020 8746 0050

## Sutton Place Safe Centre
347 Salthouse Road
Hull
HU8 9HR
01482 374186

## Swanwick Lodge
Glen Rd, off Swanwick Lane
Southampton
Hampshire
SO3 7DT
01489 581913

## Thornbury House
40 The Moors
Kidlington
Oxfordshire
OX5 2AL
01865 373153

**St John's Tiffield**
St Johns Centre
Tiffield
Northamptonshire
NN12 8AA
01604 858113

**Vinney Green Secure Unit**
Vinney Green,
Emersons Green Lane
Emersons Green
South Gloucestershire
BS16 7AA
0117 970 2286

**Watling House**
Watling Street
Gailey
Staffs
ST19 5PR
01902 798220

# Support for prisoners' families

**Action for Prisoners' Families**
www.prisonersfamilies.org.uk
*the national federation of services*
*supporting families of prisoners*

**London Head Office**
Riverbank House
1 Putney Bridge Approach
London
SW6 3JD
020 7384 1987
info@actionpf.org.uk

**Regional Office**
c/o Families House,
125 Ber Street, Norwich
Norfolk
NR1 3EY
01603 610888
mark@actionpf.org.uk

**Regional Office**
Unit 01, 2nd Floor,
Cornerstone House
Priestly Road, Basingstoke
Hampshire
RG24 9QB
01256 489021
heather@actionpf.org.uk

# Rights and legal advice

**The Children's Legal Centre**
University of Essex, Wivenhoe
Park
Colchester
Essex
CO4 3SQ
01206 873820
(mon-fri 10am-12.30)
clc@essex.ac.uk
www.childrenslegalcentre.com
*a free and confidential legal advice*
*and information service, covering*
*all aspects of the law affecting*
*children and young people*

**The Children's Law Centre**
3rd Floor, Philip House
123-137 York Street
Belfast
BT15 1AB
028 9024 5704;
freephone: 0808 808 5678
info@childrenslawcentre.org
www.childrenslawcentre.org

**Family Rights Group**
The Print House, 18 Ashwin
Street, London E8 3DL
0800 731 1696 (advice line) -
Monday to Friday 1.30pm -
3.30pm
www.frg.org.uk
*Advice, advocacy and publications*
*for families whose children are*
*involved with social services.*

**National Youth Advocacy Service**
99-105 Argyle Street
Birkenhead
Wirral
CH41 6AD
0151 342 7852;
freephone: 0800 616101
help@nyas.net
www.nyas.net
*a 'not for profit' children's charity*
*which offers socio-legal advocacy*
*services to children, young people,*
*parents, carers and professionals;*
*has an Advocacy Service for children*
*in care; lines are open 3 . 30pm - 9 .*
*30pm every week day and 2pm to*
*8pm on Saturdays and Sundays*

# Victim Support

**Victim Support and Witness Service**
0845 303 0900
www.victimsupport.org.uk
*national charity which helps people*
*affected by crime by providing free*
*and confidential support; the*
*Witness Service offers help before,*
*during and after court appearances*

**Victim Support Berkshire**
23 Prospect Street, Caversham
Reading
Berkshire
RG4 8JB
0118 947 9436
administrator@victimsupportberks
.org.uk

**Victim Support Buckinghamshire**
The Old Police Station,
23B Walton Street
Aylesbury
Buckinghamshire
HP20 1TZ
01296 396355
general@victimsupportbucksarea
.org.uk

**Victim Support Cambridgeshire**
4 Market Hill
Huntingdon
Cambridgeshire
PE29 3NJ
01480 453000
victimsupport.cambridgeshire@
uk.uumail.com

**Victim Support Cheshire**
Room C5, Cheshire Police Force
Training Centre
Salisbury Avenue, Crewe
Cheshire
CW2 6NT
01244 612332
ann.crewe@cheshirevictimsupport
.org

**Victim Support Cornwall**
Agriculture House,
Strangways Terrace
Truro
Cornwall
TR1 2NY
01872 263464
am@vscornwall.co.uk

**Victim Support Cumbria**
Lime House, The Green
Wetheral, Carlisle
Cumbria
CA4 8EW
01228 562638
victimsupport.cumbria@virgin.net

**Victim Support Derbyshire**
1st Floor, Kings Chambers
Queen Street
Derby
DE1 3DS
01332 349129
hsvsderby@aol.com

**Victim Support Devon**
Uplands, 81 Heavitree Road
Exeter
Devon
EX1 2LX
01392 678675
ado.devon@virgin.net

**Victim Support Dorset**
Barnack Chambers, 9/9A West
Street
Blandford Forum
Dorset
DT11 7AW
01258 453100
victimsupport.dorset@virgin.net

**Victim Support Durham**
5 Court Lane
Durham
DH1 3AW
0191 383 1389
victimsupport@lizleckieareaoffice.
fsnet.co.uk

**Victim Support Sussex**
Marine House, 130 Albion Street
Southwick
West Sussex
BN42 4DP
01273 870444
agvs@blueyonder.co.uk

**Victim Support Essex**
County House, 100 New London
Road
Chelmsford
Essex
CM2 0RG
01245 455979
vsessex.areamanager@virgin.net

**Victim Support Gloucestershire**
Churchdown Suite, Spreadeagle
Court
106/114 Northgate Street
Gloucester
GL1 1SL
01452 527774
albf79@uk.uumail.com

**Victim Support Bailiwick of
Guernsey**
PO Box 436, St Peter Port
Guernsey
Channel Islands
GY1 3ZH
01481 713000
victimsupportgsy@aol.com

**Victim Support Hampshire**
77 Leigh Road
Eastleigh
Hampshire
SO50 9DQ
023 8061 1177
victimsupporthampshire@uk.uum
ail.com

**Victim Support Herefordshire**
PO Box 103
Leominster
Herefordshire
HR6 8YG
01432 346767
victimsupport.herefordshire@virgin
.net

**Victim Support Isle of Man**
6 Albert Street
Douglas
Isle of Man
IM1 2QA
01624 679950
iomvictimsupport@manx.net

**Victim Support Isle of Wight**
Quay House, The Riverside
Centre
The Quay, Newport
Isle of Wight
PO30 2QR
01983 530530
albd36@uk.uumail.com

**Victim Support Jersey**
PO Box 789, St Hellier
Jersey
Channel Islands
JE4 8ZD
01534 769700
victimsupport@jerseymail.co.uk

**Victim Support Kent**
County Office, Suite 5
Caxton House, Wellesley Road,
Ashford
Kent
TN24 8ET
01233 647253
area.office@vskent.org.uk

**Victim Support Lancashire**
1 Chapel Street
Lancashire
PR1 8BU
01772 828422
victimsupport.lancs@virgin.net

**Victim Support Leicestershire
& Rutland**
2nd Floor, Alliance House
6 Bishop Street
Leicester
LE1 6AF
0116 258 0678
albn06@uk.uumail.com

**Victim Support Lincolnshire**
c/o Boston Victim Support, The
Len Medlock Voluntary Centre
St Georges Road, Boston
Lincolnshire
PE21 8YB
01652 618786/ 01205 35975
v.s.lincs@virgin.net

**Victim Support Norfolk**
Meadowview House
191 Queens Road
Norwich
NR1 3PP
01603 629577
julie.guratsky.vsnorfolk@virgin.net

**Victim Support North Yorkshire**
Knaresborough House, High
Street
Knaresborough
North Yorkshire
HG5 0HW
0845 120 9839
admin@nyvss.org

**Victim Support
Northamptonshire**
Angel Street
Northampton
Northamptonshire
NN1 1ED
01604 603477
admin@northantsvictimsupport.
co.uk

**Victim Support Northumbria**
Suite 3, 3rd Floor
Adamson House, 65 Westgate
Road
Newcastle upon Tyne
NE1 1SG
0191 230 5308
info@vsnorthumbria.org.uk

**Victim Support Nottinghamshire**
2 King Edward Court
King Edward Street
Nottingham
NG1 1EL
0115 852 3506
victimsupportnot@onetel.net.uk

**Victim Support Oxfordshire**
45 The Slade
Headington
Oxford
OX3 7HL
01865 751511
j.a.fenstermacher@btinternet.com

**Victim Support Shropshire**
Suite D1, Canon Court
Abbey Lawns, Abbey Foregate
Shrewsbury
SY2 5DE
01743 362812
victimsupport.wm@tiscali.co.uk

**Victim Support Somerset**
9a The Butts
Illminster
Somerset
TA19 0AY
01460 55535
office@victimsupport-
somerset.org.uk

**Victim Support Staffordshire**
Winton House, Stoke Road
Shelton, Stoke-On-Trent
Staffordshire
ST4 2RW
01782 414930
areaoffice@victimsupportstafford
shire.org.uk

**Victim Support Suffolk**
17 Langford Close
Stowmarket
Suffolk
IP14 1TX
01449 771020
aj.barrow@ntlworld.com

**Victim Support East Surrey**
Reigate Police Station, 79
Reigate Road
Reigate
Surrey
RH12 0RY
01737 766323

**Victim Support Epsom and District**
The Pines', 2 The Parade
Epsom
Surrey
KT18 5DH
01372 743650

**Victim Support Esher and District**
The Claygate Centre, Elm Road
Claygate, Esher
Surrey
KT10 0EH
01372 470690

**Victim Support Guildford**
PO Box 26
Guildford
Surrey
GU1 4XN
01483 503173

**Victim Support Mole Valley**
c/o Surrey Police, Moores Road
Dorking
Surrey
RH4 2BQ
01306 875866

**Victim Support North West Surrey**
80a Rydens Way
Old Woking
Surrey
GU22 9DN
01483 770457

**Victim Support Runnymede and Elmbridge**
Addlestone Police Station,
Garfield Road
Addlestone
Surrey
KT15 2NW
01932 855110

**Victim Support Spelthorne**
The Community Link Centre,
Knowle Green
Staines
Middlesex
TW18 1XA
01784 446202

**Victim Support Waverley**
Farnham Police Station
Farnham
Surrey
01428 651159

**Victim Support Warwickshire**
124 The Parade
Leamington Spa
Warwickshire
CV32 4AG
01926 450514
albf61@uk.uumail.com

**Victim Support Sussex**
Marine House, 130 Albion Street
Southwick
West Sussex
BN42 4DP
01273 870444
agvs@blueyonder.co.uk

**Victim Support Wiltshire**
31a The Brittox
Devizes
Wiltshire
SN10 1AJ
01380 729476
office@victimsupportwiltshire.org.
uk

**North East Worcestershire Victim Support**
c/o The Ecumenical Centre, 6
Evesham Walk
Redditch
Worcs
B97 4EX
01527 66462

**North West Worcestershire Victim Support**
4 Broomfield Green
Kidderminster
Worcestershire
DY11 6AJ
01562 743900

**South Worcestershire Victim Support**
PO Box 99
Worcester
WR1 2YQ
01905 28252

# Emergency services

## Police

**Home Office**
0870 000 1585
www.homeoffice.gov.uk

**Police Service**
www.police.uk

**National Crime Squad**
020 7238 2500
www.nationalcrimesquad.police.uk

**National Criminal Intelligence Service**
020 7238 8000
www.ncis.gov.uk

**Forensic Science Service**
0121 607 6800
www.forensic.gov.uk

**Centrex (national police training)**
01256 602100
www.centrex.police.uk

**HM Inspectors of Constabulary**
01527 882000
www.homeoffice.gov.uk/hmic/hmic.htm

**Interpol**
020 7238 8600
www.interpol.int

**Metropolitan Police, London**
020 7230 1212
www.met.police.uk

**Missing Persons Helpline**
0500 700700
www.missingpersons.org

**National Identification Service**
020 7230 2780
www.met.police.uk/so/nis.htm

**Northern Ireland Police Service**
028 9065 0222
www.psni.police.uk

**Northern Ireland Policing Board**
028 9040 8500
www.policingboard.org.uk

**Police Forces in Scotland**
www.scottish.police.uk

**Police Complaints Authority**
020 7273 6450
www.pca.gov.uk

**Police IT Organisation (national computer)**
020 8358 5555
www.pito.org.uk

**Police Skills and Standards Organisation**
0114 261 1499
www.psso.org.uk

## Fire

**Office of the Deputy Prime Minister**
020 7944 4400
www.odpm.gov.uk

**Fire Policy Division**
020 7944 6923

**HM Fire Service Inspectorate**
020 7944 5569

**Northern Ireland Fire Authority**
028 9266 4221

**Fire Kills campaign**
www.firekills.gov.uk

## Ambulance

**Department of Health**
020 7210 4850
www.doh.gov.uk

**Ambulance Service Association**
020 7928 9620
www.the-asa.org

**Association of Professional Ambulance Personnel**
0870 167 0999
www.apap.org.uk

## Voluntary Services

**Basics**
0870 165 4999
www.basics.org.uk
*Medical help at disasters*

**British Red Cross**
020 7235 5454
www.redcross.org.uk

**Casualties Union**
0870 078 0590
www.casualtiesunion.org.uk
*Simulated injuries for emergency exercises*

**Royal Life Saving Society**
01789 773994, 024 7621 7398
www.lifesavers.org.uk

**Royal National Lifeboat Institution**
0800 543210
www.rnli.org.uk

**St Andrews Ambulance Association**
0141 332 4031
www.firstaid.org.uk

**St John Ambulance**
0870 010 4950, 020 7324 4210
www.sja.org.uk

**Victim Support**
020 7735 9166
www.victimsupport.com
*Supports fire and crime victims*

## Local services

**Avon**
FIRE SERVICE 0117 926 2061
POLICE FORCE 01275 816350
AMBULANCE 0117 927 7046

**Bedfordshire**
FIRE SERVICE 01234 351081
POLICE FORCE 01234 842390
AMBULANCE 01234 408967

**Berkshire**
FIRE SERVICE 0118 945 2888
POLICE FORCE 01865 846000
AMBULANCE 0118 936 5500

**Buckinghamshire**
FIRE SERVICE 01296 424666
POLICE FORCE 01865 846000
AMBULANCE 01908 262422

**Cambridgeshire**
FIRE SERVICE 01480 444575
POLICE FORCE 01480 422393
AMBULANCE 01603 422700

**Cheshire**
FIRE SERVICE 01606 868700
POLICE FORCE 01244 612030
AMBULANCE 0151 260 5220

**Cleveland**
FIRE SERVICE 01429 872311
POLICE FORCE 01642 326326
AMBULANCE 01642 850088

**Cornwall**
FIRE SERVICE 01872 273117
POLICE FORCE 0870 577 7444
AMBULANCE 01392 261500

**Cumbria**
FIRE SERVICE 01900 822503
POLICE FORCE 01768 891999
AMBULANCE 01228 596909

**Derbyshire**
FIRE SERVICE 01332 771221
POLICE FORCE 01773 570100
AMBULANCE 0115 929615

**Devon**
FIRE SERVICE 01392 872200
POLICE FORCE 0870 577 7444
AMBULANCE 01392 261500

**Dorset**
FIRE SERVICE 01305 251133
POLICE FORCE 01929 462727
AMBULANCE 01202 438970

**Durham**
FIRE SERVICE 0191 384 3381
POLICE FORCE 0191 386 4929
AMBULANCE 0191 273 1212

**East Sussex**
FIRE SERVICE 0845 130 8855
POLICE FORCE 0845 607 0999
AMBULANCE 01273 489444

**Essex**
FIRE SERVICE 01277 222531
POLICE FORCE 01245 491491
AMBULANCE 01245 443344

**Gloucestershire**
FIRE SERVICE 01242 512041
POLICE FORCE 0845 090 1234
AMBULANCE 01452 753030

**Greater Manchester**
FIRE SERVICE 0161 736 5866
POLICE FORCE 0161 872 5050
AMBULANCE 0161 796 7222

**Hampshire**
FIRE SERVICE 023 8064 4000
POLICE FORCE 0845 045 4545
AMBULANCE 01962 863511

**Hereford and Worcester**
FIRE SERVICE 01905 24454
POLICE FORCE 01905 723000
AMBULANCE 01886 834200

**Hertfordshire**
FIRE SERVICE 01992 507507
POLICE FORCE 01707 354200
AMBULANCE 01234 408967

**Humberside**
FIRE SERVICE 01482 565333
POLICE FORCE 01482 326111
AMBULANCE 01482 354277

**Isle of Wight**
FIRE SERVICE 01983 823194
POLICE FORCE 0845 045 4545
AMBULANCE 01983 524081

**Kent**
FIRE SERVICE 01622 692121
POLICE FORCE 01622 690690
AMBULANCE 01622 747010

**Lancashire**
FIRE SERVICE 01772 862545
POLICE FORCE 01772 614444
AMBULANCE 01772 862666

**Leicestershire**
FIRE SERVICE 0116 287 2241
POLICE FORCE 0116 222 2222
AMBULANCE 0115 929 615

**Lincolnshire**
FIRE SERVICE 01522 553960
POLICE FORCE 01522 532222
AMBULANCE 01522 545171

**London**
FIRE SERVICE 020 7587 2000
POLICE FORCE 020 7230 2171
AMBULANCE 020 7921 5100
**Metropolitan Police. City of
London police:** 020 7601 2222

**Merseyside**
FIRE SERVICE 0151 296 4000
POLICE FORCE 0151 709 6010
AMBULANCE 0151 260 5220

**Norfolk**
FIRE SERVICE 01603 810351
POLICE FORCE 01953 424242
AMBULANCE 01603 422700

**North Yorkshire**
FIRE SERVICE 01609 780150
POLICE FORCE 01609 789000
AMBULANCE 01904 666000

**Northamptonshire**
FIRE SERVICE 01604 797000
POLICE FORCE 01604 700700
AMBULANCE 01908 262422

**Northumberland**
01670 534700
POLICE FORCE 01661 872555
AMBULANCE 0191 273 1212

**Nottinghamshire**
FIRE SERVICE 0115 967 0880
POLICE FORCE 0115 967 0999
AMBULANCE 0115 929 6151

**Oxfordshire**
FIRE SERVICE 01865 842999
POLICE FORCE 01865 846000
AMBULANCE 01865 740100

**Shropshire**
FIRE SERVICE 01743 260200
POLICE FORCE 01905 723000
AMBULANCE 01384 215555

**Somerset**
FIRE SERVICE 01823 364501
POLICE FORCE 01275 818181
AMBULANCE 01392 261500

**South Yorkshire**
FIRE SERVICE 0114 272 7202
POLICE FORCE 0114 220 2020
AMBULANCE 01709 820520

**Staffordshire**
FIRE SERVICE 01785 813234
POLICE FORCE 01785 257717
01785 253521

**Suffolk**
FIRE SERVICE 01473 588888
POLICE FORCE 01473 613500
AMBULANCE 01603 422700

**Surrey**
FIRE SERVICE 01737 242444
POLICE FORCE 01483 571212
AMBULANCE 01737 353333

**Tyne and Wear**
FIRE SERVICE 0191 235 2902
POLICE FORCE 01661 872555
AMBULANCE 0191 273 1212

**Warwickshire**
FIRE SERVICE 01926 423231
POLICE FORCE 01926 415000
AMBULANCE 01926 881331

**West Midlands**
FIRE SERVICE 0121 380 6906
POLICE FORCE 0845 113 5000
AMBULANCE 01384 215555

**West Sussex**
FIRE SERVICE 01243 786211
POLICE FORCE 0845 607 0999
AMBULANCE 01273 489444

**West Yorkshire**
FIRE SERVICE 01274 682311
POLICE FORCE 01924 375222
AMBULANCE 01274 707070

**Wiltshire**
FIRE SERVICE 01380 723601
POLICE FORCE 01380 722341
AMBULANCE 01249 443939

## Wales

### Mid Wales
FIRE SERVICE 01267 211444
POLICE FORCE 01267 222020
AMBULANCE 01745 583900

### West Wales
FIRE SERVICE 01267 211444
POLICE FORCE 01633 838111
AMBULANCE 01745 583900

### North Wales
FIRE SERVICE 01745 343431
POLICE FORCE 01492 517171
AMBULANCE 01745 583900

### South Wales
FIRE SERVICE 01443 232000
POLICE FORCE 01656 655555
AMBULANCE 01745 583900

## Scotland

### Central Scotland
FIRE SERVICE 01324 716996
POLICE FORCE 01786 456000
AMBULANCE 0131 446 7000

### Dumfries and Galloway
FIRE SERVICE 01387 252222
POLICE FORCE 01387 252112
AMBULANCE 0131 446 7000

### Fife
FIRE SERVICE 01592 774451
POLICE FORCE 01592 418888
AMBULANCE 0131 446 7000

### Grampian
FIRE SERVICE 01224 696666
POLICE FORCE 01224 386000
AMBULANCE 0131 446 7000

### Highland and Islands
FIRE SERVICE 01463 227000
POLICE FORCE 01463 715555
AMBULANCE 0131 446 7000

### Lothian and Borders
FIRE SERVICE 0131 228 2401
POLICE FORCE 0131 311 3131
AMBULANCE 0131 446 7000

### Strathclyde
FIRE SERVICE 01698 300999
POLICE FORCE 0141 532 2000
AMBULANCE 0131 446 7000

### Tayside
FIRE SERVICE 01382 322222
POLICE FORCE 01382 223200
AMBULANCE 0131 446 7000

## Northern Ireland

### HQ, Lisburn
FIRE SERVICE 028 9266 4221
POLICE FORCE 028 9065 0222
AMBULANCE 028 9040 0999

# Health

## National public agencies

**Health and Safety Executive**
Caerphilly Business Park
Caerphilly
CF83 3GG
0870 154 5500
hseinformationservices@natbrit.com
www.hse.gov.uk

**Family Health Services Appeal Authority**
30 Victoria Avenue
Harrogate
HG1 5PR
01423 530280
mail@fhsaa.nhs.uk
www.fhsaa.org.uk

**General Medical Council**
178 Great Portland Street
London
W1W 5JE
020 7580 7642
gmc@gmc-uk.org
www.gmc-uk.org

**National Institute for Mental Health in England (NIMHE)**
Blenheim House, West One
Duncombe Street
Leeds
LS1 4PL
0113 254 3811
ask@nimhe.org.uk
www.nimhe.org.uk

## Children's hospitals

**Royal Aberdeen Children's Hospital**
Cornhill Road
Aberdeen
AB25 2ZG
01224 68181

**Royal Alexandra Children's Hospital**
Dyke Road
Brighton
BN1 3JN
01273 328145

**Royal Belfast Hospital for Sick Children**
180 Falls Road
Belfast
BT12 6BE
028 9024 0503 ext 4113

**Birmingham Children's Hospital**
Steelhouse Lane
Birmingham
B4 6NH
0121 333 9999 ext 8611

**Bristol Royal Hospital for Sick Children**
Paul O'Gorman Building
Upper Maudlin Street
Bristol
BS2 8BJ
0117 927 6998

**Royal Hospital for Sick Children**
9 Sciennes Road
Edinburgh
EH9 1LF
0131 536 0070

**Royal Hospital for Sick Children**
Yorkhill
Glasgow
G3 8SJ
0141 201 0707

**Alder Hey Hospital**
Alder Hey
Eaton Road
Liverpool
L12 2AP
0151 228 4811

**Great Ormond Street Hospital**
London
WC1N 3JH
020 7813 8151

| Royal Manchester Children's Hospital | Booth Hall Children's Hospital | Sheffield Children's Hospital |
|---|---|---|
| Pendlebury | Charlestown Road | Western Bank |
| Manchester | Blackley | Sheffield |
| M27 4HA | Manchester | SO10 2TH |
| 0161 727 2903 | M9 7AA | 0114 271 7594 |
|  | 0161 220 5555 |  |

# General health

**DOH and DfES series of health websites:**
*series of sites aimed at different ages cover the main areas of personal, social and health education (PSHE) and citizenship set out in the national curriculum, the framework for PSHE and citizenship and the national healthy school standard*

**Wired for Health**
wfh@hda-online.org.uk
www.wiredforhealth.gov.uk
*for health and education professionals interested in young people's health*

**Welltown**
www.welltown.gov.uk
*for 5-7 year olds (Key Stage 1)*

**Galaxy-H**
www.galaxy-h.gov.uk
*for 7-11 year olds (Key Stage 2)*

**Lifebytes**
www.lifebytes.gov.uk
*for 11-14 year olds (Key Stage 3)*

**Mind, Body & Soul**
www.mindbodysoul.gov.uk
*for 14-16 year olds (Key Stage 4)*

**Action for Sick Children**
c/o National Children's Bureau
8 Wakley Street
London
EC1V 7QE
020 7843 6444
www.actionforsickchildren.org
*children's healthcare charity, specially formed to ensure that sick children always receive the highest standard of care possible*

**Children First**
3rd Floor, Ormond House
Boswell Street
London
WC1N 3LZ
www.childrenfirst.nhs.uk
*a national project working with children's hospitals and departments across the NHS, providing a safe place where children and young adults can access reliable, verifiable information and share their experiences*

**Muslim Youth Helpline**
Dexion House
2-4 Empire Way
Wembley
Middlesex
HA9 0EF
0870 774 3518; helpline: 0808 808 2008
help@myh.org.uk
www.myh.org.uk
*a confidential helpline for young Muslims*

**Teenage Health Freak**
48 Church Street
Chesham
HP5 1HY
0870 900 0019
charlie@baigent.net
www.teenagehealthfreak.org
*provides web-based, accurate and reliable health information to teenagers in a contemporary, cringe-free, entertaining and informative way*

**TheSite.org**
YouthNet UK, 2-3 Upper Street
Islington
London
N1 0PH
020 7226 8008
info@thesite.org
www.thesite.org
*aims to offer the best guide to life for young adults, aged 16-25; topics include sex, relationships, careers, money, health, drugs, legal and housing*

**There4me.com**
www.there4me.com
*NSPCC website for 12-16 year olds offering advice on a range of things, and the opportunity for a 'real time' chat with an NSPCC advisor*

**Youth2Youth**
helpline: 020 8896 3675
help@youth2youth.co.uk
www.youth2youth.co.uk
*telephone, email and online chat helpline run by young people for young people up to 19 years old; all helpline staff are aged between 16 and 21 years old; also you can read problems sent to Y2Y by others and the advice given in each case*

# Bereavement

## Childhood Bereavement Network
8 Wakley Street
London
EC1V 7QE
020 7843 6309
cbn@ncb.org.uk
www.ncb.org.uk/cbn/
*works to improve the range and quality of bereavement support for children throughout the UK and increase access to information, guidance and support*

## The Child Bereavement Trust
Aston House, West Wycombe
High Wycombe
Bucks
HP14 3AG
01494 446648; information & support: 0845 357 1000
enquiries@childbereavement.
org.uk
www.childbereavement.org.uk
*provides specialised training and support for professionals to improve their response to the needs of bereaved families; produces resources and information for children and families*

## Cruse Bereavement Care
Cruse House, 126 Sheen Road
Richmond
Surrey
TW9 1UR
020 8939 9530; Day by Day
helpline: 0870 167 1677
helpline@crusebereavementcare.
org.uk or
info@crusebereavementcare.org.uk
www.crusebereavementcare.org.uk
*leading charity in the UK specialising in bereavement*

## The Foundation for the Study of Infant Deaths
Artillery House
11-19 Artillery Row
London
SW1P 1RT
0870 787 0885; helpline: 0870
787 0554
fsid@sids.org.uk
www.sids.org.uk

## RD4U
Youth Involvement Project, The
Friend's Meeting House
6 Mount Street
Manchester
M2 5NS
0161 819 5810; helpline: 0808
808 1677
info@rd4u.org.uk
www.rd4u.org.uk
*a website developed by Cruse Bereavement Care's youth involvement project which aims to support young people, after the death of someone close to them*

## Winston's Wish
The Clara Burgess Centre,
Gloucestershire Royal Hospital
Great Western Road
Gloucester
GL1 3NN
01452 394377; Family Line:
0845 203 0405
info@winstonswish.org.uk
*a charity which supports bereaved children and young people*

# Mental Health

## @ease
30 Tabernacle Street
London
EC2A 4DD
020 7330 9100; National Advice
Service: 020 8974 6814
(Mon-Fri 10am-3pm)
advice@rethink.org or
at-ease@rethink.org
www.rethink.org/at-ease
*mental health resource for young people under stress or worried about their thoughts and feelings*

## British Association for Counselling and Psychotherapy
BACP House,
35-37 Albert Street
Rugby
Warwickshire
CV21 2SG
0870 443 5252
bacp@bacp.co.uk
www.bacp.co.uk

## emental-health.com
info@psychmed.co.uk
www.emental-health.com
*mental health website with information, news and discussions relevant to schizophrenia and related psychoses, Alzheimer's disease and other dementias, depression and bipolar disorder*

## Get Connected
North Acton Business Park
Wales Farm Road
London
W3 6RS
020 8896 4774; Helpline: 0808
808 4994 (1pm-11pm every day)
help@getconnected.org.uk or
admin@getconnected.org.uk
www.getconnected.org.uk
*a free, UK wide, email and telephone helpline that finds young people the best help whatever the problem*

## The Mental Health Foundation
7th Floor
83 Victoria Street
London
SW1H 0HW
020 7802 0300
mhf@mhf.org.uk
www.mentalhealth.org.uk
*UK charity working in mental health and learning disabilities*

## The Mental Health Foundation
5th Floor
Merchants House,
30 George Square
Glasgow
G2 1EG
0141 572 0125
scotland@mhf.org.uk

## Mind
15-19 Broadway
London
E15 4BQ
020 8519 2122; MindinfoLine:
0845 766 0163 (confidential help)
contact@mind.org.uk
www.mind.org.uk
*the leading mental health charity in England and Wales*

## Mind Cymru
3rd Floor, Quebec House
Castlebridge,
5-19 Cowbridge Road East
Cardiff
CF11 9AB
029 2039 5123

## Rural Minds
c/o National Agricultural Centre
Stoneleigh Park
Warwickshire
CV8 7LZ
024 7641 4366
ruralminds@ruralnet.org.uk

## YoungMinds
102-108 Clerkenwell Road
London
EC1M 5SA
020 7336 8445
enquires@youngminds.org.uk
www.youngminds.org.uk
*the national charity committed to improving the mental health of all children and young people*

## Mind Out for Mental Health
Freepost LON15335
London
SE1 1BR
www.mindout.net
*an active campaign coordinated by the Department of Health to stop the*

*stigma and discrimination surrounding mental health; has produced a resource pack for youth groups on attitudes to mental health*

## National Institute for Mental Health in England (NIMHE)
Blenheim House, West One
Duncombe Street
Leeds
LS1 4PL
0113 254 3811
ask@nimhe.org.uk
www.nimhe.org.uk

## National Phobics Society
Zion Community Resource
Centre, 339 Stretford Road
Hulme
Manchester
M15 4ZY
0870 770 0456
nationalphobic@btconnect.com
www.phobics-society.org.uk
*advice and information regarding anxiety, phobias, compulsive disorders and panic attacks*

## Read The Signs
www.readthesigns.org
*a website from Mind Out for Mental Health which targets young people aged 14-21*

## The Royal College of Psychiatrists
17 Belgrave Square
London
SW1X 8PG
020 7235 2351
rcpsych@rcpsych.ac.uk
www.rcpsych.ac.uk
*online mental health resource offering leaflets and factsheets, and details of useful books and audiotapes*

## Samaritans Central Office
The Upper Mill, Kingston Road
Ewell
Surrey
KT17 2AF
020 8394 8300
admin@samaritans.org
www.samaritans.org

## Chris
PO Box 90 90
Stirling
FK8 2SA
0845 790 9090
jo@samaritans.org
*contact details if you are in crisis and need to talk about how you are feeling*

## SANE
1st Floor, Cityside House
40 Adler Street
London
E1 1EE
020 7375 1002; Saneline: 0845
767 8000 (12noon to 2am)
www.sane.org.uk
*aims to raise awareness and respect, improve education and training, and provide information and emotional support to those experiencing mental health problems, their families and carers*

## SANE
Units 1 & 2, The Greenway Centre
Doncaster Road, Southmead
Bristol
BS10 5PY
0117 950 2140

## SANE
1 Queen Victoria Street
Macclesfield
SK11 6LP
01625 429050

---

# depression

## Aware
72 Lower Leeson Street
Dublin 2, Republi of Ireland
00 353 1 661 7211
info@aware.ie
www.aware.ie/
*provides information and support to people in Ireland and Northern Ireland*

## The Campaign Against Living Miserably (CALM)
Helpline: 0800 585858 (5pm-3am)
www.thecalmzone.net
*raises awareness of depression amongst young men (15-35) across Manchester, Merseyside, Cumbria and Bedfordshire*

## Depression Alliance
35 Westminster Bridge Road
London
SE1 7JB
020 7633 0557
www.depressionalliance.org
*a voluntary organisation which runs self-help groups, offers information and advice regarding depression, and presents workshops, seminars and conferences*

Depression Alliance Scotland
3 Grosvenor Gardens
Edinburgh
EH12 5JU
0131 467 3050

Depression Alliance Cymru
(Wales)
11 Plas Melin, Westbourne Road
Whitchurch
Cardiff
CF4 2BT
029 2069 2891

**The Manic Depression
Fellowship**
Castle Works
21 St George's Road
London
SE1 6ES
020 7793 2600
mdf@mdf.org.uk
www.mdf.org.uk
*a national user-led organisation
and registered charity for people
whose lives are affected by manic
depression*

## self harming

**The National Self-Harm
Network (NSHN)**
PO Box 7264
Nottingham
NG1 6WJ
info@nshn.co.uk
www.nshn.co.uk
*a survivor-led organisation
which campaigns for the rights
and understanding of people
who self-harm*

**Self Harm Alliance**
PO Box 61
Cheltenham
Gloucestershire
GL51 8YB
01242 578820
selfharmalliance@aol.com
www.selfharmalliance.org
*a voluntary organisation which
runs a telephone helpline, produces
monthly newsletters, provides
postal and e-mail support and
offers an advocacy service*

**Young People and Self Harm**
selfharm@ncb.org.uk
www.selfharm.org.uk
*information on a wide range of
activities and initiatives that relate
to young people and self harm*

# Family planning and sexual health

## National public bodies

**British Pregnancy Advisory Service**
Actionline: 0845 730 4030
www.bpas.org

**fpa
(formerly The Family Planning Association)**
2-12 Pentonville Road
London
N1 9FP
020 7837 5432; helpline: 0845 310 1334 (9am -
7pm Monday to Friday)
www.fpa.org.uk

**fpa Cymru (Cardiff)**
Suite D1, Canton House
435-451 Cowbridge Road East
Cardiff
CF5 1JH
029 2064 4034

**fpa Cymru (Bangor)**
Greenhouse, Trevelyan Terrace
Bangor
Gwynedd
LL57 1AX
01248 353534

**fpa Northern Ireland (Belfast)**
113 University Street
Belfast
BT7 1HP
028 9032 5488
margaretr@fpa.org.uk

**fpa Northern Ireland (Derry)**
2nd Floor, Northern Counties Building
Custom House Street
Derry
BT48 6AE
028 7126 0016

**fpa Scotland**
Unit 10, Firhill Business Centre
76 Firhill Road
Glasgow
G20 7BA
0141 576 5015; helpline: 0141 576 5088
fpascotland@dial.pipex.com

**Teenage Pregnancy Unit**
c/o 5th Floor, Skipton House
80 London Road
London
SE1 6LH
MB-Teenage-Pregnancy-Unit@doh.gsi.gov.uk
www.info.doh.gov.uk/tpu/tpu.nsf

## Internet sites

### Like It Is
likeitis@mariestopes.org.uk
www.likeitis.org.uk
*aims to provide non-judgemental sexual health information to 11-15 year olds, ranging from handling peer pressure to understanding sexually transmitted diseases*

### R U Thinking
Sexwise helpline: 0800 282930
www.ruthinking.co.uk
*website provides young people under the age of 18 advice and information on anything to do with sex, relationships or contraception*

## Brook centres

### Brook
421 Highgate Studios
53-79 Highgate Road
London
NW5 1TL
020 7284 6040; find nearest clinic: 020 7713 9000; free, confidential helpline: 0800 018 5023
admin@brookcentres.org.uk
www.brook.org.uk
*national voluntary sector provider of free and confidential sexual health advice and services specifically for young people under 25; services may include: contraception, emergency contraception, pregnancy testing, screening for infections, smear tests, Hepatitis B injections, termination referrals, counselling.*

### Brook Belfast
29a North Street
Belfast
BT1 1NA
028 9032 8866

### Brook Birmingham
59-65 John Bright Street
Birmingham
B1 1BL
0121 643 5341

### Brook Blackburn
54/56 Darwen Street
Blackburn
BB2 2BL
01254 268700

### Brook Bristol
1 Unity Street
Bristol
BS1 5HH
0117 929 0090

### Brook Burnley
64 Bank Parade
Burnley
Lancashire
BB11 1TS
01282 416596

### Brook Cornwall
60 Station Road
Pool, Redruth
Cornwall
TR15 3QG
01209 710088

### Brook Cornwall (St Ives)
The Island Centre
Island Road
St Ives
01209 710088

### Brook Cornwall (Newquay)
The Bungalow
St Thomas's Road
Newquay
TR7 1RR
01209 710088

### Brook Cornwall (Torpoint)
The Old School House
Macey Street
Torpoint
PL11 2AJ
01209 710088

### Brook Eccles
55 Regent Street
Eccles
Manchester
M30 0BP
0161 707 9550

### Brook Inverness
77 Church Street
Inverness
IV1 1ES
01463 242434

### Brook Inverness (Grant St)
MP33, 33 Grant Street
Inverness
01463 717639

### Brook Jersey
7 Nelson Street
St Helier
Jersey
JE2 4TL
01534 507981

### Brook Liverpool
81 London Road
Liverpool
L3 8JA
0151 207 4000

### Brook London (Barking)
Central Clinic, Vicarage Drive
Barking
Essex
IG11 7NF
020 8276 7021
www.brooklondon.org

### Brook London (Brixton)
374 Brixton Road
London
SW9
020 7787 5000

### Brook London (Deptford)
Waldron Health Centre, Stanley Street
Deptford
London
SE8 4BG
020 8691 0417

### Brook London (East Street)
153a East Street
London
SE17 2SD
020 7703 7880

### Brook London (Euston)
92-94 Chalton Street
London
NW1 1HJ
020 7387 8700

### Brook London (Harrow)
Harrow Young People's Centre
24a Canning Road
Wealdstone
HA3 7SL
020 8427 5505

### Brook London (Hayes)
Minet Clinic
Avondale Drive
Hayes
UB3 3PF
020 8813 7050

### Brook London (Ilford)
John Telford Clinic, 45 Cleveland Road
Ilford
Essex
IG1 1EE
020 8478 6982

**Brook London (Islington)**
The Northern Centre, 580
Holloway Road
London
N7 6LA
020 7272 5599

**Brook London (Lewisham)**
Central Lewisham Health Centre
410 Lewisham High Street
London
SE13 6LL
020 8690 3922

**Brook Manchester**
Faulkner House
Faulkner Street
Manchester
M1 4DY
0161 237 3001
info@manchesterbrook.freeserve.
co.uk

**Brook Manchester (Sale)**
Talkshop
81 School Road
Sale
M33 7YR
0161 237 3001

**Brook Milton Keynes**
Acorn House
355 Midsummer Boulevard
Milton Keynes
MK9 3HP
01908 669215
www.mkweb.co.uk/brook

**Brook Milton Keynes
(Fullers Slade)**
The Family Resource Centre,
91-92 Weaver's Hill
Fullers Slade
Milton Keynes
MK9 2BN
01908 669215

**Brook Milton Keynes
(Market Hall)**
CAB, Wheeldon House
Market Hall
Buckingham
01908 669215

**Brook Milton Keynes
(Wolverton)**
MK Dass
73 Church Street
Wolverton
01908 669215

**Brook Milton Keynes
(Bletchley)**
Spotlight on Bletchley
Serpentine Court, Lakes Estate
Bletchley
01908 669215

**Brook Oldham**
99 Union Street
Oldham
OL1 1QH
0161 627 0200

**Brook Sandwell and Dudley**
31 Priory Street
Dudley
West Midlands
DY1 1HA
01384 239001

**Brook Sandwell and Dudley
(Coseley)**
Health and Family Centre
Beyer Street
Coseley
WV14
01384 239001

**Brook Sandwell and Dudley
(Brierly Hill)**
Sure Start
175 High Street
Brierly Hill
DY5 3BU
01384 239001

**Brook Sandwell and Dudley
(Oldbury)**
Unity Centre
6 Unity Place
Oldbury
B69 4DB
01384 239001

**Brook Sandwell and Dudley
(Blackheath)**
Rowley Village Surgery
91 Rowley Village
Blackheath
01384 239001

**Brook Sandwell and Dudley
(Tipton)**
Toll End Youth Centre, Toll End
Road
Tipton
West Midlands
DY4 0HP
0121 557 1937

**Brook Wigan and Leigh**
Coops Business Centre
11 Dorning Street
Wigan
WN1 1HR
01942 760000
www.brookwiganandleigh.org.uk

**Brook Wigan and Leigh**
Leigh Connexions Centre
114 Bradshawgate, Leigh
Lancashire
WN7 4NP
01942 760000

**Wirral Brook**
Beechwood Estate Satellite
Service
Beechwood and Ballantyne
Youth Centre, Birkenhead
Merseyside
0151 670 0177
www.merseyworld.com/wirral-
brook

**Brook Wirral (Seacombe)**
Seacombe Family Centre
St Pauls Road
Seacombe
0151 630 2080

## Marie Stopes centres

**Marie Stopes International (MSI)**
Marie Stopes House
108 Whitfield Street
London
W1T 5BE
0845 300 8090
www.mariestopes.org.uk
*network of centres providing advice on abortion, emergency contraception, sterilisation and general health screening*

**MSI Reading Centre**
121 London Street
Reading
Berkshire
RG1 4QA

**MSI Leeds Centre**
10 Queen Square
Leeds
Yorkshire
LS2 8AJ

**MSI Manchester Centre**
St John Street Chambers
2 St John Street
Manchester
M3 4DB

**MSI Essex Centre**
88 Russell Road
Buckhurst Hill
Essex
IG9 5QB

**MSI Maidstone Centre**
10 Brewer Street
Maidstone
Kent
ME14 1RV

**MSI Bristol Centre**
3 Great George Street
Bristol
BS1 5RR

**MSI West London Centre**
87 Mattock Lane
Ealing
London
W5 5BJ

**MSI West Ealing Centre**
189 Uxbridge Road
West Ealing
London
W13 8AJ

**MSI South London Centre**
1a Raleigh Gardens
Brixton Hill
London
SW2 6AB

## Eating disorders

**Anorexia and Bulimia Care**
PO Box 173
Letchworth
Herts
SG6 1XQ
www.anorexiabulimiacare.co.uk
*national Christian organisation for sufferers, their families and for carers*

**The British Dietetic Association**
5th Floor, Charles House
148/9 Great Charles St, Queensway
Birmingham
B3 3HT
0121 200 8080
info@bda.uk.com
www.bda.uk.com

**Eating Disorders Association (EDA)**
103 Prince of Wales Road
Norwich
NR1 1DW
0870 770 3256; Youthline: 0845 634 7650
info@edauk.com; Youthline:
talkback@edauk.com
www.edauk.com

**The National Centre for Eating Disorders**
54 New Road
Esher
Surrey
KT10 9NU
01372 469493
www.eating-disorders.org.uk

# Illness

**Cancer Research UK**
PO Box 123
Lincoln's Inn Fields
London
WC2A 3PX
020 7242 0200
www.cancerresearchuk.org

**Sargent Cancer Care for Children**
Griffin House
161 Hammersmith Road
London
W6 8SG
020 8752 2800/2821
operations@sargent.org
www.sargent.org

c/o The White House
118 Gatley Road
Cheshire
SK8 4AD
0161 610 7150
janelewis@sargent.org

Malcolm Sargent House,
22-24 Links Road
Prestwick
Scotland
KA9 1QG
01292 671233
lorrainefinlayson@sargent.org

Cutler's Farm Business Centre,
Edstone Near Wootton Wawen
Warwickshire
B95 6DJ
01926 840128
juliajones@sargent.org

Sargent Cancer Care for Children
Scotland
Mercantile Chambers
5th Floor, 53 Bothwell Street
Glasgow
G2 6TS
0141 572 5700
glasgow@sargent.org

Sargent Cancer Care for Children
Northern Ireland
1st Floor, Albany House
73-75 Great Victoria Street
Belfast
BT2 7AF
028 9072 5780
careni@sargent.org

**Children's Cancer Web**
www.cancerindex.org/ccw
*an index of some of the key cancer-related sites and pages*

**Help Adolescents With Cancer (HAWC)**
1st Floor, Post Office Building
388 Hollinwood Avenue,
New Moston
Manchester
M40 0JB
0161 688 6244
niki@hawc.fsnet.co.uk

**Teenage Cancer Trust**
38 Warren Street
London
W1T 6AE
020 7387 1000
tct@teencancer.bdx.co.uk
www.teencancer.org

**Children's Heart Federation**
0808 808 5000 (9.30am -
9.30pm Monday to Friday)
www.childrens-heart-fed.org.uk

**The Association for Children with Heart Disorders**
01706 213632
information@heartchild.info
www.heartchild.info

**HeartLine Association**
Community Link,
Surrey Heath House
Knoll Road, Camberley
Surrey
GU15 3HH
01276 707636
heartline@easynet.co.uk
www.heartline.org.uk

**National Kidney Federation (NKF)**
6 Stanley Street
Worksop
S81 7HX
01909 487795;
helpline: 0845 601 0209
nkf@kidney.org.uk
www.kidney.org.uk
*aims to promote the welfare of persons suffering from kidney disease or renal failure and those relatives and friends who care for them; operates a young person's group*

**The Children's Liver Disease Foundation (CLDF)**
36 Great Charles Street
Birmingham
B3 3JY
0121 212 3839
info@childliverdisease.org
www.childliverdisease.org

**Children with Leukaemia**
51 Great Ormond Street
London
WC1N 3JQ
020 7404 0808
info@leukaemia.org
www.leukaemia.org

**Leukaemia CARE**
2 Shrubbery Avenue
Worcester
WR1 1QH
0845 767 3203
enquiries@leukaemiacare.org.uk
www.leukaemiacare.org

**Meningitis Trust**
Fern House, Bath Road
Stroud
Gloucestershire
GL5 3TJ
01453 768000; 24 hour nurse-led helpline: 0845 600 0800
info@meningitis-trust.org
www.meningitis-trust.org

**The Children's Transplant Foundation**
17 Veryan Close
Orpington
Kent
BR5 3NQ
01689 834906
mail@ctfl.co.uk
www.ctfl.co.uk

# Chronic conditions and disabilities

## Arthritis

**Arthritis Care**
18 Stephenson Way
London
NW1 2HD
020 7380 6500;
The Source: 0808 808 2000
(weekdays: 10am to 2pm)
thesource@arthritiscare.org.uk
www.arthritiscare.org.uk
*services for young people include a
helpline (The Source); a magazine
for 15-20 year olds (No Limits);
courses, worshops and weekends;
information and advice*

**The Arthritis Research
Campaign**
Copeman House, St Mary's
Court
St Mary's Gate, Chesterfield
Derbyshire
S41 7TD
0870 850 5000
info@arc.org.uk
www.arc.org.uk

**The Children's Chronic
Arthritis Association**
Ground Floor, Amber Gate
City Wall Road
Worcester
WR1 2AH
01905 745595
info@ccaa.org.uk
www.ccaa.org.uk

**Choices for Families of
Children with Arthritis**
PO Box 58
Hove
East Sussex
BN3 5WN
info@kidswitharthritis.org
www.kidswitharthritis.org

**Give Rheumatoid Arthritis
Children Encouragement
(GRACE)**
50 Wood Street
St Annes
FY8 1QG
01253 720303
www.fyldecoast.co.uk/grace

## ADHD and hyperactivity

**The A.D.D. & Family Support
Centre**
The Old School, Arrow
Nr Alcester
Warwickshire
B49 5PJ
01789 766453
info@addcentre.co.uk
www.addcentre.co.uk

**The National Attention Deficit
Disorder Information and
Support Service (ADDISS)**
10 Station Road
Mill Hill
London
NW7 2JU
020 8906 9068
info@addiss.co.uk
www.addiss.co.uk

**The Hyperactive Children's
Support Group**
71 Whyke Lane
Chichester
West Sussex
PO19 7PD
01243 551313
contact@hacsg.org.uk
www.hacsg.org.uk

## Allergies

**Allergy UK**
Allergy Helpline: 020 8303 8583
(9am - 9pm weekdays); Chemical
Sensitivity Helpline: 020 8303
8525 (9am - 5pm weekdays)
info@allergyuk.org
www.allergyfoundation.com

**The Anaphylaxis Campaign**
01252 542029
www.anaphylaxis.org.uk

**Asthma and Allergy
Information and Research
(AAIR)**
Department of Respiratory
Medicine, Glenfield Hospital
Groby Road
Leicester
LE3 9QP
0116 270 7557
aair@globalnet.co.uk
www.users.globalnet.co.uk/~aair

## Asthma

**National Asthma Campaign**
Providence House, Providence
Place
London
N1 0NT
020 7226 2260;
helpline: 0845 701 0203
www.asthma.org.uk

**National Asthma Campaign
Scotland**
2a North Charlotte Street
Edinburgh
EH2 4HR
0131 226 2544

**Leicester Children's Asthma
Centre**
Institute for Lung Health,
University of Leicester
PO Box 65
Leicester
LE2 7LX
0116 252 3236
jg33@le.ac.uk
www.le.ac.uk/childhealth/asthma
*a centre for the study and treatment
of asthma in children*

## Autism

**AUTISM Independent UK**
199-205 Blandford Ave
Kettering
Northants
NN16 9AT
01536 523274
autism@rmplc.co.uk
www.autismuk.com

**The Disabilities Trust**
First Floor, 32 Market Place
Burgess Hill
West Sussex
RH15 9NP
01444 239123
info@disabilities-trust.org.uk
www.disabilities-trust.org.uk

**The National Autistic Society**
393 City Road
London
EC1V 1NG
020 7833 2299
nas@nas.org.uk
www.nas.org.uk

**Autism Helpline**
0870 600 8585
autismhelpline@nas.org.uk

**Information Centre**
020 7903 3599
info@nas.org.uk

**NAS Scotland**
Central Chambers, 1st Floor
109 Hope Street
Glasgow
G2 6LL
0141 221 8090
scotland@nas.org.uk

**NAS Wales**
William Knox House, Suite C1,
Britannic Way
Llandarcy
Neath
SA10 6EL
01792 815915
wales@nas.org.uk

**NAS Services for Children**
Church House
Church Road, Filton
Bristol
BS34 7BD
0117 974 8400
services@nas.org.uk

**The Scottish Society for Autism**
Head Office, Hilton House
Alloa Business Park, Whins Road
Alloa
FK10 3SA
01259 720044
www.autism-in-scotland.org.uk

# Blindness and visual impairment

**Action for Blind People**
14-16 Verney Road
London
SE16 3DZ
020 7635 4800
info@afbp.org
www.afbp.org

**The Royal National College for the Blind**
College Road
Hereford
HR1 1EB
01432 265725; minicom: 01432 276532
info@rncb.ac.uk
www.rncb.ac.uk

**Royal National Institute of the Blind (RNIB)**
105 Judd Street
London
WC1H 9NE
020 7388 1266; helpline: 0845 766 9999
helpline@rnib.org.uk
www.rnib.org.uk

**National Blind Childrens Society**
Bradbury House, Market Street
Highbridge
Somerset
TA9 3BW
01278 764764
enquiries@nbcs.org.uk
www.nbcs.org.uk

**Micro & Anophthalmic Childrens Society**
1 Skyrmans Fee, Frinton on Sea
Essex
CO13 0RN
0870 600 6227
enquiries@macs.org.uk
www.macs.org.uk
*information about microphthalmia, anophthalmia, coloboma and related conditions*

**The National Federation of Families with Visually Impaired Children (LOOK)**
c/o Queen Alexandra College, 49 Court Oak Road
Harborne
Birmingham
B17 9TG
0121 428 5038
info@look-uk.org
www.look-uk.org

# Brain injury

**British Institute for Brain Injured Children**
Knowle Hall
Bridgwater
Somerset
01278 684060
e.wheeler@bibic.org.uk
www.bibic.org.uk
*produces tailored programmes aimed at improving the quality of life for the child and family*

**The Disabilities Trust**
First Floor, 32 Market Place
Burgess Hill
West Sussex
RH15 9NP
01444 239123
info@disabilities-trust.org.uk
www.disabilities-trust.org.uk

# Cerebral palsy

**The Hornsey Trust for Children with Cerebral Palsy**
54 Muswell Hill
London
N10 3ST
020 8444 7242
info@hornseytrust.org.uk
www.hcec.org.uk
*specialist centre and school for children with cerebral palsy*

**SCOPE**
PO Box 833
Milton Keynes
MK12 5NY
helpline: 0808 800 3333
(9am-9pm weekdays, 2pm-6pm weekends and Bank Holidays)
cphelpline@scope.org.uk
www.scope.org.uk

# Deafblindness

**A-Z to Deafblindness**
www.deafblind.com
*award winning website giving information about deafblindness and related issues*

**Deafblind UK**
National Centre for Deafblindness, John and Lucille van Geest Place
Cygnet Road, Hampton
Peterborough
PE7 8FD
01733 358100 (voice/text)
www.deafblind.org.uk

**Deafblind Scotland**
21 Alexandra Avenue
Lenzie
Glasgow
G66 5BG
0141 777 6111 (voice/text)
info@deafblindscotland.org.uk
www.deafblindscotland.org.uk

### Deafblind Northern Ireland Branch

Course Lodge, 10 Coilhill Road
Killyleagh
Co Down
BT30 9ST
028 4482 1983 (voice/text)
hazelwilson@dbni.freeserve.co.uk

### Sense

11-13 Clifton Terrace
Finsbury Park
London
N4 3SR
020 7272 7774
enquiries@sense.org.uk
www.sense.org.uk

## Deafness

### British Deaf Association

1-3 Worship Street
London
EC2A 2AB
020 7588 3520;
text phone: 020 7588 3529
helpline@bda.org.uk
www.bda.org.uk

### The National Deaf Children's Society

15 Dufferin Street
London
EC1Y 8UR
020 7490 8656
ndcs@ndcs.org.uk
www.ndcs.org.uk
Northern Ireland: 028 90313170,
nioffice@ndcsni.co.uk; Scotland:
0141 2484457,
ndcs.scotland@ndcs.org.uk;
Wales: 029 20373474,
ndcswales@ndcs.org.uk

### Royal National Institute of the Deaf (RNID)

19-23 Featherstone Street
London
EC1Y 8SL
020 7296 8000;
textphone: 020 7296 8001
informationline@rnid.org.uk
www.rnid.org.uk

### RNID Manchester Office

Manchester Technology Centre,
Armstrong House
Oxford Road
Manchester
M1 7ED
0161 242 2316
information.north@rnid.org.uk

### RNID Birmingham Office

1st Floor, Monaco House
Bristol Street
Birmingham
B5 7AS
general: 0121 622 2726;
information: 0121 622 5662;
general textphone: 0121 622
1191; information textphone:
0121 622 4354
information.midlands@rnid.org.uk

### RNID Bristol Office

10 Stillhouse Lane
Bedminster
Bristol
BS3 4EB
0117 963 0146; textphone: 0117
963 0147
information.SouthWest@rnid.org.uk

### RNID Bath Office

13B Church Farm Business Park
Corston
Bath
BA2 9AP
01225 837590; freephone for
deaf callers: 0800 622401

### RNID Scotland - Glasgow Office

Floor 3, Crowngate Business
Centre
Brook Street
Glasgow
G40 3AP
0141 554 0053;
textphone: 0141 550 5750

### RNID Scotland - Aberdeen Office

2nd Floor, 15 Union Street
Aberdeen
AB11 5BU
01224 584781; textphone:
01224 584357

### RNID Northern Ireland

Wilton House, 5 College Square
North
Belfast
Co Antrim
BT1 6AR
028 9023 9619

### RNID Cymru

RNID Suite, 1st Floor, Shaw Trust
Disability Action Centre
The Courtyard, D'Arcy Business
Park, Llandarcy
Neath
SA10 6EJ
01792 324477;
minicom: 01792 324455

## Diabetes

### Diabetes UK

10 Parkway
London
NW1 7AA
020 7424 1000; careline
counsellors: 020 7424 1030
info@diabetes.org.uk
www.diabetes.org.uk

### Diabetes UK North West

First Floor, The Boultings
Winwick Street, Warrington
Cheshire
WA2 7TT
01925 653281
n.west@diabetes.org.uk

### Diabetes UK West Midlands

1 Eldon Court
Eldon Street
Walsall
WS1 2JP
01922 614500
w.midlands@diabetes.org.uk

### Diabetes UK South West

PO Box 326
Exeter
EX2 9XJ
south.west@diabetes.org.uk

### Diabetes UK Northern Ireland

Bridgewood House
Newforge Business Park,
Newforge Lane
Belfast
BT9 5NW
028 9066 6646
n.ireland@diabetes.org.uk

### Diabetes UK Scotland

Savoy House
140 Sauchiehall Street
Glasgow
G2 3DH
0141 332 2700
scotland@diabetes.org.uk

**Diabetes UK Cymru**
Quebec House
Castlebridge, Cowbridge Road
East
Cardiff
CF11 9AB
029 2066 8276
wales@diabetes.org.uk

## Down's syndrome

**Down's Syndrome Association**
155 Mitcham Road
Tooting
London
SW17 9PG
020 8682 4001
info@downs-syndrome.org.uk

**DSA Northern Ireland**
Graham House, Knockbracken
Healthcare Park
Saintfield Road
Belfast
BT8 8BH
028 9070 4606
downs-syndrome@cinni.org

**DSA Wales**
Suite 1, 206 Whitechurch Road
Heath, Cardiff
South Glamorgan
CF4 3NB
029 2052 2511
dsa.wales@lineone.net

**The Down Syndrome Educational Trust**
The Sarah Duffen Centre,
Belmont Street
Southsea
Hampshire
PO5 1NA
023 9285 5330
enquiries@downsed.org
www.downsed.org

**The Down Syndrome Information Network**
www.down-syndrome.info

## Eczema and other skin conditions

**British Association of Dermatologists**
19 Fitzroy Square
London
W1T 6EH
020 7383 0266
admin@bad.org.uk
www.bad.org.uk

**The National Eczema Society**
Hill House
Highgate Hill
London
N19 5NA
020 7281 3553;
helpline: 0870 241 3604
helpline@eczema.org
www.eczema.org

**The Psoriasis Association**
Milton House
7 Milton Street
Northampton
NN2 7JG
0845 676 0076
mail@psoriasis.demon.co.uk
www.psoriasis-association.org.uk

## Epilepsy

**Epilepsy Action**
New Anstey House
Gate Way Drive, Yeadon
Leeds
LS19 7XY
0113 210 8800;
helpline: 0808 800 5050
epilepsy@epilepsy.org.uk
www.epilepsy.org.uk
*the working name for British Epilepsy Association*

**The National Society for Epilepsy**
Chesham Lane
Chalfont St Peter
Bucks
SL9 0RJ
01494 601300
www.epilepsyne.org.uk

**The National Centre for Young People with Epilepsy (NCYPE)**
St Piers Lane, Lingfield
Surrey
RH7 6PW
01342 832243
www.ncype.org.uk

## Facial disfigurement

**The Birthmark Support Group**
PO Box 3932
Weymouth
DT4 9YG
01202 257703
info@birthmarksupportgroup.org.uk
www.btinternet.com/~birthmark
supportgroup

**Changing Faces**
1 & 2 Junction Mews
London
W2 1PN
020 7706 4232
info@changingfaces.co.uk
www.cfaces.demon.co.uk

**Cleft Lip and Palate Association (CLAPA)**
235-237 Finchley Road
London
NW3 6LS
020 7431 0033
info@clapa.fsnet.co.uk
www.clapa.com
*provides support for new parents, and for people with the condition and their families, from infancy through to adulthood*

**Let's Face It**
72 Victoria Avenue
Westgate on Sea
Kent
CT8 8BH
01843 833724
www.letsfaceit.force9.co.uk

## Other conditions

**Birth Defects Foundation**
BDF Centre, Hemlock Business
Park
Hemlock Way, Cannock
Staffordshire
WS11 7GF
01543 468888; Here to Help
Nurse Service: 0870 070 7020
enquiries@birthdefects.co.uk
www.birthdefects.co.uk

**Children Living with Inherited Metabolic Diseases (Climb)**
Climb Building
176 Nantwich Road
Crewe
CW2 6BG
0870 770 0326
www.climb.org.uk

**The Enuresis Resource & Information Centre (ERIC)**
34 Old School House
Britannia Road, Kingswood
Bristol
BS15 8DB
0117 960 3060
info@eric.org.uk
www.enuresis.org.uk

**The Fragile X Society**
Rood End House, 6 Stortford
Road
Great Dunmow
Essex
CM6 1H7
01371 875100
info@fragilex.org.uk
www.fragilex.org.uk

**Association of Wheelchair Children**
6 Woodman Parade
North Woolwich
London
E16 2LL
0870 121 0050/0053
headoffice@wheelchairchildren.
org.uk
www.wheelchairchildren.org.uk
*provides specialist training and expert advice that will enable children to become more independently mobile*

---

# Addiction

**Substance Misuse Team**
Department of Health, Room
580D
Skipton House, 80 London Road
London
SE1 6LH
020 7972 2000
drugs@doh.gsi.gov.uk
www.doh.gov.uk/drugs

**National Drug Prevention Development Team**
New Mill, Victoria Road
Saltaire
Shipley
BD18 3LD

**ACAPS Youth Provision**
34 Electric Lane
Brixton
London
SW9 8JT
020 7737 3579
www.youth@acaps.co.uk
*counselling, advice and information on drugs and alcohol in the boroughs of Lambeth, Southwark and Lewisham*

**Addaction**
67-69 Cowcross Street
London
EC1M 6PU
020 7251 5860
info@addaction.org.uk
www.addaction.org.uk
*provides drug and alcohol treatment programmes within communities and prisons*

**Admel House**
82 Clarence Road
Windsor
Berkshire
SL4 5AT
01753 842156
*a residential service for vulnerable young people aged 16 to 25 in the Borough of Windsor and Maidenhead*

**Al-Anon**
Family Groups UK & Eire
61 Great Dover Street
London
SE1 4YF
020 7403 0888
www.al-anonuk.org.uk
*provides understanding, strength and hope to anyone whose life is, or has been, affected by someone else's drinking*

**Alcohol and Drug Abuse (.com)**
www.alcoholanddrugabuse.com
*straightforward information and useful resources related to alcohol & drug abuse, alcoholism, drug addiction, codependency, & (especially) recovery*

**Alcohol Concern**
Waterbridge House, 32-36
Loman Street
London
SE1 0EE
020 7928 7377
contact@alcoholconcern.org.uk
www.alcoholconcern.org.uk
*the national agency on alcohol misuse*

**BASE 10**
Templar Chambers
10 Merrion Street
Leeds
LS1 6PQ
0113 243 3552
info@base10drugs.org.uk
www.base10drugs.org.uk
*offers support, advice and information for young drug and alcohol users in Leeds up to 21 years of age as well as their families, carers and friends*

**Birmingham & Blackcountry Services: Drugline**
Dale House
New Meeting St
Birmingham
B4 7SX
0121 632 6363
team@birminghamdrugline.co.uk

**Bromley Community Drug Project**
35 London Road
Bromley
Kent
BR1 1DG
020 8289 1999

**The Children & Family Alcohol & Drugs Service (CAFADS)**
Unit 202, Bow House
153-159 Bow Road
London
E3 2SE
020 8983 4861
info@cafads.org.uk
www.cafads.org.uk
*offers therapeutic interventions, training and consultancy within London area; service is free and confidential*

**Druglink Hammersmith & Fulham**
The Old Coach House,
103a Devonport Road
London
W12 8PB
020 8749 6799
druglink@aol.com

**Druglink Staffordshire**
76-82 Hope Street
Hanley
Stoke-on-Trent
ST1 5BX
01782 425113

**Hungerford Drug Project**
32A Wardour Street
London
W1D 6QR
020 7437 3523
info@thehungerford.org
www.thehungerford.org

**National Association for Children of Alcoholics**
PO Box 64
Fishponds, Bristol
BS16 2UH
0117 924 8005;
helpline: 0800 358 3456
help@nacoa.org.uk
www.nacoa.org.uk
*provides information, advice and support to children of alcoholics and people concerned with their welfare*

**North Tyneside Young Persons Service**
18a Percy St
North Shields
Tyne & Wear
NE20 0AG
0191 270 4505
*works with 11- 25 year olds with drug and alcohol issues*

**SHED**
91 Division Street
Sheffield
S1 4GE
0114 272 9164
shed@turning-point.co.uk
www.shed-turningpoint.co.uk
*a drug and alcohol service for young people under 19 in Sheffield*

**Talk To Frank**
0800 776600
frank@talktofrank.com
www.talktofrank.com
*free confidential drugs information and advice 24 hours a day; translators available covering 120 languages*

**Turning Point**
New Loom House,
101 Back Church Lane
London
E1 1LU
020 7702 2300
info@turning-point.co.uk
www.turning-point.co.uk
*a social care organisation working with individuals and their communities across England and Wales in the areas of drug and alcohol misuse*

**What you need to know about...**
substanceabuse.about.com and
alcoholism.about.com
*range of information about substance abuse and alcoholism issues*

**Worcester Druglink**
35 Foregate Street
Worcester
WR1 1EE
01905 724853

# Training

## Courses

Information taken from the UCAS website with kind permission
Key to qualifications: FT = full time, FD = Foundation degree

**UCAS**
01242 222444
enquiries@ucas.ac.uk
www.ucas.co.uk
*the central organisation that processes applications for full-time undergraduate courses at UK universities and colleges*

**Applied Community and Youth Studies**
(3yr FT BA Hon)
University of Derby

**Applied Social Science - Children & Young People**
(3yr FT BA Hon)
University of York

**Applied Social Science, Community Development & Youth Work**
(3yr FT BA Hon)
Goldsmiths College (University of London)

**Child and Adolescent Studies**
(3yr FT BA Hon)
University of Luton

**Child Development**
*(with Business, Education, Health, International Studies, Law or Legal Studies)*
(3yr FT BA/BSc Hon)
University of Greenwich

**Child Nursing**
(3yr FT BSc Hon)
Coventry University

(3yr FT BA Hon)
Liverpool John Moores University

**Child Nursing Studies**
(3yr FT BSc Hon)
King's College London (University of London)

**Child Studies**
(3yr FT BA Hon)
University of Lincoln

**Child Studies & Advice, Guidance & Counselling**
(3yr FT BA Hon)
Northumbria University

**Child Young Person & Family Studies**
*(also with Applied Social Science, Business & Management, Christian Ministry, Community Health, Creative Writing, English, Environmental Geography, Environment Management, Ethics, Fine Art, Geography, Health Studies, Health Community & Lifestyle, History, I.T., Mathematics or Philosophy & Society)*
(3yr FT BA/BSc Hon)
St Martin's College, Lancaster; Ambleside; Carlisle; London

**Childhood & Youth Studies**
*(also with Critical Criminology, Education Studies, English, Social Psychology, Sociology, English, Info Tech or Management)*
(3yr FT BA Hon)
Edge Hill College of Higher Education (Lancaster University)

**Childhood & Youth Studies**
*(with American Studies, Applied Social Studies, Film & Television Studies, Cultural Studies, Dance,*
*Drama, English, Geography, Health Studies, Leisure Studies, Marketing, Music, Outdoor Studies, Philosophy, Psychology, Social Justice, Sociology, Sport or Visual Arts)*
(3yr FT BA/BSc Hon)
Manchester Metropolitan University

**Childhood and Youth Studies**
(3yr FT BA)
University of Exeter

(2yr FT HND)
West Suffolk College

**Childhood, Youth & Society**
(3yr FT BA)
University College Chichester

**Children's Intensive Care**
(3yr FT BSc Hon)
Oxford Brookes University

**Children's Nursing**
(3yr FT BSc Hon)
City University

(3yr FT BSc Hon)
Edge Hill College of Higher Education (Lancaster University)

(3yr FT BN Hon)
Keele University

(3yr FT BSc Hon)
University of Luton

(3yr FT BSc Hon)
University of The West of England, Bristol

**Church-based Community and Youth Work**
(3yr FT BA Hon)
University of Durham

**Clinical Nursing (Child Health)**
(3yr FT BSc Hon)
Bournemouth University

**Community and Youth Studies**
(3yr FT BA Hon)
Leeds Metropolitan University

(3yr FT BA Hon)
St Martin's College, Lancaster;
Ambleside; Carlisle; London

**Community and Youth Work**
(3yr FT BA Hon)
University of Sunderland

(2yr FT DipHE)
Goldsmiths College (University of London)

(2yr FT DipHE)
University of Durham

**Community and Youth Work Studies**
(3yr FT BA Hon)
University of Durham

(2yr FT DipHE)
University of Sunderland

**Community Children's Nursing**
(3yr FT BA Hon)
Oxford Brookes University

**Community Studies (also with Playwork or Youth and Community Work)**
(3yr FT BA Hon)
University of Wales College, Newport

**Community Studies (Development & Youth Work)**
(2FT FD)
University of Plymouth

**Community Youth Work**
(3yr FT BSc Hon)
University of Ulster

**Community, Play and Youth Studies**
(3yr FT BPhil Hon; 2yr FT DipHE)
University of Birmingham

**Early Childhood Education**
(2yr/4yr FT BA Hon)
Leeds Metropolitan University

**Early Childhood Studies**
*(also with  Applied English Studies, Art for Public Space, Biological Anthropology, Biology,*

*Business Studies, Childhood & Society, Childhood & the Arts, Children's Literature & Childhood, Computing, Creative Writing, Criminology, Cultural Studies, Dance Studies, Drama Theatre & Performance Studies, Education, English Language & Linguistics, English Literature, English Local History, Film Studies, French, Health Studies, History, Human Biosciences, Human Rights, Internet & Multimedia Computing, Music, Philosophy, Psychology, Religious Studies, Science of Sport & Exercise, Social Anthropology, Sociology, Social Policy & Admin, Social Science of Sport, Spanish (ab initio), Sport & Pop Culture, Theology or Translation)*
(3yr FT BA/BSc Hon)
Roehampton University of Surrey

**Early Childhood Studies with Health Studies**
(3yr FT BA Hon)
Canterbury Christ Church University College

**Family & Child Care Studies**
(3yr FT BA Hon)
Kingston University

**Health and Child Development**
(3yr FT BSc Hon)
University of Greenwich

**Health Science and Early Childhood Studies**
(3yr FT BSc Hon)
University of The West of England, Bristol

**Health Studies and Childhood Studies**
(3yr FT BA Hon)
Northumbria University

**Nursing (Child Health)**
(3yr FT BN Hon)
University of Wales College of Medicine

**Nursing (Child)**
(3yr FT BSc Hon)
University of Salford

(3yr FT BN Hon)
University of Wales Swansea

(3yr FT BSc Hon)
Anglia Polytechnic University

(3yr FT BSc Hon)
Canterbury Christ Church University College

(3yr FT BSc Hon)
De Montfort University

(3yr FT BSc Hon)
Oxford Brookes University

(4yr FT BSc Hon)
Robert Gordon University
(3yr FT BSc Hon)
University College Northampton

(3FT BSc Hon)
University of Central England in Birmingham

(3yr FT BSc Hon)
University of East Anglia

(3yr FT BN Hon)
University of Glamorgan

(3yr FT BSc Hon)
University of Greenwich

(3yr FT BHSc Hon)
University of Leeds

**Nursing Practice: Child**
(3yr FT BSc Hon)
Staffordshire University

**Nursing Studies (Child Care)**
(3yr FT BSc Hon)
London South Bank University

(3yr FT BA Hon)
Sheffield Hallam University

**Nursing Studies (Child)**
(3yr FT BSc Hon)
Northumbria University

(3yr FT BSc Hon)
University of Wolverhampton

**Nursing Studies (Child) (Pre-Registration)**
(3yr FT BSc Hon)
University of Teesside

**Nursing Studies (Registered Nurse:Child Nursing)**
(3yr FT BSc Hon)
University of Surrey

**Nursing with Registration (Adult or Child)**
(3FT BSc Hon)
University of Hertfordshire

**Nursing: Child Branch**
(3yr FT BN Hon)
University of Southampton

**Playwork**
(2yr FT FD)
Cornwall College

(3yr FT BA Hon)
Leeds Metropolitan University

(2yr FT DipHE)
Northumbria University

(2yr FT FD)
University of Plymouth

**Playwork and Youth Studies**
(3yr FT BA Hon)
University of East London

**Positive Practice with Children & Young People**
(2yr FT FD)
Blackburn College

**Psychology with Child Development**
(3yr FT BSc Hon)
London South Bank University

**Social Work, Residential Child Care**
(3yr FT BA)
University of Strathclyde

**Working with Young People**
(2yr FT FD)
Anglia Polytechnic University

**Youth & Community Work and Applied Theology**
(3yr FT BA Hon)
Oxford Brookes University

**Youth and Community**
(3yr FT BA Hon)
Manchester Metropolitan University

(2yr FT DipHE)
University College Chichester

**Youth and Community Development**
(3yr FT BA Hon)
Bradford College (University of Bradford)

(3yr FT BA Hon)
De Montfort University

**Youth and Community Education**
(3yr FT BA Hon)
North East Wales Institute of Higher Education

**Youth and Community Studies**
(3yr FT BA Hon)
Liverpool John Moores University

(3yr FT BA Hon)
University of Greenwich

(2yr FT DipHE; 3yr FT BA)
University of Luton

**Youth and Community Work**
(2yr FT DipHE)
Havering College of Further and Higher Education

(2yr FT DipHE)
Liverpool John Moores University

(3yr FT BA Hon)
Manchester Metropolitan University

(2yr FT DipHE)
North East Wales Institute of Higher Education

(3yr FT BA Hon)
The College of St Mark and St John

(3yr FT BA Hon)
University of Huddersfield

(1yr FT Cert.HE; 2yr FT FD)
Ruskin College Oxford

**Youth Studies**
(3yr FT BA Hon)
Nottingham Trent University

(2yr FT FD)
St Helens College (Liverpool John Moores University)

**Youth Studies**
*(also with Criminology, Media Studies, Psychology, Sociology or Sport & Exercise)*
(3yr FT BSc Hon)
University of Teesside

**Youth Studies and Applied Theology**
(3yr FT BA Hon)
Oxford Brookes University

**Youth Work & Community Service (SI)**
*(with Outdoor Education, Religious Studies, Sport Studies or Education Studies)*
(3yr FT BA Hon)
Trinity College Carmarthen

# Institutions

**Anglia Polytechnic University**
0845 271 3333
www.apu.ac.uk

**University of Birmingham**
0121 414 5491
www.bham.ac.uk

**Blackburn College**
01254 292936
www.blackburn.ac.uk

**Bournemouth University**
01202 524111
www.bournemouth.ac.uk

**Bradford College**
01274 433333
www.bradfordcollege.ac.uk

**University of The West of England, Bristol**
0117 344 3333
www.uwe.ac.uk

**Canterbury Christ Church University College**
01227 782900
www.cant.ac.uk

**University of Central England in Birmingham**
0121 331 5000
www.uce.ac.uk

**University College Chichester**
01243 816002
www.ucc.ac.uk

**City University**
020 7040 5060
www.city.ac.uk

**Cornwall College**
01209 616161
www.cornwall.ac.uk

**Coventry University**
0845 055 5850
www.coventry.ac.uk

**De Montfort University**
0116 255 1551
www.dmu.ac.uk

**University of Derby**
0870 120 2330
www.derby.ac.uk

**University of Durham**
0191 334 2000
www.dur.ac.uk

**University of East Anglia**
01603 456161
www.uea.ac.uk

**University of East London**
020 8223 2835
www.uel.ac.uk

**University of Exeter**
01392 263035
www.ex.ac.uk

**University of Glamorgan**
0800 716925
www.glam.ac.uk

**Edge Hill College of Higher Education**
0800 195 5063
www.edgehill.ac.uk

**University of Greenwich**
0800 005006
www.gre.ac.uk

**Goldsmiths College (University of London)**
020 7919 7766
www.goldsmiths.ac.uk

**University of Hertfordshire**
01707 284800
www.herts.ac.uk

**University of Huddersfield**
01484 422288
www.hud.ac.uk

**Havering College of Further and Higher Education**
01708 462801
www.havering-college.ac.uk

**Keele University**
01782 584005
www.keele.ac.uk

**King's College London (University of London)**
020 7836 5454
www.kcl.ac.uk

**University of Leeds**
0113 343 3999
www.leeds.ac.uk

**Kingston University**
020 8547 7053
www.kingston.ac.uk

**University of Lincoln**
01522 886060
www.lincoln.ac.uk

**Leeds Metropolitan University**
0113 283 3113
www.lmu.ac.uk

**University of Luton**
01582 489286
www.luton.ac.uk

**University of Wales College, Newport**
01633 432030
www.newport.ac.uk

**Liverpool John Moores University**
0151 231 5090
www.livjm.ac.uk

**University College Northampton**
0800 358 2232
www.northampton.ac.uk

**Nottingham Trent University**
0115 941 8418
www.ntu.ac.uk

**London South Bank University**
020 7815 7815
www.lsbu.ac.uk

**Oxford Brookes University**
01865 483040
www.brookes.ac.uk

**University of Plymouth**
01752 232137
www.plymouth.ac.uk

**Manchester Metropolitan University**
0161 247 2000
www.mmu.ac.uk

**Robert Gordon University**
01224 262728
www.rgu.ac.uk

**Roehampton University of Surrey**
020 8392 3232
www.roehampton.ac.uk

**North East Wales Institute of Higher Education**
01978 290666
www.newi.ac.uk

**Ruskin College Oxford**
01865 310713
www.ruskin.ac.uk

**University of Salford**
0161 295 5000
www.salford.ac.uk

**Sheffield Hallam University**
0114 225 5555
www.shu.ac.uk

**University of Southampton**
023 8059 5000
www.soton.ac.uk

**The College of St Mark and St John**
01752 636890
www.marjon.ac.uk

**Northumbria University**
0191 232 6002
www.northumbria.ac.uk

**St Martin's College, Lancaster; Ambleside; Carlisle; London**
01524 384444
www.ucsm.ac.uk

**Staffordshire University**
01782 292753
www.staffs.ac.uk

**University of Strathclyde**
0141 552 4400
www.strath.ac.uk

**University of Sunderland**
0191 515 3000
www.sunderland.ac.uk

**University of Surrey**
01483 681681
www.surrey.ac.uk

**University of Wales Swansea**
01792 295111
www.swan.ac.uk

**University of Teesside**
01642 218121
www.tees.ac.uk

**Trinity College Carmarthen**
01267 676767
www.trinity-cm.ac.uk

**University of Ulster**
028 7032 4221
www.ulster.ac.uk

**University of Wales College of Medicine**
029 2074 2027
www.uwcm.ac.uk

**West Suffolk College**
01284 716333
www.westsuffolk.ac.ukhe

**University of Wolverhampton**
01902 321000
www.wlv.ac.uk

**University of York**
01904 433533/433539
www.york.ac.uk